THE NEW LAW OF LAND RE

GW01018317

This book is an examination of the law of land r
in the light of the Land Registration Act 2002, a
istration is influenced by, and in turn influenc
whole. It examines the legal problems that hav. ----
registration and considers the effect of the 2002 statute, drawing extensively upon
the law in other jurisdictions and considering possibilities for future development.

This is a book which will be essential reading for students, their teachers, and
practitioners who will have to grapple with the intricacies of the new Act when it
comes into force.

The New Law of
Land Registration

Elizabeth Cooke
Professor of Law,
The University of Reading

·HART·
PUBLISHING
OXFORD AND PORTLAND, OREGON
2003

Hart Publishing
Oxford and Portland, Oregon

Published in North America (US and Canada) by
Hart Publishing c/o
International Specialized Book Services
5804 NE Hassalo Street
Portland, Oregon
97213-3644
USA

© Elizabeth J Cooke 2003

The Author has asserted her right under the Copyright, Designs and
Patents Act 1988, to be identified as the author of this work

Hart Publishing is a specialist legal publisher based in Oxford, England.
To order further copies of this book or to request a list of other
publications please write to:

Hart Publishing, Salter's Boatyard, Folly Bridge,
Abingdon Road, Oxford OX1 4LB
Telephone: +44 (0)1865 245533 or Fax: +44 (0)1865 794882
e-mail: mail@hartpub.co.uk
WEBSITE: http//www.hartpub.co.uk

British Library Cataloguing in Publication Data
Data Available
ISBN 1–84113–350–7 (hardback)

Typeset by Hope Services (Abingdon) Ltd.
Printed and bound in Great Britain by
Biddles Ltd, _www.biddles.co.uk_

Preface

The Land Registration Act 2002 is both a continuation of and an exciting new beginning for title registration in England and Wales. This book is intended, not as a commentary on the new Act, and certainly not as a practitioner's guide to its operation, but as an academic companion to it. It is quite selective in its scope, and there are a number of important aspects of the new statute that it does not address; I have endeavoured to concentrate on the nature of land ownership and the protection of the purchaser. I have tried to place the English legislation in its international context, and to highlight some issues that arise when it is considered in that context.

I hope that what I have written will be of use to quite a wide readership; advanced readers are asked to forgive some of the explanations of general land law concepts. Reference has been made to standard land law works where necessary.

Inevitably in writing about a recently enacted statute I have had to comment on the work of the individuals responsible for it, some of whom I have met, all of whom I admire very much. I hope that they will be forgive me for disagreeing with them in some respects.

I have had a great deal of help in writing this book. The most conspicuous thanks should go to Pamela O'Connor, of Monash University. Many yards of email have passed between the two of us over the last year or so, and she has taught me a great deal; if the book has succeeded in having a Torrensy flavour, it is thanks to her help. It will be seen from the notes that I have benefited greatly from what I have learnt at two conferences in particular; one at Reading in 2002, and the conference in Auckland in March 2003, 'Taking Torrens into the 21st century', organised by David Grinlinton. Chapter 9, which discusses European registration systems, is actually co-authored. Magdalena Habdas of the Silesian University of Technology, Matti Niemi of the Lappeenranta University of Technology and Lars van Vliet of the University of Maastricht, have written about registration in their own systems for me, and the sections on Scots and German law have been read and improved respectively by Jan-Bertram Hillig and by Stewart Brymer. Michael Croker, District Land Registrar at Stevenage, answered my queries and provided the sample land registers found in this book. Richard Hart has been a source of encouragement and constructive comment throughout the writing process. My colleagues in the School of Law at the University of Reading have been unfailingly patient and helpful to me in my ramblings.

It would have been impossible to write this book in time for publication in October 2003 without research leave funded by the Arts and Humanities Research Board; it is a pleasure to be able to thank them for a second time for enabling me to bring a book to completion.

My husband, John, has read the book in draft, made numerous corrections of style, typography and content and excised the worst jokes; I thank him for his patience with two rather intense book completions in the last year, and I thank him, and Gillian and Dominic, for filling my life with joy.

Lizzie Cooke
University of Reading, May 2003

Table of Contents

Table of Cases

Table of Statutory Instruments

Table of Statutes

Abbreviations

Anderson, *Lawyers 1832–1940*	S Anderson, *Lawyers and the Making of English Land Law 1832–1940* (Oxford, Clarendon Press, 1992).
Bradbrook, MacCallum and Moore	AJ Bradbrook, SV MacCallum, AP Moore, *Australian Real Property Law*, 3rd edn (Sydney, Lawbook Co, 2002).
Cooke, *Modern Studies I*	E Cooke (ed), *Modern Studies in Property Law, vol I: Property 2000* (Oxford, Hart Publishing Ltd, 2001).
Cooke, *Modern Studies II*	E Cooke (ed), *Modern Studies in Property Law, vol II* (Oxford, Hart Publishing Ltd, 2003).
Evans and Smith	PF Smith, *Evans and Smith, The Law of Landlord and Tenant*, 6th edn (London, Butterworths, 2002).
Grinlinton, *Torrens conference papers*	D Grinlinton, *Torrens in the Twenty-First Century* (LexisNexis New Zealand Ltd, 2003); papers given at a conference at the University of Auckland in March 2003.
LC 254	The Law Commission and HM Land Registry, *Land Registration for the Twenty-First Century; a consultative document* Cm 4027 (Law Com No 254) (London, The Stationery Office, 1998).
LC 271	The Law Commission and HM Land Registry, *Land Registration for the Twenty-First Century; a conveyancing revolution* HC 114 (Law Com No 271) (London, The Stationery Office, 2001).
Megarry and Wade	C Harpum, *Megarry and Wade, The Law of Real Property*, 6th edn (London, Sweet & Maxwell, 2000).
Ruoff and Roper	TB Ruoff, RB Pryer, C West, R Fearnley, *Ruoff and Roper on the Law and Practice of Registered Conveyancing* (London, Sweet & Maxwell, 1991; looseleaf, updated to September 2002).

Simpson, *Land Registration*	SR Simpson, *Land Law and Registration* (Cambridge, CUP, 1976).
Smith, *Property Law*	R Smith, *Property Law*, 4th edn (London, Longman, 2003).
Ziff, *Property Law*	B Ziff, *Principles of Property Law*, 3rd edn (Ontario, Carswell, 2000).

The expression 'the 2002 Act' always means the Land Registration Act 2002, which is referred to either thus or with its full title. Similarly, the expression 'the 1925 Act' is only occasionally used when there is no possiblity of confusion: it always refers to the Land Registration Act 1925, which is more usually referred to by its full title.

1

Modern Land Registration

L
AND REGISTRATION' IS a misleading expression. It refers to a record, not of land, but of ownership of land. It could more accurately be described as title registration; but since that label is reserved for a particular kind of record of ownership, the reader is asked to accept 'land registration' as the conventional umbrella term. It refers to a record created and maintained by the state, rather than by private enterprise; it may be publicly accessible, to a greater or lesser extent, and the state may guarantee its accuracy.

This makes land registration sound like a one-dimensional, boring list. The reality is rather different. Land law is an expression of the relationships between people with respect to their land; land registration is particularly interesting because it changes those relationships while ostensibly merely recording them. In some cases this happens without anyone intending it, as an unforeseen consequence of legislation; but in many cases it is deliberate. A whole system of land registration, or an individual provision in a statute, may be used as an instrument of legal reform.

This book is written after the enactment for England and Wales, but before the coming into force, of the Land Registration Act 2002. It heralds what its progenitor, the Law Commission for England and Wales, has called a 'conveyancing revolution'.[1] Indeed, land registration in this country in its current form has its origins in the endeavours of the nineteenth-century reformers to simplify conveyancing. But the 2002 statute is designed to change more than the procedure for sale and purchase. The consultation paper that preceded it announced that one of the objects of reform would be to bring about acceptance of 'not a system of registration of title but a system of title by registration'.[2] The new law will continue a process which can be seen to have taken place throughout the twentieth century, whereby land registration has gradually changed the nature of ownership of land.

It will do so in two phases. Unusually, the Act contemplates its own staged implementation. It is to be brought into force in October 2003. Its principal provisions will take effect immediately, replacing the Land Registration Act 1925 and

---

[1] The Law Commission Report which gave rise to the Land Registration Act 2002 was entitled *Land Registration for the Twenty-First Century; a conveyancing revolution* (Law Com No 271). It is referred to in this book as LC 271; the consultation paper which preceded it, *Land Registration for the Twenty-First Century; a consultative document* (Law Com No 254) is referred to as LC 254.

[2] LC 254, 10.43. The words are from an Australian case, *Breskvar v Wall* (1971) 126 CLR 376, 385, *per* Barwick CJ; for the significance of the case, see ch 6, text at n 110.

substituting much better-drafted provisions including some important substantive reforms. But the sections that concern electronic conveyancing require statutory instruments to activate them, and this will be done later, perhaps several years hence. For the new Act is a response to one of the most exciting developments of the turn of the twentieth and twenty-first centuries, the growth of electronic information and communication. It contains sections to enable, and eventually to make compulsory, the creation and transmission of interests in land by electronic means. And while the implementation of the main provisions of the Act in 2003 will change the law in significant respects, the introduction of compulsory electronic conveyancing will introduce a further tranche of important changes. The first set of changes is visible now; the consequences of electronic conveyancing (if indeed it does become universal) are not yet completely clear.

The purpose of this book is to reflect upon the new law, in its two stages, and to assess its effect upon ownership of land in the context of the worldwide development of land registration. For land registration cannot be regarded as a domestic matter. Its roots are centuries old, but also immensely wide-ranging. It has grown up in different forms in a number of jurisdictions, sometimes with shared origins, sometimes wholly independently. Any one system can best be understood in the light of its fellows, and may well be misunderstood if it is considered in isolation. And there is more at stake than an understanding of the operation of individual systems. As the world becomes smaller and communications (particularly by electronic means) become swifter and more effective, there is pressure for harmonisation. If a worldwide land register still seems unimaginable, a European one is not.[3] And that is quite a challenge, for, as we shall see, the English land registration system is much closer to its Australasian cousins than to its European neighbours.

Let us begin, then, by looking at the systems of land registration that have developed in Western societies.

LAND REGISTRATION: THE OPTIONS

Land registration is not at all modern. We could spend a chapter playing the game of tracing back land registration to its very earliest forms; the ancient Egyptians, for example, kept a record of ownership in documentary form, so that land could be allocated accurately when it became accessible following the annual flooding of the Nile.[4] Without going into detail about remote history, we may observe that land registration is a feature of a state with a centralised bureaucracy; and one

---

[3] The possibility of such a register was mentioned in the debate about the Land Registration Bill in the House of Lords, HL Deb 3/7/01, Col 786; plans for a European land information system are well under way. See the website of EULIS: www.eulis.org and ch 9, below.

[4] E Dowson and VLO Sheppard, *Land Registration* (London, HMSO, 1956) pp 2–3; G Husson and D Valbelle, *L'Etat et les institutions en Egypte* (Paris, Armand Colin, 1992) 91 ff. A facsimile of a papyrus register of land may be seen at http://scriptorium.lib.duke.edu/papyrus/images/150dpi/174r—at150.gif.

where a settled civilisation is content to have ownership recorded and regulated by officialdom rather than by force. In its modern forms, it is a feature of a society where individuals own and trade land as a capital asset and so need their ownership to be easily proved and efficiently transferable. Land registration is a means of achieving that end, although it is not the only way of doing so.

Land registration bites both upon ownership and on third party rights. I own land; but others may have rights in that land, for land is an asset that lots of people can do lots of things with. We can live on it, build on it, walk over it, catch fish in rivers on it, play on it, trade both on it and in it . . . Moreover, it stays where it is, unlike, say, ships; and land (although not the buildings on it) is, for all practical purposes, indestructible, unlike pension funds and horses, so we can plan ahead for people to do things with land in the future. You can use it for 10 years, then I can have a turn for another five, and so on. Thus ownership of land is complex, and a potentially infinite number of people may have rights in it. That complexity militates against easy transactions in land; it may make it difficult to know who owns a piece of land, or how many people have rights in it, or which third party rights have priority over other third party rights.

When we turn this into legal terminology, the picture becomes a diptych because Western legal systems have organised that complexity in two different ways. There are the common law systems, based on English law, and the civil law systems, descended from Roman law, and they take two quite distinct approaches to the ownership of land. In the civil law systems, there is one owner of land, while others may have subordinate rights in it; in the common law, ownership is not a unitary concept, and it may be impossible to say that any one person is 'the owner' of a piece of land. In particular, land may be held upon trust, owned by one person for the benefit of someone else, and we say that both the trustee and the beneficiary have ownership rights in the land, the one legal and the other equitable. Third party rights, too, may be either legal or equitable, and this sets up difficult questions of priority. In 1974, John Henry Merryman explained the difference between the two legal families like this:

The basic difference between Romanic ownership and the Anglo–American 'estate' or 'interest' in land can be illustrated by a simple metaphor. Romanic ownership can be thought of as a box, with the word 'ownership' written on it. Whoever has the box is the 'owner'. In the case of complete, unencumbered ownership, the box contains certain rights, including that of use and occupancy, that to the fruits of income, and the power of alienation. The owner can, however, open the box and remove one or more such rights and transfer them to others. But, as long as he keeps the box, he still has the ownership, even if the box is empty. The contrast with the Anglo–American law of property is simple. There is no box. There are merely various sets of legal interests. One who has the fee simple absolute has the largest possible bundle of such sets of legal interests. When he conveys one or more of them to another person, a part of his bundle is gone.[5]

---

[5] JH Merryman, 'Ownership and Estate', [1974] 48 *Tulane Law Review* 916, at 927; cited in S Panesar, *General Principles of Property Law* (London, Longman, 2001), at 113.

Merryman's metaphor of the 'black box' of ownership conveys the idea that in a civil law system, in answer to the question 'who owns this house?' it is supposed to be possible to point to one individual who is, unambiguously, the owner, while others may have rights of a different kind. He offers no metaphor for common law ownership, where there is no black box; we might compare something like a pack of cards which has been dealt among a number of players. For that to work the pack has to contain an infinite number of cards; better perhaps would be a strudel or other flaky pastry construct, or a chocolate flake bar, where the texture is visibly complex, the substance splittable and sharable, and the layers genuinely uncountable.[6]

This distinction between common law and civil law systems is important for any study of land registration. Land registration is, generally, inimical to fragmentation, and much more akin to a civil law system than to a common law one. One of the aims of registration is to make title more secure and easily provable. It is supposed, ideally, to set up a mirror of ownership. The mirror principle—or, rather, aspiration—is hostile to interests that do not appear on the registered title. Like many systems registration has its own momentum; it tends towards tidiness and completeness, and to the elimination, as far as possible, of interests that a purchaser cannot discover from the register. Registration seems to imply a unitary form of ownership, in much the same way that registration of ownership of shares, cars, ships or dogs is supposed to enable you to point to *the owner*.[7] One of the fundamental difficulties with registration in a common law system is: what are we to do with equitable interests? Are they to be eliminated; or registered; or enforceable despite being unregistered? It will be seen both from the detailed analysis of the current English system and from the limited comparative study attempted here that this difficulty has not been completely solved.

Against that background, then, land registration is found today in a number of forms. Broadly, there are deeds registration, interest recording and title registration.[8] Each form has been adopted in several jurisdictions, with many local variants and varying degrees of success. It is not unusual for a jurisdiction to adopt a number of forms of registration in turn, implying a search for a form that is in some way better; and we sometimes find more than one form combined within a system. Another way of classifying land registration systems is by their effect: they may be protective or dispositive. A protective system records ownership and/or other interests in land as a way of settling their relationship to each other; it affects priority, but not the actual existence of the interests. A dispositive system exercises a much tighter grip upon its users by regulating the very existence of property

---

[6] Merryman's point is discussed further by the author in 'The Land Registration Act 2002 and the nature of ownership', ch 5 of A Hudson (ed), *New Perspectives on Property Law: Obligations and Restitution* (London, Cavendish, 2003), 117.

[7] The simplifying force of registration is thoroughly demonstrated in Alain Pottage's work: see 'The Originality of Registration', [1995] 15 *Oxford Journal of Legal Studies* 371, and 'Evidencing Ownership' in S Bright and J Dewar (eds), *Land Law, Themes and Perspectives* (Oxford, OUP, 1998), 129.

[8] This is Roger Smith's three-fold classification: *Property Law* (London, Longman, 2003) (hereafter 'Smith, *Property Law*'), 214.

rights, as well as their priority. This two-fold classification cuts across the three groups mentioned above, which we now consider in turn.

Deeds Registration

There comes a time when a literate society accepts that writing is useful as evidence of a transaction; the process may be a lengthy one.[9] Common law systems have used the deed as the special form of writing by which certain transactions in land must be effected, and without which they are either invalid or of lesser validity. Accordingly, 'the deeds' of a property become an almost sacred sign of ownership; title is proved genealogically by the production of documents which trace owner-ship back from the present, showing a chain of entitlement made up of legitimate links (in modern terms, a conveyance from A to B, a mortgage by B to C, redemp-tion of mortgage by B, conveyance from B to D, death of D, probate to E and F, assent by E and F to G, etc). In theory that chain goes back to the beginning of the relevant legal system, but invariably law or custom prescribes a convenient limit.

There are two practical problems here. The first is that deeds may get lost. Without them, in the common law, we resort to possession as the ancient basis of title, which can be proved in a number of ways, none of them especially reliable. The second problem is that deeds, even a full set of them, may not give the whole picture; a prospective purchaser may not be able to ascertain from them all the rights affecting the land. Deeds registration guards against the first problem, but not the second, by setting up a record of deeds, so that there is a public record of private paperwork.

The advantage of deeds registration is that it preserves the system that people are used to. No one feels they lose anything under a deeds registration system; regis-tration adds security and, depending upon the precise details of the system, pub-licity, which in turn generates a confident market. The main disadvantage is that it is cumbersome. Individual deeds must still be found in the records; there may be a great many to find. Title is not simplified by deeds registration; and the pro-duction of proof of ownership (called by conveyancers 'deducing title') is still done by tracing ownership from the present day, through the various transactions recorded in different deeds, back to a legally acceptable starting point (called, in a common law system, a 'root of title'). Thus one of the important features of a deeds registration system is its index, which will make it more or less easy to find a particular document. A further disadvantage is that interests in land may exist apart from deeds; deeds registration has no effect upon such rights, and cannot make them any more secure or more easily discoverable.

Deeds registration may be merely protective, so that a deed can only have pri-ority over subsequent transactions if it is registered, or it may also be dispositive, so that it is of no effect at all unless registered. The protective or dispositive effect

---

[9] A Pottage, 'Evidencing Ownership', n 7 above, at 130.

acts as a form of compulsion; without compulsion, deeds registration will not 'catch on', however useful the system may be as a convenient central record of documents. Another important feature of a deeds registration system is the place of notice in the rules relating to its protective effect, expressed in the answer to the question: is a purchaser bound by an unregistered deed of which he has knowledge?

Deeds registration operated in Yorkshire and Middlesex from the eighteenth to the twentieth centuries. Its effect was protective; unregistered deeds were of no effect against later purchasers, whether or not those purchasers knew of the transaction recorded in the deed.[10] We do not know why only these areas of England had this form of registration; the registries were eventually closed with the advent of title registration. Deeds registration was set up in Ireland contemporaneously with the English registries, and the deeds registration systems of Ireland and Northern Ireland are still in operation, only slowly being replaced by title registration.[11]

However, all the US jurisdictions operate a system of deeds registration, and so successfully that there seems no prospect of any other system taking over.[12] The effect of the various systems is protective, not dispositive, and they differ in their treatment of a purchaser's knowledge, being divisible into three forms: 'race', 'notice' and 'race-notice'.[13] In race systems, deeds take priority purely in order of registration, while in notice systems they do so only if the purchaser has no notice of the earlier deed;[14] in a race-notice system a purchaser without notice of an earlier unregistered deed takes priority over it only if his own deed is registered.[15] The issue whether notice, of whatever kind, should be relevant despite lack of registration has to be addressed by any registration system, and can arouse strong emotions.[16] The twin disadvantages of deeds registration, its cumbersomeness and its inability to be comprehensive, are tackled by means of two forms of private enterprise. First, there are the abstract companies, who search the registries, often developing specialised local knowledge of titles and their own databanks parasitic upon the public registries. Thus the individual conveyancer does not have to search the registries. Second, there is title insurance, whereby the risk of undiscoverable interests can be met by insurance.[17] In Canada, deeds registration

---

[10] See ch 2 below, text at n 21.

[11] See ch 9, text following n 4.

[12] See ch 11 of RA Cunningham, WB Stoebuck and DA Whitman, *The Law of Property* (St Paul, West Publishing Co, 1993), 823 ff.

[13] The same terminology is used in Canada, where there are a number of deeds registration systems: B Ziff, *Principles of Property Law* 3rd edn, (Ontario, Carswell, 2000) (hereafter 'Ziff, *Property Law*'), 420 f.

[14] Thus A mortgages his land to B, and then to C. B fails to register. In a race system, C's mortgage takes precedence over B's, from the point of the creation of C's mortgage. In a notice system, it does so only if C had no notice of B's mortgage.

[15] In the example above, C's mortgage takes priority over B's once C's is registered.

[16] See ch 5, below, at n 75.

[17] For a discussion of title insurance, see G Morgan, 'Title Insurance: Its Relevance to Lenders' in P Jackson and D Wilde (eds), *Contemporary Property Law* (Aldershot, Ashgate, 1999), 168; and J Flaws, 'Compensation for loss under the Torrens system—Extending State Compensation with Private Insurance' in D Grinlinton, *Taking Torrens into the Twenty-first Century*, forthcoming; papers given at a conference at the University of Auckland in March 2003 (hereafter 'Grinlinton, *Torrens conference papers*').

coexists with title registration in Ontario, Manitoba and the Maritime States, but is being supplanted by title registration.[18]

Conspicuous for their successful and accurate deeds registration systems are South Africa[19] and Scotland.[20] These systems differ from the US ones in two important respects. First, they both operate upon civil law, rather than common law jurisdictions. Thus in neither case are there equitable interests potentially lying behind a legal title; both operate on the basis that there is one *dominus* who owns the land, no matter how many others have interests in it. Second, in both cases the registration system is dispositive, rather than merely protective. A disposition has no effect until it is registered. In Scotland, title registration is now taking over from the earlier system;[21] there is no such development in prospect in South Africa. Indeed, it is claimed that the South African deeds registration system incorporates the accuracy and comprehensiveness of a title registration system;[22] first, because the registrar is under a duty to check the accuracy of deeds presented for registration, rather than simply taking them as he finds them, and secondly because of the antiquity of the system. David Carey Miller points out[23] that South African conveyancing is descended from the Dutch system of public transactions[24] so that South Africa has never had a system of private conveyancing to generate inaccuracies.[25]

It is perhaps surprising, given the prevalence in Europe of title registration on the German model, to find that France operates what is in effect deeds registration with protective, not dispositive, effect.[26] Moreover, while the Australian jurisdictions and New Zealand operate very successful title registration systems, their deeds registration systems, which predate title registration, and are still operative in respect of those titles that remain unregistered.[27]

---

[18] Ziff, *Property Law*, 420.

[19] DM Carey Miller, *Land Title in South Africa* (Cape Town, Juta, 2000), 45 ff.

[20] RRM Paisley, *Land Law* (Edinburgh, W Green, 2000), 92 ff.

[21] Land Registration (Scotland) Act 1979; title registration is being made compulsory by area, as it was in England and Wales.

[22] SR Simpson *Land Law and Registration* (Cambridge, CUP, 1976) (hereafter 'Simpson, *Land Registration*'), at 105: 'We suggest that it is misleading to classify the South African system as a deeds system in any way comparable with the deeds systems of, for example, the United States. To all intents and purposes it is registration of title.'

[23] See n 19 above, p 48.

[24] Of the same nature as the Hanseatic states; see n 42 below. The modern Dutch system is related to the French deeds registration system; see ch 9.

[25] The same might perhaps be said of Scotland, where deeds registration, in the Register of Sasines, has been compulsory since 1617: RRM Paisley, see n 20 above, 100.

[26] J Bell, S Boyron, S Whittaker, *Principles of French Law* (Oxford, OUP, 1998), 289 ff. At 290: 'France has a system of registration of transactions, but this procedure does not affect their validity, merely their effectiveness against third parties.' See also J Bell, 'Property and Legal Culture in France' in P Birks and A Pretto (eds) *Themes in Comparative Law in Honour of Bernard Rudden* (Oxford, OUP, 2002), 83. Other European jurisdictions using deeds registration are Iceland, Italy, Lithuania, Luxembourg, San Marino and Greece—the latter is in the course of transition to a register of titles—according to the UNECE *Inventory* (see n 46 below).

[27] It was Robert Torrens' work as registrar-general of deeds for South Australia, from 1853, that convinced him that title registration was essential: T Mapp, *Torrens' Elusive Title* (Alberta, University of Alberta, 1978), 1.

Interest Recording

An interest recording system records rights rather than documents; it is closely related to deeds registration, but it enables a purchaser to look at a single record to see what are the current interests in a piece of land (although not necessarily all the details that he needs to know about them). But the system registers third party rights in land, not ownership; and although usually protective, it is not dispositive. This apparently rather odd system has worked well in areas where ownership itself is stable and easy to prove, but where third party rights have generated problems of complexity or discoverability. We have two such systems in England and Wales. First, there is the register under the Land Charges Acts;[28] it has been, since its inception, an obviously temporary system, being set up in a way that invites abolition.[29] It regulates priority strictly according to registration.[30]

Second, there is the system of recording interests within the title registration system. As will be seen, title registration records and guarantees ownership, and can guarantee some third party rights as well; but there are generally interests that cannot be given the full protection of registration, and one of the important policy decisions for a new title registration system is which interests can be included and which cannot. An interest recording system within one of title registration is a compromise between comprehensiveness and practicability. Both the 1925 and 2002 Land Registration Acts provide that interests in land, the title to which is registered, may be recorded on the register as interests adverse to the proprietor. The priority of recorded interests is protected, without any guarantee as to their validity being given.[31] The same sort of provision is found in the Torrens systems, where unregistrable interests are protected by caveat. This takes one of two forms. In some jurisdictions, generally the older statutes,[32] the effect is neither protective nor dispositive, but merely ensures that a disposition inconsistent with the caveated interest cannot be registered until the caveator has had an opportunity to establish his claim.[33] In others,[34] the caveat has protective effect, as does the notice in the English system.

---

[28] Originally 1925, now 1972.

[29] See ch 2 below.

[30] Although the rules are not entirely straightforward; see ch 2 below, n 66.

[31] Land Registration Act 1925, s 52; Land Registration Act 2002, s 32. See ch 5, n 21.

[32] For example, New Zealand and South Australia; see P O'Connor, 'Registration of Title in England and Australia: A Theoretical and Comparative Analysis' in E Cooke (ed), *Modern Studies in Property Law, vol II* (Oxford, Hart Publishing Ltd, 2003) (hereafter 'Cooke, *Modern Studies II*'), 81, 94.

[33] The effect is thus that of a caution under the English statute of 1925.

[34] Such as Alberta, discussed in T Mapp, *Torrens' Elusive Title* (see n 27 above), 62 and ch 7; and see Ziff, *Property Law*, 433.

Title Registration

This is a different animal altogether. It consists of a tabular, not genealogical, record of ownership,[35] wherein the state of the title can be seen without the necessity for further tracing or investigation, at least so far as concerns those interests in land that a given title registration system purports to comprehend. Thus it is not an index or collection of traditional documents, but substitutes a new form of record. Anyone interested in the state of the title to a piece of land need not, and indeed must not, look behind that new record in order to check or supplement the information it gives about registered rights.[36] He need not, because only the register confers title. It is not merely a record of something else. It is dispositive, not by preventing the traditional documents from operating until they are registered,[37] but by preventing them from operating at all; once a transaction is registered, it is the register itself that confers the right in question.[38]

Thus Theodore Ruoff, a former Chief Land Registrar from 1963 to 1975, explained title registration as encapsulating three principles:[39]

—The mirror principle
—The curtain principle
—The insurance principle

The mirror principle means that the register reflects the state of the title; the curtain, that 'the register is the sole source of information for proposing purchasers, who need not and, indeed, must not concern themselves with trusts and equities which lie behind the curtain'.[40] Thus the register screens the purchaser from information which he does not need; the implication, of course, is that those trusts and equities cannot affect him. The insurance principle is:

that the register is deemed to give an absolutely correct reflection of title but if, through human frailty, a flaw appears, anyone who thereby suffers loss must be put in the same position, so far as money can do it, as if the reflection were a true one.[41]

We might say that title registration is inspired, consciously or otherwise, by a myth, which goes something like this:

---

[35] The terminology belongs to Alain Pottage: 'The Originality of Registration' (1995) 15 *Oxford Journal of Legal Studies* 370 at 383.

[36] Not all rights are registrable; but the register is the complete record for those which are.

[37] This is how some deeds registration systems have dispositive effect (nn 19, 20 above).

[38] English lawyers have found this deeply counter-intuitive. Alain Pottage, in 'The Originality of Registration' (1995) 15 *Oxford Journal of LegalStudies* 370 at 381, notes how for some years after 1925 solicitors had their clients execute both a registered charge and a traditional mortgage document in order, as they saw it, to ensure that the mortgagee had sufficient powers. It may be that this reluctance to see that the register confers title may explain why English law has found it so difficult to tackle the issue of indefeasibility; see ch 6, below.

[39] In *An Englishman Looks at the Torrens System* (Sydney, Law Book Company, 1957), 8 ff.

[40] *Ibid*, p 11.

[41] *Ibid*, p 13. We shall have a lot to say about this (see ch 6 below); for the moment, an easy example of a 'flaw' is where the land is incorrectly described or the plan is incorrect, so that someone is registered as the proprietor of part of someone else's land.

Picture the ideal title register. It is a complete mirror of title: every interest in the land in question is encapsulated in the one record. The record has taken complete control of title: it is impossible to create or deal with any interest in land without proper use of the register, but once registered an interest is valid and enforceable against the world, and cannot be compromised by any event outside the register. The register is therefore infallible; it does not merely record the title, it generates and defines the title.

That is only a myth, and the reality is far removed from this Plato-esque fantasy; but it is the ideal that leads to the supposition that title registration is a good thing. A complete and infallible register would make conveyancing simple by eliminating the work of investigating a title from documentary and physical evidence; it would eliminate risk for all parties because it would be impossible to be caught by an undiscoverable interest, and because the holder of a registered interest is completely invulnerable to any off-register events. But no title registers are complete and infallible. All leave open the possibility of off-register interests; all are vulnerable to human error and, to some extent, to fraud. It is in the extent to which the registered title is vulnerable to off-register interests or events that some of the most useful points of comparison between title registration systems lie.

Deeds registration, at least in its protective, non-dispositive forms, and interest recording, reflect a system where dealings with land are essentially private transactions, of which a public record may be made. Title registration originated in the middle ages in what are now Germany and the Netherlands, in the Hanseatic cities where sales of land were public events, which could not take place without the involvement of the relevant city authorities. Essentially, these powerful trading cities constituted islands of independent legal regulation, distinct from the feudal hinterland surrounding them. From the late thirteenth century onwards land transactions took place in public ceremonies before the relevant city Council and were recorded in the City books.[42] These local registers are the ancestors of the modern German *Grundbuch*,[43] and of most of the title registration systems of Europe and Scandinavia.[44] These, of course, are civil law systems, untroubled by equity.[45] Another striking difference between the European registration systems and the common law ones is that the former co-exist with a cadastre, a national register of land units compiled for fiscal purposes, recording land use and, so far as possible, ownership. This can be a source of confusion for the English observer.

---

[42] The system is described by Murray Raff in *The True Meaning of the Torrens System and Environmental Responsibility: A Comparative Study of German Real Property Law* (paper delivered at the Real Property Teachers' Conference, Melbourne, 2001; copy with the author). See also P Butt, *Land Law* 3rd edn, (Sydney, Law Book Co, 1996), 687; and P O'Connor, see n 32 above, 97, fn 105.

[43] N Foster, *German Legal System and Laws* 2nd edn, (London, Blackstone, 1996), 278 ff.

[44] Matti Niemi, in 'The Public Trustworthiness of Land Registers in the Nordic Countries' in E Cooke (ed), *Modern Studies in Property Law, vol I: Property 2000* (Oxford, Hart Publishing Ltd, 2001) (hereafter 'Cooke, *Modern Studies I*'), 329, comments, at 330, on the different systems within the Nordic 'family group', modelled on the German system.

[45] It was pointed out above that it was this sort of system that gave birth to South African deeds registration, which is thus unlike common law deeds registration systems. On the European systems, see further ch 9 below.

Generally, we can say that the Germanic systems of title registration form a much more integral part of the legal tradition of the European countries that employ it than do the other systems discussed below, partly due to their antiquity and partly due to an absence of a peculiarly English love of privacy in land transactions.[46]

Title registration was thus already old when it was re-invented in the mid-nineteenth century, almost simultaneously in England and in Australia.[47] It has therefore been said that there are three families of land registration systems:[48] the English, the Torrens system which originated in Australia but is found in many forms worldwide, and the Germanic systems. Modern scholarship takes the view that the English and Torrens systems are not in fact so far apart as has been supposed[49] and indeed both have roots in the German system.[50] Both are highly successful systems of registration, existing in different forms in many jurisdictions. Both have had to grapple with, and all the variants have found different answers to, the problem of the fragmentation of ownership within the common law system. The Land Registration Act 2002 is the most robust approach yet seen to that difficulty within the English title registration tradition. It is argued in this book that the biggest challenge for the English system is now the issue of indefeasibility, i.e. the extent to which the title of the registered proprietor of land is guaranteed and protected from defects which would make it void or voidable in unregistered land. As will be seen, the English system stands apart from the Torrens and the German-based systems in this respect.

By contrast, title registration has been a failure in America. It ran into constitutional difficulties soon after its introduction in the late nineteenth century, and of course is the object of hostility from the title insurance companies.[51] Although a few states have title registration statutes, they operate only on a voluntary basis and title registration has never been widespread. By contrast, title registration systems, based both on the English and the Torrens model, operate successfully in Canada.[52]

Inevitably, the subject matter of this book is really title registration. This is the most complete form of registration, and the only one that can come anywhere near to the myth of the ideal register. It has defeated deeds registration in England, and is the prevalent form in Europe, Australasia and Canada. Much of the rest of this book is devoted to the analysis of the current system of title registration in England

---

[46] For a survey of the European systems, see *Inventory of Land Administration Systems in Europe and North America* 3rd edn, 2001, a survey produced for the United Nations Economic Commission for Europe (UN/ECE), financed and published by HM Land Registry in London on behalf of the UNECE Working Party on Land Administration, to be found at http://www.unece.org/env/hs/wpla/docs/wpla_inv3.pdf

[47] See ch 2, below.

[48] Simpson, *Land Registration*, 124.

[49] P O'Connor, see n 32 above.

[50] Sir Robert Torrens acknowledged the German precedent: *The South Australian System of Conveyancing by Registration of Title* (Adelaide, 1859), Preface and 22; in England, contemporary acknowledgement of the German influence on the English system is harder to find.

[51] See Cunningham, Stoebuck and Whitman, see n 12 above, at 880 ff.

[52] Ziff, *Property Law*, 432.

and to comparison between that system and others. Equally inevitably, the closest points of comparison for the English system are drawn from the Torrens systems, similar yet different as they are, and closely related to each other. In summary, the differences between them can be said to be in their respective approaches to:

—Indefeasibility. The Torrens systems take this much more seriously than has the English one.[53]

—Overriding interests, that is, rights which remain valid and binding in spite of lack of registration. The Torrens systems do have these; they do not have the notorious feature of the English system, namely the provision that the rights of everyone in actual occupation of the property are overriding.[54]

—Recorded interests. As already noted,[55] the English system employs a different terminology from that used in the Torrens systems for the recording of certain unregistered interests, and the effect of recording under the English system differs from that in some, but not all, Torrens systems.[56]

—Adverse possession. Until the 2002 Act, the English law of adverse possession in registered title was substantively, though not procedurally, similar to that in unregistered land. In this respect it differed from some, but not all, Torrens systems.[57]

Before we move into a detailed analysis of the new law, we need to call to mind what we might call the ethical dimension of any land registration system, in view of the premise stated above, that land registration changes rights and relationships.

LAND REGISTRATION: THE ETHICAL DIMENSION

Registration is a consumer product. It is immensely good for those whose rights are registered, and for those who have the ability to acquire registered rights. Registration, in whatever form, is an instrument both of practical security, making land more marketable, and of intellectual satisfaction—the more so the nearer it approaches the perfect, infallible register that is the aim of title registration. Yet the perfect register should cause us some misgivings. However satisfying it is in theory, as soon as it is translated into the reality of a human legal system it is seen to have an appalling potential for oppression. It is simply not possible for all dealings with land to be carried out on the register; accordingly, the more complete the register, the less protection is given to people who cannot use it. And there will always be people who, because of ignorance, poverty, or discrimination, cannot use a register of title and who therefore cannot acquire rights, or are deprived of those they hold.

---

[53] See ch 6 below.
[54] See ch 5 below.
[55] See nn 32–34, above.
[56] See ch 5 below.
[57] See ch 7 below.

Land registration has always been an export product of the colonial powers,[58] not always to happy effect.[59] Many countries are still grappling with the tension between the attractions of registered ownership and the value of traditional land-holding patterns which registration cannot reflect.[60] The most extreme example of this is probably South Africa. The policy of the Apartheid regime was to confine the non-white population, not only to small and, in some cases, undesirable areas of land, but also to inferior, insecure and unregistered property rights:

[Under Apartheid] Black South Africans were precluded from obtaining and holding rights in land . . . Instead, a host of legislative and administrative measures forced blacks to resort to forms of land control that were not recognised or effectively protected. These included tribal rights and statutory land rights based on a variety of permits. . . . In effect, these so-called 'black' land rights were ostracised from the markets and invisible within the economic infrastructure. The Deeds Registries Act's support of the supremacy of ownership within a system of land rights (wittingly or unwittingly) perpetuated the differentiation between 'black' and 'white' land control mechanisms.[61]

The challenge for the democratic regime is to reverse the injustices of the past, to give rights in the land to a greater spectrum of people, and to ensure that everyone has a home. Somehow the South African registration system must be harnessed or adapted in order to turn insecure statuses into secure and marketable rights; we have yet to see how this will be achieved, but there is inspiration here for other jurisdictions where land registration has created hardship.

Back in the West, this aspect of registration must not be forgotten as systems undergo the inevitable process of revision and updating. In the context of recent reform in this country, one commentator has called for attention to be given to the 'ethical element' of land registration,[62] and one of the challenges for the courts in this jurisdiction over the next generation will be to assess how far they can respond to the land registration legislation in a way that is both principled and ethical, without undermining the undoubted good effect and achievement of the statutory scheme. That will become a matter for even greater concern as we move towards the second stage of the implementation of the 2002 Act, when under the system of

---

[58] Simpson's book on land registration, and before it Dowson and Sheppard's *Land Registration* (HMSO, London, 1952 and 1956), were written as guides to the introduction of title registration in developing countries that had formed part of the Empire: Simpson, *Land Registration*, xvii.

[59] Thus while Simpson in 1976 mentions with approval the introduction of title registration in Kenya (xxi, and ch 15 passim), it seems that the land register very quickly became out of date there: PL Delville, *Harmonising formal law and customary land rights in French-speaking West Africa* (International Institute for Environment and Development, Issue Paper 86, 1999), 20.

[60] PL Delville, see n 59 above; KB Ghimire (ed), *Land Reform and Peasant Livelihoods* (London, ITDG, 2001), passim. In Grinlinton, *Torrens Conference Papers*, see RP Boast, 'The Implications of Indefeasibility for Maori Land' and J Mugambwa, 'Transportation of the Torrens System to Developing Countries: Uganda and Papua New Guinea experiences'.

[61] N Mostert, 'The Diversification of Land Rights and its Implications for a New Land Law in South Africa' in Cooke, *Modern Studies II*, 3, 6. See also CG van der Merwe and JM Pienaar, 'Land Reform in South Africa', in *The Reform of Property Law*, see n 8 above, 114.

[62] G Battersby, 'Informal Transaction in Land, Estoppel and Registration' (1995) 58 *Modern Law Review* 637, 655, cited at LC 254, 3.45.

electronic conveyancing certain interests, and even contracts relating to land, will, apparently, completely cease to exist outside the registration system.

We need to have these factors in mind as we turn, first, to an examination of the development of land registration in England, and then to a detailed analysis of the current title registration system, while making comparison with other systems.

2

The Road to Title Registration in England and Wales

EARLY REGISTRATION SYSTEMS

ONE OF THE questions we can ask about a record of land ownership is: who is it for? The earliest such record in England, at least on anything like a national scale, must have been made in Roman times, and its purpose and beneficiary are clear; for some at least of the period of Roman rule an annual *tributum capitis* (poll tax) and *tributum soli* (land tax) will have been levied, as it was throughout the empire,[1] and the information needed for the administration of the tax system was gathered in a periodic census to ascertain land holdings and liability.[2] We have some indication of the sort of information that had to be provided on these occasions, encompassing both the location and, in some detail, the productivity of the land.[3] The cadastre maintained in many modern European states but not in the UK is the descendant of this system, in scope and purpose.

Records of land holdings during the centuries following the Romans' departure may have been based on the Roman records.[4] We have to leap ahead to the eleventh century to find another strong, successful, centralised administration making comprehensive records, again for taxation purposes. William I's efforts to draw together his new realm included the compilation of Domesday Book .[5] The record for the land in Berkshire where Reading University now stands reads as follows:

Shinfield. Saxi held it in freehold from King Edward. Then for 5 hides, now for nothing. Land for 6 ploughs. In lordship one [plough?]; 8 villagers and 5 smalholders with 7 ploughs. 2 slaves; a mill at 5 shillings and 150 eels; meadow, 16 acres; woodland at 90 pigs. The value was £7; now £8.[6]

---

[1] AK Bowman, P Garnsey and D Rathbone (eds), *Cambridge Ancient History, vol XI* (Cambridge, CUP, 2000), 282 ff.

[2] *Ibid*, 287. Perhaps the best-known Roman census is that hinted at in Luke ch 2, 1.

[3] Digest 50:15:4, '. . . the number of vines in a vineyard; the number of *jugera* [acres] in an olive orchard, as well as the number of trees; where there are meadows, the quantity of hay cut from them within the last ten years. . .', SP Scott, *The Civil Law, vol IX* (New York, AMS Press, 1973), 257.

[4] E Dowson and VLO Sheppard, *Land Registration* (London, HMSO, 1956), 4–5.

[5] See Simpson, *Land Registration*, 112–4.

[6] P Morgan (ed), *Domesday Book 5, Berkshire* (Chichester, Phillimore, 1979) 1, 18.

The wish to control is stamped all over Domesday, in its detail and its geographical extent. This was a work carried out by the king, for the king and not for the people, and it bolstered his control over his country by giving him information about population and productivity. Its most basic motivation was the collection of taxation; but the detailed information collected goes beyond that, and must have enabled the conqueror mentally to grasp his new realm.[7] Like the Roman census, although it was a record of land-holding, it was a snap-shot (although it does give some idea of changing values by its careful notes of the situation in King Edward's time, before the conquest). There was no obligation to up-date the record when holdings changed, and so it would eventually go out of date. Even so, it remained accurate far longer in that relatively immobile society than would a similar survey done today; and we might add that doubtless the land was much more important to the king than the people who worked it. 'Ownership' of land by the people was meaningless in this feudal society, where land belonged to the king (as his title, *dominus rex*, precisely indicates[8]); the king's vassals held from him as his tenants in chief[9] and theirs held from them, in return for various forms of service. Land holding, and its passing from one person to another, was controlled by the feudal system that bound society together more closely than could any documentary record.

Despite its original purpose, and the hostility it engendered,[10] it seems that Domesday Book became more a facility for the people than a tool of the king and the treasury. It became an invaluable source of publicly available evidence for land holdings and feudal status.[11] In a feudal society the value of being able to see precisely what one's grandfather's holding had been is obvious. An instrument of conquest and oppression became a valuable practical record for the people, and remained so long after it ceased to be of use to the king.

The germ of a different and potentially more potent record is seen, curiously enough, in one element of the feudal system: the unfree, villein tenure of the medieval serf became, in the fourteenth and fifteenth centuries, copyhold tenure, whereby those who held land from the lord of the manor were recorded in his court roll, and held a copy of that roll as proof of their status.[12] One became a copyhold tenant by a surrender and admittance made in the lord's court, and by no other means; here, on a very local scale, is a record of land-holding which is, itself, the instrument by which the holding is created and transferred. Thus here is an early form of dispositive registration; it was actually among the precedents for the nineteenth century developments in title registration.[13] Copyhold was not

---

[7] P Morgan (ed), *Domesday Book 5, Berkshire* (Chichester, Phillimore, 1979) Introduction.

[8] Latin for an owner of land is *dominus*.

[9] Latin *tenens*, one who is holding.

[10] EM Hallam, *Domesday Book through nine centuries* (London, Thames and Hudson, 1986), 36–7.

[11] *Ibid*, 52 ff; and D Roffe, *Domesday, The Inquest and the Book* (Oxford, OUP, 2000) 17 ff.

[12] C Harpum, *Megarry and Wade, The Law of Real Property* (London, Sweet & Maxwell, 2000) (hereafter '*Megarry and Wade*'), 2–034.

[13] Sir Robert Torrens, in *The South Australian system of conveyancing by registration of title* (Adelaide, 1859), 11, refers to copyhold as 'an admirable illustration of the security and economy

abolished until 1925; thus it is still possible occasionally to find traces of it in unregistered titles.

The feudal system in its complete form did not last long; it began to disintegrate with the passing of the statute *Quia Emptores* in 1270, which prevented further subinfeudation;[14] by the end of the middle ages we find ourselves in a different world where, despite the technical talk of 'holding' land, what actually happened was something much more like ownership. By the sixteenth century, many of the feudal services have disappeared or have been commuted for a money payment; there is a reasonable degree of testamentary freedom; and land has become a commercial asset. But the structure of feudalism remains. Henry VIII, hungry for revenues, sought to halt its decline and to seize the wealth which it should have brought him but which the ingenuity of lawyers was denying him, particularly by the employment of the 'use' or trust. Land held on trust could pass from one beneficiary to another without payment of feudal dues; as is well known, the Statute of Uses of 1536 was intended to put a stop to this by executing the use, that is, passing the legal estate direct to the beneficiary. With it was passed the Statute of Enrolments, which provided that from 31 July 1536:

no manors, lands, tenements or other hereditaments, shall pass, alter or change from one to another, whereby any estate of inheritance or freehold shall be made or take effect . . . by reason only of any bargain and sale thereof, except the same bargain and sale be made by writing indented, sealed and inrolled in one of the King's courts at Westminster, or else within the same county or counties where the same manor, lands, or tenements so bargained and sold, lie or be, before the *Custos Rotulorum* and two justices of the peace.

Here was a nationwide register of dealings with land; the idea was to ensure that conveyancing was public so that feudal dues could be collected.[15] The mechanism takes some inspiration from copyhold, but seems startlingly modern in its endeavour to ensure that conveyancing simply did not happen without registration.[16] The statute is, however, very brief; it provides that no lands etc shall pass unless the document is enrolled within six months. Was it intended to be valid initially, but to become invalid if it was not in fact enrolled within the time limit?[17] Whatever its detailed operation should have been, the Statute of Enrolments did not work as

attending transfer by registration'. Stuart Anderson, in *Lawyers and the Making of English Land Law, 1832–1940*, (Oxford, Clarendon Press, 1992) (hereafter 'Anderson, *Lawyers 1832–1940*'), notes in his discussion of the evidence given to the House of Lords Select Committee on the Burdens of Land ((1846) HLP xxii 1) that copyhold was referred to as a useful precedent for a registration system.

[14] AWB Simpson, *A History of the Land Law* (Oxford, Clarendon Press, 1986), 54, 58.

[15] The Statute of Uses made it necessary; the device of executing uses could be employed deliberately as a means of passing a legal estate without the public act of livery of seisin.

[16] It is a shock to find this statute only a page or two from statutes such as 31 H8 c14, 'An act for the abolishing of diversity of opinions concerning christian religion', which is achieved by the simple expedient of setting out six articles of faith and prescribing death by burning to anyone holding or teaching a contrary opinion. The modern and medieval worlds are here cheek by jowl.

[17] Thus providing a very early precedent for s 123 of the Land Registration Act 1925 and s 7 of the Land Registration Act 2002.

intended; it took only a short time for lawyers to find ways round it, in particular by inventive use of leases.[18]

The tale of registration now changes; not so very long after Henry VIII's reign we find new plans being made for registration with a wholly different purpose.

DEEDS REGISTRATION: A SYSTEM FOR THE CONSUMER

The seventeenth century saw the breakage of the monarchy as an autocracy; it also saw repeated demands for the introduction of a register of dealings with land.[19] These demands were made by members of the landowning classes; registration has suddenly taken on a new complexion. The system envisaged, but imperfectly realised, by the Statute of Enrolments is clearly the inspiration for the new demands; the difference is that registration is being demanded as a service rather than resented as an imposition. The demands seem to have been unsuccessful during the turbulence of the seventeenth century, but bore fruit early in Queen Anne's reign where we find a statute whose preamble ran as follows:[20]

Whereas the West riding of the county of York is the principal place in the North for the cloth manufacture, and most of the traders therein are freeholders, and have frequent occasions to borrow money upon their estates for managing their said trade, but for want of a register find it difficult to give security to the satisfaction of the money lenders (although the security they offer be really good) by means whereof the said trade is very much obstructed, and many families ruined: for the remedying whereof may it please your most excellent Majesty . . . that it may be enacted . . . That a memorial of all deeds and conveyances, which from and after the [9th September 1704] shall be made and executed, and of all wills and devises in writing made or to be made or published . . . *may* at the election of the party or parties concerned, be registered in such manner as is herein after directed . . . (emphasis added)

This was the first of a series of statutes[21] setting up the Deeds Registries of Yorkshire and Middlesex, which functioned until the last of them closed in 1976.[22]

[18] Because the statute spoke only of freehold conveyancing; hence the invention of the device of conveyance by lease and release, which continued until the nineteenth century; AWB Simpson, see n 14 above, 189 ff. The statute 5 Anne 18 (see n 21 below) comments in its preamble upon other shortcomings of the Statute of Enrolments: the clerk who keeps the records is not made to give any security for their safekeeping, nor is he under any penalty for mistakes, nor is there any place for the keeping of the records. It seems that the Statute of Enrolments failed both because of its own practical shortcomings and because ways to evade it were so easily devised.
[19] J Howell, 'Deeds Registration in England: a Complete Failure?' [1999] *Cambridge Law Journal* 366 at 371–2, traces a remarkable number of bills seeking to establish a register during the seventeenth century. The establishment of deeds registries was one of Oliver Cromwell's projects; WS Holdsworth (*A History of English Law* (London, Methuen, 1924) at 416 and 423) suggests that it could not go ahead because it needed the co-operation of lawyers, to whom the Commonwealth was 'distasteful'.
[20] 2 & 3 Anne, c 4 (1703).
[21] There followed 5 Anne c 18, 6 Anne c 35 and 7 Anne c 20 (the latter is known as the Middlesex Registry Act 1708). Registration in Yorkshire was eventually governed by the Yorkshire Registries Act 1884, which repealed the earliest statutes.
[22] The deeds registries closed when title registration became compulsory for their areas: J Howell, see n 19 above at 376.

These local schemes, confined to two small areas of the country, were wholly modern in their purpose: that of providing a service to the individual landowner, so as to improve the commercial value of his land. Notice that conveyancing itself does not, on the face of the statute, seem to be a problem; the mischief addressed is the difficulty of using land as security for loans. Why Yorkshire and Middlesex? We may never know; doubtless there were local and political factors, now undiscoverable, at work.[23]

The mechanics of deeds registration in Yorkshire and Middlesex was consistent with the motivation of the legislation. The scheme of the statutes was to prescribe that deeds and wills executed after a certain date might (not must) be registered; and that any registrable deed not so registered was void for the purposes of priority. Thus, again, registration is not dispositive—conveyancing works perfectly well without it; but the registration system changes and rationalises the position on priorities. This is consistent with its aim of making land more readily mortgageable.

Priorities have bedevilled the law of unregistered land and have given rise to volumes of difficult case law. The problem is simple: given an offer of land by way of security for a loan, and a heap of title deeds in the possession of the borrower, how can the lender know that there is not already a mortgage subsisting? A first mortgagee would be expected to have the title deeds,[24] but it was not unknown for that right not to be exercised;[25] second and subsequent mortgages were easily concealed.[26] Land would be much more acceptable as security if the lender knew that the title was unencumbered. This was achieved by the provision that an unregistered deed was void against a later, registered one;[27] thus if the lender searched the register[28] and found no mortgage registered there he could accept a mortgage with confidence, provided that he then registered it promptly.[29] Thus the ancient rule that the first in time wins, while very acceptable in a relatively static society, is taken over by a registration-based rule of priority once land has become a traded asset.[30]

---

[23] That local registration was not, however, unique to Yorkshire and Middlesex can be seen in the second of the two sections of the Statute of Enrolments of 1536, which states that that Act does not apply to land in a city or town 'wherein the mayors, recorders . . . or other officers . . . have authority or have lawfully used to inroll any evidence, deeds or other writings within their precincts or limits.' Might there perhaps have been a closer parallel between practice in England and the city-based registration systems of the Hanseatic States (see ch 1 n 42) than has been realised?

[24] He now has that right by statute: Law of Property Act 1925 s 85(1); before 1925, the first legal mortgagee had the fee simple and thereby would take the title deeds. Where the first mortgage was equitable, the mortgagee could protect himself by custody of the deeds: *Megarry and Wade*, 19–035.

[25] *Clarke v Palmer* (1882) 21 Ch D 124.

[26] Particularly if a second mortgagee kept the documentation himself rather than insisting on its being kept with the title deeds; the writer recalls, from practice during the 1980s, second mortgagee clients adopting this policy despite advice not to do so.

[27] 2&3 Anne c 4, s 1: 'shall be adjudged fraudulent and void against any subsequent purchaser or mortgagee for valuable consideration'. Yorkshire Registries Act 1844, s 14: 'all assurances entitled to be registered under this Act shall have priority according to the date of registration thereof'.

[28] Against the name of the borrower; see below.

[29] The idea of a search with a priority period was an invention of the twentieth century.

[30] See P O'Connor, 'Information, Automation and the Conclusive Land Register', in Grinlinton, *Torrens Conference Papers*.

This reassuringly clear position was then skewed by a decision in 1747 that a mortgagee was, nevertheless, bound by a prior, unregistered, mortgage of which he had constructive notice.[31] The effect of that decision was to create a race-notice system. This was repealed, for the Yorkshire registry, by statute, which provided that the purchaser was not to lose priority by reason of notice, actual or constructive, 'except in cases of actual fraud';[32] it is not known how much difficulty it caused in Middlesex.

The registers were indexed, and therefore searched, by names; the record is based on people rather than properties. Searching was therefore by no means a one-stop affair and could take many hours, perhaps days for a complex title.[33] This was inevitable in the absence, until the mid-nineteenth century, of an adequate map for the whole of England and Wales.[34]

The Yorkshire and Middlesex deeds registries remained in operation after 1925, and explicit provision was made for them in the 1925 legislation.[35] They worked well; they must be regarded as precursors of the Land Charges Act 1925. They might have formed the basis of a nationwide system had not title registration caught the attention of the nineteenth century reformers. Jean Howell has argued that there was nothing intrinsically wrong with the deeds registry system.[36] Certainly, legislation could have amended weaknesses and made the registries more comprehensive, in particular by tightening up compulsion; but deeds registration could not, by itself, have made title simpler. Searching the registry, and interpreting what one found there, still demanded time and all the skills of the traditional conveyancer. We do not know how accurate were the complaints about complexity of title in the nineteenth century; certainly it cannot have been irrelevant to the debate that deeds registration perpetuated the ancient, dynastic system of deducing title,[37] while title registration offered something wholly different.

THE NINETEENTH CENTURY AND THE LAW OF PROPERTY ACT 1925

The nineteenth century was a time of tremendous legal reform, as the law struggled to emerge from its still medieval formulas into something that could make

---

[31] *Le Neve v Le Neve* (1747) Amb 436, citing earlier cases such as *Blades v Blades* (1727) 1 Eq Cas Abr 358. The case demonstrates just how difficult it is, morally and emotionally, to accept the logic of registration in the face of sharp practice (in this case, a later marriage settlement of properties already settled on the issue of an earlier marriage).

[32] Yorkshire Registries Act 1884, s 14. Yorkshire thus became a 'race' system (since fraud is defined so as to be narrower than notice), in the terminology now used to describe the American and Canadian systems: see ch 1, text at n 13.

[33] J Howell, [1999] CLJ 366 at 380.

[34] J Howell, [1999] CLJ 366 at 381; A Pottage, 'The Measure of Land' (1994) 57 *Modern Law Review* 361.

[35] The now repealed s 11 of the Law of Property Act 1925.

[36] [1999] CLJ 366.

[37] Dynastic because entitlements must be traced back along one or more branches, not unlike a family tree; the term is Alain Pottage's. See 'The Originality of Registration' (1995) 15 *Oxford Journal of Legal Studies* 370.

sense to the people of the industrial revolution as well as the landed gentry. Amidst the reform of the franchise, the abolition of the ancient forms of action, and the revolution in the organisation of the courts, a great debate rolled onwards about the future of the land law. The culmination of that debate was, of course, the six property statutes of 1925; of these, the most important for our purposes are the Law of Property Act 1925, the Land Charges Act 1925 and the Land Registration Act 1925.[38]

The problem was complexity.[39] Then as now, the money earned by lawyers out of the complexity of the law, and the time spent in achieving transactions, was a matter for discontent; and although there was doubtless some exaggeration at work, it was clear that something had to be done about the difficulty of deducing title to property and of passing a clean title to purchasers.[40] There was frustration about the duplication of work involved in the fact that an unregistered title must be investigated afresh every time there was a dealing with the property. The legal and political debate that surrounded the land law in the nineteenth century is well documented elsewhere.[41] We know that originally there were plans to extend the systems of deeds registration, and that a number of Bills for such a system were prepared, but that title registration swiftly took over as the ideal from the early 1850s onwards.[42] But registration was not the only item on the agenda. Reform of the underlying law of real property proceeded with less drama and rather more success until the early years of the twentieth century, when reform began to be seen as a competition between simplification and registration.[43] Hence the multiple system we have inherited, to the dismay of all students of land law. The Law of Property Act 1925 both codified and simplified the earlier law; the Land Charges Act 1925 added on to that law a system of interest recording; and the Land Registration Act 1925 built on the system of title registration which had already been the subject of nineteenth century experiment.

The 1925 legislation is still in force, with amendments but largely in its original form. Few statutes have had so long a shelf-life; and the Law of Property Act 1925

---

[38] The others are the Settled Land Act 1925, the Trustee Act 1925 and the Administration of Estates Act 1925.

[39] There is debate about this. Anderson says: 'In England neither debt not complexity was the issue, only repetitive re-examination of title' (Anderson, *Lawyers 1832–1940*, 91). Not all titles were complex. Some were; some unregistered titles remain unpleasantly complex today. Many were very long, giving an impression at least of potential complexity; certainly length meant time spent by lawyers. Torrens himself (see n 13 above) was quite clear that complexity was a big problem, yet Australian titles cannot, in general, have been as complex as English ones.

[40] HM Land Registry's *Annual Report and Accounts, 1991–92* (London, HMSO, 1992) reports (with a picture) the registration of the title to Prudential Building at 442 Holborn Bars, London EC1: 'The site comprised 36 unregistered freehold titles, 16 registered freehold titles and several unregistered leasehold titles stored in several large boxes of deeds. These have been replaced by a 4-page computerised register'.

[41] In particular: A Offer, *Property and Politics 1870—1914* (Cambridge, CUP, 1981); Anderson, *Lawyers 1832–1940*.

[42] Anderson, *Lawyers 1832–1940*, 76—84. The Royal Commission on Registration of Title was appointed in 1854.

[43] *Ibid*, 283, 291.

will continue to be the bed-rock of land law for (probably) many years to come. It has been described as 'a compendium of answers to particular questions' rather than a set of principles;[44] yet we must use it as a generator of principle and, indeed, it has not done too badly as such. At this distance from the preoccupations of the time it is not easy to get a clear view of what the Law of Property Act 1925 did, and any account, including this one, is coloured by the experience of nearly three generations of legal practice.

Without attempting a complete account of its provisions,[45] we can say that the main achievement of the Law of Property Act 1925 was to settle the relationship between legal and equitable rights in land.

The co-existence of multiple ownership rights in the same land is the distinguishing feature of the common law; it is what sets us apart from our Roman neighbours. The uniquely common law expression of this diversity is the recognition of both legal and equitable ownership, through the institution of the trust. This means that the question 'whose is this?' may be easy to answer in the case of a piano or a hamster, but very difficult in the case of land in a common law jurisdiction. This is still a very English issue, despite the apparent reception of the concept of the trust in European law. The definition of a trust in the Hague Trusts Convention means that it encompasses a number of concepts that are not trusts at all in the English sense, and where ownership remains unitary.[46]

The 1925 legislation was a valiant, and remarkably successful, attempt to put the law on a better, more user-friendly footing. It brought to a conclusion nearly a century of debate about the role that equitable interests should play in a reformed land law. The closing chapters of Stuart Anderson's book[47] demonstrate how difficult it was to achieve that conclusion, and how much of the success of the 1925 Act has depended upon subsequent interpretation of its compromised and at times loosely drafted provisions. For example, it is not clear from the statute (as it was in the original draft of the 1922 legislation) that all equitable interests must henceforth exist behind the curtain of a trust;[48] but that is what the draftsman wanted, and that is what the courts have achieved.

The Law of Property Act 1925 limited the number of legal estates in land to two:[49] the fee simple absolute in possession, and the term of years absolute. This was a dramatic change, affecting not so much the day-to-day reality of ownership but the form of transactions in land. Legal form of ownership was boiled down to

---

[44] *Ibid*, 331.

[45] The reader is referred to the standard works on English Land Law, and in particular to *Megarry and Wade*.

[46] See M Lupoi, 'Effects of the Hague Convention in a Civil Law Country', in *The Reform of Property Law*, P Jackson and D Wilde (eds), (Aldershot, Ashgate, 1997), 222. More generally, see DJ Hayton, SCJJ Kortmann, HLE Verhayen, *Principles of European Trust Law* (The Hague, Kluwer Law International, 1999).

[47] Anderson, *Lawyers 1832–1940*.

[48] *Ibid*, 292, 297, 309, 313. Thus the Act does not state that there is a trust when a sole legal owner holds land on trust for himself and another; but the desired conclusion was reached in *Williams & Glyn's Bank v Boland* [1981] AC 487.

[49] Law of Property Act 1925, s 1.

two things: the freehold and the lease; and from 1926 onwards these formed the basis of conveyancing. Conveyancing, in this context, is the ancient deeds-based system, whereby title is proved by the production of a heap of deeds. In theory the chain of ownership goes back to 1066, but the law requires documents to be produced only as far back as a 'good root' of title. This is a document which deals with the whole of the legal and equitable interest in the land, describes the property fully, and casts no doubt on the title.[50] Statute sets out the required age of the root of title (in 1925 it was 60 years, and it is now 15);[51] the length of time prescribed is intimately connected to the limitation period.[52] A seller of land who holds a 'paper title' must be able to show that he has owned it for at least as long as the time needed in order to acquire what is colloquially known as squatters' rights to the land (of which more later), in other words title by adverse possession. The effect of the cutting down of the number of legal estates was, primarily, that the conveyancer would be concerned with much less material. But it also meant that a range of property rights were downgraded.[53]

Another change, this time a small one, takes the streamlining further: the maximum possible number of holders of a legal estate was reduced to four;[54] and legal co-owners must hold as joint tenants, not as tenants in common.[55]

A further important element in the scheme of the Law of Property Act 1925 was overreaching. This has often been supposed to have been an invention of the Law of Property Act 1925, but it was not.[56] It is a fundamental feature of modern English land law; the essence of the idea is that a transaction which meets certain qualifications will have the effect not only of transferring a legal title to a purchaser but also of stripping the property of certain equitable interests. Thus the purchaser gets a clean title; and the holder of the equitable interest has a claim, not against the property but against the proceeds of sale in the hands of the vendor. The conditions for an overreaching transaction where land is held on trust are set out in section 2 of the Law of Property Act 1925: the sale must be made by two legal owners, or a trust corporation. This means that all sales or mortgages of property where there are successive or concurrent beneficial interests *may* be overreached provided those conditions are met. Thus if A and B are the legal owners of land, but hold it on trust for C and D, then when they convey it to P the two beneficiaries, C and D, will have no further claim against the land. That remains the case even if P knew of their equitable ownership and so would, according to the usual rules, be bound by it.

[50] One learns this by rote; the authority given by *Megarry and Wade* at 12–076 is TC Williams and JM Lightwood, *A Treatise on the Law of Vendor and Purchaser*, 1936, 124.
[51] Law of Property Act 1925, s 44(1) and Law of Property Act 1969 s 23.
[52] M Dockray, 'Why Do We Need Adverse Possession?' [1985] *Conveyancer* 272.
[53] Sch 1 Part I to the Law of Property Act 1925 made the transitional provision that those whose rights had been transformed from legal to equitable would not lose priority or enforceability.
[54] Law of Property Act 1925, s 34(2).
[55] *Ibid* s 34(1); for the problems with the drafting of this section see Smith *Property Law*, 305–6.
[56] C Harpum, 'Overreaching, Trustees' Powers and the Reform of the 1925 Legislation', [1990] *Cambridge Law Journal* 277.

Overreaching is actually rather complex. Pre-1925 case law establishes that overreaching cannot happen unless the transaction is within the powers of the owner(s), or *intra vires* as the legal shorthand has it. Charles Harpum's seminal article in 1990[57] demonstrated that overreaching is a feature of dispositions by owners whose powers are limited. They may hold the legal estate, as trustees, and so have the ability to transfer it but, because of the terms of the trust, have only limited authority to do so.[58] Or they may be mortgagees, who do not actually hold the legal estate but nevertheless have the ability, and a limited authority, to transfer it to others. Harpum has demonstrated that the rule was clear: a transaction that was outside the transferor's powers, or involved a misapplication of the purchase moneys, would not overreach. A purchaser would therefore be bound by the beneficiaries' interests if he had notice of them; and the rules of notice were so strict that a purchaser could easily find himself deemed to know something that he really was not aware of.[59] Harpum showed that the 1925 legislation facilitated overreaching by endeavouring to ensure that in all cases where land was held upon trust, that fact would be obvious. Warned of the trust, the purchaser could then check that the disposition was within the trustees' powers.[60]

Unfortunately, as Harpum demonstrated, the law developed in such a way that land may be held upon trust in circumstances where the purchaser cannot be aware of that fact; in particular, if land is held by a sole trustee.[61] The position is now governed by the Trusts of Land and Appointment of Trustees Act 1996, where section 16 protects the purchaser who takes land innocently from a trustee who is acting in excess of his powers and ensures that overreaching will nevertheless take place—as was intended in the 1925 scheme.[62]

The overall effect of the Law of Property Act 1925 is thus to limit the number of possible interests, to set up a structure where it is clear whether they are legal or equitable, and to facilitate the removal of equitable interests from the land by overreaching. The system set up in the Law of Property Act 1925 forms the bedrock upon which are built two systems of registration.

---

[57] N 56 above. Harpum's approach was endorsed by the Court of Appeal in *State Bank of India v Sood* [1997] Ch 276.

[58] This is discussed in more detail in ch 4, following n 12.

[59] Harpum, n 56 above, at 283–285.

[60] Harpum, n 56 above, 290 ff. In addition, s 17 Trustee Act 1925 states that the purchaser need not be concerned about the application of the proceeds (and this seems to have been relied upon to ensure that overreaching happened in the landmark decision *City of London Building Society v Flegg* [1988] AC 54, HL, despite the trustees' misuse of the money in that case; Harpum, n 56 above, 309; cf, Anderson *Lawyers 1832–1940*, 330. Ferris and Battersby, n 62 below, argue that the wording of s 2 of the Law of Property Act 1925 also relieves the purchaser from any concern that the trustees' powers may be being used for an improper purpose. Thus the draftsman is doing everything possible to ensure that the awkward eventualities that might prevent overreaching are eliminated, *provided* the purchaser knows there is a trust and checks the trustees' powers.

[61] *Bull v Bull* [1955] 1 QB 234, CA; Harpum, n 56 above, 301 ff.

[62] G Ferris and G Battersby, 'The Impact of the Trusts of Land and Appointment of Trustees Act 1996 on Purchasers of Registered Land' [1998] *Conveyancer* 168 at 176, discussing the effect of s 16 on purchasers of unregistered land. The problem of overreaching in registered land is discussed in ch 4, below.

THE LAND CHARGES ACT 1925: INTEREST RECORDING

The Law of Property Act 1925 stills leaves us with a system where a multitude and variety of rights can co-exist in land, so that an owner very rarely has the whole thing; it is likely that someone else has an interest in his property, or that someone else is, to a greater or lesser extent, an owner of it. In terms of a transaction, that means that a purchaser is at risk. The documentary title shown to him should give him details of everything that affects the title being sold; but it may not be complete. Any legal rights in the property will endure beyond a sale and so bind him (for example an easement; or a mortgage if it is not redeemed on the sale); any equitable rights will bind him but only by notice. The rules of constructive notice are such that he may be found to have known something he did not know but should have known. The other side of the coin is that for holders of those equitable rights a sale of the property always involves a risk that their rights will be lost. Title registration embodies, or seeks to embody, the ideal that all interests in land can be seen in one record; the Land Charges Act 1925 introduces a hybrid—it is tempting to say half-hearted—approach to that ideal, namely interest recording, where ownership remains provable by deeds, but certain other interests are recorded in a public register.

The advantage of this is privacy (assuming that to be an advantage). The register does not reveal who owns Bleak House; but if I have, say, an equitable easement over Bleak House, I must protect it by registration or risk losing it when the land is sold. Moreover, if I am buying Bleak House I know that I must take my information about the legal estate from the deeds, but I have additional protection and help from the Land Charges Register which will reveal to me certain interests that may or may not otherwise have affected me, but which I might not have otherwise discovered.

This system of interest recording is by no means straightforward. It is not purely a matter of protecting the holders of equitable rights who would otherwise have lost their interests, because some legal interests are protected too,[63] while not all equitable interests are registrable. Notably, beneficial ownership, existing behind a trust, is not registrable; the intention was that such rights should be overreached, so that registration was not necessary to protect purchasers nor relevant to protect beneficiaries. Nor is land charges registration simply a matter of protecting purchasers from undiscoverable legal interests, because most such interests are not registrable. So it does not exactly tidy up the land law. Nor is it dispositive, any more than deeds registration was; it has no effect upon the creation of the registrable rights, which remain perfectly valid between the original parties. Equally, if

---

[63] Notably, a legal mortgage not protected by deposit of title deeds. Without the Land Charges Act 1925, this is a legal right, automatically binding upon the purchaser unless redeemed on the sale (as it normally would be). Such mortgages are second mortgages, because of course the deeds would be with the holder of the first legal mortgage (see n 24 above). By providing for the registration of such mortgages as a land charge the statute ensures that they are binding only where they are discoverable.

an interest is invalid, perhaps because of inadequate documentation, registration does not make it valid (although registration will turn it into a conveyancing nuisance). Registration affects enforceability only.

Compulsion works just as it did in the Middlesex and Yorkshire deeds registration systems. Registration under the Land Charges Acts constitutes actual notice to all the world,[64] so that a purchaser is bound by all land charges, even if he would not otherwise have been bound because they are equitable and he had no notice of them. Moreover, interests which *can* be[65] registered as land charges *must* be so registered or be void against (broadly) most purchasers.[66] The rule is strict; an unregistered land charge is void even if the purchaser knew about it, indeed even if the purpose of the conveyance was to defeat the interest.[67] Interestingly, the statute thus speaks in the old language of notice,[68] even though what is binding is registration. More interesting: even in this to us now rather primitive system of registration, we are seeing something much more subtle than a mere record of the truth. This is a changing of the truth. Equitable interests become binding automatically despite their equitable status; and some legal interests fail to bind when they are unregistered, despite being legal. The written record has made a fundamental change to that which it is recording.

The Land Charges Acts[69] could never be more than a temporary measure, indeed they almost seem to pre-suppose a short-term operation because, like Domesday, they create a snapshot. The register records interests by the name of the person against whom they are created, and contains no mechanism for referencing them to the current ownership of property. Thus if I buy unregistered land now, and an estate contract was registered against a purchaser in 1930, the title deduced to me will probably contain no evidence of that 1930 owner and I will never actually find the registration. That does not matter because doubtless the contract is long defunct; but a restrictive covenant might well not be, and it is easy to see how a purchaser could be caught by pre-root encumbrances. There is now a scheme of compensation for any one so caught.[70]

---

[64] Law of Property Act 1925, s 198.

[65] The list is now in s 2 of the Land Charges Act 1972.

[66] The precise rule is perversely complex: an unregistered land charge of Classes A B, C(i), (ii), (iii) and F is void against any purchaser of the land or of any interest in it; an unregistered C(iv) or D is void against a purchaser for money or money's worth of a legal estate in the land; s 4 Land Charges Act 1972. In any event a donee of the land takes it just as it was in the hands of the giver.

[67] *Midland Bank Trust Co Ltd v Green* [1981] AC 513. What is now s 14 of the Law of Property Act 1925 (which states that 'this Part of this Act shall not prejudicially affect the interest of any person in possession or in actual occupation of the land') is a re-enactment of s 33 of the Law of Property Act 1922, where it stood with the provisions on land charges registration; thus the original intention seems to have been that occupiers' interests should bind purchasers even if they could have been registered but were not. That would reverse the result in *Midland Bank v Green*, and would achieve consistency with the Land Registration Act 1925! (Harpum, see n 56 above, at 318, n 22; and Hayton, *Registered Land*, (London, Sweet & Maxwell, 1981), 16).

[68] The provision is an echo of s 15 of the Yorkshire Registries Act 1844.

[69] The current statute is the Land Charges Act 1972.

[70] The scheme has been scarcely used: Smith, *Property Law*, 217. Far less fundamental to the scheme of the Act is the silliness of a computer system that requires a search against names and cannot cope

Land Charges registration is, therefore, an incomplete and inaccurate form of interest recording, because it records only a selected number of interests, and does so in a way that may make them undiscoverable. This is not to say that it has been a failure; it has in fact functioned surprisingly well. But we could not expect it to survive any thoroughgoing reform.

THE LAND REGISTRATION ACT 1925: TITLE REGISTRATION

Title registration in England and Wales was by no means new in 1925. The Land Registration Act 1925 was the latest in a series of statutes that progressively refined the system of title registration, beginning with the Transfer of Land Act 1862 and continuing in the Land Transfer Acts 1875 and 1897.

The Appointment of a Royal Commission on Registration of Title in 1854 meant that title registration was being explored in this jurisdiction at just the same time as it was in Australia; in both jurisdictions there was some awareness of the precedent of the Hanseatic states.[71] Sir Robert Torrens was elected Prime Minister of South Australia in 1857, on the basis of his promise to introduce registration, which he did in the statute of 1858; and in his pamphlet of 1859 he acknowledged the similarities between his scheme and that recommended by the Royal Commission, while disclaiming plagiarism.[72] It is not hard to imagine how reluctant would be the nineteenth century English legal profession and Parliament to take a precedent from a colony. The system introduced in the 1862 Act was nevertheless not so far removed from the Australian system, and it does seem that the two systems started off in similar form, almost independently but with common Germanic roots. But three features set the systems apart in 1862. One substantive difference was the absence of provision in the 1862 and 1875 statutes for an indemnity fund, to enable compensation to be made for errors in the register. This meant that the standard of title that an owner must prove in order to be awarded 'title absolute' was almost unattainably high.[73] Second, the English system was not compulsory. There were no events triggering registration; the idea was that registration should be its own reward, offering such advantages to the landowner that he would register voluntarily. Again, only a little knowledge of the characteristics of the English propertied classes in the nineteenth century makes it easy to imagine how fiercely compulsion was resisted. Indeed, resistance was very sensible. Registration was expensive because of the standard of title to be proved; and the procedure involved detailed inquiries of neighbours about boundaries, and thus

with variant spellings, nor with the addition or subtraction of middle names. Thus there is extensive case law about the consequences of searching the wrong version of a name, or not searching against a name that would have been undiscoverable anyway because incorrectly recorded. We can only hope that a system invented today would be more flexible.

[71] See ch 1 above, text at n 42.

[72] *The South Australian System of Conveyancing by Registration of Title* (Adelaide, 1859), Preface.

[73] S 5 of the 1862 Act requires a title 'such as a Court of Equity would hold to be a valid marketable title' which, as Anderson explains, was a much stricter standard than was commonly accepted by purchasers (Anderson, *Lawyers 1832–1940*, 115).

risked provoking disputes which would not otherwise have arisen. The combination of a voluntary system and an excessively high standard for titles meant that the first two English statutes could not possibly work. Third, although forms were provided for dealings with registered land, the landowner was free to deal with it by deed and to produce the deed in due course for notation by the registrar.[74] Thus registration was not even properly dispositive; even if the 1862 Act had induced universal registration, the system would have collapsed swiftly.

Compulsion was finally conceded in the 1890s,[75] and when it was introduced in the Act of 1897 the attempt precisely to define all boundaries had been abandoned, the standard of title required was far more pragmatic and realistic, and there was a scheme of compensation for loss caused by the operation of the system; thus the English system now involved at least a rudimentary form of insurance, which is not logically essential to title registration but is regarded, as we have seen, as one of its standard features. Even then, land came on to the register extremely slowly; contrast the situation in Australia where, in the mid-nineteenth century, grants of land were still being made directly from the Crown, registration was compulsory on grant or conveyance, and trade in land was brisk. Small wonder that registration rapidly became the norm rather than the exception in South Australia, the other Australian states that rapidly followed its example, and New Zealand, on a scale that did not happen in this jurisdiction until the last quarter of the twentieth century.

The 1897 Act did not work very well, and a Royal Commission on the Land Transfer Acts was appointed in 1908 in order to investigate why so few titles were being registered. It reported in 1911. But it was not until after the 1914–1918 war that it was feasible to introduce the large-scale legislation that was needed. The process was fraught with controversy. One fascinating thread running through the development of title registration—and a major reason why it took so long—is the hostility it aroused in the breasts of at least some lawyers, charted by Avner Offer and Stuart Anderson in their respective books and from their different perspectives. Some of it was linked to the fear of lost conveyancing revenue; some of it must have been emotional. Even today, many of us feel wistful about the loss of deeds, and of the pleasure of investigating them. In the light of the very early precedents for registration it is interesting to note that some of the resistance to reform arose from the fear of taxation and of tyranny fostered by centrally-held information;[76] there was a scheme for registration of title to form part of a cadastre-like central record which could be used for taxation purposes, actually called a 'Domesday scheme'.[77] That idea came to nothing, and the scheme of title registration in the 1925 legislation continued in a more or less familiar form.

---

[74] The same problems occurred in Ireland; see A Dowling, 'Of Ships and Sealing Wax: the Introduction of Land Registration in Ireland', (1993) 44 *Northern Ireland Legal Quarterly* 360 at 362, and ch 9, text at n 7.

[75] Anderson, *Lawyers 1832–1940*, 115, 205.

[76] *Ibid*; A Offer, 'The Origins of the Law of Property Acts 1920–1925' (1977) 40 *Modern Law Review* 505, 507 ff.

[77] Anderson, *Lawyers 1832–1940*, 251.

The 1925 statute was still intended as an experiment; initially, registration was possible only in Greater London. The plan was for it to be reviewed in a few years' time, when an assessment would be made of its success or otherwise, and a decision taken as to whether or not it would continue. Meanwhile, the Privy Council's power to extend areas of compulsory registration was unavailable for 10 years.[78] In fact no assessment took place, no decision was ever taken, and registration was simply extended gradually, until in 1989 the whole of England and Wales became subject to compulsory registration.[79] Thus for nearly a century we have had to be familiar with two versions of land law, according to whether or not title is registered. The aim now, of government and Land Registry, is to finish the job and eliminate the dichotomy. Thus the Land Registration Act 1997 introduced further triggering events, so that now nearly (but not quite) everything one does with unregistered land will trigger first registration. The Land Registration Act 2002 adopted the new tactic of making registered title explicitly better (that is, more secure) than unregistered land with the aim of inducing voluntary registration; and the Law Commission has recommended that if this is not effective to bring the whole of land in England and Wales on to the register in, say, five years' time, further measures should be considered.[80]

Title registration is thus the winner in the battle of different forms of registration in this jurisdiction; the Middlesex and Yorkshire deeds registries are closed, and in another generation the Land Charges Acts will almost certainly have become a matter of history. Why? It is a measure of the success of the nineteenth century reforms and of the Law of Property Act 1925, as well as of the problems with the Land Registration Act 1925, that doubt has been expressed quite recently as to whether title registration offers any benefit at all.[81] Victory for title registration was not inevitable; even after 1925, it could have suffered the same fate as it did in America.[82] There are several reasons why that did not happen.

First, title insurance has never become prevalent in this jurisdiction, and so has not been present either as a source of commercial opposition to title registration or as a way of making unregistered title safer. Second, the extension of areas of compulsory registration has proceeded slowly but steadily, so that eventually there was no point in not completing the job (whereas in none of the American states has title registration been compulsory).[83] Those two factors alone would ensure

---

[78] Land Registration Act 1925, s 120(2).

[79] SI 1989 No 1347.

[80] LC 271, 2.13.

[81] 'We are left with the unpalatable conclusion that the registered system makes conveyancing more expensive without any useful improvement in the quality of titles.' R Smith, *Property Law* 3rd edn, Longman, 2000), 248. In the fourth edition of the same book, (Smith, *Property Law*, 273) the author is more positive about registration, but notes that registered conveyancing is still more expensive than unregistered because of land registry fees, and does not seem to have made the sale of land any quicker: 'Although the delays in the Land Registry have been eradicated, it is difficult to conclude that registration has much improved the speed or efficiency of dealings with land'.

[82] See ch 1, n 51.

[83] RA Cunningham, WB Stoebuck and DA Whitman, *The Law of Property* (St Paul, West Publishing Co, 1993), 881.

the eventual success of title registration, for better or for worse. But alongside the process of extension of compulsory registration, the substantive law itself has been developing. With the growth in volume of land registration and its consequent growing practical importance has come a shift in attitude: the acceptance of the law of registered title as a separate system independent of registered land. This has happened gradually. It was perfectly natural for registered title to take root as a derivative of unregistered title. There has even been some confusion caused by the famous idea that the title register is a mirror;[84] there has been a temptation to see that as meaning that the register mirrors the state of the title as it was or would be without registration, whereas of course the expression is intended to convey the idea that the register mirrors the title itself. To some extent, similarity with unregistered title ensured acceptance of the system after 1925; thus the provisions of section 70(1)(g) of the 1925 Act[85] were slightly different from the old doctrine of notice, but nevertheless reassuringly close. Only with the passing of decades has come the confidence to affirm the independence of registered title. Famously, this was made explicit in *William & Glynn's Bank Ltd v Boland*[86] when the House of Lords rejected argument that section 70(1)(g) was to be construed so as to reach a result consistent with the position that would have obtained in unregistered land.[87] In another difficult case on registered title, *Spectrum Investment Co v Holmes*,[88] this time on adverse possession, Browne-Wilkinson J (as he then was) summed up the decision in *Boland* as a statement that:

if the words of the Land Registration Act 1925 are clear, they are to be given their natural meaning and not distorted so as to seek uniformity in the substantive law as between registered and unregistered land.[89]

Applying that principle, he went on to reach a decision in *Spectrum* that could not have been made if title had not been registered, and explained:

I approach this question on the basis that one would expect that substantive legal rights would be the same whether the land is registered or unregistered but that clear words in the Act of 1925 must be given their natural meaning even if this leads to a divergence.[90]

The tide of independence ebbed and flowed; as late as 1988 we find the Law Commission advocating a provision for rectification of the register:

[84] The expression was coined by TB Ruoff, in *An Englishman Looks at the Torrens System* (Sydney; Law Book Company, 1957), 8.
[85] Proprietary rights of those in actual occupation of a property, and of those receiving rent from it, are overriding interests and bind the purchaser unless he has made enquiry of the interest-holder and the latter has failed to disclose his rights.
[86] [1980] 3 WLR 138
[87] Although in fact, in that instance, it is clear that the law of unregistered title has now followed that in registered title.
[88] [1981] 1 WLR 221.
[89] *Ibid* at 230B.
[90] *Ibid* at 230B.

if the title to the registered interest as shown by the register does not correspond to the title which would subsist to that interest if the registered estate had not been registered.[91]

Such a provision is unimaginable to anyone who has read LC 254, LC 271, and the Act of 2002; yet on closer examination of the law of rectification we find that English law is still closely tied to the principles of unregistered land in the area of indefeasibility.[92]

Nevertheless, in the Land Registration Act 2002 and the Law Commission documents that preceded it we find the divergence of registered from unregistered title affirmed with confidence and reinforced. It has finally been appreciated that title registration can be used to manipulate the nature of title; for the first time we see real legislative enthusiasm for title registration not merely because of its accuracy or its potential benefit to conveyancers, but also because of its ability to change the law relating to land ownership. In the following chapters we shall be looking at the detail of the new law, and we shall see how that law reform potential is being harnessed in the 2002 statute. The focus of the following chapters will therefore be on the nature and the security of ownership, rather than on the detailed mechanics of conveyancing or on the 2002 Act's administrative procedures.[93]

A final factor that has ensured the success, and the take-over, of title registration is the demand for electronic conveyancing. This is the electronic age; if I can buy books, music and holidays through my computer, why not a house? For some years now the stock market has been computerised, with purchases and payments orchestrated through the CREST system. And naturally the Land Registry has moved from typewriters to word processors, so that data is in electronic form. Two further steps will make the system fully electronic; first, electronic access to the register, so that it can be searched from a solicitor's desk, and second, the ability to carry out transactions electronically, so that the click of a solicitor's mouse would both complete and register the transaction. What ensured the passage of the Land Registration Act 2002 through Parliament was its provisions for electronic conveyancing; there are votes in conveyancing reform.[94]

---

[91] *Property Law: Fourth Report on Land Registration* (Law Com No 17), (London, HMSO, 1988) cl 46(1) to the draft Bill. See R Smith, 'Land Registration: Reform at Last?' in P Jackson and D Wilde (eds) *the Reform of Property Law* (Aldershot, Ashgate, 1997).

[92] See ch 6, below.

[93] In particular, the new office of the Adjudicator, the procedure for making rules under the Act, and the administration of the Land Registry.

[94] Electronic conveyancing is discussed in ch 8, below.

3

The Registrable Estates

T HIS CHAPTER EXAMINES the registered title. We ask what can be registered, when it has to be registered, and what the register of title looks like. The effect of registration is considered in chapters 4 and 5. The analysis in this chapter is based upon the 2002 statute, but explains where that statute differs from its 1925 predecessor (which, of course, it has repealed). In particular, the 2002 Act permits the registration of a wider range of estates; but it is suggested that the principal change has been a considerable gain in clarity.

THE 1925 HIERARCHY OF PROPERTY RIGHTS IN LAND

As is well known, lawyers deal not in land, but in interests, or rights, in land. It is the possibility of the co-existence of so many different types of rights in land that makes dealing with it potentially complex. Much was done in the nineteenth century to organise and simplify this, but the modern starting point is the Law of Property Act 1925, which made the fee simple and the lease the only possible legal estates in land (an estate being the lawyer's term for an ownership right: the right to hold land for a time). The fee simple, often called the freehold,[1] and the lease were thus made the basis of conveyancing. To that end, its opening section set up a hierarchy of proprietary rights in land:

—Legal estates (there are two of these, the fee simple and the lease)[2]
—Legal interests (these are set out in an exhaustive list)[3]
—Equitable interests (everything else).[4]

---

[1] This is a confusion of terms, although now deeply engrained in our language. The fee simple is the right to hold land and pass it on to one's heirs without restriction—almost an open-ended ownership right. 'Freehold' refers to the quality of the holding in feudal terminology, and now means that the land is held from the Crown; contrast the leasehold, held from an intermediate landlord. Technically one holds an estate in fee simple, of freehold tenure, but the terms have been conflated.

[2] S 1(1).

[3] S 1(2): in summary, legal easements, rentcharges, legal mortgages and rights of entry. The definitions are thus circular by their use of the term 'legal', and import an understanding of the conditions for the creation of a legal interest, in particular the law relating to formalities.

[4] S 1(3). There is no list, and the category is an open one, subject to the limitation in s 4(1) that restricts equitable interests to those that could have been created before 1925, so that we are not free to invent new ones. This is known as the *numerus clausus* of property rights; see B Rudden, 'Economic Theory v Property Law: The Numerus Clausus Problem' in J Eekelaar and J Bell, (eds), *Oxford Essays in Jurisprudence*, 3rd series (Oxford, OUP, 1987) 244.

The division into legal and equitable rights has been an anachronism ever since the courts of law and equity were merged in 1873; in 1925 the abandonment of the old labels would have been unthinkable, but perhaps a future Law of Property Act might describe legal and equitable interests for what they are—two different classes of rights, the one stronger than the other. Thus legal estates and interests in land are (outside the registration systems) enforceable against everyone; equitable interests are enforceable only against those who have notice of them. Equitable interests are further subdivided, by section 2 of the Law of Property Act 1925, into those that can and cannot be overreached, that is, lifted off the land and transferred to the proceeds of a transaction so that a purchaser cannot be affected by them. Roughly, those that cannot be overreached are equitable mortgages, equitable interests generated by contracts to sell land,[5] easements and covenants, all of which we might describe as broadly commercial in nature; all other equitable interests—and that means mostly family-type interests under trusts of land—are overreachable. We have seen[6] how the 1925 legislation facilitated overreaching in unregistered land by making it easier for purchasers to detect defects in the transaction that would prevent overreaching; overreaching was one of the cornerstones of the structure set up in 1925 and must be constantly borne in mind in any examination of English conveyancing.

A particular bugbear for the draftsmen of the 1925 legislation was the mortgage;[7] if the fee simple was to be the basis of conveyancing, then the owner of land must have a fee simple, but how was this to be achieved when the effect of a mortgage of land had always been to vest the fee simple in the mortgagee, leaving the owner with an 'equity of redemption'—that is, his ancient right to have his land back on payment of the debt? The difficulty was solved by leaving the fee simple or long lease with the landowner; a mortgage would be achieved either by granting a long lease to the mortgagee (or sublease, for a mortgage of a lease), known as a mortgage by demise, or by giving him 'a charge by deed expressed to be by way of legal mortgage', now known simply as a legal charge, which gave him the same rights and remedies as if he had a mortgage by demise.[8] To the lawyer of the 1920s, the mortgage by demise probably felt reasonably safe. The legal charge must have seemed strange indeed. Where was the mortgagee's estate? To the modern law student, content with the notion that property is a bundle of rights and less accustomed to reify his legal concepts, the charge feels normal and the device of a long lease unnecessary.

---

[5] One who has agreed to purchase a legal estate in land has an equitable interest in it until completion of the transaction.

[6] In ch 2, at n 56 ff.

[7] Anderson, *Lawyers 1832–1940*, 284–5: a scheme for resolving the difficulties of real property by converting all ownership to leasehold was abandoned, but contained the germs of the solution for the problem of mortgages.

[8] Law of Property Act 1925, ss 85, 86 and 87.

THE REGISTRATION HIERARCHY

Title registration under the Acts of 1925 and 2002 also operates on the basis of a hierarchy, but a different one; or rather, it takes the one from the Law of Property Act 1925 and re-shuffles it, so that the traditional division into legal and equitable rights no longer operates as it used to and no longer tells the whole story. A hierarchy of rights in a registration scheme has to cope with the fact that some rights in land can be registered, while some cannot; and with the fact that some rights that can be registered nevertheless may not be. The basis of the hierarchy, not surprisingly, is this:

—Certain rights can be registered,
—The rest cannot be.

That beguilingly simple formula can be unpacked as follows:

—Certain legal estates can be registered. It is convenient to call these the 'registra-ble estates'.[9] Note that the term 'legal estates' is used here, as in the 1925 and 2002 Act, to mean both legal estates and legal interests.[10]
—Anything else cannot be registered but
  —Certain listed rights are overriding interests, and bind the land in spite of the fact that they are not (and in some cases cannot) be registered.[11] Of these, many can be overreached so as to leave a purchaser free of them.
  —All except certain listed exceptions may be recorded on the register, which means that their validity is not guaranteed but their priority is protected (i.e. they have protective but not dispositive registration, known as interest recording).[12]

The registrable estates, the upper level of the hierarchy, are the subject of this chap-ter. They key into the hierarchy of the Law of Property Act 1925 in that they are legal estates and interests—but not all legal estates and interests are registrable. The lower level is composed mainly, but not exclusively, of equitable interests; as burdens on the registered title, they are examined in detail in chapter 5.

We must now look more closely at that upper division, the registrable estates.

---

[9] The 2002 Act uses the term in s 6 to refer to estates that *must*, in the context of that section, be registered; here, the term is used to refer to estates that *may* be registered.

[10] This is so in both the Land Registration Acts 1925 and 2002; the former defines the term in s 3(xi), while the latter imports the definition in the Law of Property Act 1925, which by s 205(1)(x) defines 'legal estates' as 'the estates, interests and charges, in or over land (subsisting or created at law) which are by this Act authorised to subsist or to be created as legal estates'.

[11] 1925 Act, s 70(1); 2002 Act, schs 1 and 3. The 1925 list was obscurely drafted, so that we could be surprised by new ones, as in *Celsteel Ltd v Alton House Holdings Ltd* [1985] 1 WLR 204.

[12] 1925 Act, s 52; 2002 Act s 32.

THE SCOPE OF TITLE REGISTRATION

The scope of title registration' is the heading to section 2 of the 2002 Act, and it is to this section that we must turn for a list of those estates that can be registered. Section 2 of the Land Registration Act 1925 simply provided that only legal estates in land could be registered.[13] The new section 2 is rather different:

'This Act makes provision about the registration of title to-
  (a) unregistered legal estates which are interests of any of the following kinds-
      (i) an estate in land
      (ii) a rentcharge
      (iii) a franchise
      (iv) a profit à prendre in gross, and
      (v) any other interest or charge which subsists for the benefit of, or is a charge on, an interest the title to which is registered; and
  (b) interests capable of subsisting at law which are created by a disposition of an interest the title to which is registered.

So the Act is going to make provision, first for the registration of certain unregistered legal estates (recall that that term includes estates, interests and charges) and, second, for the registration of certain interests arising from dispositions of registered estates—thus it provides both for first registration and for what we might call next-generation registration.

If 'legal estate' includes, by section 132, 'estates, interests and charges' then it is difficult to see the point of the words 'which are interests' in the opening words of the section. In LC 254, the Law Commission did promise a definition of estates and interests;[14] it may have been felt that the existence of section 205(1)(x) precluded the introduction of a definition for use only in this statute. But the drafting of section 2 is unpleasant as a result. A reformed Law of Property Act, which must surely come, may be able to mend this. If property rights are all, indeed, bundles of rights, their characterisation as estates or interests may indeed be pointless.

Section 2(a)(i) refers simply to the legal estates of section 1(1) of the Law of Property Act 1925,[15] our old friends the freehold and the lease. Note that the list in section 2 is not quite definitive, since not all legal leases can be registered. Sections 3 and 4 reveal that, at present and with a few awkward exceptions, only leases with more than seven years to run at the point of registration can come on to the register (the shorter ones cannot be registered at all, either voluntarily under section 3 or compulsorily under section 4); this is a big reduction from the current

---

[13] The wording of the section is 'estates capable of subsisting as legal estates in land'. The opening of the Land Registration Act 1925 is nowhere near so clear as is that of its cousin the Law of Property Act 1925. We do not know the details of who drafted what; Benjamin Cherry was careful to point out that he did not draft all six statutes (BL Cherry and JRP Maxwell, *Prideaux's Forms and Precedents in Conveyancing*, 22nd edn, (London, Stevens and Sons Ltd, 1926), vol 1, 3).

[14] Para 3.2

[15] The drafting feels strange; but note that while 'legal estates' is defined to include both estates and interests (see n 10 above), 'estates' by itself is free simply to mean 'estates'.

threshold of 21 years. Why? The motivation is to bring more land on to the register; the political spin is the simplifying of conveyancing.[16] Thus it was claimed in debate in the House of Lords that registration would save two-and-a-half hours per transaction, which has to be dismissed as ridiculous.[17] The specification of seven years is a balancing exercise; in the interests of not doing too much too quickly the figure could have been set at 14. Amendments both to reduce the figure to three and to extend it to 14 were advocated in the House of Lords when the Land Registration Bill was debated, and were rejected.[18] Section 118 enables the Lord Chancellor by order to reduce the figure of seven years, and the intention is that a threshold of three years[19] will eventually be substituted.[20] The effect of this on commercial leasing practice has yet to be seen. As we shall see, short leases which are not registrable estates cannot be protected on the register at all, but are overriding interests.

Section 2(a)(ii)–(v) covers rights which are not legal estates within section 1(1) of the Law of Property Act 1925. The newcomers in the 2002 Act are the rentcharge, the franchise and the profit à prendre in gross. The rentcharge is a sum of money payable on a freehold. They are common in a few areas of the country, such as Bristol and Manchester; many are uneconomic to collect and remain only as an inconvenience to conveyancers. They will nearly all be extinguished in 2037.[21] A franchise is a privilege, originally a royal grant, for example to hold a market or to recover treasure trove.[22] A profit is a right to take something from someone else's land, such as fish or game; they behave like easements in many respects except that they can exist in gross, that is, as a freestanding right rather than being for the benefit of a particular piece of land.[23] None of these are everyday occurrences, but they are now to be capable of substantive registration

---

[16] LC 271, 3.14 to 3.17, 2.6, 2.9.

[17] HL Deb 17/7/01, col 1384. The work of assigning an unregistered lease of, say, business premises, is largely involved in securing a licence to assign. The actual conveyancing involves perusal of the lease and drafting a very simple assignment. The freehold title is not usually involved in a short business lease, particularly where the lessor is a large organisation. Registration would add time and expense. The ability to grant and assign business leases electronically may be a benefit (LC 271, 3.16); but the transaction (as opposed to the negotiation of terms) is so simple that the procedural demands may outweigh the benefit. The motivations of bringing land on to the register, and making information about land publicly available (LC 271, 3.16) have outweighed considerations about the simplicity of transactions. It is significant that the Law Commission admits that this was the only area in which their recommendations went against the views expressed on consultation (LC 271, 3.14).

[18] HL Deb 17/7/01, cols 1394 and 1384. The House actually divided on the question of an amendment to increase the figure to 14, but the amendment was not agreed to.

[19] For leases of three years or less, written formality is not required: s 54(2) Law of Property Act 1925.

[20] LC 271, 3.17: 'It is likely that, when electronic conveyancing is fully operative, the period will be reduced to include all leases that have to be made by deed—in other words, those granted for more than three years.'

[21] See *Megarry and Wade* 4–048 to 4–051 and 18–014 ff.

[22] See *Megarry and Wade* 18–013 ff, and the discussion in Appendix F of The Law Commission, *Third Report on Land Registration* (HC 269) (London, HMSO, 1987).

[23] See *Megarry and Wade* 18–040 ff. Easements, by contrast, cannot exist in gross.

following responses to the consultation exercise of LC 254. We shall see from sections 3 and 4 that, at the moment, they *may* be registered but never have to be.

One entity that can no longer be registered is a manor. These are the survivors of the key landholdings of the Middle Ages, existing now as mere titles without any effect upon the land to which they refer. They have been registrable,[24] but are no longer, and section 119 of the 2002 Act contains provision for the removal from the register of those that have been on it on the application of the registered proprietor of the manor (it is not clear why he would apply for de-registration).

Section 2(a)(v) provides for the registration of legal interests, that is, the interests falling within section 1(2) of the Law of Property Act 1925: thus easements, profits not held in gross and, most importantly, charges.[25] Section 59 tells us that these have a dependent form of registration, appearing as a part of the title to another registered estate. Naturally an easement or a profit may appear as a 'credit' or 'debit' entry; that is, the benefit of an easement may be noted on one title while the burden appears against another.[26] Charges are the subject of special provision in the statute (in sections 48 to 57). Up until the coming into force of the 2002 Act chargees have had the privilege of holding a 'Charge Certificate', that is, a copy of the individual register given to the chargee; during the currency of the charge the registered proprietor did not hold a Land Certificate. This of course reflected the mortgagee's ancient right to hold the deeds of the property, and the modern superstition that all properties have 'deeds'; under the 2002 statute Charge Certificates are no longer issued, and the Land Certificate will be of reduced importance.[27]

Section 2(b) provides for the registration of legal estates derived from registered estates: thus the new lease, or the sub-lease, of land or, equally, of a franchise or of a profit à prendre in gross. When all the legal estates in section 2(a) have been registered (still only a theoretical possibility), the only new registrations will be under section 2(b).

At present there are about 5 million unregistered estates which may be the subject of first registration, either following a voluntary application for registration, or after an event which has triggered compulsory registration, and we now examine how they come on to the register.

---

[24] LC 271, 3.21; Land Registration Rules 1925, rr 50, 51. Manors are bought and sold as curios; their status as registrable estates felt extremely odd, and must have been a waste of registry time.

[25] The list of legal interests in s 1 of the Law of Property Act 1925 includes rentcharges, which are given separate mention here, and 'rights of entry' connected with a mortgage or rentcharge; see *Megarry and Wade* 4–053 and 4–054.

[26] Note that s 13 provides for registration where, of the two properties, one is registered and the other is not.

[27] Sch 10, para 4.

THE REGISTRATION OF REGISTRABLE ESTATES

Section 3 lists the interests in respect of which one may (not 'must') apply to be registered as proprietor. This is a sub-set of the registrable estates.[28] Here is the parallel with section 21 of the 1925 Act, but the list has expanded. There are, of course, the familiar legal estates—the fee simple and the lease. A lease is registrable only when the right to possession is continuous, thus excluding time-shares,[29] and only when it has more than seven years to run.[30] Section 3 is the basis for voluntary registration of the estates there listed.

Section 4 tells us when certain registrable estates *must* be registered. The sub-set is smaller again than the set in section 3, and the registrable estates listed become subject to the requirement of registration on the occurrence of certain events. This 'triggering' mechanism has been familiar since the Land Transfer Act 1897; the class of triggering events has been progressively expanded during the twentieth century as a way of extending registration so that, following the Land Registration Act 1997, nearly (but not quite) everything one does with a legal estate in land activates the registration requirement. The 2002 Act uses the same scheme, and, indeed, there are no new triggering events.[31] But section 4 looks complicated because the reduction in the qualifying term for leases has necessitated some exceptions. In detail, its provisions are as follows:

First, note that section 4 operates on 'qualifying estates',[32] namely a freehold, or a leasehold which has more than seven years to run. The newcomers to the registrable estates, the franchise, the rentcharge and the profit à prendre in gross, are not subject to compulsory registration; but section 5 gives the Lord Chancellor power to bring them in. One can imagine this being done for the sake of completeness. The innovation is the compulsion for shorter leases, which may be registered, and must be registered if they have more than seven years to run.[33]

Thus freeholds, and leaseholds with more than seven years to run, are qualifying estates. Section 4 lists a range of events which give rise to 'the requirement of registration', which can be summarised as follows:

---

[28] See n 9 above.

[29] S 3(4).

[30] S 3(3).

[31] More land could be brought onto the register by a provision adding the appointment of new trustees to the list of triggers, or by requiring registration of the freehold on the grant of a long lease, but neither step has been taken. To a suggestion in the House of Lords that the latter be enacted, Baroness Scotland gave among the reasons for not doing so the fact that it might force the registration of a very large estate on the grant of a lease of a small part of it, and that this was felt to be 'disproportionate' (HL Deb 17/7/01, col. 1390). If registration is a benefit, why would this be a problem? One answer is cost, which would inevitably be passed on to the lessee in that case.

[32] S 4(2).

[33] Legal interests in land, by contrast with legal estates, cannot be included within s 3 or s 4 because they are registrable only as burdens on registered estates; s 13.

—a qualifying estate is transferred (for valuable or other consideration,[34] by way of gift, pursuant to a court order, or by an assent,[35] but not by operation of law[36])

—the grant of a lease of land for more than seven years out of a qualifying estate (which need not itself be registered; but thus not a lease of, or granted out of, a lesser interest such as an easement or of a franchise etc).

—the grant, out of a qualifying estate, of a lease taking effect in reversion,[37] ie where possession is to be given more than three months after the date of the grant. The rationale for this is that reversionary leases are harder to discover by inspection because until possession takes effect there is no-one there.[38] The hassle of registration will, however, doubtless be avoided by making a contract now to grant a lease in three months' time.

—The creation of a first legal mortgage of a qualifying estate.[39]

—The transfer of a qualifying estate, or the grant of a lease out of an unregistered estate, which leads to a person no longer being a secure tenant, pursuant to section 171A of the Housing Act 1985.[40]

—The grant out of an unregistered estate of a lease pursuant to the 'right to buy' provisions of Part 5 of the Housing Act 1985.[41]

Much of the list is thus concerned with the familiar cases of the transfer of freeholds, the transfer and assignment of leases, and first legal mortgages. Note that grants and transfers of leases that are in fact mortgages do not trigger registration.[42] The threshold length for leases is reduced, as already discussed; and four special kinds of lease are mentioned in sections three and four together. These are: a lease of a landlord's reversion triggering section 171A of the Housing Act 1985, a lease granted pursuant to the right to buy, a reversionary lease taking effect in possession more than three months from the grant, and a lease where the right to possession is discontinuous. All are voluntarily registrable; all but the fourth trigger compulsory registration; the grant of any of the four out of a registered estate

---

[34] Including circumstances where the estate has a negative value; s 4(6).

[35] S 4(1)(a).

[36] S 4(3); for example, when a deceased's property vests in his executors; LC 271, 3.25.

[37] S 4(1)(d).

[38] LC 271, 3.32.

[39] S 4(1)(g). The sub-section reads 'a protected first legal mortgage', and sub-section (8) explains that this means that the mortgagee must be entitled to the title deeds of the mortgaged land, and must rank ahead of all other mortgages. Thus it must be first in time, or first because an earlier mortgagee has agreed to be postponed.

[40] S 4(1)(b) and (f). This happens when housing is privatised by the transfer of a public sector landlord's estate to a private sector landlord; s 171A of the Housing Act 1985 nevertheless preserves the tenant's right to buy. The point here is that the new landlord's estate is registrable; the tenant's position is seen in the next point.

[41] S 4(1)(e). The right to buy is an important asset of public sector tenants; see PF Smith, *Evans and Smith, The Law of Landlord and Tenant* (London, Butterworths, 2002) (hereafter '*Evans and Smith*'), 438 ff. The right is more usually exercised by the purchase of a freehold, which of course falls under s 4(1)(a) above. It is hard to imagine that a lease granted in pursuance of the right to buy would be shorter than seven years, except perhaps as a device to avoid registration.

[42] S 4(4) and (5); see nn 7, 8 above.

must be completed by registration.[43] The addition of reversionary leases raises the possibility of very short leases being registered, including those with a term of less than three years.

One class of leases is not registrable: the PPP lease. These are a creation of the Greater London Authority Act 1999, enabling partnerships of public and private bodies to run the London underground while preventing the disposal of 'key system assets'.[44] Section 90 has the effect that a PPP lease, whether granted out of registered or unregistered land, cannot be registered. Nor can it even be protected on the register by a notice. It is an untouchable, an outcaste of the registration system. Section 90(5) states that Schedules 1 and 3 'have effect as if they included a paragraph referring to a PPP lease'; thus, of course, only section 90 need be repealed if PPP leases cease to exist. A more effective way of expressing lack of confidence in a creature of statute could scarcely be imagined.

Sections 6 and 7 impose the familiar penalty for non-registration[45] where section 4 applies; after two months, the relevant transaction becomes void as regards the legal estate. Section 8 obliges the transferor (etc) to re-convey where necessary; but the registrar is enabled, by section 6(5), to extend the period, and will doubtless continue to be willing to do so in order to get estates registered (thus re-transferring the legal estate by magic).

Section 5 enables the Lord Chancellor by order to add further triggering events to section 4; this may include bringing into compulsion the new members of the class of registrable estates, namely the rentcharge, the franchise and the profit à prendre in gross.

THE CLASSES OF TITLE

When the registrable estate is registered, like eggs and apples it goes through a grading process. Obviously the title is examined by the registrar's staff, and requisitions are raised if anything seems amiss. For freeholds and leases, the 2002 Act, like its predecessors, offers a number of classes of title. The estates submitted to the registration process are not of uniform quality, yet the registered title system seeks to yield from that variable raw material a uniform product whose quality is instantly recognisable. Thus freehold and leasehold titles may be absolute, qualified, or possessory; leasehold titles may in addition be 'good leasehold'.[46] What is the significance of these titles, which stamp the quality of the estate held by the registered proprietor?

---

[43] S 27. For a while, any of these four kinds may still exist in unregistered form, because they were granted before the Act came into force; they are not always overriding interests. See ch 5, nn 46, 47.

[44] LC 271, 8.11 ff.

[45] By transferee, grantee etc; note in particular that where the trigger is the grant of a mortgage, it is the transferee of the charged estate who must apply: s6(2).

[46] Ss 9(10) and 10(1).

On the top shelf is 'title absolute'. This is the best the Land Registry has to offer. It is not absolute, but the use of the word can be said to embody the myth of the perfect register. It is defined in section 11(2):

A person may be registered with absolute title if the registrar is of the opinion that the person's title to the estate is such that a willing buyer could properly be advised by a competent professional adviser to accept.

Eligibility for absolute title is thus still defined in terms of advice, opinion and professional competence.[47] Title qualifying for registration with absolute title is thus defined as something that need not be perfect; and sections 9(4) and 10(4) state specifically that title may be defective provided that the registrar 'is of the opinion that the defect will not cause the holding under the title to be disturbed'. For absolute leasehold title, there is the additional requirement that the registrar is satisfied that the lessor has title to grant the lease.[48]

Qualified title is very rare. It is issued when title would be absolute but for an identifiable flaw on the title—for example, an unbarred interest prior to the one barred by an adverse possessor[49]—which can then be specifically excepted from the effect of registration.[50]

The relationship between absolute and possessory title has been crucial to the operation of the register since its inception. Recall that in the first two land registration statutes, the standard of title to be deduced in order to achieve an absolute title was set too high, so that landowners shied away from voluntary registration. However, at the same it was possible to register what was known as a 'good holding title' in order to qualify for a possessory title, which could in due course be upgraded to an absolute title. Voluntary registrations with possessory title were a little more popular than the unattainable title absolute, although as we have noted registration did not take off until compulsion began in 1897. But note that those early possessory titles were designed for landowners who did have a documentary title, albeit with flaws that the register could not tolerate. By contrast, now, the possessory title is in practice the domain of the squatter, the applicant who has no paper title; the description simply states that he must be in possession of the land or in receipt of the rents and profits of the land.[51] Section 62 of the 2002 Act states that the registrar may upgrade titles less than absolute when he is satisfied as to the title to the estate; 12 years must elapse before a possessory title is upgraded.

Good leasehold says something very specific: that the registry is satisfied as to the validity of the lease but knows nothing about the superior title, and thus about the landlord's ability to grant it. This arises where the freehold is unregistered, and

---

[47] Compare the 1862 and 1875 Acts; ch 2 at n 46.
[48] S 10(2)(b).
[49] See ch 7.
[50] Ss 9(4) and 10(5). Where the registered title is leasehold, the flaw may be on that title or on the reversion.
[51] Ss 9(5) and 10(6).

the lessee has not had the superior title deduced to him.[52] A lease registered with good leasehold title may, therefore, be a tenancy by estoppel.[53]

THE INDIVIDUAL REGISTER

As indicated above,[54] there is a division within the upper layer of the registration hierarchy, because the registrable estates are divided into those that can be registered independently and those that can only be noted against the title to another registered estate. Thus 'the register of title' referred to in section 1 of the 1925 and 2002 statutes is, rather confusingly, made up of thousands of individual registers (the terminology does not make life easy). Their existence is implied by the statute, but their form and structure is left to the land registration rules.[55] When a right is registered thus it is given a title number, and an individual register (sometimes called, in paper terminology, a 'folio').

The fact that some registrable estates may not have their own individual register but can only be registered on that of another registered estate is not instantly obvious from the 2002 Act; it is unimportant in the statute, while fundamental from a practical point of view. The relevant provision is section 59, which states that those which exist for the benefit of or as a charge upon a registered estate—thus corresponding to those interests falling within section 2(a)(v)—must be registered by an entry 'in relation to' ie on the individual register of, that estate. The heading to section 59 calls such estates 'dependent estates'.

The individual register is divided into three parts: the property register, the proprietorship register and the charges register, describing respectively the property, the proprietor and some of the rights to which it is subject. The property register describes the property; if it is leasehold it contains the short particulars of the lease (the parties, the term and the rent); if there are any rights benefiting the property, such as an easement, they appear here. The proprietorship register gives the names of the registered proprietor(s), states the class of title they hold, and sets out any restriction on their powers of disposition.[56] In the charges register are found, not surprisingly, registered charges; but also notices recording unregistered interests, pursuant to section 32. Note, therefore, that the third part of the register contains both registered and recorded interests (eg both legal easements and rights of pre-emption); the register itself does not indicate which is which, and one has to work this out from the statute according to the nature of the interest.

The individual register is thus a collection of information in three parts, represented on paper or on screen as a tripartite chart. We can see the title in tabular,

---

[52] He has no right to insist on this. Where the title is well-known locally it is not seen as a problem; in other cases, the lessee may not have the bargaining power to require it.

[53] See *Megarry and Wade*, 14–095 ff.

[54] Text at n 26.

[55] Land Registration Rules 2003, rules 2 to 9.

[56] See ch 4, below.

rather than genealogical form.[57] There is nothing to trace back,[58] historical depth is gone, and interests affecting the land are all seen in the one document. Indeed, as the register has changed from a typed record to a computer generated one, our concept even of the registered title has changed. Very old land certificates (being the proprietor's copy of the individual register)[59] showed old entries deleted, even though no information about the present state of the title needed to be taken from the deleted entries. Previous proprietors, discharged mortgages, etc, were all visible, if irrelevant; once the register, and corresponding certificate, could be automatically updated whenever a change was made so that the history of the registered title could no longer be seen, our view of the title became much more one-dimensional. Everything is now in the present tense.[60] There is something of a loss here; but section 69 gives the registrar the power to provide, on application, information about the history of a registered title, and it is to be hoped that this power will be exercised for the benefit of historians where appropriate.

On pages 46–51 are two sample individual registers (Example 1 and Example 2), kindly provided for use in this book by HM Land Registry; both relate to the same property and the same proprietors and accordingly the plan, on page 51, relates to both.

THE REGISTER OF CAUTIONS

A caution against first registration relates to land as yet unregistered, and is a way of notifying the registrar that, when there is an application for first registration, the cautioner has a claim to be heard. The effect of a caution is that when an application is made, the cautioner must be informed, and given a period to substantiate his claim. Examples might be: a squatter who has completed his 12 years' adverse possession, but does not wish to make his own application for registration; or someone who, correctly or otherwise, feels he has a right in the land arising from informal dealings. Thus there is an element of labour-saving or perhaps conflict avoidance about the caution against first registration; the cautioner does not want to bother now, but does not want his claim to be overridden by sections 11 and 12 which, as we shall see, have the effect that only certain rights will survive first

---

[57] Ch 1, above, n 35.

[58] Except where the charges register contains an entry of the infuriating kind: 'a conveyance of 29th September 1922 contains covenants'. The difficulties this sort of thing used to cause are being hugely ameliorated as the Registry computerises its archived documents so that they can be readily referred to on screen; the point remains that in complex cases it is simply not possible to have everything visible, literally, at a glance.

[59] It is proposed that these be phased out, or at least reduced to an abbreviated form; see above, n 27.

[60] Originally, the price for each transfer was seen on the register, so that it was a very interesting, but inaccessible, record of economic history. The price was no longer recorded when the register became a public document open to inspection by all, in the interests of privacy; now, again, prices are being shown, but as computerisation means that only the latest proprietor is shown, so only the latest price is visible.

registration. The cautions register is now regulated by sections 15 to 22;[61] but with the important proviso that anyone who is entitled to be registered as proprietor of a freehold or leasehold estate may not use it to protect his position.[62] If he wants protection, he must go for voluntary first registration instead. This was hotly resisted by the Charities' Property Association during the Bill's passage through Parliament, providing an interesting illustration of how much certain sections of the community would like their land to remain unregistered.[63]

[61] And rules 39 to 53 of the Land Registration Rules 2003.
[62] S 15(3) of the 2003 Act.
[63] HL Deb 17/7/01, cols 1412–1415. This was the only issue on which a vote had to be taken at Committe stage in the House of Lords.

HM Land Registry

Title Number : CS72510

Edition Date : 30 October 1998

A: Property Register

containing the description of the registered land and the estate comprised in the Title.

CORNSHIRE : MARADON

1.   (19 December 1989)   The **Freehold** land shown edged with red on the plan of the above Title filed at the Registry and being 13 Augustine Way, Kerwick, (PL14 3JP).

2.   (19 December 1989)   The land has the benefit of a right of way on foot only over the passageway at the rear leading into Monks Mead.

B: Proprietorship Register

stating nature of the Title, name and address of the proprietor of the land and any entries affecting the right of disposal

Title Absolute

1.   (31 August 1990)   **Proprietor : PAUL JOHN DAWKINS and ANGELA MARY DAWKINS** both of 13 Augustine Way, Kerwick, Maradon, Cornshire PL14 3JP.

C: Charges Register

containing charges, incumbrances etc. adversely affecting the land

1.   (19 December 1989)   The passageway at the side included in the title is subject to rights of way on foot only.

END OF REGISTER

NOTE A: A date at the beginning of an entry is the date on which the entry was made in the Register.
*NOTE B: This certificate was officially examined with the register on **30 October 1998**.*

Page 1

Example 2 47

HM Land Registry

Title Number : **CS72510**

Edition Date : 30 October 1998

A: Property Register
containing the description of the registered land and the estate comprised in the Title.

CORNSHIRE : MARADON

1. (19 December 1989) The **Freehold** land shown edged with red on the plan of the above Title filed at the Registry and being 13 Augustine Way, Kerwick, (PL14 3JP).

2. (19 December 1989) The land has the benefit of a right of way on foot only over the passageway tinted brown on the filed plan.

3. (19 December 1989) The land has the benefit of the following rights granted by the Transfer dated 3 May 1968 referred to in the Charges Register:-

   "TOGETHER WITH the rights set out in the First Schedule hereto :-

   THE FIRST SCHEDULE before referred to

   The right for the Transferee in common with the Transferor and all other persons who have hereafter the like right

   (a) to take water electricity gas and other appropriate services and to the passage of water and soil through the pipes cables sewers and drains and other contributing media respectively now laid or to be laid within the Perpetuity Period in or under any land included in the Estate the Transferee contributing a due proportion of the expense of keeping and maintaining the said pipes cables sewers and drains and other conducting media in good repair

   (b) to enter on the land of the land forming the Estate for the purpose of

   (i) laying connecting to maintaining replacing and inspecting the said pipes cables sewers and drains and other conducting media

   (ii) renewing repairing and inspecting the walls of any house garage or other structure which may be built on the boundary line of the said land

   The Transferee making good all damage which may be done in the exercise of such powers as specified in this sub-clause (b) at his own cost and without unnecessary delay"

   NOTE:- The Perpetuity Period refered to is 80 years from 1 January 1984.

Continued overleaf

Title Number : CS72510

B: Proprietorship Register

stating nature of the Title, name and address of the proprietor of the land and any entries affecting the right of disposal

Title Absolute

1. (31 August 1990)   **PROPRIETOR:** PAUL JOHN DAWKINS and ANGELA MARY DAWKINS both of 13 Augustine Way, Kerwick, Maradon, Cornshire PL14 3JP.

2. (31 August 1990)   **RESTRICTION:** No disposition by a sole proprietor of the land (not being a trust corporation) under which capital money arises is to be registered except under an order of the registrar or of the Court.

3. (31 August 1990)   **RESTRICTION:** Except under an order of the registrar no disposition by the properitor(s) of the land is to be registered without the consent of the proprietor(s) of the Charge dated 29 July 1990 in favour of Weyford Building Society referred to in the Charges Register.

4. (1 February 1992)   **CAUTION** in favour of Paul Mitchell of 3 Rusty Lane, Aberville, Cornshire, DL8 2NJ.

C: Charges Register

containing charges, incumbrances etc. adversely affecting the land

1. (19 December 1989) A Conveyance of the land in this title and other land dated 19 May 1924 made between (1) Allen Ansell (Vendor) and (2) Frances Amelia Moss (Purchaser) contains the following covenants:-

    "And the Purchaser for herself her heirs executors administrators and assigns hereby covenants with the Vendor his heirs and assigns that she will perform and observe the stipulations set out in the First Schedule hereto so far as they relate to the hereditaments hereby assured

    THE FIRST SCHEDULE above referred to

    (a) No caravan shall be allowed upon the premises and the Vendor or owner or owners of adjoining premises may remove and dispose of any such caravan and for that purpose may forcibly enter upon any land upon which a breach of this stipulation shall occur and shall not be responsible for the safe keeping of any such caravan or for the loss thereof or any damage thereto or to any fence or wall

    (b) No earth gravel or sand shall at any time be excavated or dug out of the land except for the purpose of excavations in connection with the buildings erected on the land and no bricks or tiles shall at any time be burnt or made nor any clay or lime be burnt on the land."

2. (19 December 1989)   A Transfer of the land in this title and other land dated 3 May 1968 made between (1) Gareth Jones (Transferor) and (2) Ann Leigh and David Leigh (Transferees) contains covenants details of which are set out in the schedule of restrictive covenants hereto.

Continued on next page

Example 2 49

C: Charges Register continued

3. (19 December 1989) The land is subject to the following rights reserved by the Transfer dated 3 May 1968 referred to above:-

    "EXCEPT AND RESERVED the rights and other matters set out in the Second Schedule hereto

    THE SECOND SCHEDULE before referred to

    (Rights Excepted and Reserved)

    (a) to enter on the said land for the following purpose:

    (i) to lay maintain and replace inspect and connect into such pipes cables sewers and drains and other conducting media

    (ii) to repair and inspect the facing walls of any house garage or other structure built upon any adjoining land and upon the boundary line of the said land

    All damage which may be done in the exercise of such powers as specified in this sub-clause being made good without unnecessary delay at the cost either of the Transferor or other the person so entering"

4. (19 December 1989) The land is subject to rights of way on foot only over the passageway tinted blue on the filed plan.

5. (31 August 1990) **REGISTERED CHARGE** dated 29 July 1990 to secure the moneys including the further advances therein mentioned.

6. (31 August 1990) **PROPRIETOR:** WEYFORD BUILDING SOCIETY of Society House, The Avenue, Weyford, Cornshire CN12 4BD.

7. (19 February 1994) An Agreement under hand dated 22 December 1993 made between (1) Hilary Jones and Leslie Jones and (2) Paul John Dawkins and Angela Mary Dawkins relates to the ownership of a boundary wall on the north western boundary of the land in this title.

    NOTE :- *Copy Filed*

Continued overleaf

Schedule of Restrictive Covenants

1.   The following are details of the covenants contained in the Transfer dated 3 May 1968 referred to in the Charges Register.

"For the benefit and protection of the land comprised in the Estate and each and every part thereof and so as to bind the land into whosesoever hands the same may come the Transferee hereby covenants with the Transferor and also as a separate covenant with every other person who is now the owner of any part of the Estate that the Transferee will henceforth and at all times hereafter observe and perform the restrictions and stipulations set out in the Third Schedule hereto but not so as to render the Transferee personally liable in damages for any breach of a restrictive covenant after it shall have parted with all interest in the said land.

THE THIRD SCHEDULE before referred to

1.   The Transferee will not use or permit to be used the said land or any buildings thereon for the carrying on of any trade or business whatsoever and will use the same as private dwellinghouse only

2.   The Transferee will not mutilate or remove any trees and/or shrubs which may be planted within the boundary of the land

3.   The Transferee will maintain the garden area surrounding the property as a garden and will not allow erections thereon or any trees shrubs plants or otherwise to exceed a height of 600mm."

END OF REGISTER

NOTE A: A date at the beginning of an entry is the date on which the entry was made in the Register.
NOTE B: This certificate was officially examined with the register on **30 October 1998.**

H.M. LAND REGISTRY		TITLE NUMBER
		CS72510
ORDNANCE SURVEY PLAN REFERENCE	AP2948	SECTION B	Scale 1/1250 Enlarged from 1/2500
COUNTY CORNSHIRE	DISTRICT MARADON	© Crown copyright 1977

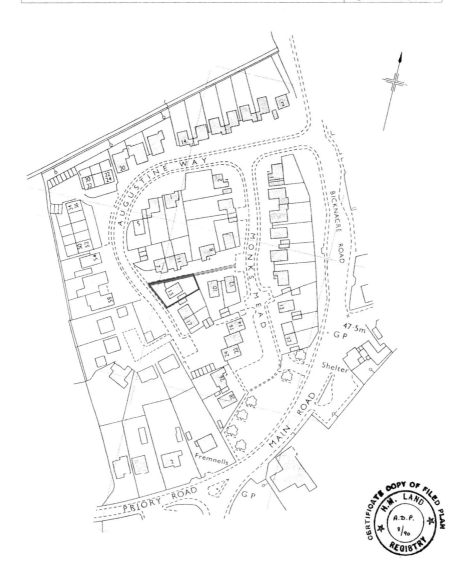

4

The Effect of Registration I: Vesting, Powers and Dispositions

W‌E HAVE SEEN in chapter 3 which estates can be registered, and how they may arrive on the register by first registration. We now ask: what is the effect of registration? More specifically, what are the consequences of a given estate's being a *registered* estate, for its proprietor, for a potential purchaser and for others?

This chapter looks at some of the effects of registration on the registered proprietor: the vesting effect of registration, the powers of the registered proprietor, and the regime of registrable dispositions. In chapter 5 we look at the burdens on the registered estate. As we examine these aspects of registration we must keep in mind the fact that title registration functions as a mirror and a curtain;[1] the mirror reveals, the curtain hides. The strange thing about this mirror is that it is an active one; what it reveals has been made true, at least to some extent, by the register itself. And just as domestic mirrors are designed to assist a specific type of viewer (humanoids with heads about 1.8 metres from the floor), so is the land register: it is designed to assist purchasers. It is designed so as to fashion and display that particular facet of truth which most tends to make a purchaser secure, although what it shows is also informative and useful to others. What the register hides are things that the purchaser does not need to know, because the law of registration has ensured that they cannot affect him, although they may be of the first importance to others. In particular, they concern those who hold equitable interests in the land; the registered proprietor himself (and today's purchaser is tomorrow's registered proprietor); and those to whom a registered estate may pass but who are not purchasers—the technical term is 'volunteers'.

So although this chapter is, apparently, *about* the registered proprietor we shall find that the mirror is rather selective in what it reveals, and that its selections are aimed at its most favoured viewer, the purchaser.

THE VESTING EFFECT

True for all—the purchaser, the volunteer, the registered proprietor himself—is the vesting effect of registration. Whoever is shown by the register to be the proprietor of a registered estate does indeed have vested in him that legal estate. The

---

[1] Ch 1, text at n 39. Its insurance function is the subject of ch 6.

registered proprietor holds it however he came on to the register—by first registration, by registered disposition, by fraud, by forgery. Whatever his provenance, section 58 of the 2002 Act (headed 'Conclusiveness') states:

If, on the entry of a person in the register as proprietor of a legal estate, the legal estate would not otherwise be vested in him, it shall be deemed[2] to be vested in him as a result of the registration.

Thus where the wrong person is registered as proprietor of a legal estate (because of an error or a forgery), he nevertheless holds the legal estate so long as he remains so registered, unless and until the register is amended. This is a fundamental principle of title registration.[3]

The unavoidable exception to this occurs when the registered proprietor dies. Clearly the estate cannot then be vested in him; it passes to his personal representatives, who must produce a death certificate and a grant of probate in order to transmit the registered estate to those entitled to it, or to sell it.[4]

Section 58 says nothing about equitable interests. It does not need to. The point is simply that the registrable estates are legal estates—so says section 2—and if X is the registered proprietor of a registered estate, that means that it is vested in him. The answer to 'what about the beneficial interest?' is that it depends who is asking. The answer to a prospective purchaser is quite simply 'none of your business *except* as provided by sections 29 and 30', which tell him that if he acquires a registered estate or charge by registered disposition[5] he will acquire the whole of the legal and beneficial interest in the land subject only to the matters set out in those sections. The substance of those matters is discussed in chapter 5. The curtain ensures that the beneficial interest in the registered estate does not concern the purchaser because it cannot bind him except as provided by the Act. If the registered proprietor asks the question, by contrast, the answer to him is slightly different; again, this is discussed in chapter 5.

The registered proprietor may be one or more individuals. There may not be more than four, because a maximum of four people can hold a legal estate in land.[6] Whenever there is more than one, the legal estate is being held upon trust, whether for one person, for the legal owners themselves, or for one or more third parties,

---

[2] The Court of Appeal has held that the word 'deemed' is of no significance: *Morelle Ltd v Wakeling* [1955] 2 WLR 672 (discussing the same wording in s 69(1) of the 1925 Act). See TBF Ruoff, 'Registered Proprietors and the *Morelle* Cases', (1955) 19 *Conveyances* 190, at 192 where Ruoff points out that s 20 of the 1862 Act used the words 'be and be deemed to be'.

[3] See ch 6 below.

[4] If there are no personal representatives because the deceased did not appoint any, the registered estate vests in the Public Trustee (see *Megarry and Wade* 11–125, and fn 35). Where the deceased held the registered estate jointly with another registered proprietor as joint tenants at law, the right of survivorship operates to vest the estate in the survivor. See *Megarry and Wade* 9–003. A purchaser in these circumstances need only see the death certificate to be satisfied of the position, provided there was no restriction on the register to indicate that the proprietors held as tenants in common (subject to the problem mentioned below at n 9).

[5] I use the term 'registered disposition' to mean 'a registrable disposition which is duly completed by registration'; see below.

[6] Law of Property Act 1925, s 34(2).

perhaps even for successive beneficiaries. Rules[7] dictate that where there is more than one registered proprietor, they must state in their application for registration whether or not they are to hold the registered estate as joint tenants for themselves in equity. If they are not, the registrar is obliged to enter a restriction stating that no disposition can be registered unless there are at least two registered proprietors.[8] Restrictions are provided for in section 40 of the 2002 Act; as we shall see, they have more than one use. The purpose of *this* use is to ensure that overreaching will take place. If two registered proprietors, say, hold for themselves as joint tenants in equity, then when one dies the other will be entitled to the whole estate. This is the effect of the right of survivorship, the essential characteristic of joint tenancy. The sole survivor can sell the land without there being any possibility of equitable interests that might possibly bind a purchaser.[9] If the equitable owners hold as tenants in common, a sale by a sole survivor is not safe. That survivor may not own the whole of the equitable title, but is not able (as a sole trustee[10]) to overreach the beneficial interests in the land.[11] So if joint proprietors purchase as tenants in common in equity, a restriction is entered, warning the next purchaser: do not take a transfer from just one of these two. This ensures that, whatever is happening in equity, the beneficial interests will be overreached. Note that this is a protection for purchasers, not for beneficiaries.

THE POWERS OF THE REGISTERED PROPRIETOR: (A) LEGAL ABILITIES

A further effect of registration is that the registered proprietor has certain powers to deal with his registered estate or charge.[12] Section 23 of the 2002 Act states that

---

[7] See for example Form TR1 (transfer of whole) in Schedule 1 of the Land Registration Rules 2003.

[8] The wording of standard forms of restriction is set out in Sch 4 of the Land Registration Rules 2003. The appropriate one in this case would be Form A:
'No disposition by a sole proprietor of the registered estate (except a trust corporation) under which capital money arises is to be registered unless authorised by an order of the court'.
(And see entry no 2 in the Proprietorship Register in Example 2, on p 48).

[9] Provided, that is, that the equitable joint tenancy has not been severed in a way that has not come to the attention of the registrar—for example by a course of conduct or by alienation of the equitable interest of one party (see *Megarry and Wade* 9–036 ff). This problem was solved for unregistered land by the Law of Property (Joint Tenants) Act 1964 but not for registered land because it was not believed at the time that interests under trusts for sale (the then prevalent form of joint ownership) were interests in land that could therefore bind a purchaser as an overriding interest. The writer cannot see that this lacuna has been filled in the 2002 Act, for s 26 cannot enable a sole proprietor to overreach (see below, n 34).

[10] S 2 of the Law of Property Act 1925 prescribes that for overreaching to happen there must be at least two trustees, or a trust corporation.

[11] Although there would in fact be no problem if one equitable tenant in common had died and, by his will, left his share to the survivor.

[12] S 58 refers to registration as proprietor of a legal estate, which must include all the registrable estates listed in s 2. S 23 distinguishes between a registered estate and a registered charge; the former is defined, in s 132, 'a legal estate the title to which is entered in the register, other than a registered

he has 'owner's powers', which means that he can do anything permitted by the general law *except* effect certain forms of mortgage.

This is the successor to section 18 of the Land Registration Act 1925.[13] The general law permits the owner of a legal estate in land to do all sorts of things with it— sell it, lease it, mortgage it, create an equitable interest in it, etc. He does not have carte blanche entirely, as he must comply with the structures imposed by law; for example, he cannot create a lease for an uncertain term,[14] or a legal lease for a life,[15] nor can he create a legal life estate,[16] nor, now, an entail of any kind.[17] In the same way, a land registration statute must state what the proprietor of a registered estate can do with it.[18] The 2002 Act follows the 1925 Act in allowing the registered proprietor to do with his registered estate pretty well anything he could do with an unregistered legal estate.[19] However, he may not now create a mortgage by demise. This was the result of responses to consultation following LC 254; it was widely felt that giving the mortgagee a long lease or sub-lease was virtually obsolete.[20] The prohibition of mortgages by demise in registered land is a welcome modernisation, and we may anticipate that it will be followed in the general law at some stage.[21]

We have to add the proviso that the statute prescribes, in section 27, the method for certain exercises of the owner's powers. The registered proprietor may transfer his legal estate to another, or create a legal estate[22] out of his own, but these are 'registrable dispositions' and only work if completed by registration. It is hardly surprising to find that once a legal estate is on the register, provision is made to ensure that it stays there, and that any legal estates derived from it are registered. We shall have more to say about such dispositions later, because they act as a mechanism for protecting a purchaser from some rights adverse to the registered estate. In the present context, the point is simply that the requirement that certain dispositions be registered regulates the way in which owner's powers can be exercised.

charge'. The distinction enables the making of separate provision for registered charges where appropriate, as in s 23, but causes some duplication, as in ss 29 and 30.

[13] This statement begs the debate as to whether s 18 contained legal abilities or equitable authorities; see the postlude to this chapter.

[14] Provided the period is not of uncertain duration: *Prudential Assurance Co Ltd v London Residuary Body* [1992] 2 AC 386, HL.

[15] Law of Property Act 1925, s 149(6).

[16] Law of Property Act 1925, s 1.

[17] Trusts of Land and Appointment of Trustees Act 1996, Sch 1, para 5.

[18] That 'must' begs a question; it assumes that a registered estate is not the same thing as an unregistered legal estate; that something happens to it when it is registered. That is the conclusion English writers have slowly reached during the past century; see for example D Jackson, 'Registration of land interests—the English version' (1972) 88 *Law Quarterly Review* 93 at 96.

[19] In addition, he has the ability to 'charge the estate at law with the payment of money' (s 23(2)). This form of charge, unique to registered estates, is derived from the Land Transfer Act 1875; see LC 271, 7.2.

[20] LC 271, 4.7. See ch 3, text at n 8.

[21] One further change in s 23 is the specification of only one permitted form of sub-mortgage, ie a mortgage of a mortgage; the sub-mortgage can only be of the indebtedness secured by the mortgage LC 271, 7.11.

[22] Recall that the term includes legal estates and interests: ch 3, n 10.

But registered proprietors may be subject to limitations upon their powers which would prevent their conveying a legal estate if their land were unregistered, making any purported conveyance void. A registered proprietor may be bankrupt, and so without any powers of disposition; or if the proprietor is not a natural person, there may be statutory limitations upon what it is permitted to do, as in the case of public bodies. Thus in *Hounslow LBC v Hare*[23] the local authority sold a flat to the lady who had been tenant of it, in the belief that she had the right to buy. She had not, and had the land been unregistered the conveyance would have been void; section 69(1) of the Land Registration Act 1925 (the equivalent of the section 58 of the 2002 Act) nevertheless vested the legal estate in the purchaser. Charities, too, are subject to controls as to the dispositions they may make.[24] Accordingly, section 40 of the Land Registration Act 2002 provides that where there are such limitations, a restriction may be entered on the register. This not only brings the limitation to the purchaser's attention, but prevents the registration of any disposition that contravenes it.[25]

So what happens if a registered proprietor is subject to a limitation which would prevent his conveying a legal estate in unregistered land, but makes a transfer because, by mistake, no restriction has been entered on the register? Section 26 gives a very clear answer:

(1) Subject to subsection (2), a person's right to exercise owner's powers in relation to a registered estate or charge is to be taken to be free from any limitation affecting the validity of a disposition.
(2) Subsection (1) does not apply to a limitation–
    (a) reflected by an entry in the register, or
    (b) imposed by, or under, this Act.
(3) This section has effect only for the purpose of preventing the title of a disponee being questioned (and so does not affect the lawfulness of a disposition).

Section 52 does the same job for the proprietors of registered charges (and references here to section 26 are to be taken to include section 52). Section 26 states clearly that if the registered proprietor makes a disposition in excess of his legal abilities, the purchaser's title cannot be questioned. Section 26(3) preserves the liabilities that the transferor may incur by making the unlawful disposition, but leaves the purchaser secure. That this is one of the intended effects of the sections is clear from LC 271.[26]

---

[23] (1990) 24 HLR 9.

[24] See *Megarry and Wade* 20–030. Charities are no longer, however, required to obtain the consent of the Charity Commissioners in all circumstances; the restrictions on disposition are now found in s 36 of the Charities Act 1992.

[25] So this is the second use we have encountered for a restriction; see n 8 above. This one, too, is a protection not for the owner of an equitable interest, but for the purchaser.

[26] LC 271, 2.15. A direct consequence of this must be that where a transfer takes place in the absence of a restriction that should have prevented it, there can be no question of alteration/rectification of the register to correct the situation, since the purchaser's title cannot be questioned. See ch 6 below. Thus the result in a case where the facts matched those of *Hounslow LBC v Hare* (n 23 above) would be the same as it actually was in that case, but on wholly different principles.

Note that the protection for a purchaser who takes a transfer or other disposition from a bankrupt registered proprietor when, for some reason, there was no restriction to prevent this, is slightly more complex and is found in section 86(5). Because of the need to make this provision consistent with those of the Insolvency Act 1986[27] the purchaser in these circumstances is not protected unless he acted in good faith and had no notice of the bankruptcy. This serves to stress the point that in all other cases, even if the purchaser had notice of the registered proprietor's lack of ability to make the disposition he is still protected by section 26.

THE POWERS OF THE REGISTERED PROPRIETOR:
(B) AUTHORITY IN EQUITY

Section 26 does another and rather more subtle job. For a registered proprietor may be affected by a different sort of restriction on his powers. If he is a trustee, he is prevented by the law relating to trusts, and may be further prevented by the terms of the trust itself, from carrying out certain transactions. For example, section 6 of the Trusts of Land and Appointment of Trustees Act 1996 sets out the authority of all trustees of land and prevents them from selling the land without having regard to the interests of beneficiaries.[28] And the trust deed may forbid them to sell the property without a certain beneficiary's consent, for example.[29] The contravention of such limitations does not make the disposition void at law where the land is not registered; but it is a contravention of the terms of the trust and an exceeding of the trustee's powers.[30] Recent academic literature has adopted terms to distinguish the two kinds of power: abilities and authority. A legal owner has the ability to convey the legal estate; a trustee has authority to do so in accordance with the terms of the trust.[31] Another way of putting this is to say that a disposition by a registered proprietor may be ultra vires, that is, beyond his powers, in two senses: ultra vires at law, or ultra vires in equity.[32]

How do these equitable limitations upon the owner's powers affect a purchaser, who is supposed to be curtained off from equitable matters? Quite simply, if a vendor sells without ability, the purchaser would not get a legal estate if it were not for the protection of section 26; but if trustees sell without authority, even though the requirements of section 2 of the Law of Property Act 1925 are met, the interests of the beneficiaries will not be overreached. If they are not overreached the purchaser

---

[27] See LC 271, 11.44.

[28] S 6(5).

[29] Trusts of Land and Appointment of Trustees Act 1996, s 8(2).

[30] Graham Ferris and Graham Battersby have just the right analogy: I have the ability to punch you in the face, but I am not allowed to do so ('The General Principles of Overreaching and the Reforms of 1925', (2002) 118 *Law Quarterly Review* 270, at 274 fn 28).

[31] G Ferris and G Battersby, 'The Impact of the Trusts of Land and Appointment of Trustees Act 1996 on Purchasers of Registered Land' [1998] *Conveyancer* 168, 181.

[32] G Ferris, 'Making sense of s 26 of the Land Registration Act 2002' in Cooke, *Modern Studies II*, 101, at 105.

will be bound by them, by notice in unregistered land or, where land is registered, if the interests are overriding because of the beneficiaries' occupation of the land.

The position in unregistered land was discussed in chapter 2, where we saw how the 1925 legislation assisted purchasers by making overreaching happen more readily.[33] Today, section 16 of the Trusts of Land and Appointment of Trustees Act 1996 protects purchasers of unregistered land from any disposition in excess of the trustees' authority provided the purchaser has no notice of the problem. The position in registered land is much simpler. First, any limitation on the registered proprietor's authority will be reflected by a restriction if the registrar is aware of it. Restrictions may therefore record these two sorts of limitations on owner's powers—those that affect the ability to make a disposition that is valid at law, and those that forbid a trustee to do something that would nevertheless be legally valid. Second, if by some mischance there is no restriction to record and enforce the limitation on the proprietor's authority, section 26 has the additional function of protecting the purchaser from the effect that an ultra vires disposition would otherwise have. It draws the curtain between the purchaser and the equitable authorities of the trustees, and ensures that overreaching happens despite any lack of authority.[34]

That this was the intention behind section 26 is, again, clear from LC 271.[35] Again, the proviso in sub-section (3) preserves the registered proprietor's liability for any unlawful disposition; thus if the deal was ultra vires in equity the beneficiaries still have their remedies against the trustee. Indeed, the purchaser himself may incur personal liability, if the circumstances of his purchase are such as to render him liable to the beneficiaries as a constructive trustee for them.[36]

Section 26 thus uses the word 'power' to mean two rather different things; but it achieves its purpose with considerable economy of expression. And of course it does not matter to a purchaser whether the limitation on the registered proprietor's powers is legal or equitable; he simply needs to know that if there is no restriction recording a limitation on the registered proprietor's powers—in either sense[37]—then he can safely assume that the registered proprietor is free to make the disposition contemplated.[38]

---

[33] See C Harpum, 'Overreaching, Trustees' Powers and the Reform of the 1925 Legislation', [1990] *Cambridge Law Journal* 277; and ch 2, n 56 ff.

[34] S 26 cannot remove any other requirement for overreaching. If there is only one trustee, and no restriction to ensure that a second one is appointed (see above, n 8), overreaching will not happen—not because of any lack of power on the part of the trustee, but because he is not exercising that power in the manner prescribed for overreaching to take effect. The writer thus agrees with the conclusions of G Ferris and G Battersby, in 'The General Principles of Overreaching and the Modern Legislative Reforms 1996–2002' (2003) 119 *Law Quarterly Review* 94 at 121.

[35] LC 271, 4.8–4.11.

[36] LC 271, 4.11. It is clear that much more than notice is required. How much more depends upon how seriously the courts are prepared to take the protection given to a purchaser in registered land. Notorious still is the decision in *Peffer v Rigg* [1977] 1 WLR 285, which made the purchaser liable far too readily.

[37] G Ferris, 'Making sense of s 26', n 32, above, at 113.

[38] This chapter ends with a comment upon the corresponding provisions in the 1925 Act; the problem, which has been the subject of fierce debate, has no effect upon the construction of the 2002 Act.

It will be recalled that overreaching may also be jeopardised if the transaction is within the trustees' powers, but the proceeds are misapplied; and that the 1925 legislation provided protection in this instance in section 17 of the Trustee Act 1925; this still acts to protect the purchaser of a registered estate. One matter that must be regarded as still open to question is the sale at an undervalue by a trustee. Owner's powers must include the ability to give the land away; but this is nevertheless a breach of trust. In the absence of a restriction forbidding the registered proprietor to give the land away or to sell it at an undervalue—and such a restriction would not be usual—can a purchaser safely take land at a bargain price from one whom he knows to be a trustee? It is suggested that he can; that the plain words of the statute state that in the absence of a restriction, a limitation on the registered proprietor's powers, in any sense, does not affect the purchaser.[39]

So the register tells a prospective purchaser whether or not the current registered proprietor of the land has the power to make the disposition contemplated. Next, we need to say a little about registrable dispositions, which regulate the way in which certain transactions can be effected by a registered proprietor.

REGISTRABLE DISPOSITIONS

Some of the debate, in the nineteenth century, about the form that registered title might take centred upon the issue of the form of dispositions once title was registered. Should registration be a one-off event, cleansing the title, after which transactions would take the same form they had always taken? If, as seemed more plausible, dispositions would themselves appear on the register, how would that be managed? The two very different precedents of copyhold, on the one hand, and of the German systems on the other, dictated a form of dispositive registration: certain transactions could only be effected through the register itself. If this control was imposed, how tight would control be?

Registered Dispositions in the Land Registration Act 1925

In true British fashion a compromise evolved, and was represented in the Land Registration Act 1925 by the provisions that the registered proprietor could deal with his estate just as he could if it was unregistered,[40] but that certain dispositions were *registered dispositions* and could take effect at law only if they were registered. Thus documentation would be executed (in the form prescribed by the Land

---

[39] Note that if the land is given away, or sold for nominal consideration (how much is that? See ch 5, n 1) the acquirer is a volunteer. S 26 is not limited to purchasers, and so will still protect him. But he will not have the protection of s 29; nor will overreaching operate in his favour as the conditions of s 2 of the Law of Property Act 1925 are not met because he is not a purchaser. (Contrast *State Bank of India v Sood* [1997] Ch 276, where no money was involved, but the mortgagee was nevertheless a purchaser).

[40] Land Registration Act 1925, s 101(1).

Registration Rules where applicable),[41] and would purport to transfer a legal estate; but only when sent to the Land Registry with the appropriate form and recorded on the register did the legal estate or interest actually pass.[42] Moreover, registered dispositions had 'special effect or priority',[43] which meant that they took effect in favour of a purchaser subject only to matters on the register and to overriding interests[44] and that the person entitled to the benefit of the resulting entry in the register would have the benefit of the indemnity provisions where appropriate.

Other dispositions—both those that did not purport to create legal estates, and registered dispositions before they were registered[45]—took effect in equity.[46] The consequence of this was, of course, that they would be overridden by subsequent transactions if not protected by a notice on the register.[47] In addition, the register did not guarantee the validity of interests created in this way; even if they were recorded by notice on the register, their priority was protected but only insofar as they were valid.[48]

Registrable Dispositions in the Land Registration Act 2002

The new statute preserves the existing position, but with considerably more clarity in its drafting. Section 27 sets out the transactions that must be completed by registration, now called 'registrable dispositions', and states simply that they do not operate at law until registered. They are:

—transfers of registered estates;[49]
—grants of leases of registered estates, except leases of land that do not themselves require substantive registration pursuant to section 4, but including a lease where the right to possession is discontinuous;[50]

---

[41] As it was for transfers but was never, for example, for charges.

[42] Thus what is seen in conveyancing transactions as *completion* is in fact nothing of the sort. S 19 of the Land Registration Act 1925, and its counterpart for leases, s 22, reads: 'A transfer . . . shall be completed by the registrar entering on the register the transferee as the proprietor of the estate transferred . . .'.

[43] S 3(xxii) of the 1925 Act.

[44] S 20 of the 1925 Act; there were obvious qualifications in the case of qualified and possessory titles: s 20(3) and (4). S 23 makes the parallel provision for dispositions of registered leaseholds.

[45] Thus the term 'registered disposition' is inappropriate, as is noted in LC 254, 2.21, fn 69; the 2002 statute substitutes the more precise 'registrable dispositions'.

[46] S 101 of the 1925 Act.

[47] S 20(1)(a) of the 1925 Act. Despite the provision in s 101 that minor interests take effect in equity, they did not, of course, bind by notice. But they behaved like equitable interests for the purposes of priority.

[48] S 101 of the Land Registration Act 1925.

[49] S 27(2)(a).

[50] S 27(2)(b) and (c). Note that time-shares granted out of registered estates must themselves be registered even though they do not attract compulsory registration when granted out of an unregistered estate, see s 4.

—grants of most legal interests;[51]
—legal charges of registered estates, and dealings with charges.[52]

Transfers within the above groups occurring by operation of law are registrable dispositions, except transfers on death, on bankruptcy, or on the dissolution of a corporate proprietor, and except for the creation of a legal charge which is a local land charge.[53]

The effect of registering registrable dispositions is of course primarily that the interest transferred or created by the disposition stays on the register and has its validity and priority guaranteed. But registrable dispositions are immensely important for a quite different reason, namely that they are the key to two different protections for a purchaser from certain third-party rights.

First, because registrable dispositions are the only way to create legal estates, they are the only way that registered land can be acquired with the benefit of over-reaching. This is the vital protection of purchasers from interests under trusts, which we have highlighted as one of the most important features of the 1925 legislation. More of this in chapter 5. Recall that we have seen two uses of restrictions aimed at ensuring that overreaching takes place: restrictions preventing dispositions by a sole trustee where there have been joint proprietors,[54] and restrictions recording a limitation upon the registered proprietor's powers of disposition.[55] Second, registered dispositions are stated, in sections 29 and 30, to take effect subject only to certain interests. This is a question of priorities. The priority of interests is in general unaffected by registration[56] (to be discussed).[57] But registered dispositions have privileged status, and take effect subject *only* to interests seen on the register, to Schedule 3 interests, and to interests appearing from the register to be excepted from the effect of registration. They thus leapfrog, and override, interests which do not fall into this category, ie anything that could be on the register and is not and does not fall within Schedule 3.[58]

Accordingly, if a registrable disposition is not actually registered it will have no effect at law; the transaction will not attract the protection of sections 29 or 30 so that it takes effect subject to interests that would not otherwise have affected it; overreaching will not happen; and any interest created by it will not itself be

---

[51] S 27(2)(d), (e): effectively, everything within s 1(2)(a)–(e) of the Law of Property Act 1925 except for interests capable of registration under the Commons Registration Act 1965, and except for the enigmatic sub-section (2)(d), as to which see *Megarry and Wade*, 4–053. The creation of easements by s 62 of the Law of Property Act 1925 is not an express grant for these purposes (s 27(7)).

[52] S 27(2)(f) and 27(3).

[53] Not discussed in this book; see *Megarry and Wade*, 5–132 ff.

[54] Note 8 above.

[55] Note 25 above.

[56] S 28 of the 2002 Act.

[57] Ch 5.

[58] The terminology of minor interests, used in the 1925 Act to refer to interests which are not registered estates nor registered charges, nor overriding interests, has gone, and with it an unnecessary layer of terminology. We no longer have to speak of interests transforming from being minor to being something else, but can speak more simply of their position vis-à-vis the register—registered, recorded, overriding or unprotected.

protected and so will be overridden by the next registered disposition (unless actual occupation makes it an overriding interest).[59] Notice that the problems arising where registrable dispositions, through some oversight, are not actually registered, will disappear with the advent of electronic conveyancing; it will then only be possible to carry out such a disposition through the medium of registration.[60]

In chapter 5 we look at the burdens on the registered estate, and will have a clearer view of the importance of the protection that hangs upon registrable dispositions.

RESTRICTIONS

Finally, we have to mention in a more collected form a factor that has already been the subject of discussion in this chapter, namely restrictions. These are closely linked with dispositions, since their function is precisely to prevent the registration of dispositions—and to do no more than that, although they serve a number of quite different purposes. Section 40 provides that a restriction 'is an entry on the register regulating the circumstances in which a disposition of a registered estate or charge may be the subject of an entry in the register'. It goes on to explain that the restriction may prohibit the making of an entry in respect of any disposition at all, or in respect of a specified kind of disposition. The prohibition may be indefinite, for a specified period, or until the occurrence of a specified event.

Notice, then, what a restriction prevents. It is a trip-wire to prevent the making of an *entry* of a disposition; it does not actually prevent the making of the disposition itself. Thus it does not prevent a transfer of a registered estate in contravention of the terms of the restriction; but the transfer could then not be registered, and so could not actually transfer the legal estate, would not overreach anything, and would not confer any protection on the purchaser pursuant to section 29. Contravention of a restriction does not prevent a disposition but makes the disposition disastrous for the purchaser. Obviously the advent of electronic conveyancing, when disposition and registration will be one, will mean that restrictions prevent the disposition itself.

Section 42 gives the registrar power to enter a restriction for three purposes:

—to prevent invalidity or unlawfulness
—to ensure that overreaching will take place
—to protect a right or claim in relation to a registered estate or charge.

---

[59] We need an example. A is the registered proprietor of Blackacre. He purports to grant a 10-year lease to B, who fails to register the registrable disposition; and he then grants a mortgage to C, who also fails to register. At this point C has an equitable mortgage, and is subject to B's interest (an equitable lease); where the equities are equal, the first in time prevails. If A now sells to D, who registers the transfer, D takes free of B's lease and C's mortgage. However, if, say, B is in actual occupation, para 2 of Sch 3 makes the lease an overriding interest and the lease has priority over the transfer, pursuant to s 29.

[60] The priority problem of the previous note will thus disappear. The dispositions to B and C must be done electronically, and completion will effect registration. See ch 8, below, text following n 26.

The first two of these we have met already. The first was encountered in our discussion of the powers of the registered proprietor, when we noted that a limitation on those powers may be recorded by a restriction (and, in the absence of a restriction, does not exist so far as the purchaser is concerned). Thus a restriction may ensure that a bankrupt proprietor makes no disposition at all; or that a disposition by a local authority will be within its powers; or that a disposition by a trustee will comply with some provision of the trust instrument, for example that he obtain a consent before selling. The second purpose has also been mentioned, as this is the restriction used when there are joint proprietors who hold otherwise than for themselves as beneficial joint tenants. These two uses of restrictions benefit a purchaser. The second use, to prevent overreaching, is the one instance where the registrar has a duty to enter a restriction where necessary: section 44. The third is slightly different in that it benefits a third party. Section 42(3) explains that a restriction may be entered to protect a person who claims to have an interest in the land under an implied trust—ie one that has arisen through the conduct of the parties and is likely to be the subject of dispute—or someone who is entitled to the benefit of a charging order in relation to an interest under a trust. This happens when one of two joint owners contracts a debt which, eventually, has to be recovered by enforcement proceedings against that person's interest in land.[61] What these claims have in common is that they cannot have their priority protected by notice on the register;[62] but they require some form of protection. A restriction does not protect their priority directly, but ensures that the claimant's rights will be satisfied before a disposition is registered.[63] This third use of restrictions takes over a function of the caution against dealings under the 1925 Act, now abolished.[64]

The Act provides that restrictions may be entered on the application of the registered proprietor, anyone with his consent, or anyone with sufficient interest in the making of the entry.[65] Rules will provide that trustees have a *duty* to apply for a restriction where there is any limitation in the trust instrument on the exercise of their owner's powers.[66] Where the application is not an obligatory one and is made by someone other than the registered proprietor and without his consent, the registered proprietor must be notified of it,[67] and has the opportunity to object to it. Disputes may be referred to the Adjudicator.[68] Some statutes require the

---

[61] See *Megarry and Wade* 9–074 ff.

[62] See below, ch 5, text at n 27.

[63] No restriction can be entered in respect of any interest whose priority *can* be protected by notice: s 42 (2).

[64] But cautions remain on the register from before the 2002 Act; see entry no 4 of the Proprietorship Register in Example 2, on p 48.

[65] S 43. Land Registration Rules 2003, r 93.

[66] Land Registration Rules 2003, r 94.

[67] S 45; LC 271, 6.54 ff.

[68] S 73.

entry of a restriction;[69] the court may order the entry of a restriction.[70] A court order will be made in bankruptcy proceedings, in order to prevent the bankrupt dealing with his property; under the 1925 Act this was achieved by an inhibition, which froze the register. A restriction may do the same job, but is obviously more flexible. Such an order *may* prevent the registration of dispositions whose priority is already protected by a search or a notice, but will not automatically do so.[71]

Restrictions may be disapplied by the registrar on the application of anyone with a sufficient interest in it: section 41. The point is that restrictions often take an 'unless' form, for example that no disposition be registered unless a consent has been obtained; there has to be provision for registration to go ahead once the pre-condition has been complied with. There is also provision for the withdrawal of restrictions on application, in section 47.

Restrictions are gate-keepers. They prevent the registration of a disposition which would prove disastrous—usually, disastrous for the purchaser. Even the use of restrictions to protect claims can be seen in this way, as they prevent the purchaser from buying a lawsuit.

POSTLUDE:
THE POWERS OF THE REGISTERED PROPRIETOR AND THE PURCHASER'S
PROTECTION UNDER THE LAND REGISTRATION ACT 1925
(THE 'FERRIS AND BATTERSBY EFFECT')

The debate about the problem that has come to be labelled the 'Ferris and Battersby effect' is now strictly irrelevant, and does not belong in the main text because it does not really shed light upon the construction and effect of the 2002 Act; but it is not really possible to resist commenting upon it.

The tale begins with Charles Harpum's very important article in 1990.[72] That article demonstrated the close link between overreaching and the powers of limited owners, and has since had the endorsement of the Court of Appeal.[73] 'Powers' here refers to equitable authority; a transaction by trustees of land (trustees for sale, before 1996) must be within their authority as trustees because if it is not, the legal estate will pass but the beneficial interests will not be overreached, with disastrous results for the purchaser.

We have discussed Harpum's explanation of the steps taken by the 1925 legislation to ensure that this danger was minimised in unregistered land: the draftsman worked on the basis that the existence of a trust would always be clear on the title,

[69] LC 271, 6.46 mentions the Housing Act 1985, s 157(7); Sch 9A, paras 4, 5(2); Housing Act 1988, ss 81(10), 133(9); Local Government and Housing Act 1989, s 37(8); Charities Act 1993, ss 37(8), 39(1B), each as amended by Sch 11 of the 2002 Act.
[70] S 46.
[71] S 46(3); LC 271, 6.52–53. See ch 5 at n 78.
[72] 'Overreaching, Trustees' Powers and the Reform of the 1925 Legislation' [1990] *Cambridge Law Journal* 277.
[73] *State Bank of India v Sood* [1997] 1 All ER 169, *per* Peter Gibson LJ at 172.

so that the purchaser could then check the trustees' powers and ensure that the disposition was intra vires. He would find those powers both under the general law, where they were set out in section 28 of the Law of Property Act 1925, and in the trust instrument, which he could demand to have disclosed to him. We have seen that this protection was upgraded in 1996, when the Trusts of Land and Appointment of Trustees Act 1996 updated the trustees' powers (= authority) and gave to purchasers of unregistered land explicit protection if a disposition was ultra vires. Provided the purchaser had no actual notice of the fact that it was ultra vires, overreaching would take place. We have also discussed the even stronger protection now available for purchasers of registered land, where there is no requirement of absence of notice.

This digression concerns the area so obviously missing from the account given so far: to what extent was the purchaser of *registered* land protected from a failure of overreaching where a disposition was ultra vires? The Land Registration Act 1925 did not provide for restrictions to record a limitation upon the registered proprietors' powers.[74] So what, if anything was the purchaser's protection from the trustees' contravention of a limitation of their powers, either in the trust instrument or in the general law?

Harpum's answer to this was that the protection set up for the purchaser of registered land was entirely different from that in unregistered land. In registered land, he argued, trustees' powers, in the sense of their equitable authority, derived not from section 28 of the Law of Property Act 1925, but from section 18 of the Land Registration Act 1925. This set out the powers of the registered proprietor. It did not limit the powers of registered proprietors who were trustees. Accordingly the trustees' powers were unlimited in registered land, and a purchaser could safely proceed on that basis.[75]

The Trusts of Land and Appointment of Trustees Act 1996 proceeded on the same basis. It did not give any protection to purchasers of unregistered land on the grounds that full protection was available already.

Graham Ferris and Graham Battersby, in their article in 1998, questioned this argument.[76] They asserted that section 18 of the Land Registration Act 1925 dealt only with legal abilities, not with equitable authority.[77] The latter was, from 1925 onwards, governed by section 28 of the Law of Property Act 1925, and the purchaser of registered land had no protection additional to or different from that of the purchaser in unregistered land. Moreover, they argued, the equitable authority of trustees was now governed by section 6 of the Trusts of Land and Appointment of Trustees Act 1996. That section limited trustees' powers in ways which were immensely difficult to check—how does a purchaser ascertain if the

---

[74] It did provide for the usual restriction for joint proprietors; see above n 8, and Harpum, n 72 above, at 305.

[75] Harpum, see n 72 above, at 308.

[76] 'The Impact of the Trusts of Land and Appointment of Trustees Act 1996 on Purchasers of Registered Land', [1998] *Conveyancer* 168.

[77] *Ibid*, at 181.

vendor trustees have had regard to the interests of beneficiaries, or have contra-
vened any rule of equity?[78] Thus, therefore, the purchaser could far more easily
now be caught out by an ultra vires disposition which would not overreach. The
argument was startling and had grave implications;[79] it has never been wholly
refuted.

The truth about the scheme for overreaching in the Land Registration Act 1925
may lie in the draftsman's intentions. The idea that the purchaser was supposed to
have protection from the effects of ultra vires dispositions which would, in the
absence of protection, prevent overreaching rings true. And we know that there
are a number of places where the draftsman did not say, or did not say clearly, what
he meant to say;[80] to some extent the culprit was the frantic operation, doubtless
behind closed doors in smoked-filled rooms late at night in Lincoln's Inn, to rescue the legislation from the hijack perpetrated in Parliament upon the Law of
Property Act 1922.[81] The debate depends upon the view taken of the function of
section 18 of the Land Registration Act 1925, and its relationship with section 28
of the Law of Property Act 1925. Did section 18 govern both legal ability and equitable authority, as stated by Harpum (though not in those terms); or does it govern only legal ability, leaving the trustees' authority to be covered by section 28 of
the other statute, as argued by Ferris and Battersby? The latter contention has the
merit of being in accordance with the construction of the Court of Appeal.[82]

Obviously section 18 could not be primarily a statement about equitable
authority—such a statement would have no place in a land registration statute.
Trusts are not its business. Nor did Harpum say it was. But Harpum's argument
that the draftsman intended the purchaser to be able to proceed with trustees as he
could with absolute owners, on the basis that their authority was co-extensive with
their ability, is utterly consistent with the whole tenor of the Act's provisions,
which is, as we can see in this chapter and the next, to skew reality in order to protect purchasers. Thus section 18 sets out the registered proprietor's legal abilities;
*and the purchaser can safely and must assume that his equitable authority is co-
extensive.* The trouble was that there was no express statement of those italicised
words. Benjamin Cherry would, surely, have testily suppressed with a common 'oh
of course not'[83] any suggestion that the purchaser could be tripped up by ultra

---

[78] Trusts of Land and Appointment of Trustees Act 1996 s 6(5), 6(6).

[79] As is acknowledged in *Megarry and Wade*, 8–155, fn 6.

[80] For example, the notorious ambiguity of s 34 of the Law of Property Act 1925, which looks as if
it prohibits tenancy in common in any form at all, at law or in equity, but cannot have been intended
to do that. See Smith, *Property Law* at 305–6; and Harpum, n 72 above, at 300.

[81] Anderson, *Lawyers 1832—1940*, 310–11. It would by no means be the last time decent legislation
was wrecked by Parliament; witness the Family Law Act 1996.

[82] *City of London Building Society v Flegg* [1988] AC 54; discussed by Harpum, n 72 above, at 307 ff,
and by Ferris and Battersby n 31 above, at 181 and in 'Overreaching and the Trusts of Land and
Appointment of Trustees Act 1996—a reply to Mr Dixon' [2001] *Conveyancer* 221 at 222. The latter is
a reply to Martin Dixon's casenote on *Birmingham Midshires Mortgage Services Ltd v Sabherwal
(Sudesh)*, at [2000] *Conveyancer* 267.

[83] This is getting to be rather an old joke, and comes from a contract case: *Shirlaw v Southern
Foundries Ltd* [1939] 2 KB 206, *per* MacKinnon LJ at 227.

vires dispositions in registered land. But the 1925 Act did not say what Cherry and his colleagues must have meant.[84] Harpum's argument must be perfectly correct as to the draftsmen's intention; Ferris and Battersby (and the Court of Appeal in *Flegg*) are right about what the 1925 legislation actually says.

The issue is now wholly academic, in the light of the provisions of the 2002 Act.

---

[84] Following the enactment of the Trusts of and Appointment of Trustees Act 1996 the Land Registration Rules 1825 were amended (see rr 59A and 106A(1)) to make restrictions available to record limitations in the trustees' powers (see n 74 above), and to impose a duty upon trustees to apply for them but the argument remains the same—there was no explicit statement that the purchaser was safe in the absence of such a restriction.

5

The Effect of Registration II:
Burdens on the Registered Estate

IN CHAPTER 4 we looked at the effect of registration in terms of the registered proprietor and his powers. In this chapter we look at the burdens upon, or interests adverse to, the registered estate. This is immensely important, and arises from the complexity of land. Scarcely any land is simply owned, unaffected by third-party rights. One of the principle motivations of title registration is to display third party rights simply, in a tabular document, so as to get rid of the need for an historical investigation of deeds. And so it does; but the picture we see from the register may nevertheless be complex and may not be a one-stop affair. Moreover, in this chapter even more than in chapter 4 we shall find that the information displayed by the register is fashioned so as to be most useful to the purchaser. Accordingly we examine the mirror of title from the point of view of the different people who may look into it: the purchaser, the registered proprietor, and anyone who receives the land as a gift. We look briefly at priorities of interests between themselves. The chapter ends with a discussion of the relationship between overriding and overreaching, since overreaching is vital to the function of the 2002 Act, as it was to the 1925 Act, although it is not the subject of the Act's provisions.

THE MIRROR OF TITLE: WHAT THE PURCHASER SEES

One thing the register does *not* do is to show all the interests subject to which the registered estate is held. For one thing, it does not show overriding interests; but at least they are listed in the statute and we know about them as a category. For another, it does not show rights that could be registered but are not. Trivial and obvious as that seems, it leads us to the important point that the registered estate, at any point, may be held subject to proprietary interests which affect the registered proprietor, but will have no effect upon a purchaser. And so the logical place to start when looking at the burdens on the registered estate is *not* the current state of the title at any time, but what the register actually reveals: the interests to which it *will* be subject if a purchaser invests in it.

'Purchaser' is not defined in the 2002 Act, but is used here as a shorthand for one who buys land, or an interest in it. 'Buys' is a shorthand for 'takes for valuable consideration', and 'valuable consideration' (according to section 132) 'does not include marriage consideration or a nominal consideration in money'.[1] 'Purchaser' includes, of course, a mortgagee. Once a registered charge is in place, the registered estate will have two aspects: the title so far as the registered proprietor is concerned and the title so far as the mortgagee is concerned, because interests adverse to the former may not affect the latter.

The vital question for a prospective purchaser is not 'to what burdens is the land subject at the moment?' but rather 'to what burdens will it be subject if I buy it?'. For the Act has a sieving effect; whatever are the burdens on the land at any point, only some will survive and affect a purchaser. Section 29 states:

(1) If a registrable disposition of a registered estate is made for valuable consideration, completion of the disposition by registration has the effect of postponing to the interest under the disposition any interest affecting the estate immediately before the disposition whose priority is not protected at the time of registration.
(2) For the purposes of subsection (1), the priority of an interest is protected–
　　　　(a) in any case, if the interest–
　　　　(i) is a registered charge or the subject of a notice in the register,
　　　　(ii) falls within any of the paragraphs of Schedule 3, or
　　　　(iii) appears from the register to be excepted from the effect of registration, and
　　　　(b) in the case of a disposition of a leasehold estate, if the burden of the interest is incident to the estate.

Section 30 does exactly the same for dispositions of registered charges (note that in the Act, 'registered estate' is defined as 'a legal estate the title to which is entered in the register, other than a registered charge'[2]) and hereafter registered charges are to be taken as included by implication. Thus the purchaser knows that if he buys the land, or an interest in it (a new lease; an assignment of a registered charge, etc), interests affecting the registered estate immediately before the disposition will be postponed to his interest as the new registered proprietor[3] *except* the following, by which he will be bound:

—Everything that appears on the charges register of the title (section 29(2)(a)(i));
—Overriding interests in Schedule 3 (section 29(2)(a)(ii));
—Anything which appears from the register to be excepted from the effect of registration, if the title is less than absolute (section 29(2)(a)(iii)); and
—If the land is leasehold, the obligations in the lease.

For the sake of simplicity this discussion assumes that the registered estate is freehold, so that the purchaser will take the land subject to (or 'be bound by', as it is

---

[1] Where is the line drawn for nominal consideration? £10? £100? In *Midland Bank Trust Co Ltd v Green* [1981] Ac 513 (a case on the Land Charges Acts) Lord Wilberforce commented, at 532, that it would be inappropriate 'to equate "nominal" with "inadequate" or even "grossly inadequate" '; he took it to refer to something like a peppercorn where there is really no payment at all. See n 80, below, for further reference to *Midland Bank*.

[2] S 132. This enables separate provisions to be made for registered charges.

[3] Anything created after the disposition but before registration will also be postponed to him because he will have protected his position by making a search with priority; see below, text at n 28. This will cease to be an issue when electronic conveyancing unites disposition and registration.

sometimes put) just the three matters in section 29(2)(a). We have to add that the purchaser also knows, from the general law, that he will *not* be subject to any trust interests in the land that are overreached by the disposition to him; and we know that the facilitation of overreaching was a major policy of the 1925 legislation.[4]

The wording of section 29 entails that it, and it alone, determines the interests subject to which the registered estate will be held by a purchaser. It states that the interests listed above (items on the charges register, overriding interests, and excepted interests) are the *only* items to which the registered estate is subjected following a registered disposition. Section 30 does the same for registered charges. The implication from those two sections is that if a given interest does not fall into one of those categories, the registered estate or charge is held free from it. Admittedly the combined effect of those categories is very wide, because of the scope of the overriding interests; but the two sections are drafted so as to be exhaustive.[5] In chapter 6 we shall have to examine the extent to which that apparently exhaustive list is supplemented by the provisions relating to alteration of the register.

Let us examine each of these aspects of title in turn.

RIGHTS EXCEPTED FROM THE EFFECTS OF REGISTRATION

First, because we have already dealt with them, the rights excepted from the effect of registration. These have been discussed in chapter 3, when we considered the various classes of title.[6] We know that a qualified title may be awarded because the registrar is aware of a specific flaw in the title; that a good leasehold title is given where the registrar does not know whether or not the landlord had power to grant the lease; that a possessory title

does not affect the enforcement of any estate, right or interest adverse to, or in derogation of, the proprietor's title subsisting at the time of registration or then capable of arising.[7]

Thus the titles less than absolute each involve saving certain rights from the effect that registration would otherwise have upon them.[8] A purchaser always takes subject to these rights.

---

[4] Ch 2, n 56 ff.

[5] Note s 29(4), whose effect is that where a lease is granted out of a registered estate, but is too short to require registration (currently seven years or less, but doubtless intended to be three eventually; see ch 3, n 19), the grant counts as a registrable disposition, completed by registration at the time of the grant. Thus the tenant under a fixed-term five year lease, say, where the lessor is a sole proprietor and also a trustee, takes it free of the interest of any beneficial owner who is not in occupation of the land. The point applies only to leases of land, s 27(2)(b)(i); the grant of a lease of a registered franchise or manor is registrable in any event, s 27(2)(c).

[6] Ch 3, text at n 45 ff.

[7] Ss 12(7) and 13(8), for freeholds and leaseholds respectively.

[8] The implication of s 29(2)(a)(iii) is that if there is a right which should have been excepted from the effect of registration, eg by rendering the title qualified, but was not, perhaps because nobody knew about it, then it does not bind the registered estate. Whether or not, if such a right comes to light later, the register can be altered so as to subject the registered estate to it, is an important issue of principle. See ch 6, generally, and ch 7 at nn 83 and 112.

INTERESTS SEEN ON THE CHARGES REGISTER

This is the easy bit, from the practical point of view of the purchaser inspecting the register and from the point of view of academic analysis. Most interests affecting a registered estate may be recorded by notice on the register, and it is safe to say that the registered estate is held at any point subject (inter alia) to any burdens seen on the register; here is the tabular representation of title. But even so it is not quite as simple as that.

Registered Estates as Burdens

Some of the burdens on the registered estate are themselves registered estates, whose validity is guaranteed by the registry; for practical purposes these are leases, registered charges and easements created by registered disposition. One of the virtues of a title registration system is that one does not have to say very much about such interests; they can only be created by registration, and once registered their validity is guaranteed and their priority protected. Moreover, leases created by registrable disposition have their own title number and individual register, but also appear as burdens on the lessor's title, in a notice on the lessor's charges register.

Recorded Interests

Third party rights in registered estates which are not themselves registered estates may appear on the register but are not *registered*. They are recorded, but they are not the subject of title registration and their validity is not guaranteed.[9] The 2002 Act is unhelpful in defining the term 'registered' to mean simply 'entered in the register',[10] which tends to obscure this distinction. The recording of such interests is protective[11] in that the priority of the interest (if valid, which is not guaranteed) is protected when a registered disposition takes place.[12] But recording is not dispositive; any disposition that is not registrable can be done without recording the resulting interest on the register and will remain perfectly valid, but any interest created will be overridden by the subsequent registration of a registrable disposition.[13]

---

[9] S 32. See entries 1 and 2 (restrictive covenants) and 7 (an estate contract) of the Charges Register in Example 2, on pp 49–50.

[10] S 132(1).

[11] See the terminology in ch 1, text following n 8.

[12] S 32(3).

[13] Thus A is the registered proprietor of a freehold estate in land. He grants to B an option to buy the land; B does not protect the option by notice on the register. If A then sells to C, C is not bound by the option; but B can still sue A for breach of contract. Note, of course, that if B is in occupation of the land then his option *does* bind C, because his occupation makes it an overriding interest: Sch 3, para 2: *Webb v Polmount* [1966] Ch 584.

The Land Registration Act 1925 called these rights 'minor interests';[14] the term is not used in the 2002 Act, nor in the new Land Registration Rules, and there is no authority for its continued use. It is more helpful to be able simply to say what is the position of a given interest vis-à-vis the register—is it registered, recorded, overriding or unprotected?—and, in any case, is it overreachable?

The Interface Between Registration and Recording

There is something of an overlap between registered estates as burdens, and recorded burdens. For if the registrar is not satisfied as to the validity of an easement or charge, he will record it by notice without guaranteeing its validity. Thus the same interest may be registered or recorded, depending upon its provenance. The difficulty here is that many lawyers are unaware of the difference. It is expressed on the register by the use of different forms of wording; thus a recorded, but not registered, easement may be the subject of a notice in words such as 'the land *is expressed to be* subject to the easements set out in a deed dated etc'. Accordingly, unless the reader of the register has a detailed knowledge of the implications of certain forms of words, interests that are only recorded actually appear to be registered. Recording thus gives a sort of mythological protection.

Agreed and Unilateral Notices

Those familiar with the 1925 legislation will appreciate that section 32 represents a change. Under the Land Registration Act 1925, interests could be protected by notice on production of the registered proprietor's land certificate and therefore only with his consent. If consent was not forthcoming—essentially, therefore, where the claim was disputed—the interest could be protected not by a notice but by a caution. And the caution neither guaranteed validity nor protected priority. It functioned as the caveat does in most Torrens systems.[15] The presence of the caution simply staked a claim; it meant that when an application to register a disposition was made, the cautioner must be 'warned off', ie given 14 days to substantiate his claim before the disposition was registered nevertheless (thus overriding his claim by virtue of section 29/30, unless the cautioner happened to have an overriding interest).[16]

---

[14] 1925 Act, s 3(xv). The term also included registrable estates which were not actually registered eg when the purchaser failed to register the transfer to himself, or an attempt was made to create a legal easement without registration.

[15] Ziff, *Property Law*, 433–4; AJ Bradbrook, SV MacCallum, AP Moore, *Australian Real Property Law* 3rd edn (Sydney, Lawbook Co, 2002) (hereafter '*Bradbrook, MacCallum and Moore*'), [4.81].

[16] The effect of a caution was thus rather weaker than that of a restriction. There is a caution on the Proprietorship Register of Example 2, on p 48, since this imaginary title was prepared before the implementation of the 2002 Act.

The fact that a caution did not affect priority was not widely appreciated—despite the clear statement to that effect in *Ruoff and Roper*.[17] So the decision in *Clark v Chief Land Registrar*[18] came as something of a surprise. Thus where a charging order was protected by a caution, and the registry failed to give notice to the chargee of the forthcoming registration of a mortgage, the charging order was overridden by that mortgage.[19] *Clark* was heard together with another action,[20] where an estate contract had been protected by a caution. The cautioner was warned of the impending registration of a mortgage and consented to it; only to find that its interest was therefore postponed to the registered charge.

Now, however, the position has changed. Cautions have gone. Burdens that are not registered estates are all protected by notice, whether or not the registered proprietor agrees;[21] but notices entered pursuant to an application[22] are either 'agreed' or 'unilateral', so that a purchaser can see whether or not there is a dispute about the interest claimed.[23] The warning off procedure has also gone; thus the effect of section 29/30 is simply that the purchaser takes the registered estate subject to all interests protected by notice, *insofar as they are valid.*

Interests That Cannot be Protected by Notice

Section 33 states that no notice can be entered in the register in respect of certain interests. These include leases too short to be registrable; this exclusion must be read with the restrictions, discussed below, upon the eligibility of such leases for overriding status in Schedule 3. Taken together, these provisions are intended to ensure that a purchaser need *never* be concerned about a reversionary lease.[24] The other exclusions are restrictive covenants in leases,[25] certain commons rights and mining rights[26] and, most important of all, interests under trusts of land and under Settled Land Act settlements.[27] Section 90(4) adds that no notice may be

---

[17] 1991 edition, 7–03; see the table of abbreviations for the current edition.

[18] [1994] Ch 370.

[19] This meant, of course, that the chargee was entitled to an indemnity; had the decision been otherwise, the subsequent mortgagee would have been entitled to an indemnity. This is the classic case of the mistake which is bound to happen sometime, for which the alteration and indemnity provisions are designed; see ch 6.

[20] *Chancery Plc v Ketteringham* [1994] Ch 370.

[21] 2002 Act ss 34–36; Draft Land Registration Rules 2003, r 80 ff.

[22] As opposed to a notice entered by the registrar on first registration.

[23] Save that some non-consensual matters have to be recorded by an agreed notice; draft Land Registration Rules 2003 r 80. In particular, this applies to a notice under the Access to Neighbouring Land Act 1992, and to a matrimonial home rights notice, recording the spouse's right of occupation under the Family Law Act 1996, s 30. The purpose of this is to ensure that such entries cannot be cancelled on the application of the registered proprietor under s 36 of the 2002 Act.

[24] S 33(b). This is explained in detail at n 46, below.

[25] As these bind successors in title under leasehold law in any event: *Evans and Smith* 94 ff.

[26] *Megarry and Wade*, 18–179 ff.

[27] S 33(a) (i) and (ii). No new settlements under the Settled Land Act 1925 can be created following the Trusts of Land and Appointment of Trustees Act 1996. Interests under trusts may be protected by restrictions (see ch 4, n 8), and may be overriding interests (see below, at n 54).

entered in respect of an interest under a PPP lease, in accordance with the 2002 Act's policy of ostracism for such leases.[28]

Interests That Now *Can* be Protected by Notice

Section 115 of the 2002 Act ensures that a right of pre-emption functions as a proprietary right in registered land; it can be protected by notice, or can be an overriding interest by virtue of actual occupation. Under the old law, the position seemed to be that a right of pre-emption did not become a proprietary right until the owner of the land decided to sell it, at which point the right of pre-emption became an option.[29] The trouble with that was that it made the right of pre-emption unprotectable up to the point when it crystallised into a right in the land. The new status for such rights avoids that difficulty.[30]

Section 116 does something rather startling. It promotes two interests, in registered land only, to the status of proprietary rights that can, again, be protected by notice or have overriding status: the 'equity by estoppel' and the 'mere equity'.

The equity by estoppel is the interest, whatever it be, of the beneficiary of an estoppel *before* his entitlement has been determined by a court. Thus Mr Crabb, in *Crabb v Arun DC*,[31] was promised a right of way over the District Council's land. The promise was broken after Mr Crabb had relied upon it to his detriment. From that point until the court's decision, Mr Crabb had an equity, sometimes called an inchoate equity. He had the standing to ask the court for relief, and the right to whatever the court might award him, be it an estate in land, financial compensation, or whatever. Regarding this as an estate in land is not entirely straightforward;[32] the point is now resolved in any event by the provisions of the new Act. Thus where A claims relief based upon an estoppel raised by the conduct of B in connection with B's land, he may seek to enforce his right to relief against C, the new proprietor of the land concerned.

Obviously in many instances C will take free of A's interest because it is not protected by notice and is not an overriding interest by virtue of actual occupation. But suppose A is in occupation of the land when C buys it. The response to estoppel is discretionary, guided by principles of equity,[33] and the outcome of A's claim is unknown until the court has determined what relief the claimant should have vis-à-vis B (although if the elements of estoppel are satisfied the court will tend

---

[28] See ch 3, n 44.
[29] *Pritchard v Briggs* [1980] Ch 338.
[30] LC 271, 5.26 ff.
[31] [1976] Ch 179.
[32] LC 271, 5.29 ff. See for example G Battersby, 'Informal Transactions in Land, Estoppel and Registration' (1995) 58 *Modern Law Review* 637; R Smith, 'How Proprietary is Proprietary Estoppel?' in FD Rose (ed) *Consensus ad idem* (London, Sweet & Maxwell, 1996); and E Cooke, *The Modern Law of Estoppel* (Oxford, OUP, 2000) at 131 ff.
[33] S Gardner, 'The Remedial Discretion in Proprietary Estoppel' (1999) 115 *Law Quarterly Review* 438.

towards relief that matches A's expectation). The implication of section 116 is that once the court determines the relief that A should obtain from B, he may in these circumstances seek it from C.[34] We are not supposed to have too much sympathy for C; for he will only be bound by an overriding interest based upon occupation if that occupation was reasonably obvious; but we all know that mortgagees do not inspect. We also have to ask whether or not an equity by estoppel could be overreached, so as to rule out any possible claim against C; it has been suggested that this will have to be determined on the basis of a consideration of what the claimant is eventually awarded by a court hearing his estoppel claim.[35] On that basis, if A is awarded an equitable interest in the land which in fact could be overreached, then, if the conditions for overreaching are met, it will be found to have been overreached.

Similarly promoted to proprietary status is the 'mere equity', the right to apply for equitable relief, for example for rectification of a document for mistake, for rescission of a transaction for undue influence, or for relief against forfeiture of a lease. Such rights function a little like equitable interests, but with a more shadowy and uncertain status and with inferior rights to priority.[36] Now, like the equity by estoppel, they are proprietary rights in registered land, they behave in the same way as other equitable interests for priority purposes, and they will be defeated by the registration of a registrable disposition unless protected by a notice or given overriding status by actual occupation. Thus their promotion does not necessarily give them any additional protection.

OVERRIDING INTERESTS: SCHEDULE 3

A debate central to any theory of title registration is: how far can the system dispense with interests that bind the land without being recorded on the register? The answer, embodied in the 1925 legislation and adhered to in discussion ever since, is that there will always be rights which it is unfair or impracticable to expect the holder to register but which the system must protect. Overriding interests have been described as the crack in the mirror of title;[37] they are the main reason why the perfect register can only ever be a myth. This is so in most, probably all systems of registered title; it is sometimes supposed in this country that the Torrens systems are not plagued by overriding interests, but that is not the case, although the list in such systems is shorter.[38] It is only fair to add that the 2002 Act does not use the term 'overriding interests', but lists in two schedules 'unregistered interests

---

[34] There is no room, on principle, for a fresh exercise of discretion to decide whether or not C should be liable; s 116 has already done that job.

[35] S Baughen, 'Estoppels over land and third parties', (1994) 14 *Legal Studies* 147 at 154.

[36] See below.

[37] DJ Hayton, *Registered Land*, 3rd edn (London, Sweet & Maxwell, 1981), 76.

[38] Ziff, *Property Law*, 432; *Bradbrook, MacCallum and Moore*, [4.51] to 4.62]; P O'Connor, 'Registration of Title in England and Australia: A Theoretical and Comparative Analysis' in Cooke, *Modern Studies II*, 81 at 89.

which override first registration' and 'unregistered interests which override registered dispositions'. This has the merit of clarity, but the term 'overriding interests' will probably still be used colloquially.

The 1925 Act listed overriding interests in section 70(1)(g). The list was long, in paragraphs (a) to (m), and in parts had a distinctly feudal ring. Many of them obsolesced early in the lifetime of the 1925 Act and are unknown to modern practitioners.[39] The most striking feature of the list of overriding interests in Schedule 3 of the 2002 Act (Schedule 1 is discussed below) is that it has been slimmed down. There are far fewer words, slightly fewer items; and some—in paragraphs 10 to 14 of the Schedule—are transitional only, and will cease to be overriding 10 years after the coming into force of the Schedule.[40] Gone are the umpteen different ways of saying 'easement' in section 70(1)(a) of the 1925 Act; gone are the rights of squatters—their rights can only override under paragraph 2. Gone are obligations to repair chancels, now that the Court of Appeal has outlawed them on human rights grounds.[41] It all looks cleaner and simpler.

The list in Schedule 3 is not quite self-contained; for section 90 provides that it takes effect as if it included a reference to a PPP lease. This is the only protection given to PPP leases in the 2002 Act, and it is obviously designed to be easily repealable without messing up the numbering of paragraphs in the Schedule.

The following call for special comment:

Paragraph 1: Short Leases

The Land Registration Act 1925 included among the list of overriding interests[42] leases granted for a term of not more than 21 years.[43] The word 'granted' was interpreted to mean that the lease must be legal.[44] The new provision duplicates this, substituting 'seven' for '21'. Legal leases for seven years or more can only be created out of a registered estate by registered disposition; whether or not created out of a registered estate they must, of course, be registered with their own title as well as being entered on the register of the reversion.[45]

---

[39] S 70(1)(g) of the Land Registration Act 1925 is reproduced at p 78.

[40] S 117. Careful thought has been given to possible human rights implications here: see LC 271, 8.81 ff.

[41] *Aston Cantlow PCC v Wallbank* [2002] Ch 51.

[42] S 70(1)(k).

[43] The provision originally included the requirement that the lease be granted in possession and at a full market rent, which left some short leases unprotected. *Strand Securities Ltd v Caswell* [1965] Ch 958.

[44] *City Permanent BS v Miller* [1952] Ch 840; see *Megarry and Wade* 6–066 ff.

[45] What happens when a lease for more than seven years is granted out of a registered estate and not registered? It will fail to be legal; it cannot be an overriding interest under para 1 of Sch 3; it could be protected by notice but almost certainly would not be; so whilst it will continue to be enforceable against the grantor it will only affect a purchaser if the lessee is in actual occupation—as he normally would be. Where such a lease is granted out of unregistered land but not registered, the provisions of s 7 mean that it will cease to be a legal lease when the period for registration expires; as an equitable lease it will bind purchasers of the reversion by notice.

Land Registration Act 1925

70 Liability of registered land to overriding interests

(1)   All registered land shall, unless under the provisions of this Act the contrary is expressed on the register, be deemed to be subject to such of the following overriding interests as may be for the time being subsisting in reference thereto, and such interests shall not be treated as incumbrances within the meaning of this Act, (that is to say):—

(a) Rights of common, drainage rights, customary rights (until extinguished), public rights, profits à prendre, rights of sheepwalk, rights of way, watercourses, rights of water, and other easements not being equitable easements required to be protected by notice on the register;

(b) Liability to repair highways by reason of tenure, quit-rents, crown rents, heriots, and other rents and charges (until extinguished) having their origin in tenure;

(c) Liability to repair the chancel of any church;

(d) Liability in respect of embankments, and sea and river walls;

(e) . . . , payments in lieu of tithe, and charges or annuities payable for the redemption of tithe rentcharges;

(f) Subject to the provisions of this Act, rights acquired or in course of being acquired under the Limitation Acts;

(g) The rights of every person in actual occupation of the land or in receipt of the rents and profits thereof, save where enquiry is made of such person and the rights are not disclosed;

(h) In the case of a possessory, qualified, or good leasehold title, all estates, rights, interests, and powers excepted from the effect of registration;

(i) Rights under local land charges unless and until registered or protected on the register in the prescribed manner;

(j) Rights of fishing and sporting, seignorial and manorial rights of all descriptions (until extinguished), and franchises;

[(k) Leases granted for a term not exceeding twenty-one years;]

(l) In respect of land registered before the commencement of this Act, rights to mines and minerals, and rights of entry, search, and user, and other rights and reservations incidental to or required for the purpose of giving full effect to the enjoyment of rights to mines and minerals or of property in mines or minerals, being rights which, where the title was first registered before the first day of January, eighteen hundred and ninety-eight, were created before that date, and where the title was first registered after the thirty-first day of December, eighteen hundred and ninety-seven, were created before the date of first registration;

[(m) any interest or right which is an overriding interest by virtue of paragraph 1(1) of Schedule 9 to the Coal Industry Act 1994:]

Provided that, where it is proved to the satisfaction of the registrar that any land registered or about to be registered is exempt from land tax, or tithe rentcharge or payments in lieu of title, or from charges or annuities payable for the redemption of tithe rentcharge, the registrar may notify the fact on the register in the prescribed manner.

Again there are exceptions. A lease whose grant, in unregistered land, triggers first registration cannot be an overriding interest when granted out of a registered reversion,[46] and any lease for seven years or less whose grant is nevertheless a registrable disposition[47] cannot be an overriding interest.

Paragraph 2: The Interests of Persons in Actual Occupation

Paragraph 2, corresponding to the notorious section 70(1)(g) of the 1925 Act, is different in function from the other paragraphs of Schedule 3. The other paragraphs each pick on a particular interest and give it overriding status. Paragraph 3 operates on *any* proprietary interest provided a certain factual situation obtains— namely that the holder of the interest is in actual occupation of the land. This provision is one of the unique features of English title registration; it does not seem to appear in Torrens systems[48] nor in those based on the German paradigm.[49]

The original provision in the 1925 Act attracted little comment when it was enacted,[50] but it was found to have potential for dramatic effects. An estate contract, for example, could take on overriding effect if the person with the benefit of the contract was occupying the land.[51] For the paragraph is not limited in its operation to interests which could not be protected otherwise (as are now paragraphs 1 and 3[52]); the effect is to give overriding importance to occupation, even where registration requirements are not met. Its scope was widened hugely in 1981, when the House of Lords' decision in *William & Glyn's Bank Ltd v Boland*[53] established that interests under trusts for sale were interests in land and could be overriding interests.[54]

---

[46] S 4(1)(d), (e) or (f). Thus short leases that are required to be registered do not fall within para 1 of Sch 3 ie they cannot override a registered disposition by reason of their shortness; moreover, reversionary leases cannot be overriding by virtue of actual occupation—Sch 3, para 2(d); see below, text at n 62.

[47] S 27(2)(b)(ii)–(v)—again, the lessee should have complied with the requirement, and gained the protection, of registration. Note that the grant of a lease where the right to possession is discontinuous does not trigger first registration, but is a registrable disposition. So a timeshare cannot be an overriding interest if granted out of a registered estate; if granted out of unregistered land, it *is* an overriding interest once the reversion is registered.

[48] See ch1, n 54.

[49] See ch 9, below.

[50] There had been no parallel to this provision in the statutes of 1862, 1875 and 1897. Anderson, *Lawyers 1832*—1940, 277–89, reproduces debate about a proposed provision about actual occupation, in the proceedings of the First Royal Commission on the Land Transfer Act in 1909; the pre-occupation seems to have been with cellars and drains. Harold Potter (sic), *Registered Land Conveyancing* (London, Sweet & Maxwell, 1934), 270, suggested that it might protect tenancies at will or on sufferance, or leases subject to an absolute prohibition on assignment (which were not at that date capable of registration). The first edition of RE Megarry and HR Wade, *The Law of Real Property* (London, Stevens and Sons Ltd, 1957) devotes 18 pages to registration of title and makes no comment on s 70(1)(g).

[51] *Bridges v Mees* [1957] Ch 475.

[52] See above and below.

[53] [1981] AC 487.

[54] Since then, the suggestion has been made that it be widened further, by extending its scope to include *any* right of an occupier, personal as well as proprietary: L Tee, 'The Rights of Every Person in

There is so much more to say about the relationship between trust interests, overriding and overreaching that this is postponed to a note at the end of this chapter. For the purposes of this general discussion of overriding interests, we must note simply that trust interests are overriding interests when the beneficiary is in actual occupation of the land; but that those interests will not bind a purchaser if they are overreached, because overreaching trumps overriding. If the conditions for overreaching are met, overreaching takes place.[55]

Again, there are exceptions. First, an interest under the Settled Land Act 1925 cannot be an overriding interest. This replicates the 1925 provision; there it was part of the legislator's policy of drawing a curtain in front of trusts and ensuring that beneficial interests could not affect a purchaser. Interests under Settled Land Act settlements could not trouble a purchaser because they could not be protected by notice[56] and could not be overriding interests;[57] in the absence of wrongdoing the rules would be complied with and the interests overreached.[58] And interests under trusts for sale would not bind a purchaser because legal doctrine in 1925 regarded them as interests in personalty so that they could not possibly be overriding interests under the then section 70(1)(g); again, they could not be protected by a notice;[59] the expectation was that they be overreached in any event. The curtain was heavy and effective in 1925; but the explicit provision that interests under Settled Land Act trusts could not be overriding interests was (for reasons obvious at the time) not matched by a similar provision for interests under trusts for sale. If it had been, the development of land law in the twentieth century would have been very different.[60]

Second, an interest will not override if the occupier is asked about his rights and makes no disclosure of them. Again, this replicates the provision in section 70(1)(g) of the 1925 Act; the idea is based on something like estoppel. For if the vendor's wife is asked 'do you have any proprietary right in this house?', and does not say she has, it is unfair for her to claim one later when the purchaser has relied on her silence or her denial. The provision has not been tested in litigation—what would happen if it were challenged by someone who had denied that she had rights

Actual Occupation: An Enquiry Into S 70(1)(g) of the Land Registration Act 1925', (1998) 57 *Cambridge Law Journal* 328. Acceptance of this suggestion would mark a huge, and probably impracticable, change in the Act's policy of protecting purchasers. For further comment on this, see see R Smith, 'The role of registration in modern land law' in L Tee (ed), *Land Law: Issues, Debates, Policy* (Willan Publishing, 2002), 58 ff. Tee's other suggestion, that the rights of occupiers should only bind a purchaser if the occupation is apparent, reinforces the 1925 Act's purchaser protection and has been followed in the 2002 Act; see text at n 61 below.

  [55] *City of London BS v Flegg* [1988] AC 73.
  [56] See above, n 27.
  [57] S 86(2) of the 1925 Act provides that beneficial interests under the Settled Land Act 1925 'shall take effect as minor interests and not otherwise'.
  [58] Law of Property Act 1925, s 2(1)(i).
  [59] S 49(2) Land Registration Act 1925.
  [60] For a fuller discussion of this development see the final section of this chapter. The prohibition on interests under Settled Land Act trusts being overriding interests was debated in Parliament during the passage of the Bill that became the 2002 Act, without appreciation of the historical reason for its presence in the 1925 Act; HL Deb 17/07/2001, Col 1403.

because she did not know she had them? Or denied through fear of the legal owner? Should a purchaser make sure that the occupier has taken legal advice before replying? Such enquiries are made as a matter of routine in nearly every conveyancing transaction, for it is part of the protection evolved by conveyancers and lending institutions in the wake of the decision in *Boland*. If adult occupiers are asked to confirm that they have no rights in the property, and/or consent to the proposed transaction, the purchaser has nothing to fear from what is now paragraph 2 of Schedule 3.

Third, in a provision new to the 2002 Act, occupation will not bestow overriding status on an interest if the occupation is not known to the purchaser and is not reasonably obvious. This was something of a lacuna in the 1925 Act, which gave rise to the dilemma: if occupation is undiscoverable, why should the occupier be protected, when in unregistered land the purchaser would not have had constructive notice of something he truly could not have discovered and so would not have been bound?[61] The 2002 Act tidies up the problem, and reinforces the protection of the purchaser.

Fourth, a reversionary lease taking effect in possession more than three months from the grant—which we already know cannot be an overriding interest by virtue of its shortness under paragraph 1—cannot be overriding either by virtue of actual occupation if the lease has not taken effect in possession at the date of the disposition.[62]

The 2002 Act changes the law by excluding from this paragraph those in receipt of the rents and profits from the land, who featured in section 70(1)(g) of the 1925 Act.[63] And it further tidies the law by providing that where someone is in occupation of only part of the land, their interest is overriding in respect only of that part; this reverses the decision in *Ferrishurst Ltd v Wallcite Ltd*.[64]

Paragraph 3: Easements

Only legal easements and profits à prendre can override now. Under the 1925 Act it was a shock to find that the wordy description of easements in section 79(1)(a)

---

[61] In fact the rules of constructive notice were so strict that occupation, however hard to discover, would almost always give rise to it. See *Kingsnorth Finance Ltd v Tizard* [1986] 1 WLR 783; and the discussion at LC 254, 5.71—5.73.

[62] For example: two year lease dated 1st January, to take effect 1st June. The lessee-to-be is in occupation already as a licensee. Sale takes place 1st March; the lessee-to-be does not have an overriding interest by virtue of his lease, because of paras 1 and 2 of Sch 3; nor does he have protection under para 2 because his licence is not a proprietary interest. The only protection available to him is supposed to be compliance with the requirement of registration in s 27(2)(b)(ii). By contrast, the unusual short leases in s 27(2)(iii), (iv) and (v) can be overriding interests by virtue of actual occupation, even though they should have been registered. Note that a contract now to grant a lease in six months' time *will* be an overriding interest if the prospective lessee is in actual occupation, and so the apparent determination to leave unregistered reversionary leases unprotected is easily evaded.

[63] See LC 271, 8.18. Transitional provisions ensure that rights which were overriding interests by virtue of the receipt of rent before the implementation of the 2002 Act will retain their overriding status: Sch 12, para 8.

[64] [1999] Ch 355; see LC 271, 8.55 ff.

included equitable easements openly exercised,[65] for the purchaser of unregistered land is not bound by these unless they are registered as land charges.[66] Now only legal easements override. We have to put this together with the provision that legal easements can only be expressly created out of registered land by registered disposition;[67] and easements thus created will appear on the register. So the legal easements that override will be ones arising by implication (easements of necessity, easements arising by common intention, through the rule in *Wheeldon v Burrows*[68], through the operation of section 62 of the Law of Property Act 1925[69]) or by prescription.[70,71]

Again, there are exceptions. Paragraph 3 of Schedule 3 is a model of correct punctuation; but the sense would have been clearer if brackets had been used instead of the third and fourth commas. Unpacking it step by step: despite the general rule in paragraph 3, legal easements or profits à prendre are *not* overriding if both (a) the purchaser does not actually know about them, and (b) they would not have been obvious on a reasonably careful inspection of the land affected, *unless* the easement has been exercised during the year before the disposition. So the purchaser *is* bound by a drainage easement that he did not know about and could not have noticed—say, an underground pipe—but which is in regular use; but he is *not* bound by a right of way that he did not know about, could not have spotted, and that has not been used for a year. The onus of proving use lies with the person entitled to the benefit of the easement. The same goes for profits à prendre, provided they are not registered under the Commons Registration Act 1965.[72] The aim is to reduce the number of overriding interests by eliminating undiscoverable rights that are not in regular use.[73]

---

[65]   *Celsteel Ltd v Alton House Holdings Ltd* [1985] 1 WLR 204.

[66]   As a Class Diii land charge under s 2 of the Land Charges Act 1972.

[67]   Ch 3, n 25.

[68]   (1879) 12 Ch D 31.

[69]   As to all these, see *Megarry and Wade* 18–097 ff. The Law Commission is currently examining the law of easements; it is to be hoped that one outcome of their deliberations will be a provision making the creation of easements by implication much simpler.

[70]   See *Megarry and Wade* 18–121 ff. Another desirable result of the Law Commission's project— indeed, surely the least they can do—must be the simplification of the rules relating to prescription.

[71]   Also overriding will be legal easements created expressly before first registration, that have never found their way onto the register. Anecdotal evidence indicates that this has happened frequently where the relevant information was not with the deeds submitted for first registration.

[72]   There are too many double negatives here. A profit à prendre which the purchaser does not know about and could not have spotted, and has not been used for over a year, *does* bind the purchaser nevertheless if it is registered under the 1965 Act.

[73]   Easements that are thus disqualified as overriding interests do not, of course, thereby cease to be proprietary rights; but they will only bind a purchaser if protected on the register. Again, transitional provisions retain the overriding status of easements that were overriding before the Act came into force and would otherwise lose that status: Sch 12 para 9.

WHAT THE PURCHASER SEES: SUMMARY

To summarise what we have said so far: a purchaser inspecting the register knows that he will take the land subject to the categories of interest listed in sections 29/30 *unless* they are overreached; and the intention is that the well-informed, properly advised purchaser will make sure that overreaching takes place where it is needed. A fuller discussion of the interaction of trust interests, overreaching and overriding is given in the last section of this chapter as it involves some history and some far-reaching points of principle.

Given this information on the register for the purchaser, one more protection is needed for him:

The Search with Priority

Reverting for a moment to the terminology used in deeds registration systems,[74] a purchaser of registered land is faced with a race system.[75] He will be bound, at the moment of his own registration, by interests that reached the register before his did. The trouble with races is that you may not be the fastest runner. Early conveyancing practice following the 1925 legislation involved completions at the District Land Registry and last minute searches;[76] when this became impracticable the solution devised was the search with priority, now an essential feature of English conveyancing.[77] The practice is simple; after exchange of contracts and before completion, the purchaser carries out a search of the register, and his search certificate gives him priority for the purpose of the disposition he is contemplating. This means that after his search, the register is frozen for 30 days. Nothing else can be registered during the priority period. When his disposition is registered, he takes the register as he found it when he searched.[78]

[74] See ch 1, n 13.

[75] The 1925 Act, specifically ruled out any possibility of race-notice, in s 50(6); but the issue was muddied by the definition of 'purchaser' as 'a purchaser *in good faith* and for valuable consideration' (s 3 (xxi), emphasis added). On occasion the courts found it impossible to resist the temptation to hold that a purchaser with notice of an unregistered interest was bound by it: *Peffer v Rigg* [1971] 1 WLR 285. The 2002 Act does not define 'purchaser'. The Land Registration Rules 2003 retained the old definition, referring to 'good faith', but this has been corrected in the final version so that there is no possibility of the use of that definition to circumvent the Law Commission's clear intentions (r 131). However, there is more to say about this, as the statute must leave room for the imposition of personal liability on the purchaser in extreme circumstances: see text following n 86 below, and ch 6, below, text at n 15 ff.

[76] A Pottage, 'The Originality of Registration' (1995) 15 *Oxford Journal of Legal Studies* 371.

[77] It is a surprise to find that it is not in general use in Australia and New Zealand; some of the concerns there about electronic conveyancing, (see for example, R Thomas, 'Fraud, Risk and the Automated Register', in Grinlinton, *Torrens Conference Papers*) would be readily eliminated by the use of searches with priority. The plan for electronic transactions in this jurisdiction is that searches with priority in electronic transactions will be implemented automatically at the point when contracts are released: see the Land Registry website, www.landregistry.gov.uk.

[78] Land Registration Rules 2003, r 151 ff. The search can be extended if completion is delayed; and when one solicitor acts for both buyer and mortgagee, he searches in the mortgagee's name and

The Ethics of Racing

In chapter 1 reference was made to Graham Battersby's warning of the need to consider the ethical aspect of registration;[79] his remark arose in the context of the race system for registered and recorded interests under the Land Registration Act 1925. For the problem with a strict race system is that it may produce results which seem unbearable from an ethical standpoint. It means that a purchaser may take free of an interest which he knows perfectly well would have bound him if it had been registered.

The most conspicuous example of this is of course *Midland Bank Trust Co Ltd v Green*,[80] a case on the provisions of the Land Charges Acts.[81] The facts were, simply, that a farmer granted his son an option to purchase his farm. The option was not registered under the Land Charges Act 1925. Subsequently there was a family quarrel, and the father sold the farm to his wife for £500; he did this in order to defeat the option, having checked that it was not registered. His wife knew all this; the court found that the £500 was in fact paid to the farmer. Since the Land Charges Act 1925 made no reference to any requirement that a purchaser be in good faith, the House of Lords refused to hold that the mother was bound by the option.[82] The Court of Appeal (Lord Denning among those sitting) had come to the opposite conclusion, importing a requirement of good faith into the statute; but the House of Lords refused to do so.

The Land Registration Act 1925 is intended to operate as a race system just as the Land Charges Acts have done. There has been at least one occasion when the courts have been unable to tolerate this, in contrast to the robust approach of the House of Lords in *Midland Bank*.[83] The possibility of introducing what we might call a race-actual-notice system was advocated by Graham Battersby in 1995;[84] it was given careful consideration in LC 254,[85] and rejected in the interests of consistency and of the protection of purchasers, and in view of the difficulty in assessing actual notice to the exclusion of constructive notice.

To make the move Battersby suggested would be a tremendous about-turn in the policy of land registration and would have been unthinkable in a statute whose tendency is to reinforce the security of purchasers in the interests of marketability. Alongside this must be borne in mind two things. First, the protection given by

---

thus protects both parties. The same system, incidentally, operates under the Land Charges Acts: Land Charges Act 1972, s 11(5), (6).

[79] See ch 1 n 62.
[80] [1981] AC 513, HL.
[81] See ch 2.
[82] Perhaps it is worth bearing in mind that at the date of litigation both mother and son were dead; and that at the date of trial the son's estate had already obtained a judgment in negligence against his solicitor, because of the non-registration of the option, which would be payable if he lost the House of Lords case.
[83] *Peffer v Rigg* [1971] 1 WLR 285; see n 75 above.
[84] 'Informal Transactions in Land, Estoppel and Registration' (1995) 58 *Modern Law Review* 637.
[85] At 3.39 ff.

paragraph 2 of Schedule 3 to those in actual occupation of land. This protection has flavoured and qualified nearly everything said in this chapter, and it will in every case give protection to the interest-holder against a purchaser, unless the interest is overreached. This unique feature of English title registration gives powerful protection to an interest associated with someone's occupation.

Second, it is possible for a purchaser to have so much more than notice of an unregistered right that he incurs a personal liability. In the Torrens systems this is called fraud, and is an express exception to the equivalent, in the various Torrens statutes, of our sections 29/30.[86] In the 2002 Act there is no express provision for this, and the authors of LC 254 were very wary of including anything so productive of litigation as have been the Torrens provisions.[87] Nevertheless, they explain the basis of a purchaser's personal liability in case-law, noting that a purchaser may take as a constructive trustee if he is aware that the vendor is acting in breach of trust[88] or if he has taken land in circumstances such as those in *Lyus v Prowsa Developments Ltd*.[89] The latter case has had a bad press,[90] but the principle it expresses is an essential one if we wish to see an ethical control to the race system. The facts, briefly, were that a purchaser who took land expressly subject to an unregistered option, and paid a reduced price because of the option, was found to have taken the land upon constructive trust for the option-holder. Subsequently it has been stressed that for such a trust to arise, the circumstances must be very persuasive indeed;[91] the possibility of imposing such a trust must not be allowed to jeopardise the fact that liability on the basis of notice is supposed to be eliminated in registered land.[92] It is suggested that if the facts of *Midland Bank Trust Co Ltd v Green*[93] were replicated in registered land, with a purchaser taking with knowledge

---

[86] The Alberta provision, Land Titles Act 1980 s 64(1) (quoted in Ziff, *Property Law*, 424), reads: 'The owner of land in whose name a certificate of title has been granted shall, except in case of fraud wherein he has participated or colluded, hold it, subject . . . to the encumbrances, liens, estates and interests that are endorsed on the certificate of title, absolutely free from all other encumbrances [etc.] . . .' The definition in the Land Registration Act 1925 of a purchaser as 'in good faith' (see n 75 above) is said in LC 254, at 3.41, to have been 'legislative accident'.

[87] LC 254, 3.40. The Torrens concept of fraud is wide, and there is an overlap with what is known as the *in personam* exception to indefeasibility, which refers to personal liabilities incurred by the registered proprietor; see *Bradbrook, MacCallum and Moore*, [4.40] ff and [4.68] ff. The distinction between the two is immaterial here, the point is simply that a purchaser may incur a personal liability that disqualifies him from winning the race. This is an important issue in the context of indefeasibility; see ch 6.

[88] LC 254, 3.38, citing *Eagle Trust Plc v SBC Securities Ltd* [1993] 1 WLR 484.

[89] *Lyus v Prowsa Developments Ltd* [1982] 1 WLR 1044, confirmed in *Ashburn Anstalt v Arnold* [1989] Ch 1 at 22. Compare the New Zealand case of *Bahr v Nicolay (No 2)*, (1988) 164 CLR 604, whose facts were very similar to those of *Lyus v Prowsa*, and where the result was, again, that the purchaser was held to be a constructive trustee for the prior option-holder. *Lyus v Prowsa* was cited by Wilson and Toohey JJ, at 638. See L Stevens and K O'Donnell, 'Indefeasibility in decline: the *in personam* remedies' in Grinlinton, *Torrens Conference Papers*.

[90] *Megarry and Wade* 10–022.

[91] *IDC Group v Clark* [1992] EGLR 187 at 190, *per* Browne-Wilkinson VC.

[92] Which is what is wrong with *Peffer v Rigg*, n 75 above.

[93] See above, n, 80.

of the earlier right and in a transaction expressly designed to defeat it, the result should be the imposition of a trust on the purchaser.[94]

THE MIRROR OF TITLE: WHAT THE PROPRIETOR SEES

So far, we have discussed the burdens on the registered estate from the point of view of a purchaser—because that, essentially, is what the register is for. So what about the proprietor himself—what does registration mean to him? When he looks in the mirror by inspecting the register, one of the things he sees is himself. And the register does not tell him quite the whole story about the interests subject to which he holds the land. If he acquired his land or his interest through a registered disposition, he knows that the land is held subject to everything appearing on the register (insofar as it is valid), overriding interests (unless they were overreached by his purchase), and matters excepted from the effect of registration, for that is what the register promised him beforehand. But he may know of other matters to which he alone is subject; trusts he has declared, for example, that do not appear on the register but bind him as trustee; or an equitable mortgage, which remains unregistered and unprotected but binds him by contract. He may also know that his title is vulnerable because he obtained it through undue influence. Thus the register does not protect him from liabilities he has himself incurred in the course of acquisition of the registered estate or after registration.

Moreover, if he is a first registered proprietor there may be other matters to which he, but not a future purchaser, is subject. First registration is different from the registration of dispositions; it is not dispositive, it does not confer the legal estate. The registered proprietor had the legal estate already, by purchase shortly beforehand or as a long-standing owner who has registered voluntarily. Registration is a transforming process; what comes out is not quite what goes in. But different considerations apply to first registration from those operative on the registration of a disposition of already-registered land.[95]

The proprietor immediately following first registration holds the estate on the terms set out in section 11,[96] which tells us that the effect of registration as proprietor of a freehold estate is that the estate is vested in the proprietor 'together with all interests subsisting for the benefit of the estate'.[97] It makes the same provision for three categories of interest to have priority over the registered estate, familiar to us from section 29,[98] but with the following differences:

---

[94] Note that the protection for purchasers under s 26 of the 2002 Act is also qualified by the possibility of personal liability of the purchaser; see ch 4, at n 36, and LC 271, 4.11.

[95] LC 271, 8.3 ff.

[96] S 12 does the same, *mutatis mutandis*, for first registration of leases.

[97] S 11(3); thus easements etc.

[98] Text preceding n 2 above: interests protected on the charges register, overriding interests, rights excepted from the effect of first registration.

—he holds the estate subject to the overriding interests listed in Schedule 1, not Schedule 3
—he holds it pursuant to section 11, which lists a couple of matters additional to those in section 29, namely:
    —any relevant interests of squatters under section 11(4)(c)
    —any relevant beneficial interests under section 11(5).

Looking at these in order:

Schedule 1 Interests

The Land Registration Act 1925, and its predecessors, had one list of overriding interests. The 2002 Act has two, one applicable on first registration and the other on subsequent transactions. This was not envisaged in LC 254, and is intended to reflect the special considerations applicable on first registration.[99]

Schedule 1 differs from Schedule 3 in only three respects:

—Paragraph 1 omits the exception for leases whose grant constitutes a registrable disposition; for the land up to this point has not been registered and so no dispositions can have been registrable.[100]
—Paragraph 2 omits the proviso about enquiry and the exception where occupation is undiscoverable, on the basis that the rights of occupiers should not be prejudiced by first registration.[101]
—Paragraph 3 takes effect without the exception, again because legal easements should not be prejudiced by first registration.

Interests Acquired Under the Limitation Act

Section 11(4)(c) adds that he holds the estate subject to

interests acquired under the Limitation Act 1980 of which the proprietor has notice.

Squatters as such do not appear in Schedule 1 (nor in Schedule 3[102]); by contrast, their rights (whether or not adverse possession had endured for the 12 years necessary to displace the registered proprietor's title) were overriding interests under the Land Registration Act 1925. But most squatters will be in actual occupation of the land and so their interest, whatever it is, will override first registration as a

---

[99] LC 271, 8.3 ff.
[100] Note that s 90 applies to Sch 1 as well as to Sch 3; so PPP leases are treated as included.
[101] See LC 271, 8.21. However, if first registration immediately follows a purchase, there will already have been a filtering process, since some trust interests may have been overreached, and others may have ceased to bind the land because the purchaser is a bona fide purchaser of the legal estate without notice.
[102] But why does not s 11(4)(c) simply appear as an additional item in Sch 1?

result of paragraph 2 of Schedule 1.[103] How strong the squatter's interest is will depend upon how much time he has clocked up. If he has completed his 12 years before the documentary owner is registered he can apply to be registered as proprietor of the land he holds; if he has not completed his 12 years, he falls into the new regime where there is no limitation period for recovery of a registered estate.[104] Section 11(4)(c) operates to preserve the position of a squatter who is not in actual occupation but of whose interest the proprietor has notice; it is only likely to be relevant when he has completed his 12 years and is entitled to apply to be registered as proprietor (since otherwise his moving out of occupation would probably mean the discontinuance of his adverse possession).

The intention, as LC 271 explains,[105] is to clear off the title squatters who have abandoned their land at some point after the paper owner's title has been extinguished.[106] Suppose A takes adverse possession of one of B's fields for 12 years; some time later A abandons the field and B resumes possession; B never noticed the adverse possession and there is nothing to tell him that his own title has been extinguished. Three years later he sells to C who applies for registration. The registered title will include A's field. A may never have realised that he owned the field; even if he did, he may no longer want it, as his abandonment implies. But restoring his land to the paper owner in this way is not only a novel way to create a legal estate but also certainly a deprivation of property within the first paragraph of Article 1 of the First Protocol of the European Convention for the Protection of Human Rights and Fundamental Freedoms. The squatter is unlikely to complain, and the public interest can be invoked to justify the removal from someone of the legal title to property he does not want and has abandoned. But there is the potential for challenge here.

More seriously, section 11(4)(c) is not drafted in these terms. Not being in actual occupation (so as to come within Schedule 1 paragraph 2) is not legally equivalent to having abandoned property, and there is a danger that clause 11(4)(c) will take property away from a squatter who still wants it and is aware that he has it. Issues may arise about the meaning of actual occupation.[107] Certainly this provision may throw up some interesting cases on the meaning of actual occupation, and risks reviving a lot of case law about notice.[108] It is an incentive for large landowners to register their title voluntarily, as this may regain for them land which they did not know they had lost.

[103] Leaving aside the practical issue of how the proprietor managed to get himself registered with a squatter *in situ*, particularly if registration followed a purchase. It is easiest to imagine a squatter in a very small corner of a large estate.
[104] Discussed in ch 7, below, as are the transitional provisions, which are complex.
[105] Para 3.46.
[106] The point was raised by Roger Smith, 'Land Registration: Reform at Last?' in P Jackson and D Wilde, eds, *The Reform of Property Law* (Aldershot, Ashgate, 1997) 129 at 139.
[107] These may take some inspiration from the original wording of the description of actual occupation in the second paragraphs of Schs 1 and 3 in the Land Registration Bill, to include occupation by an employee or agent.
[108] LC 271, at para 3.47 explains that notice means actual and constructive, except where the Act makes clear that only actual notice is meant.

Note that the protection given to squatters under section 11(4)(c) is effective only on first registration. So the sub-section tells a first registered proprietor how he holds the land; and tells the intending purchaser of unregistered land how he *will* hold it when he has purchased and registered. But once the estate is registered, the sub-section tells the intending purchaser nothing; he need only look to Schedule 3, and will find that squatters' rights override a disposition only if the squatter is in actual occupation. We have spent some paragraphs on this new and slightly strange provision, but its practical importance is minimal.

Beneficial Interests Binding the Proprietor Personally

Section 11(5) reads:

(5) If the proprietor is not entitled to the estate for his own benefit, or not entitled solely for his own benefit, then, as between himself and the persons beneficially entitled to the estate, the estate is vested in him subject to such of their interests as he has notice of.

This is expressed to affect only the registered proprietor and the relevant beneficiaries; it is of no concern to a purchaser after first registration.[109] First registration obviously leaves the registered estate subject to any trust interests that are overriding, pursuant to paragraph 2 of Schedule 1; so section 11(5) is relevant only where beneficiaries are not in occupation. If first registration follows a purchase, then any such beneficial interests in the land may have been overreached on that purchase (while the land was unregistered); even if they were not, the purchaser may have taken free of them because he was 'equity's darling', taking the land as a bona fide purchaser of the legal estate without notice. So section 11(5) bites on trust interests that survived the purchase that preceded first registration because the purchaser had notice of them (in which case he is not entitled to the land for his own benefit), even where they are not overriding interests under paragraph 2 of Schedule 1. Moreover, where first registration is voluntary, section 11(5) acts to ensure that the newly registered proprietor remains subject to trust interests of which he has notice even though the beneficiaries are not in actual occupation and so do not fall within paragraph 2 of Schedule 1—for it would be unacceptable for a trustee to be able to evade his liabilities by registration.

Note that where joint proprietors apply for registration, they are required to state the nature of the trust on which they hold the land,[110] so that if they hold the land on any terms other than for themselves as beneficial joint tenants a restriction can be entered to prevent any disposition of the land by a single proprietor.

---

[109] Although of course it is to a volunteer; see below.
[110] See ch 4, text at n 8.

WHAT THE REGISTERED PROPRIETOR SEES: SUMMARY

The registered proprietor is concerned with rather more than the register tells him. He will have been registered under the terms of sections 29/30, or under sections 11/12, and subject to the categories of interests listed there;[111] but he holds the registered estate subject to any liabilities he may have incurred in the course of the disposition or since then, which will not necessarily be reflected on the register. Those liabilities bind him, and, if they have given rise to proprietary rights, they will bind volunteers who may acquire the land from him, even if they are not among the rights that may affect a purchaser.

THE MIRROR OF TITLE: WHAT THE VOLUNTEER SEES

The point laboured in this chapter is that the intended user of the mirror of title is the prospective purchaser, who intends to acquire land or an interest in it under a registered disposition. For him, the register gives a complete list of the categories of interest subject to which he will take it (admittedly, paragraph 2 of Schedule 3 is a yawning chasm, but he does have a complete list of *categories*). It also tells him whether or not the registered proprietor has the power to effect the transaction contemplated; for he can rely upon the absence of any statement on the register that the owner's powers are restricted.

For the registered proprietor himself, inspecting the register after acquisition (whether immediately afterwards or after many years) a less complete picture emerges; for the register tells him nothing about liabilities he has incurred through his own actions. He may have acquired the registered estate through undue influence; or he may have declared a trust over it or granted to someone else an option that has not been protected by notice on the register. Only he knows.

And for anyone proposing to acquire the registered estate, or an interest in the land, other than as a purchaser, this is crucial. For the volunteer does not have the protection of section 29. Nothing is sieved for him; he takes the registered estate exactly as it stands in the hands of the registered proprietor, vulnerabilities, trusts and all; and unless the registered proprietor tells him what those matters are, he cannot know.

Note that in some registration systems the volunteer *is* protected just like a purchaser;[112] but not in this one. The purchaser thus has the protection of section 29; the registered proprietor has in addition his own knowledge of what has happened to the registered estate; the volunteer has neither.

---

[111] Unless he took the land as a volunteer; see below.

[112] The Torrens systems vary: see *Bradbrook, MacCallum and Moore* [4.64]. Contrast the decision of the Victorian Supreme Court in *King v Smail* [1958] VR 273 (volunteer takes the property subject to everything that affected the donor) and the decision of the New South Wales Court of Appeal in *Bogdanovich v Koteff* (1988) 12 NSWLR 472 (volunteer takes the title just as a purchaser would take it).

PRIORITIES OF INTERESTS *INTER SE*

This chapter has been about priorities; we have asked which interests take priority over, and therefore bind, the registered proprietor, whether following purchase, following a first registration, or following a volunteer acquisition. Indeed, sections 29 and 30, with which we have been largely concerned, use the terminology of priority and postponement. Now we move on to ask about the priority between themselves of interests, other than registered estates with their own title number— roughly, third party rights.

This involves slightly more awkward questions. It is easy to ask: if I buy this land, will I be bound by that easement? But if I have the benefit of an easement, what does it mean to ask if I have priority over that lease, or that mortgage? The answer has to be unpacked for individual instances. If an easement has priority over a mortgage, then if the mortgagee takes possession and sells the land, the land will be sold with the burden of the easement. If an easement takes priority over a lease, the lessee must not interfere with its exercise. If mortgage A takes priority over mortgage B, then mortgagee A takes his money first from the sale proceeds; and in our real-property-mortgaged-to-a-building-society-owning democracy,[113] the priority of mortgages between themselves is immensely important (especially if the market falls and there is not enough money to pay all the mortgagees).

It is not proposed to spend a great deal of time on this, in the interests of pursuing the main theme of the book, security of ownership. Yet mortgagees are among the most important purchasers of registered estates, so a brief discussion is needed. As we might expect, in line with its general policy the trend in the 2002 Act is towards simplicity and, above all, visibility. Purchasers are not supposed to have nasty shocks.

Priority: Registered Estates

Some third party rights are themselves registered estates even though we would not describe them as ownership rights. Legal easements and mortgages created by registered disposition are seen on the charges register of another's title. Between themselves they rank in order of registration—that is simply the result of the provisions of sections 29/30.[114] It also follows from sections 29/30 that registered estates take effect subject to any interest that is not a registered estate but is

---

[113] *Pettitt v Pettitt* [1970] AC 777 at 824, *per* Lord Diplock.
[114] The 2002 Act contains provisions for mortgagees' rights to tack and to consolidate. These are rather specialist matters not dealt with in detail here. The right to tack is the right for, say, a first mortgagee to lend additional money to the borrower, after the date of his first charge and after a second charge has been granted to another lender, but to tack the later advance on to the earlier so that it has the same priority. The right to consolidate is the right of the lender who holds more than one charge to insist that if any one is redeemed, they all be redeemed. The provisions are found in ss 49 and 57; see LC 271, 7.18 ff and 7.44.

recorded on the register; again priority operates on a simple race system, in order of registration.

Transactions that are not registered dispositions[115] do not fall under the provisions of section 29/30, and for them a general rule operates:

Priority: The General Rule

The general rule is stated in section 28, that the priority of interests affecting a registered estate or charge is determined by the order of their creation, not their registration. Thus a restrictive covenant created on 1st January takes priority over an equitable easement created on 15th January, whenever either is recorded and whether or not either is recorded. Interests that are not recorded, and are therefore overridden by registered dispositions, nevertheless remain valid between the parties themselves, and remain proprietary rights which may take priority to other interests under the general rule.

Note that the change in status of 'mere equities', by virtue of section 116, changes the priority rules; formerly, mere equities were overridden by the purchaser of an equitable interest without notice of the equity. Now, mere equities rank in order of creation along with other equitable interests; this effects a welcome simplification.

OVERRIDING AND OVERREACHING

Finally, then, a closer look at the relationship between overriding and overreaching, touched on briefly above. This is something of an historical excursus; but in seeing how we arrived where we now are, we see also how social change has effected legal change; how legal change has been accommodated by legal practice; and how the balance between proprietor and purchaser, so carefully fixed in the 1925 legislation, has been shifted. That shift has had a knock-on effect which we shall see in the next chapter.

The point at issue here, then, is the question when, if ever, a purchaser is bound by interests under a trust of land existing before he bought it.

The 1925 Scheme

Recall that one of the changes effected by the Law of Property Act 1925 was to demote certain interests from law to equity. In particular, all the freehold estates except the fee simple—thus in particular the life estate and the entail—became equitable interests under section 1 of the Law of Property Act 1925 and could only

---

[115] Using that term, again, to mean registrable dispositions that are completed by registration.

exist behind a trust. Trusts relating to land were, at that date, in one of three kinds;
the strict settlement, the trust for sale, and the bare trust.

In a strict settlement pursuant to the Settled Land Act 1925 the legal fee simple
was vested in the life tenant, while the trustees' role was to receive purchase
monies. Section 2 of the Law of Property Act 1925 ensures that, provided the
purchase money, if any, is paid to the trustees, the interests under the trust will
be overreached. Thus, jumping over to registered land, they should not survive a
registered disposition because (a) in the absence of wrongdoing overreaching
will take place and (b) even if something goes wrong and overreaching does not
take place the Act provides that interests under Settled Land Act trusts cannot be
overriding interests and cannot be protected by notice.[116]

Until 1996, trusts for sale were the normal form of landholding in cases of concurrent or successive co-ownership.[117] Statute decreed, for example, that legal co-
owners held upon trust for sale[118]; it rapidly became the preferred form of trust for
successive interests, rather than the settlement under the Settled Land Act 1925;
case-law established that where one person held land at law, upon trust for more
than one person in equity, there was a trust for sale.[119] The trust for sale was in origin a device for holding investment property. It was literally the form of ownership
used in the nineteenth century for land intended to be sold for profit, not lived in.
As a consequence, the interests of beneficiaries were held to be interests not in the
land itself, but in the proceeds of sale. They were personalty, not realty.[120] This was
called the doctrine of conversion. It made perfect sense for investment property,
but became increasingly odd when the subject of the trust was the family home
and would often remain unsold for years, perhaps for more than one generation.
Nevertheless, the extension of this mode of land holding in 1925 fitted the philosophy of keeping trust interests away from the title and expressing them in monetary terms wherever possible. Thus interests under trusts for sale, which could not
be protected on the register by notice, could not possibly be overriding interests
either. There was no explicit prohibition as there was for Settled Land Act settlements, but there was no need; interests under trusts for sale were not interests in
land and therefore could not be elevated to overriding status by section 70(1)(g)
of the 1925 Act. Again, the intention was that they should be overreached, and the
legislation contained provisions designed to facilitate this; in any event they were
not supposed to trouble the purchaser of registered land.[121]

Only the beneficiary of a bare trust, who held the equitable fee simple *in the
land*, could conceivably find that interest protected as an overriding interest. This

---

[116] See above, text at n 27.

[117] See ch 2, n 48.

[118] S 36(1) of the Law of Property Act 1925, in its original version.

[119] *Bull v Bull* [1925] 1 QB 234.

[120] See the description of such rights in *Irani Finance Ltd v Singh* [1971] Ch 59, by Cross LJ at 79–80
(quoted in *City of London Building Society v Flegg* [1987] 2 WLR 1266 at 1280).

[121] See ch 2, n 56 ff; leaving aside now the controversy as to whether or not the Land Registration
Act 1925 actually achieved this. S 2 of the Law of Property Act 1925 of course originally referred to
trusts for sale, but has been amended to provide for trusts of land.

would be a rare case. The intention behind the Law of Property Act 1925 was to simplify conveyancing by ensuring that trust interests were lifted off the land by overreaching. The intention of its cousin the Land Registration Act 1925 was that for all practical purposes, the purchaser of registered land would *never* be caught by trust interests that he did not know about. This had been the intention from the early stages of English title registration. In *Re Odell* in 1906[122] Vaughan Williams LJ was able to say with confidence:

[The Land Transfer Act 1875 as amended] relieves [purchasers] from responsibility in regard to subsisting settlements, trusts and equities affecting the vendor's or mortgagor's title.

This was the true extent of the curtain—far thicker than we find it now; thus we find Benjamin Cherry, in 1926, urging conveyancers to study registration even if they were practising outside London, 'for this Act illustrates the working of the curtain system'.[123] The effect was truly radical. It remains so in most Torrens systems, untroubled—or unblessed—as they are by any equivalent to our provisions giving overriding status to those in actual occupation of the land.

The Rise of Equitable Co-ownership and the Decision in *Boland*

The world changed after 1925 in ways that Benjamin Cherry and his colleagues could not have imagined. In 1925 a very small proportion of the population owned their own home; in the early years of the twentieth century married women were legally barred from the nursing and teaching professions and would have been readily sackable, on their marriage, from other employment, so that within the sector of society where home ownership might be on the increase, few women had independent means. All that changed. On the one hand, the employment of women increased hugely, and the marriage disqualification vanished, so that more women had money. On the other hand, attitudes to ownership and partnership in marriage changed so that it became normal, perhaps around the 1960s and 1970s, for couples to be joint legal owners of their home. The common intention constructive trust was invented/discovered in the 1970s,[124] opening the road to home ownership for those who were not legal owners and could not meet the pre-requisites of the resulting trust. The incidence, across properties in England and Wales, of the trust for sale increased during the twentieth century in a way that could not have been imagined in 1925. This meant that a homeowner might, without realising it, hold land on trust for himself and another, and might sell land without having any awareness of the need to activate the overreaching machinery. And so we

---

[122] [1906] 2 Ch 47 at 70.
[123] BL Cherry and JRP Maxwell, *Prideaux's Forms and Precedents in Conveyancing* 22nd edn, (London, Stevens and Sons Ltd, 1926), vol 1, 29.
[124] *Gissing v Gissing* [1970] AC 886.

come to the decision in *Boland*,[125] about what happens when a purchaser takes land in circumstances where there is an interest under a trust for sale that is not overreached.

The facts of *Boland* are simple. Mr Boland owned a house, with registered title. Mrs Boland had contributed to the purchase price. According to equitable principles by then well-established, she held a beneficial interest under a resulting trust. Mr Boland mortgaged the house without his wife's knowledge, and defaulted on the repayments; Mrs Boland argued that she had an equitable interest in the property, which was an overriding interest by virtue of her actual occupation of the land, and had not been overreached by the mortgage by a sole trustee. The argument was controversial; for the doctrine of conversion meant that interests under trusts for sale were personalty not realty, and were not interests in the land. The House of Lords, in a decision that seems obvious to today's students but was by no means obvious then, held that Mrs Boland's interest was indeed a proprietary right in the land.[126]

Boland thus had a huge effect upon the law's treatment of the scope of section 70(1)(g) of the Land Registration Act 1925. Trust interests, which could not be protected by notice under the 1925 Act[127] just as they cannot under the 2002 Act,[128] could nevertheless have overriding effect.

The immediate aftermath was panic. The Law Commission made a special report to Parliament; among its recommendations was that the interests of bene-ficiaries in actual occupation of land should not be overreached without their con-sent, a suggestion that would have further bolstered their position and jeopardised purchasers.[129] The report was never implemented; conveyancing practice took over. First, conveyancers became aware of the need never to accept a conveyance from a sole married vendor. Second, enquiries are always made of the vendor as to the presence of adult non-owning occupiers of the property; and any such occu-piers are always asked to consent in advance to the disposition. 'Always' is perhaps too strong a term. Not all conveyancers are perfect. But the procedure is followed sufficiently often, and problems arise so rarely, that we can say that the effects of *Boland* have been minimised in the normal purchase.

It is suggested, however, that the *Boland* episode reflected one trend, and started another. It reflected the trend towards protection of those who did not hold for-mal interests in land; the invention of the common intention constructive trust

[125] *Williams & Glyn's Bank Ltd v Boland* [1981] AC 487. The prevalence of joint ownership by spouses makes this scenario increasingly unlikely where the vendor is married (and it is easy for a con-veyancer to act upon the mantra 'never take a conveyance from a sole married vendor'); it remains a trap for purchasers from cohabitants.
[126] As late as 1974, SNL Palk, in 'First Registration of Title—Just What Does It Do?' [1974] *Conveyancer* 236, could express genuine doubt as to whether an equitable interest under a trust for sale could possibly be an overriding interest under s 70(1)(g) of the Land Registration Act 1925.
[127] S 49(2).
[128] S 32.
[129] Law Commission, *Property Law: The implications of William and Glyn's Bank Ltd v Boland*, Law Com No 158 (London, HMSO, 1982).

was the most obvious symptom of this. It was part, we have to say, of the Denning era. Where that trend has gone now is hard to say. *Boland*'s effects have been minimised. Concern for those without formal rights has re-surfaced in a different form, in the huge series of cases protecting those who did not really wish to consent to mortgages of their homes.[130] But *Boland* started another trend, namely a readiness to see overriding interests in unexpected places. In the next chapter we shall see the effect of this.

Overriding Versus Overreaching

What is the relationship between overriding and overreaching? A further limitation upon the effects of *Boland* is that the decision has no effect upon the overreaching machinery. If a purchase is made from two trustees, overreaching takes place whether or not the trust interests concerned are overriding. This was the decision in *City of London Building Society v Flegg*,[131] where a mortgage was granted by two joint legal owners who, unknown to the mortgagee, held on trust for themselves and the wife's parents, who lived with them and had contributed to the purchase price. Were the parents' interests overreached by the mortgage advance to the two trustees? The judge at first instance said yes, the Court of Appeal said no; the House of Lords gave a very firm yes. It dismissed arguments based on section 14 of the Land Registration Act 1925;[132] its reasoning was founded on the effect of section 70(1)(g), which makes an interest overriding but does not change its nature. Therefore it does not make it cease to be overreachable.

The decision in *Flegg* was not forced. The Court of Appeal came rationally to the opposite conclusion. But if we look at the policy of the 1925 legislation, we can see without doubt what was meant to happen by the draftsman. Trust interests were not supposed to affect purchasers. Benjamin Cherry would have been surprised to find that an interest under a trust for sale could be overriding; but it would never have entered his wildest dreams that it would not in any event be overreached if normal conveyancing procedure was followed.[133]

Thus *Flegg* further restores the balance that the Act strikes between the security of owners and the protection of purchasers—between static and dynamic security.[134] The 1925 legislation weighted it heavily in favour of the purchaser. *Boland*

---

[130] *Barclays Bank Plc v O'Brien* [1994] 1 AC 180; see *Megarry and Wade* 19–159 ff.

[131] [1988] AC 73.

[132] The arguments dismissing it were not very strong; but we have seen that this provision is probably an accident.

[133] But in the 1925 edition of *Wolstenhome and Cherry's Conveyancing* Statutes (BL Cherry, J Chadwick and JRP Maxwell (London, Stevens and Sons, 1925)), s 70(1)(g) is mentioned, at 40, as a potential protection for equitable interests in the context of overreaching. Thus although Cherry could not have contemplated interests under a trust for sale being overriding interests, he was aware that interests under a bare trust could be overriding (other commentators seem to have missed this, see n 50 above). Therefore had the issue arisen in the context of a bare trust, Cherry himself might well have come to the conclusion opposite to that reached in *Flegg*.

[134] Discussed further in ch 6, below.

skewed this; conveyancing practice, and the confirmation in *Flegg* of the power of overreaching, have largely reversed the effect of *Boland*. But *Boland* changed our minds for ever; and it is thus no surprise to find that the law on indefeasibility, such as it is in this jurisdiction and discussed in the next chapter, has been irredeemably muddied by a preoccupation with overriding interests.

6

Indefeasibility—The English Version

THIS CHAPTER IS the obverse of chapter 5. In chapter 5 we assessed the accuracy of what has been called the 'negative warranty' of the register: that there is nothing affecting the title that is not seen on the register. This chapter concerns the affirmative warranty: that ownership is as shown by the register. The terminology of warranties derives from JE Hogg:

> The warranty of title given by the statutory conclusiveness of the register operates in two ways, and the register has two functions, affirmative and negative respectively. Affirmatively, the register warrants that the title of the owner is as stated on the register; and negatively, the warranty is that the owner's title is not affected by anything that is not stated on the register.[1]

Theodore Ruoff, in *An Englishman Looks at the Torrens System*,[2] draws attention to Sir Robert Torrens' assertion[3] that a title registration system must be 'reliable, simple, cheap, speedy and suited to the needs of the community'. Ruoff equated reliability with security and accuracy. Another way of contrasting chapters 5 and 6 is to say that chapter 5 has been concerned with accuracy, asking the question: how accurate is the information given by the register about the burdens on the registered title? This chapter is about the security of the registered title.

A book about a Torrens registration system would give prominence to a discussion of the affirmative warranty, or of 'indefeasibility', regarding it as one of the most important features of the system, while conceding that indefeasibility can never be complete.[4] Not all English texts contain a section headed 'indefeasibility'; in several we find, before 2002, discussions of 'rectification and indemnity', usually as one of the final topics considered within the whole framework of registration. Students are often glad to miss it out. But the extent of indefeasibility is a key issue in any title registration system.

The question behind a discussion of indefeasibility, or security, or the affirmative warranty, is: can I be sure that, if I purchase a registered estate, I will be able to keep it without fear that I will lose it because of something already existing that

---

[1] JE Hogg, *Registration of Title to Land Throughout the Empire* (Sydney, Law Book Co, 1920). See Pamela O'Connor's discussion in 'Registration of Title in England and Australia: A Theoretical and Comparative Analysis', in Cooke, *Modern Studies II*, 81. I am grateful to Pam for spending a great deal of time discussing with me the issues in this chapter, and explaining a number of things to me.

[2] Sydney, Law Book Company, 1957, at 6.

[3] Ruoff's citation is *Speeches* 1858–9.

[4] Thus *Bradbrook, MacCallum and Moore*'s discussion is the second section of their long chapter on the Torrens system: 120 ff; and [4.12], [4.20] ff explaining the limitations to indefeasibility.

I do not know about? Indefeasibility is a policy issue. The shape of the law, and the answer to any ambiguities in it, must depend upon whether preference is to be given to a proprietor of land or to a purchaser; that is, to static or dynamic security.[5] Dynamic security means that the purchaser can be confident that he will get a good title, and this generates a confident market; static security means that someone who owns or has an interest in land can be sure he will not be deprived of it against his will. The two are in tension. If we say that an innocent purchaser P, who has obtained registration of a forged transfer, must be able to keep his land (while compensating O who has lost it due to fraud or forgery by a third party, who of course is not worth suing), P may be happy now, but he will be less than happy if another rogue forges P's signature and transfers the land to P2, to whom the same principle will also give a good title, while compensating P. The system must therefore find an acceptable compromise between dynamic and static security; but different systems find the balance at different points. In chapter 5 we saw that the preference, so far as concerns the negative warranty of the English register, is for dynamic security; the system is weighted so as to protect the purchaser. We might reasonably expect, as a matter of consistency, that the response of the English registration system to the question of indefeasibility might be to favour dynamic security and favour the purchaser.

In fact the answer in the English system is far from clear. The 1925 statute, as interpreted by the courts, gives the same sort of response to many, but not all, factual situations as do the Torrens systems; but on a completely different basis of principle. In the Torrens systems, by contrast, the answer to the question of indefeasibility is very clear indeed; dynamic security prevails. What the answer will be under the 2002 Act is extremely unclear because the drafting of the relevant parts of the statute is very much open to interpretation. If we seek consistency—and a love of consistency beams from the pages of LC 271—we might want to interpret the 2002 Act so as to move closer to the position of the Torrens systems. But we have to be careful; whatever their merits on principle, the Torrens systems generate far more litigation on indefeasibility than does the English system. Much of this comes up as litigation under the exceptions to indefeasibility (eg fraud, in personam) because it is very hard to challenge the rule of immediate indefeasibility itself.

What we have to do in this chapter is to spend a considerable time looking at the working of the 1925 statute. We are very much in the dark as to how the 2002 Act will work,[6] and it is impossible to assess how the courts may interpret the new law

[5] The terms belong to R Demogue: 'Security' in A Fouillee, J Charmont, L Duguit and R Demogue (eds), *Modern French Legal Philosophy* (Boston, The Boston Book Co, 1916 (republished by AM Kelley, New York, 1968)), Ch XIII. Again, see Pamela O'Connor's discussion, n 1 above.

[6] As this book is being finished (May 2003), *Ruoff and Roper* has not yet been fully updated in the light of the provisions of the 2002 Act (TB Ruoff, RB Pryer, C West, R Fearnley, *Ruoff and Roper on the Law and Practice of Registered Conveyancing* (London, Sweet & Maxwell, 1995; looseleaf, updated to September 2002); once it is, and it must be by the time this book is published, we shall have an authoritative view as to how the new provisions will work. We might expect to have one already, in the shape of the Joint Working Party's views on LC 271; but LC 271 says very little indeed on the

without first seeing how the old law has worked. Accordingly, after first examining some of the issues of principle, this chapter will look at the development of the law on indefeasibility under the 1925 Act, and then consider how the 2002 Act may function. The suggestion will be made that the policy of the Act demands that we move closer to the Torrens systems, making a decisive break with the pre-2002 case-law, while preserving one especially valuable feature of the English system, the protection of the proprietor in possession.

Indefeasibility will be the most challenging area for the courts under the 2002 regime.

INDEFEASIBILITY: THE ISSUES

The sort of sequence of transactions we have to discuss looks like this:

X to Y to Z

X, Y and Z are successive registered proprietors. The transfer, or mortgage, from X to Y is flawed, without any fault on X's or Y's part; it was forged by a third party, or it was procured by the fraud of a third party, or it involves a mistake—perhaps it is a sale of part and the boundaries are wrong. Z may have bought the land from Y; if Y was a buyer, he may be Y's mortagee. X, of course, wants his land back. Is Y's title safe? And what about Z? And of course while it does not matter in principle whether Y or Z are buyers or mortgagees, it matters a lot in practice; most buyers are interested primarily in the land, while the mortgagee's needs are financial.

The common law has rules to deal with these problems; they result in dispositions being wholly or partly void or voidable. A forged transfer is void. A conveyance that accidentally includes land that the vendor does not own simply does not convey that land. A conveyance obtained through undue influence, fraud or misrepresentation is voidable, that is, it can be rescinded at the demand of the vendor and at the discretion of the court; the vendor is said to have an 'equity' to seek rescission.[7] The design of a title registration system must involve a decision as to whether or not it will follow these rules. If it does, there is a problem of principle; for registration is supposed to be a tabular, at-a-glance portrayal of title. And for

---

crucial issue of forgery and leaves much of the detail open to interpretation. The current *Ruoff and Roper* comments briefly on the new provisions at 40–35, saying: 'The position with regard to rectification under the Land Registration Act 2002 will be broadly similar to that under the Land Registration Act 1925, although there are some changes . . .'

[7] See ch 5, text at n 36.

all the qualifications we had to admit to the negative warranty in chapter 5, what the purchaser does not have to do is to investigate the title prior to the registered proprietor in order to ascertain the existence of burdens on it. Sections 29/30 give him an assurance that he need only look at the present. But if the system then replicates the common law rules as to whether or not a title is void or voidable, the purchaser must look back at the disposition to the current proprietor, perhaps to previous dispositions as well, in order to be sure about the positive warranty. And so the Torrens systems have reached a solution which protects him from having to do so, ensuring that the register's affirmative, as well as its negative, warranty is given without the need for historical investigation.

The Torrens statutes tend to contain a statement about indefeasibility, without always using that term. It corresponds to our sections 29/30, and says (with variations from one jurisdiction to another) something like: the registered proprietor shall, except in cases of fraud and other listed exceptions (corresponding to our overriding interests), hold the land subject only to interests noted on the register.[8]

Armed with such provisions, the Torrens systems have evolved two answers to our question. One is immediate indefeasibility, the other is deferred indefeasibility. Looking at the example in the box above, where the transfer from X to Y is forged, but Y is innocent; he is registered as proprietor. Later he sells or mortgages to Z, who then registers. Immediate indefeasibility protects Y; deferred indefeasibility does not, but protects Z. After some decades of a preference for deferred indefeasibility, the Torrens systems of New Zealand and Australia have opted for immediate indefeasibility, following the privy Council decision in *Frazer v Walker*.[9] This was a New Zealand case, but the Australian courts have followed it;[10] the exception for fraud in the section 29/30 equivalent is thus restricted to fraud by the purchaser himself. Immediate indefeasibility therefore ensures that a purchaser who takes innocently under a forged transfer, or who takes a transfer of land whose registered title contains an error (say, a restrictive covenant has been omitted), or who takes under the second in a double transfer series,[11] will receive what the register said he was going to receive. The section that defines the title as he will take it (our 29/30) is complete, and can only be jeopardised by his own wrongdoing.[12] The innocent transferor who may lose out by this—the victim of forgery, for example—is compensated; he takes the money, the purchaser takes the land. And that is precisely why Thomas Mapp called his book 'Torrens' Elusive Title'; the dynamic security implicit in the system threatens static security and makes the title given to the reg-

    [8] For a quoted example, see ch 5, n 86; and, generally, *Bradbrook, MacCallum and Moore* [4.20] ff.
    [9] [1967] 1 AC 569. In terms of our example above, the case involved X and Y; Y was a mortgagee. The land was held by joint proprietors, X1 and X2; X1 negotiated the mortgage and forged X2's signature on the document.
    [10] For example in *Breskvar v Wall* (1971) 126 CLR 376; see generally *Bradbrook, MacCallum and Moore* [4.31] ff. For the Canadian approach, where deferred indefeasibility predominates, see Ziff, *Property Law*, 426 ff . 'The majority of Canadian decisions on the subject of forgery indicate a preference for deferred indefeasibility': vol 2, [758].
    [11] X sells to Y1 and then sells the same land to Y2.
    [12] We touched on this in ch 5 (text at n 86), and see below; it encompasses what the Torrens writers call fraud, and the *in personam*, or *inter partes*, exception.

istered proprietor elusive; he may lose it when the system protects the purchaser.[13] To the English lawyer, immediate indefeasibility is startling; it is a glaring exception to the rule *nemo dat quod non habet*, you cannot give what you do not have; to the lawyer in a Torrens system it is fundamental to the ethos of the system.[14]

Before we go any further, we need to identify, and to some extent clear off, two different issues. The first relates to personal liabilities of the purchaser connected with the transaction, and the second relates to events subsequent to registered dispositions.

Personal Liabilities of the Purchaser Incurred in the Course of Purchase

A purchaser may incur a personal liability in the course of his purchase; it may be a criminal offence such as forgery, or a civil wrong such as undue influence. It may be a liability to the holder of a prior interest,[15] or it may be a liability to the vendor. The victim must be allowed to enforce his rights against such a purchaser, and the title registration system must accommodate this. This takes us into the areas which writers on the Torrens systems classify as, on the one hand, fraud, and on the other as the '*in personam* exception'.[16] English law has set its face against anything so wide-ranging as the Torrens concept of fraud, but it is clear that a purchaser's personal liabilities are not compromised by the registration system. He may be liable as constructive trustee, in exceptional circumstances, for the holder of a prior interest; more straightforwardly, if he has forged a transfer, he is liable to the innocent transferor.[17] A prominent example in recent years is the case of *Barclays Bank Plc v O'Brien*[18] and the numerous cases following it, where a mortgage has been rescinded, in whole or in part, because of misrepresentation or undue influence in the transaction itself. These cases, insofar as they involve registered land, have never been regarded as having anything to do with the reliability of the register, and rightly so.

English writers have not generally used the term *in personam*,[19] but the terminology is very useful as a way of pointing out a vital conceptual gulf between two

---

[13] (Alberta, Alberta Institute for Law Research and Reform, 1978); indefeasibility/defeasibility is really the subject of the book. See in particular pp 67–8.

[14] For the downside of this, see R Boast, 'The Implications of Indefeasibility for Maori Land' in Grinlinton, *Torrens Conference Papers.*

[15] Discussed in ch 5 under 'The ethics of racing'.

[16] Bruce Ziff's explanation (Ziff, *Property Law*, 428–32) implies that fraud relates to a liability to a previous interest-holder while *in personam* rights arise vis-à-vis the vendor, but in Australia that distinction is by no means clear. See *Bradbrook, MacCallum & Moore* [4.40] ff on fraud and [4.68] ff on rights *in personam*; note the comment at [4.46] about the overlap between the two, and note that the fact of *Bahr v Nicolay (no 2)* (1988) 164 CLR 604 (see ch 5, n 89) gave rise to both.

[17] See ch 5, at n 91.

[18] [1994] AC 180. For an Australian perspective on these issues see R Chambers, 'Indefeasible Title as a Bar to a Claim for Restitution' [1998] *Restitution Law Review* 126, discussing *Pyramid Building Society v Scorpion Hotels* [1988] VR 188.

[19] Or *inter se/inter partes*, since the rights referred to do not have to be personal: Ziff, *Property Law*, 431. But see R Smith, 'The role of registration in modern land law' in L Tee (ed), *Land Law: Issues, Debates, Policy* (Cullompton, Willan Publishing, 2002), 29.

very different types of title problem. A problem involving the transaction by which the purchaser took the land may be corrected without compromising indefeasibility. It is about wrongdoing, not about the reliability of the register.[20] True issues of indefeasibility concern the innocent purchaser's right to rely on the register, and to take what the register says he will get, even if there has been a problem one or more transactions ago in which the purchaser was not involved. If his title is not secure in that instance, indefeasibility is compromised.

Events Subsequent to Registered Dispositions

Titles change with time. A registered proprietor may die; he may go bankrupt; his lease may be forfeited; someone may record an interest adverse to him; that adverse interest may become invalid or may be shown to have been invalid all along. *Of course* the register must be able to be changed in order to reflect these events. No special substantive provisions should be needed for this, only an administrative ability derived from somewhere in the system; and this has no effect at all on indefeasibility of title. In itself it affects only the current registered proprietor. It has no bearing on the provisions which describe the interests subject to which the next registered proprietor will take the registered estate, unless by mistake that updating is not done and the register becomes misleading.

This type of amendment of the register can be called 'bringing the register up to date', or 'administrative alteration'. It forms part of the mirror principle; the register mirrors the title, and of course external events may change that title, and the register must reflect these.

Back to Indefeasibility

Let us now go back to the question which is the subject of this chapter: the question of indefeasibility from the point of view of a purchaser who has not been involved in any wrongdoing, and before he has done anything to change or jeopardise his own title. We have seen the Torrens answer: the purchaser is protected from any mistake or wrongdoing that is not reflected in the section 29/30 equivalent. If there has been such a mistake or wrongdoing, he takes the land, while the innocent transferor is protected.

---

[20] R Chambers, *An Introduction to Property law in Australia* (LBC Information Services, 2001) at 456–7: 'Indefeasibility of title is about the priority of rights and has nothing to do with their creation. The in personam exception is an "exception" to indefeasibility only because a registered right can be affected by the creation of a new right.'

THE ENGLISH VERSION OF INDEFEASIBILITY

The English system developed under the 1925 legislation does it the other way. The English system expresses indefeasibility in money, not in land. The common law rules are replicated in the registration system; transactions are void or voidable just as they would be at common law, and the register may (it is discretionary) be rectified (in the terminology of the 1925 statute) to reflect this. The purchaser takes the money, the innocent transferor gets his land back.

This gives rise to a problem of principle, whether or not one actually likes indefeasibility. It means that a purchaser can be affected by defects in earlier transactions, which he therefore ought to investigate; and that is precisely what title registration is supposed to eliminate.

The problem is ameliorated in two ways. First, errors and wrongs in the chain of title tend to be discovered relatively quickly or not at all, so we do not in practice find that matters have to be resolved by an investigation of more than one transaction. Indeed, they cannot be; the mechanics of registration mean that it is not possible for Z to find out whether or not the transaction from X to Y was flawed. Institutional lenders, who (as we shall see) are most at risk, can divert the problem to insurance; the lack of indefeasibility, which would cause consternation to a Torrens lawyer, is met by risk allocation rather than by the complex process of risk avoidance by investigation of title. Second, and very importantly, the replication of the common law rules is qualified by the provision that protects the proprietor in possession, section 82(3) of the 1925 Act and paragraphs 2(2) and 6(2) of Schedule 4 of the 2002 Act. And registered proprietors usually are in possession. Thus in most cases where the rules dictate that the register may be rectified, in fact it is not, because of this protection. In such cases the purchaser keeps the land and the innocent transferor loses it but is compensated by the indemnity fund. This yields the same result as immediate indefeasibility, but via a wholly different route.

What makes matters much worse is that the interpretation of the 1925 statute has bifurcated. We reach something not too far from immediate indefeasibility, starting from common law principles, but via two parallel routes. Each route has problems of its own.

INDEFEASIBILITY UNDER THE 1925 ACT: THE STATUTORY ROUTE

The Early Statutes

The Land Transfer Act 1862, inept as it was, did start off with the right sort of idea: it declared the registered title to be 'absolute and indefeasible'. The Act did not work because the standard of title required was too high, and landowners did not generally have sufficient incentive to go through the trauma of registration.[21] But

---

[21] See ch 2, n 73.

because that standard was too high, there was no provision in the statute for the correction of mistakes, as it was assumed there would be none, nor for the compensation of anyone who suffered loss through the registration system, as it was assumed this would not happen. The 1875 Act added a new provision, enabling anyone aggrieved by registration to apply to the Court, which could rectify the register but not to the prejudice of any rights or estates acquired by registration under the Act. So there was really no threat there to the reliability of the registered title.[22]

The 1897 Act marked a new departure, making registration compulsory and thereby giving it a chance of being workable, albeit in a very limited geographical area; and it set up an indemnity fund to compensate anyone suffering loss through an error or omission in the register. It also gave the Court wider powers to rectify the register; it has been said that this marked the abandonment of the principle of indefeasibility in English registered title.[23] In particular, it provided that the register must be rectified if the transfer to the registered proprietor was void. That may be said to be the starting point for the present law.

Then came *Re Odell*[24] which, in the words of a later Chief Land Registrar,[25] 'drove a coach and four through the indemnity in public confidence' as well as being 'a shock to those responsible for the drafting and for the administration of the 1897 Act.' In *Re Odell* it was held that an innocent registered chargee who held under a forged disposition (our Y) was not entitled to indemnity when the register was rectified against him because he had never been the rightful owner and therefore had suffered no loss. The interesting thing about the English view of title registration is that the shock was the unavailability of indemnity for Y, not the loss of Y's title. The drafting of the statute made indefeasibility in this respect an impossibility, and no-one seems to have found this the slightest bit surprising.

The Land Registration Act 1925

Typically, the 1925 Act provided sticking plaster for the *Re Odell* indemnity problem, rather than major corrective surgery to address the issue of indefeasibility. It provided that in such a case the registered proprietor who claims in good faith under a forged disposition shall, if his title disappears in the rectification exercise, be deemed to suffer loss, and so can receive an indemnity (section 83(4)). But it retained the structure of the 1897 Act in providing a list of cases, in section 82, where the register can be rectified, at the court's discretion, but with a proviso restricting the availability of rectification against a proprietor in possession.

---

[22] S 96; and s 98 stated that transactions which would have been fraudulent and void in unregistered land are fraudulent and void in registered land, 'subject to the provisions in this Act with respect to registered dispositions for valuable consideration'.

[23] Law Commission Working Paper no 45, *Transfer of Land, Land Registration (Third Paper)* (London, HMSO, 1972), 39, para 63.

[24] (1906) 2 Ch 47.

[25] JS Stewart-Wallace, *Introduction to the Principles of Land Registration* (London, Stevens & Sons, 1937), 47.

Sections 82 and 83 are reproduced here on pages 108–110, in their current rather than their original form (the points of principle to be made remain the same). Note that rectification may be effected by the court or the registrar, but that in two cases a court order is necessary (section 82(1)(a) and (b)).[26]

Remarkably few cases have been thrown up by section 82. Comment upon it tends to proceed subsection by subsection, and this can obscure the principles at work. This is made worse by the fact that the rectification provisions in section 82 have been used for all of the following, conceptually quite different, purposes:

A. To enable the register to be rectified so as to give effect to an overriding interest;[27]
B. To give effect to the purchaser's own liabilities, incurred by his own agreement or wrongdoing; for example where the registered proprietor has obtained his title by forgery or fraud;[28]
C. To up-date the register to give effect to off-register events subsequent to registration, such as bankruptcy or forfeiture or the fact that a caution can no longer be justified;[29]
D. To correct the register because a disposition was wholly or partly void because of an innocent mistake.[30]
E. To correct the register because of an innocent mistake of detail, e.g. the omission of a restrictive covenant.[31]
F. To correct the register following a disposition which was void or voidable because of a wrong such as forgery or fraud,[32] where the registered proprietor was not at fault.

It will be appreciated from what has been said so far that only items D and F are relevant to the core issue of indefeasibility, the qualifications if any to the register's affirmative warranty; and item E is closely linked to D. Thus issue A follows from the section stating that the purchaser takes the land subject to overriding interests (section 20 in the 1925 Act).[33] Issue B concerns the registered proprietor's own wrongdoing (fraud and the *in personam* exception, in Torrens terminology);

---

[26] The Land Registration Rules 1925 gave the registrar further powers to amend the register in trivial instances—where street numbers have changed (r 283), for example, or to correct clerical errors without detriment to the registered interest (r 13); or, by r 48, when the proprietor has in error been registered as proprietor of land he does not own. The power is exercised when there is no dispute about the error; on correction, the legal estate just slips quietly back to where it should be.

[27] *Re Chowood's Registered Land* [1933] Ch 574.

[28] *Norwich & Peterborough Building Society v Steed* [1993] Ch 116.

[29] *Lester v Burgess* (1973) 26 P & CR 536.

[30] *Re 139 Deptford High Street* [1951] Ch 884; *Re Sea View Gardens* [1967] 1 WLR 134.

[31] *Freer v Unwins* [1976] 1 Ch 288.

[32] Or it may be void for *non est factum* brought about by B; this is rare and difficult to prove. See *Saunders v Anglia Building Society* [1971] AC 1004; *Ruoff and Roper* 1995, 40–13A.

[33] That is why *Re Chowood's Registered Land* [1933] Ch 574 is not discussed in this chapter (but pause to be amused by the title to the case; in 1933 registered land was still a rare beast). However, in that case and probably in others an overlap has been assumed; and therefore s 82(3) makes it clear that the special protection for a proprietor in possession does not apply where rectification gives effect to an overriding interest; and s 83 ensures that no indemnity is available in those circumstances.

Land Registration Act 1925

82 Rectification of the register

(1) The register may be rectified pursuant to an order of the court, or by the registrar, subject to .111 appeal to the court, in any of the following cases, but subject to the provisions of this section:–

   (a) Subject to any express provisions of this Act to the contrary, where a court of competent jurisdiction has decided that any person is entitled to any estate right or interest in or to any registered land or charge, and as a consequence of such decision such court is of opinion that a rectification of the register is required, and makes an order to that effect;

   (b) Subject to any express provision of this Act to the contrary, where the court, on the application in the prescribed manner of any person who is aggrieved by any entry made in, or by the omission of any entry from, the register, or by any default being made, or unnecessary delay taking place, in the making of any entry in the register, makes an order for the rectification of the register;

   (c) In any case and at any time with the consent of all persons interested;

   (d) Where the court or the registrar is satisfied that any entry in the register has been obtained by fraud;

   (e) Where two or more persons are, by mistake, registered as proprietors of the same registered estate or of the same charge;

   (f) Where a mortgagee has been registered as proprietor of the land instead of as proprietor of a charge and a right of redemption is subsisting;

   (g) Where a legal estate has been registered in the name of a person who if the land had not been registered would not have been the estate owner; and

   (h) In any other case where, by reason of any error or omission in the register, or by reason of any entry made under a mistake, it may be deemed just to rectify the register.

(2) The register may be rectified under this section, notwithstanding that the rectification may affect any estates, rights, charges, or interests acquired or protected by registration, or by any entry on the register, or otherwise.

(3) The register shall not be rectified, except for the purpose of giving effect to an overriding interest [or in order of the court], so as to affect the title of the proprietor who is in possession—

   [(a) unless the proprietor has caused or substantially contributed to the error or omission by fraud or lack of proper care; or

   (b) ...

   (c) unless for any other reason, in any particular case, it is considered that it would be unjust not to rectify the register against him.

(4) Where a person is in possession of registered land in right of a minor interest, he shall, for the purposes of this section, be deemed to be in possession as agent for the proprietor.

(5) The registrar shall obey the order of any competent court in relation to any registered land on being served with the order or an official copy thereof.

(6) On every rectification of the register the land certificate and any charge certificate which may be affected shall be produced to the registrar unless an order to the contrary is made by him.

83 Indemnity for errors or omissions in the register

(1) Where the register is rectified under this Act, then, subject to the provisions of this Act—

(a) any person suffering loss by reason of the rectification shall be entitled to be indemnified; and

(b) if, notwithstanding the rectification, the person in whose favour the register is rectified suffers loss by reason of an error or omission in the register in respect of which it is so rectified, he also shall be entitled to be indemnified.

(2) Where an error or omission has occurred in the register, but the register is not rectified, any person suffering loss by reason of the error or omission shall, subject to the provisions of this Act, be entitled to be indemnified.

(3) Where any person suffers loss by reason of the loss or destruction of any document lodged at the registry for inspection or safe custody or by reason of an error in any official search, he shall be entitled to be indemnified under this Act.

(4) Subject to the following provisions of this section, a proprietor of any registered land or charge claiming in good faith under a forged disposition shall, where the register is rectified, be deemed to have suffered loss by reason of such rectification and shall be entitled to be indemnified under this Act.

(5) No indemnity shall be payable under this Act—

(a) on account of any loss suffered by a claimant wholly or partly as a result of his own fraud or wholly as a result of his own lack of proper care;

(b) on account of any mines or minerals, or the existence of any right to work or get mines or minerals, unless it is noted on the register that the mines or minerals are included in the title; or

(c) on account of any costs or expenses (of whatever nature) incurred without the consent of the registrar, unless—

(i) by reason of urgency it was not practicable to apply for the registrar's consent before they were incurred, and

(ii) the registrar subsequently approves them for the purposes of this paragraph.

(6) Where any loss suffered by a claimant is suffered partly as a result of his own lack of proper care, any indemnity payable to him shall be reduced to such extent as is just and equitable having regard to his share in the responsibility for the loss.

(7) For the purposes of subsections (5)(a) and (6) above, any fraud or lack of proper care on the part of a person from whom the claimant derives title (otherwise than under a disposition for valuable consideration which is registered or protected on the register) shall be treated as if it were fraud or lack of proper care on the part of the claimant (and the reference in subsection (6) to the claimant's share in the responsibility for the loss shall be construed accordingly).

(8) Where an indemnity is paid in respect of the loss of an estate or interest in or charge on land, the amount so paid shall not exceed—

(a) where the register is not rectified, the value of the estate, interest or charge at the time when the error or omission which caused the loss was made;

(b) where the register is rectified, the value (if there had been no rectification) of the estate, interest or charge, immediately before the time of rectification.

(9) Subject to subsection (5)(c) above, as restricted by section 2(2) of the Land Registration and Land Charges Act 1971—

(a) an indemnity under any provision of this Act shall include such amount, if any, as may be reasonable in respect of any costs or expenses properly incurred by the claimant in relation to the matter; and

(b) a claimant for an indemnity under any such provision shall be entitled to an indemnity thereunder of such amount, if any, as may be reasonable in respect of any such costs or expenses, notwithstanding that no other indemnity money is payable thereunder.

(10) Where indemnity is paid to a claimant in respect of any loss, the registrar, on behalf of the Crown, shall be entitled—

(a) to recover the amount paid from any person who caused or substantially contributed to the loss by his fraud; or

(b) for the purpose of recovering the amount paid, to enforce—

(i) any right of action (of whatever nature and however arising) which the claimant would have been entitled to enforce had the indemnity not been paid, and

(ii) where the register has been rectified, any right of action (of whatever nature and however arising) which the person in whose favour the register has been rectified would have been entitled to enforce had it not been rectified.

(11) Subsection (10) above does not prejudice any other rights of recovery which by virtue of any enactment are exercisable by the registrar where he has made a payment of indemnity.

(12) A liability to pay indemnity under this Act shall be deemed to be a simple contract debt; and for the purposes of the Limitation Act 1980, the cause of action shall be deemed to arise at the time when the claimant knows, or but for his own default might have known, of the existence of his claim.

(13) This section applies to the Crown in like manner as it applies to a private person.

Y cannot expect the protection of registration, and Y's liability to rectification does not threaten the security of the register so far as purchasers are concerned.[34] Issue C concerns events subsequent to registration, which of course may change the title and are not issues about purchase.[35] Only items D, E and F are in any way controversial. The others just have to happen. But the mixing up of all these different concepts must have contributed to the difficulty that English lawyers have felt in getting to grips with the issue of indefeasibility.

Taking that issue by itself, the overall effect of the provisions in the Land Registration Act 1925 (and therefore the result in cases D, E and F) is as has been stated above: that any event, whether an error or a wrong, that can impeach a title in unregistered land by making it void or voidable will have just the same effect in registered land. Even had the other paragraphs of subsection (1) not been interpreted in this way, sub-section 82(1)(g) clinches it:

[The register may be rectified] Where a legal estate has been registered in the name of a person who if the land had not been registered would not have been the estate owner.

This is subject to three qualifications. First, the fact that section 69 of the 1925 Act gives the registered proprietor the legal estate nevertheless, so that rectification of the register is needed to put the legal title back where it should, on unregistered principles, be. Second, that rectification is discretionary. Third, that it is available subject to the protection given by section 82(3) to the registered proprietor in possession (unless the registered proprietor has been at fault, or the rectification gives effect to an overriding interest, or it is unjust not to rectify).[36] Thus English law has neither deferred nor immediate indefeasibility; but there is a preference for not rectifying a title so as to deprive of his land the registered proprietor in possession.[37]

Examples

Let us unpack this by looking at a number of different cases within instances D to F above where X, Y and Z are successive registered proprietors.

D1.
The transfer is void at common law because of an innocent mistake about the extent of the land; Y is still the registered proprietor. At one extreme, the boundaries are

---

[34] See n 20 above.

[35] See above, p 104.

[36] The sub-section also says that the protection is not available when rectification is made to give effect to an order of the court; it is not clear what that wording is for, and it is not discussed here as the issue disappears in the 2002 Act where the wording is not replicated. The interpretation of it in *Kingsalton Ltd v Thames Water Developments Ltd* [2001] EWCA Civ 20 is unique and cannot be right. As to when it would be unjust not to rectify, there is very little guidance about this; monetary considerations, such as the inadequacy of indemnity in the circumstances (*Hounslow LBC v Hare* (1990) 24 HLR 9), or the fact that the proprietor has spent money on the land, will be relevant.

[37] As Pam O'Connor (see n 1 above) puts it 'There is . . . a mile-wide immunity from rectification for the proprietor in possession.'

inexact, so a small piece is included that should not have been; at the other, the whole transfer is the second in an instance of double conveyancing.[38] Under the 1925 Act, the registered disposition from X to Y vests the registered estate in Y, subject to the matters listed in section 20. But section 82(1)(a) has been read as allowing the register to be rectified in X's favour where the court has decided that he is entitled to the land; and section 82(1)(g) in any event makes that result inevitable. It was held without a great deal of discussion in *Re 139 High Street Deptford* and in *Re Sea View Gardens*—both cases of a double conveyance as to part of the land conveyed, by mistake—that if the disposition would have been void at common law, there must be a right to rectification under section 82(1)(a) or (g).[39] Accordingly the court *may* rectify the register against Y (who will in that event receive an indemnity under section 83) unless he is in possession of the land—and of course he usually will be.

In a number of cases rectification has been ordered because the registered proprietor is not in possession. The cases have concerned parts of non-residential property—an awkward boundary strip, where clear acts of possession are difficult,[40] or a piece of commercial property which might reasonably have nothing happening upon it for a while.[41] The protection of section 82(3) works excellently to protect someone's home—and of course it is precisely in such cases that monetary compensation is inadequate. Notice that commercial or agricultural property is far more likely to be the subject of a double conveyance by mistake than is a house; and there is a far greater chance that the registered proprietor of such property will not have the protection conferred by possession. But he will be compensated.[42]

D2.
As D1, but Z has purchased the land from Y, and so is once removed from the flawed transfer. The answer seems to be the same as in D1, ie rectification is available— section 82(1)(g) alone would achieve this—but subject to the protection for the proprietor in possession.[43]

---

[38] In cases where this has happened, as in *Epps* (see n 68), the first in the double conveyance sequence had not been registered when the second transaction took place, because the area had in the meantime become one of compulsory registration. It is almost impossible for double conveyancing to happen when all titles are registered, particularly if the map is computerised.

[39] The 1925 Act as drafted overdid the exceptions to the protection of the proprietor in possession. The effect of the original wording was that a proprietor lost his protection if he innocently registered a forged transfer, and therefore in fact, in *Re 139 High Street Deptford* [1951] Ch 884 and in *Re Sea View Gardens* [1967] 1 WLR 134 the register was rectified. The problem was exposed in an article by S Cretney and G Dworkin, 'Rectification and Indemnity: Illusion and Reality' (1968) 84 *Law Quarterly Review* 528 and corrected by the Administration of Justice Act 1977, s 24(b). The cases remain authority on the effect of s 82(1).

[40] *Kingsalton Ltd v Thames Water Developments Ltd* [2001] EWCA Civ 20.

[41] *Malory Enterprises v Cheshire Homes (UK) Ltd* [2002] EWCA Civ 151, [2002] Ch 216.

[42] S 83.

[43] *Epps* (see n 68) is an example of this; and the result must be the same as where the transfer X to Y was void for forgery, on which see below (example F2).

E.

There is a mistake in the transfer, but one of detail which does not render it void. This was seen in *Freer v Unwins Ltd*,[44] where the burden of a restrictive covenant affecting a freehold shop was not recorded when the title came to be registered; the covenant was of the kind designed to prevent competition between traders in a parade of shops, and forbade the owner to trade as a tobacconist.[45] The shop was let in 1969, and the lease assigned in 1974 to a lessee who set up in business as a tobacconist. The plaintiff, who had the benefit of the covenant, sought an injunction to prevent his trading. When he discovered the state of the register, from the lessee's defence, the plaintiff contacted the registrar, who amended the register of the freehold title, recording the covenant by a notice dated September 1975. The plaintiff then pursued his action for an injunction, but the court held that the lessee was not affected by the rectification. From the lessee's point all was well.[46] But note that the rectification of the freehold title was not challenged.[47] The freeholder thus suffered a rectification which contradicted the negative warranty of registration; a burden has found its way on to the title, being one which section 20 of the 1925 Act explicitly stated would not bind him.[48]

F1.

The transfer from X to Y is void because of wrongdoing, eg because of a forgery by a third party; Y is innocent. This is unusual; it is of course what happened in *Re Odell*,[49] under the rather different wording of the 1897 Act. It is more likely to happen if Y is a mortgagee; for example, Mr and Mrs X own the house, and the wife forges her husband's signature on the mortgage. The outcome follows, a fortiori, from case D1 above; again, if the transfer is void then the register may be rectified to reverse the transaction.[50] Sections 82(1)(a) and (g) would be still be seen to cover the case, and where there is forgery of the transfer itself, paragraph (d) must also be relevant.[51]

The forgery of the joint mortgage is one of the strongest cases for rectifying the register and *not* giving an indefeasible title to Y. We do not want Mr X to find himself liable to make mortgage payments to Y! That is what would happen under most Torrens systems; X would get an indemnity, of course, but he might actually

[44] [1976] 1 Ch 288.
[45] Newsagent/sweet-shop etc.
[46] Note that the lease was a short one and not registrable, but behaved as if it was; it is an example of the provision in s 29(4), mentioned in ch 5 at n 5.
[47] Although the judge, Walton J, expressed 'very great surprise' about it, no doubt because the rectification prejudiced the proprietor in possession.
[48] S 20 of the 1925 Act corresponds to s 29 of the 2002 Act. The freeholder at the time of the decision was not the first registered proprietor.
[49] (1906) 2 Ch 47.
[50] See *Ruoff and Roper* 40-13; however, a forged transfer will be effective to sever a beneficial joint tenancy and to transfer the forger's equitable interest—*Ahmed v Kendrick and Ahmed* [1988] 2 FLR 22 (where the victim of the forgery, the wife, was not living at the property and was therefore only interested financially; rectification was not claimed).
[51] *Norwich & Peterborough BS v Steed*, [1993] Ch 116, at 134.

lose his home, since he might not receive the indemnity until Y had obtained possession against him. Whatever the intellectual consistency of this, we do not want it; and in this jurisdiction such a result would probably be regarded as incompatible with protection to home and possessions given by the Human Rights Act 1998.[52] In any move to make the English system more consistent with the Torrens systems in this respect we must bear this in mind.

F2.

Taking the transaction on one stage—what of Z, the innocent purchaser following a registration based upon a void disposition? Can we find in the Act a principle of deferred indefeasibility that would safeguard Z? In *Argyle Building Society v Hammond*,[53] which was decided on the assumption that the transfer from X to Y was forged by B, the view was expressed that Z would lose his title through rectification.[54] In that case Z was Y's mortgagee, and the Court of Appeal saw no reason why subsequent purchasers should have a title any more reliable than Y's—unless, of course, they were proprietors in possession.

Ruoff and Roper quote the case of Haigh, the acid-bath murderer, who forged the signature of one of his victims on a transfer to himself, and then sold on. They explain that the purchaser was not disturbed, and the victim's estate was compensated:

The reason for this was that, despite the fact that there were valid grounds for rectification, the innocent purchaser was in possession and had not been guilty of fraud or lack of proper care.[55]

F3.

The transfer from X to Y was procured by the fraud, misrepresentation or undue influence of Y, and Z is now registered proprietor (by purchase or as a mortgagee).

The transfer from X to Y is thus voidable, not void, at common law.[56] Y was of course liable to lose the land, and that is not a problem. Z is innocent. What is his position? If he has bought the land, can he keep it? If he is a mortgagee, X can get the land back, but will he take it subject to Z's mortgage?

---

[52] In particular, Art 8, and Art 1 of the First Protocol. See Smith, *Property Law*, 16 ff.

[53] (1984) 49 P & CR 148.

[54] The case was remitted for re-hearing, and became *Norwich & Peterborough BS v Steed* (n 28 above); by then the forgery claim had been dropped, and the case was decided on the basis that fraud made the X–Y transaction voidable.

[55] *Ruoff and Roper*, 40–13. It is apparent that the registrar is able to, and frequently does, deal with cases on this basis without recourse to the courts. The wide powers vested in the registrar are at least part of the reason why indefeasibility cases are litigated far less frequently than they are in Australia.

[56] This only happens when Y is at fault; so we do not have to ask what happens if a transaction is voidable but Y is innocent. However, note that the law has developed during the last few years so as to make it much easier to find that Y has been guilty of misrepresentation or undue influence when the wrongdoing originated with another: *Barclays Bank Plc v O'Brien* [1994] 1 AC 180 and the line of cases thereafter; see *Megarry and Wade* 19–159 ff.

The answer seems to be that in this case, and in contrast to case F2, the register will not be rectified against Z.[57] This instance was considered in *Norwich & Peterborough Building Society v Steed*,[58] where Z was a mortgagee. The court's reasoning was to consider the effect in unregistered land. Where a document is voidable, the aggrieved party has an equity of rectification; an equity is the right to seek a discretionary remedy from the court.[59] In unregistered land a bona fide purchaser of a legal estate for value without notice takes free both of equitable interests and of mere equities. So Z in this case is not bound by X's equity to seek rectification of the transfer, and so takes the land free of it.

It is very unsatisfactory to have the matter determined by unregistered rules in this way.[60] Why should we not simply look at section 20 of the 1925 Act, check off the matters subject to which Z takes the land, and ascertain that X's equity is not among them? But at least the answer in *Norwich & Peterborough* is clear; it accords with the answer that would be given simply by section 20; and it accords with principle, in that Z as the purchaser of registered land takes a title that is not affected by a blemish in a prior transaction.

The other use of *Norwich & Peterborough Building Society v Steed*[61] is to confirm that section 82(1)(h) does *not* confer a general discretion to rectify the register where it is just to do so. It is not fair that X takes subject to Z's charge, but that is held to be unavoidable despite the apparently general terms of section 82(1)(h); thus dynamic security prevails over static security.

EVALUATION OF THE STATUTORY ROUTE

The position so far is reasonably clear. Unregistered rules rule. An innocent purchaser under a void disposition, or even once removed from it, has no protection under the 1925 Act unless he is in possession of the land. That proviso protects the static security of ownership (although it may not be very helpful outside domestic property). So while the stress in chapter 5, where we looked at the negative warranty of registration, was on dynamic security, we find that the English approach to the positive warranty is not so clear, tending more to static security or at least to a compromise between the two. Whether or not this is a problem is a matter of policy; it is also a matter of human rights,[62] and also of practical efficiency: the English system generates far, far less litigation about indefeasibility than do the Torrens systems. The English approach actually generates good results on a basis of rather unsatisfactory principle.

[57] *Ruoff and Roper* 40–12.
[58] [1993] Ch 116.
[59] See ch 5 above, at n 36; such an equity now has effect as an interest that may be protected by a notice on the register, under s 116 of the 2002 Act.
[60] *Norwich & Peterborough* (n 28 above, passim); and note the reference at 132H to the 'substantive law', by implication contrasting the law relating to registration as if it were merely procedural.
[61] [1993] Ch 116.
[62] The protection of possessions/property tends very much towards static security.

There is a further problem. Section 82 has been read as if it stood alongside, and supplemented, section 20 of the 1925 Act.[63] This entails that the statute states: registered dispositions give the estate to the purchaser subject only (a) to matters listed in section 20 and (b) to a liability to rectification in any of the events listed in section 82(1). It does appear that the draftsman intended that interpretation, because the Act has been read thus from the earliest cases and texts. But that is not what the statute says. Section 20 of the 1925 Act is drafted in terms of exclusivity: the land is held subject *only* to etc. The standard interpretation of section 82 thus involves a contradiction. The Torrens statutes do not generate this problem, because their negative warranty sections make an exception for fraud (which the courts interpreted as giving first deferred, and then immediate, indefeasibility). This point is going to recur when we look at the 2002 Act, where we have noted[64] that the negative warranty sections, 29/30, are again drafted in exclusive terms.

A way round this is to say: 'a void disposition is not a "registered disposition" and so section 20 does not apply'. This has been suggested by Roger Smith,[65] and adopted by the court in *Malory Enterprises Ltd v Cheshire Homes Ltd*.[66] This is an available construction of the 1925 Act; for section 18 refers to dispositions by the proprietor, so a forgery can be said not to be a registered disposition. It is not a necessary construction; for we can say that section 20 refers to the *disposition*, without reference to who made it. At any rate that construction will only justify the overriding of section 20 in our example F; in D1, there is nothing unauthorised about the disposition, it is merely mistaken, and in D2, F2 and F3 there is nothing wrong with the disposition to Z and so he should have the protection of section 20, whatever Y's position.

INDEFEASIBILITY BY THE OTHER ROUTE: THE TRUST ANALYSIS

It may be that an awareness of the contradiction between sections 20 and 82[67] lies behind the development of the alternative analysis found in a number of cases on indefeasibility. And if the statutory route generates some tension of principles, the case-law route is even worse.

Epps v Esso Petroleum Co Ltd[68] concerned a double conveyance—our type D1. Briefly, a Mr Clifford owned under one conveyance adjoining plots on which stood, respectively, No 4 Darland Avenue (a house), and Darland Garage. In 1955

---

[63] And, for that matter, s 5; but for the sake of simplicity first registration is not discussed here. This view of s 82 is implicit in the account given by JS Stewart-Wallace, see n 25 above, 44–52, and in the Law Commission's 1972 working paper (see n 23 above).

[64] Ch 5, text preceding n 5.

[65] R Smith, 'Forgeries and Land Registration'(1985) 101 *Law Quarterly Review* 79 at 93.

[66] [2002] EWCA Civ 151 *per* Arden LJ at [65] 'the transfer to [Y] could not in law be of any effect in itself, [and could not] constitute a "disposition" of the . . . land and accordingly s 20 cannot apply.'

[67] Highlighted in D Jackson, 'Registration of Land Interests—The English Version' (1972) 88 *Law Quarterly Review* 93. The title to this chapter echoes that title, as it echoes some of the disquiet expressed there.

[68] [1973] 1 WLR 1071.

he sold No 4 to X. The sale included a strip outside its garden wall, on which X wished to build an outbuilding. X never did so. In 1959 Clifford sold the garage to Y (Esso's predecessors); the conveyance included, in error, the additional strip. Title to the garage was registered. In 1964 the title to No 4 was registered following another sale, to Mr and Mrs Epps, and the double conveyance came to light. Now the strip was included in Esso's title, when it should have been part of No 4. The second of a double conveyance sequence has come first on to the register.

Now, according to the principles stated above, in line with the standard analysis of section 82 in example D1, Y (that is, Esso's predecessor) would have been liable to rectification unless he could claim the protection of section 82(3) because he was proprietor in possession. Esso (Z in our example D2) is equally vulnerable, but with the same protection. To defeat Esso, Mr and Mrs Epps must simply establish that Esso was not in possession of the strip—and as matters stood, despite the position of the wall, there was some doubt about it. The strip was not being used by the garage owners; and it was claimed that in 1955 the purchaser of No 4 had been parking a car there, which would seem to argue against Esso's being in possession. In the event, Templeman J (as he then was) held that Esso was the proprietor in possession and that, far from its being unjust not to rectify the register in their favour, justice lay on their side. The Epps' predecessors should have moved the boundary fence, as they had ample opportunity to do; whereas neither Y nor Esso could have discovered the double conveyance.[69]

So far the decision is uncontroversial. And so should have been the argument. But counsel for Mr and Mrs Epps argued not only that Esso was not the proprietor in possession, *but also* that the Eppses held the beneficial interest in the strip, which was an overriding interest by virtue of their actual occupation. Accordingly, it was argued, the register must be rectified in their favour.

But how could the Eppses have held the beneficial interest? If they did, the disputed strip was held by Y upon trust for them. To find a trust is the English lawyer's knee-jerk reaction to a situation where legal ownership and what-ought-to-have-happened are out of kilter.[70] But in fact there is no precedent for the Eppses' keeping the beneficial interest in the strip. There is no suggestion of it in the earlier cases on mistaken conveyances.[71] No possible precedent could arise from unregistered land, in the very different situation where the legal interest does not pass. And there is no justification on principle for their doing so either. Equitable interests do not detach themselves from the legal estate just because

---

[69] Originally X owned the two properties under one title. The rules of unregistered conveyancing required him in 1955 to endorse upon his own title deeds the sale of part to the new owners of No 4. And he did; but as is usual, there was no plan with the memorandum; and Y's advisers did not ask for one because the boundary of the garage was clear on the ground.

[70] Compare the drafting of s 75 of the Land Registration Act 1925; see ch 7 below, text preceding n 20.

[71] *Re 139 Deptford High Street; Re Se View Gardens;* see n 39 above. There may be a precedent in *Re Boyle's Claim* [1961] 1 WLR 339, which concerned an inaccuracy in a boundary; see *Ruoff and Roper* 40–20.

their doing so would express some kind of justice;[72] they only do so if there is a trust. How could Y possibly have taken as a trustee? He was wholly innocent; there are no grounds for imposing a constructive trust upon him.[73] Yet, astonishingly, Templeman J accepted that the transfer in 1959 had passed only a bare legal title to the strip, and that the then owners of No 4 had retained the beneficial interest in it.[74] Had they been in actual occupation of the strip, their beneficial interest would have survived section 20 and bound Esso.

The trust analysis may well stem from an awareness of the contradiction involved in reading section 82 as a supplement to section 20. And if it worked, it would eliminate the contradiction. If the Eppses had held the beneficial interest in the strip in 1959, their interest could have survived section 5 of the 1925 Act[75] as an overriding interest if they were in actual occupation. But it simply does not work in any case where Y, the first transferee, is innocent.

Where it could be made to work is where Y is himself a forger. Then, to be sure, it is appropriate to regard him as a constructive trustee for X.[76] We know that he is liable in any event, and that no special rectification provisions are needed to give effect to Y's personal liabilities. But the imposition of a trust is not the normal cause of action against a forger and seems an unnecessary importation of equitable concepts into a straight common law wrong.

Let us look at the trust analysis in our numbered cases:

D1 and F1.

Y takes innocently under a void disposition (whether void for mistake or because of forgery). If Y, despite his innocence, can be regarded as a constructive trustee (as was the innocent Y by implication in *Epps*), then X retains the beneficial interest in the land. He can call for a re-transfer under the rule in *Saunders v Vautier*[77] and

---

[72] And even if they did, the justice in this case was found to lie with the garage proprietors.

[73] The cases of *Leuty v Hillas* (1858) 2 De G & J 110, and *Craddock Brothers v Hunt* [1923] 2 Ch 136, cited in *Blacklocks v JB Developments (Godalming) Ltd* [1982] Ch 183, might possibly be used to support the imposition of the trust. They were only briefly considered in that case, and DG Barnsley, in his analysis at [1983] *Conveyancer* 361 (see n 84 below) demonstrates that they cannot properly be used in this way.

[74] Note that Templeman J did *not* hold that s 11, on first registration, in general passes only the bare legal title to the property; nor did counsel for the Eppses so argue. To that extent Simon Palk's article is tilting at a windmill ((SNL Palk, 'First Registration of Title—Just What Does It Do?' [1974] *Conveyancer* 236; and see Roger Smith's comment, in *Property Law* at 224). Counsel's point was that *in this case* and because of the particular facts, a beneficial interest was retained, which survived s 11 as an overriding interest. And if that indeed had been the case, s 11 would have conferred a bare legal title (as it might do if a registered proprietor held the property upon a common intention constructive trust for his wife).

[75] In a registered disposition case, s 20.

[76] The circumstances are far stronger than in *Lyus v Prowsa Developments Ltd* [1982] 1 WLR 1044. Compare *Breskvar v Wall* (1971) 126 CLR 376 (High Court of Australia). It was held, in circumstances similar to our forgery example, that X retained his beneficial interest, to which Y took subject, but that Z, the innocent purchaser, took the equitable interest in the property; *per* Barwick CJ at 387.

[77] (1841) Beav 115.

the protection of the proprietor in possession is by-passed.[78] The result is the same as in most cases taking the statutory route, but the different principle means that that important statutory protection is eliminated.

D2 and F2.

Z is the purchaser once removed from the void disposition. He is only bound by X's beneficial interest if X is still in actual occupation; if that is the case, then X can retrieve the land under trusts rules as above. The result is the same as that reached by the statutory route.[79] Z is in any event perfectly safe if he purchases from Y + another; if X does have a beneficial interest, it will in that event be overreached. So it is not safe to buy from one forger, but fine to buy from two. This is an absurd way of managing forgery.

D3.

Z is the purchaser once removed from a voidable disposition. The reasoning in *Epps* really cannot work here, because it is well-established that all Z has is an equity to seek rectification of the transfer itself; that would seem sufficient precedent to establish that he does not have the full-scale beneficial interest in the land.

The reasoning in *Epps* is thus very odd. It is suggested here that it does not work in any case where Y is innocent. The standard reading of section 82 makes it unnecessary in all cases: even where Y is himself the forger, Y's personal liability makes X's position secure vis-à-vis Y; and if the land has passed on to Z the result is the same as under the statutory analysis but can be destroyed by overreaching. It must also destroy much of the indemnity mechanism, since it is well-established that no indemnity is available if rectification gives effect to an overriding interest.[80]

Why go to these lengths to criticise the analysis in *Epps* when the decision on the point was *obiter*? Templeman J found that the Eppses did not have an overriding interest because they were not in actual occupation, and Esso won. A number of writers, including *Megarry and Wade*, ignore the overriding interest analysis. So do some subsequent cases: *London Borough of Hounslow v Hare*;[81] and *Kingsalton Ltd v Thames Water Developments Ltd.*[82] But unfortunately it has been followed and developed.

---

[78]   There is no need for X to be in actual occupation for Y to be liable; this is a trust imposed directly on Y, it is not one of the interests existing immediately before the transaction, to which the negative warranty (s 20 of the 1925 Act) applies.

[79]   Again, Z has no protection as proprietor in possession because the register is being rectified to give effect to an overriding interest (s 82(3)); but *ex hypothesi* Z cannot be in possession because he is only bound by X's interest if X is in actual occupation.

[80]   *Re Chowood's Registered Land* [1930] 2 Ch 156.

[81]   (1990) 24 HLR 9.

[82]   [2001] EWCA Civ 20; but only because it was not argued because the claimant was not in actual occupation: *per* Sir Christopher Slade at [51]. The point also appears in *Goodger v Willis* [1999] EGCS 32.

Malory v Cheshire Homes Ltd[83]—the Overriding Interest Idea Developed

The facts of *Malory* do not precisely match any of our examples, but they come within our type F, where there has been a forgery or other invalid transaction. M Ltd was registered proprietor of land in Manchester. M2 Ltd managed to get itself registered as proprietor instead. There was no relationship between the companies, they just had similar names. We are not told in the report how the registration was achieved, but the implication is that the manoeuvre would have had no effect at common law. Cheshire then bought the land; M Ltd now wanted it back.

M Ltd used the argument from *Epps*, that it retained the beneficial interest in the land, and that by virtue of its occupation that beneficial interest was an overriding interest in the land. The argument was successful, and the register was rectified in M Ltd's favour. However, M Ltd also argued that its right to apply to have the register rectified was also an overriding interest; and Arden LJ, *obiter*, agreed. The matter was not discussed at length in her judgment, nor in those of Clarke and Schiemann LJJ; but their lordships made it clear that they did refer to a right to seek rectification of the register, not to the right to seek rectification of a document. They also made it clear that they appreciated that an application for rectification might not always be successful (rather like an estoppel claim), but they decided that the right to seek it was proprietary nonetheless.

There may be some precedent for the argument that the right to seek rectification of the register can be an overriding interest in the very difficult decision in *Blacklocks v JB (Developments) Godalming Ltd*.[84] But it is very hard indeed to see the point of this argument in *Malory* itself. If a defrauded claimant in the position of X in our examples F1 and F2 can indeed claim a beneficial interest in the property, what ever is the need to claim that the right to seek rectification of the register is *also* an overriding interest? The two arguments were maintained together on the claimant's behalf in *Malory*, but only the one was needed (if either; section 82(1)(a) would have done the job). If the point were wholly superfluous we could ignore it, but it is not; if the right to seek rectification of the register is indeed a proprietary right which can be an overriding interest then it is available also to X in our cases D1, D2 and F3. This is because it is not the full beneficial fee simple in the property, and therefore does not require, for its existence, a finding that Y is a constructive trustee. It is simply an equitable proprietary right (like the benefit of a restrictive covenant).

---

[83] [2002] EWCA Civ 151. *Ruoff and Roper* accept the trusts analysis, derived from *Epps*, on the authority of *Malory*; 40–41.

[84] [1982] Ch 183. The case is generally regarded as an authority concerning the equity of rectification, ie the right to apply to the court to have a document rectified. But it has been argued by DG Barnsley in 'Rectification, Trusts and Overriding Interests' [1983] *Conveyancer* 361 that what was actually decided concerned an equity to seek rectification of the register; and this seems to be what counsel had argued: see [1983] *Conveyancer* 169 and 257. A reading of the judgment suggests that the judge simply failed to distinguish the two.

Can this reasoning be correct? It is certainly available. It was held in *Berkeley Leisure Group Ltd v Williamson*[85] that the benefit of a right to seek rectification of the register is transmissible; to hold that the burden may bind land is consistent with, but certainly not a necessary consequence of, that decision. Yet the reasoning is quite hard to attack. One way in is to say that the right is not sufficiently substantial to be proprietary; Arden LJ dealt with this,[86] but it is clearly a point on which opinions may differ substantially. It feels deeply wrong, because of its policy connotations. We have just found yet another means of attacking the security of the registered proprietor; the reasoning in *Malory* constitutes a further inroad into dynamic security. It begs the whole question of indefeasibility by ensuring that if a defrauded former owner is in occupation of the land he has lost—and recall how readily this may be found in commercial or agricultural property—he may recover it from a purchaser no matter how many times removed from the flawed disposition. We shall have to look again at this when we examine the provisions in the 2002 Act and consider whether or not it is desirable.

RECTIFICATION UNDER THE LAND REGISTRATION ACT 1925: SUMMARY

The position so far, then, is that under the 1925 statute anything which renders a disposition void or voidable at common law may lead, at the court's discretion, to rectification, subject to strong (but not absolute) protection for the proprietor in possession. This is how section 82 of the statute has been interpreted. It has the disadvantage of using, within registered land, reasoning appropriate to unregistered land; and of involving direct contradiction with section 20. Moreover, we have seen that the courts have also adopted an alternative line of reasoning: that where a transaction has taken place which would be void at common law, the innocent proprietor taking under the void disposition is a trustee for the former proprietor. This is contrary to principles of trust law. And it means that the former proprietor can demand the land back under the *Saunders v Vautier* principle, thus by-passing the protection of the proprietor in possession. The beneficial interest of the victim of the mistake or forgery will bind successive purchasers of the registered title provided that he remains in actual occupation of the land in question, and provided his interest is not overreached by a transfer by joint registered proprietors. And this reasoning has been extended, in *Malory*, to encompass the 'right' to seek rectification of the register, with the consequence that the victim of a voidable disposition, if he remains in occupation, can enforce his right against a subsequent purchaser, which represents a major change in the law.

[85] [1996] EGCS 18.
[86] At [67].

THE LAND REGISTRATION ACT 2002

The New Provisions

The consultation paper LC 254 that eventually gave rise to the 2002 Act focused on the fact that, as we have observed, section 82 does a great deal of work that it need not do. In particular, it was felt that there was no need for a provision about rectification to give effect to rights that have arisen after a proprietor has been registered,[87] and that the main function of special provisions for rectification was to deal with cases of mistake. 'Mistake' is not defined, but it is clearly intended to include more than merely the consequences of innocent error: paragraph 8.15 states that the registration of a forged transfer is a mistake. LC 271 develops this, explaining that a new terminology has been adopted for the 2002 Act, restricting 'rectification' to the narrow circumstances where a mistake is corrected *and* the title of the registered proprietor is prejudicially affected.

Thus there is now no counterpart to the catch-all section 82 in the 1925 Act. Instead, Schedule 4 makes provision for the register to be 'altered', and certain instances of alteration are defined as 'rectification'. Provision is made in paragraphs 2 to 4 for alteration by the court and, in paragraphs 5 to 7, by the registrar. Paragraphs 5 to 7 very nearly, but not quite, match paragraphs 2 to 4, so there is a lot of repetition, which this discussion will try to avoid.

Rectification, the sub-set of alteration, is defined in paragraph 1 of Schedule 4:

In this Schedule, references to rectification, in relation to alteration of the register, are to alteration which—
  (a) involves the correction of a mistake, and
  (b) prejudicially affects the title of a registered proprietor.

Paragraph 2 then states that the court may make an order for alteration of the register for the purpose of

(a) correcting a mistake,
(b) bringing the register up to date, or
(c) giving effect to any estate, right or interest excepted from the effect of registration.

Paragraph 3 goes on to provide that if an alteration amounts to rectification, no order for alteration is to be made without the proprietor's consent in relation to land in his possession unless

(a) he has by fraud or lack of proper care caused or substantially contributed to the mistake, or
(b) it would for any other reason be unjust for the alteration not to be made.

Paragraph 3 also provides that if the court has power to order alteration under paragraph 2, it must do so unless there are exceptional circumstances which justify its not doing so.

---

[87] LC 254, 8.12.

That, in essence, is it. The court *must* order alteration if it can, except in exceptional circumstances, and unless it amounts to rectification in which case there remains the strong protection for the proprietor in possession. The provisions for alteration by the registrar, in paragraphs 5 to 7, give him the additional power to remove superfluous entries; LC 271 explains that these will become more of a problem once the implementation of electronic conveyancing gives practitioners the power to make entries on individual registers in the course of a transaction.[88] Looking ahead to the provisions on indemnity in Schedule 8, note that alteration that is not rectification does not qualify for indemnity; so rectification and indemnity now are truly the two sides of a coin. Indemnity follows rectification and/or is available in cases where someone suffers loss because there could have been rectification, but no order was made in order to protect the proprietor in possession.

Unpacking the New Provisions

If we go back to our list of the types of amendment of the register that section 82 of the 1925 Act has been employed to cover, we may expect to find that the majority of them do not now constitute rectification. What is slightly difficult is that one has to pick up, from very brief examples in the relevant chapters of LC 271 and LC 254, just where the particular examples are now supposed to fit. In particular, there is no more than a very brief mention of forgery in LC 271, and no discussion of what is to happen to a purchaser once removed from a flawed transaction (our Z). What we can say is that the first three of our examples would appear to work like this under the new law:

A. To give effect to an overriding interest.

Such an amendment of the register, we are told, 'does no more than update the title'; it therefore falls within alteration but not rectification. The registered proprietor took the land subject to overriding interests, and so it is felt that he should not have any special protection, nor any indemnity. [89]

B. To give effect to the *in personam* exception to indefeasibility, where the registered proprietor has obtained his title by forgery or fraud.

We have to split this into two cases here.

---

[88] The drafting is very strange. The reader is referred to the full text at p 244. Why does para 3(3) not form part of para 2, where we should expect to find it, with a proviso that it takes effect subject to para 3? Why is the wording of para 3(2) very slightly mismatched with para 6(2)? Most of all, why not omit para 3(1), and commence the para with the words 'No order may be made for rectification without the proprietor's consent etc'—since 'rectification' is already defined? The opening words of para 3(1) do not even quite match the definition. The same comments arise, *mutatis mutandis,* in para 6.

[89] LC 271, 10.7 (2) at note 27; this puts into effect the point made about *Re Chowood's Registered Land* at n 33 above. It is uncontroversial that no indemnity is appropriate in such a case; but the fact that no indemnity is given makes the trust analysis of rectification, in *Epps v Esso Petroleum Ltd* (n 68 ff above) all the more objectionable.

Where the proprietor has obtained his title by fraud, ie by a valid but voidable disposition, this, we are told, is another instance that requires no special rectification provisions. Again, it is a matter of bringing the register up to date. For example, if Y was registered as proprietor, but X obtains an order setting aside the transfer to Y on the grounds that Y procured it by fraud on X; there was no mistake in the registration of Y, but the order made since requires that the register be altered. Because there is no mistake, this is not rectification.[90] There is no mention in LC 271 of the term '*in personam* exception'; it is a well-known term in writings on Torrens legislation, and the writer has borrowed it for use here. This treatment of fraud in the new law accords well with our expectations.

However, if the registered proprietor is guilty of forgery, correction of the register does involve rectification, because LC 271 regards forgery as a mistake. The transfer was void, and should not have been given effect by registration. But because the transferee is guilty of the forgery, he will have no protection as a registered proprietor in possession, and rectification will be ordered.

This, too, accords with our expectations. It is slightly odd to find alteration of the register so as to reflect the fault of the registered proprietor dealt with in two conceptually different ways, but there is no difficulty in the practical outcome.

C. To up-date the register to give effect to off-register events subsequent to registration, such as bankruptcy or forfeiture.

This, again, needs no special provision, and falls into the category of keeping the register up-to-date. The example given in LC 271 is of a decision of the court that someone has acquired an easement by prescription over the registered land.[91]

Again this accords with our expectations. This is not an issue about indefeasibility.[92]

The remaining cases were these:

D. To correct the register because a disposition was wholly or partly void because of an innocent mistake.
E. To correct the register because of an innocent mistake of detail, e.g. the omission of a restrictive covenant.
F. To correct the register following a disposition which was void or voidable because of a wrong such as forgery or fraud, where the registered proprietor was not at fault.

All three cases are regarded by LC 271 and LC 254 as cases of mistake. If they prejudicially affect the title of the proprietor in possession they are instances of rectification, and the proprietor has strong but not absolute protection. But the new provisions simply do not tell us enough to enable us to predict the detail. By them-

---

[90] LC 271, 10.7 (1), fn 23.
[91] LC 271, 10.7 (1), fn 22.
[92] See above, text at nn 27–29.

selves they are open to a number of interpretations, and even using LC 254 and LC 271 as guidance as to what is intended there is room for uncertainty.

The intention is clearly to change very little, while making the law clearer by sep-arating out cases that are not true instances of rectification (our cases A to C).[93] Turning to the remaining cases, consider case E and something like *Freer v Unwins Ltd*.[94] Simplifying the facts and looking just at the freehold title, take the registered proprietor who has bought a shop whose registered title does not record a restric-tive covenant. The facts of *Freer v Unwins Ltd* led to the discovery that there had been a mistake on first registration, one transaction removed from this propri-etor's purchase. Should the register be rectified against him? There are two pos-sible answers under the new law:

(a) Take the approach used in *Freer*: the covenant should have been recorded when the land came to be registered, and was omitted by mistake. Therefore the mistake should be corrected. But this is an instance of rectification because it prejudicially affects the title of the proprietor in possession (Schedule 4 paragraph 6(2)[95]), who is not at fault; therefore unless there are other circumstances making it unjust not to rectify, the title should be left unaltered.[96]

(b) Alternatively, look at the title of the current freeholder. He was promised, in section 29, that he would take the registered estate subject to the matters listed there. The restrictive covenant is not seen on the register and therefore he takes free of it. There is no mistake, and therefore no question of rectification.

The two routes lead to similar results, on two wholly different conceptual bases. Either is a permissible construction of the statute; but route (b) is consistent with the rest of the statute. Route (a) depends upon the use of pre-2003 precedent and involves overriding section 29. There is something of a dilemma here, and a choice between unregistered and registered thinking. And as we analyse the remaining examples drawn from our cases D and F we shall find a similar dilemma.[97]

D1. The transfer is void at common law because of an innocent mistake about the extent of the land; Y is still the registered proprietor.

Here is a nice clear mistake, and one case where there is no difficulty about apply-ing Schedule 4 very simply. A mutual mistake about boundaries, or the accidental inclusion of an extra field in a sale of part, will be corrected by alteration of the

---

[93] LC 271, 10.4: 'We considered that the main task of any new legislation should be to recast the leg-islation in a much more transparent form.'

[94] [1976] Ch 288; see above, text at n 44

[95] If this is being dealt with by the registrar; otherwise para 3(2).

[96] Recall that the judge was very surprised that the register had been rectified against the freeholder, presumably because the protection of the proprietor in possession had been ignored. It may be that the difficult situation between competing traders would be considered a reason to rectify the freehold title.

[97] Thus Roger Smith in *Property Law* at 261 refers to an analysis, corresponding to route (b) here, which 'links mistake with the outcome in registered land: there is no mistake if the register accords with registered land outcomes and priorities'.

register, but (in general) not so as to prejudice the proprietor in possession. The latter may well, of course, have contributed to the mistake, and it may be right simply to put things back where they should have been.[98] LC 271 calls this qualified indefeasibility;[99] it might be more accurate to call it qualified defeasibility.

D2. As D1, but Z has purchased the land from Y, and so is once removed from the flawed transfer.

Again, there has been a mistake. We can follow two routes here:

(a) Follow the pre-2003 precedent and correct the mistake (despite the inconsistency with section 29), subject to the protection of the proprietor in possession (which could go either way, depending whether or not the mistake has left possession out of step with ownership[100]).

(b) Look at the registered title Z has purchased. There is no mistake in *this* transaction and therefore the register should not be altered. This route gives deferred indefeasibility.

If land of X was transferred to Y and is still occupied by X, there is the third option of adopting the reasoning in *Epps* and saying that X is still beneficial owner of the land and has an overriding interest. This is unprincipled. There are no grounds for constituting Y a constructive trustee for X. And it would be wrong to deprive Y of his indemnity, when he took the land in good faith.

F1. The transfer from X to Y is void because of wrongdoing, e.g. because of a forgery by a third party; Y is innocent.

Following LC 271 and regarding forgery as a mistake then the result is the same as in D1. X regains the land and Y is compensated, unless he is the proprietor in possession. There is nothing in the statute itself to compel this construction, and 'mistake' is not the most natural way to describe a forgery; but this is clearly what is intended. And recall that this example encompasses the strongest case for altering/rectifying the register to undo the forgery—the mortgage created by forgery of one of two joint owners. There seems no doubt that the result will continue to be as it has been under the old law. English human rights thinking simply would not countenance the home-owning victim of forgery being postponed to the financial institution. The tradition of protecting the individual against moneyed might is too strong; it certainly did not retire with Lord Denning.

F2. The disposition from X to Y is void because of wrongdoing, whether Y's fault or another's. Z, an innocent purchaser, is now the registered proprietor.

---

[98] Schedule 4 paras 3(2)(a) and 6(2)(a).

[99] LC 271, 10.13 ff.

[100] Just as the result in *Epps* depended upon who was in occupation of the disputed strip; facts at n 68 above.

Again we have the dilemma:

(a) Follow what little precedent there is under the old law: principle dictates that the transaction be unscrambled, while protecting the proprietor in possession. This is the *Haigh*/acid-bath case again; Z will normally be protected unless he is not in possession.
(b) Look at section 29, and the guarantee it gave to Z. There is no mistake in *this* transaction and Z's title is secure.

Again, a third analysis is possible: if X is in occupation, he can argue that he has an overriding interest. This will only work if Y is *not* innocent and it is possible to regard him as a constructive trustee. This will be the argument most strongly urged if route (b) is argued, and it will force the Adjudicator, or the court, to confront head-on the issue of indefeasibility and the balance between dynamic and static security. The suggestion made here is that the Adjudicator's and the courts' priority must be to outlaw the trusts analysis found in *Epps*, and the treatment of the equity of rectification as an overriding interest in *Malory*.[101] Neither analysis is referred to in LC 271,[102] and clearly alteration and rectification are intended to proceed without reference to them. Both are unnecessary. The trusts analysis involves an unwelcome distortion of the protection of the proprietor in possession;[103] and the use of overriding interests against successors in title risks the unexpected intrusion of overreaching, as well as depriving of compensation innocent parties involved in the rectification process.

Voidable Transactions

We have to deal separately with voidable transactions, because they can now clearly not be the basis of rectification. Thus where the transaction from X to Y was flawed by Y's fraud or undue influence, we have seen that this does not fall within the idea of 'mistake'.[104] The transaction was valid until avoided and therefore it was properly registered. Obviously X still has his remedy against Y, and the register will be brought up to date if the transaction is rescinded.

But there is a major change in the law where Z has purchased from Y before the transaction was avoided. We saw, above,[105] in our example F3 that Z should be safe even on unregistered land principles, because the purchaser of the legal estate would not be bound by an equity. However, the equity to rectify a document is now a fully fledged proprietory right in registered land, following section 116.[106]

---

[101] Whatever the decision in *Malory*, if it goes to the House of Lords, that decision will be distinguishable as being made under the 1925 statute.

[102] Which pre-dates *Malory* but not *Blacklocks* (see n 84 above).

[103] See n 36 above.

[104] See above, n 90.

[105] Text at n 60 above.

[106] See ch 5 n 36 above. The provision embodies one interpretation of the *Blacklocks v JB Developments (Godalming) Ltd* [1982] 183.

It can therefore be an overriding interest if promoted to that status by actual occupation. The result in our instance F3 may now be different; the purchaser one disposition removed from a voidable one *is* vulnerable to alteration if the person with the equity is in actual occupation. The result in *Norwich & Peterborough BS v Steed*[107] is reversed. This does make for fairness in an instance like *Steed*, and gives greater static security than does the common law. It is perhaps a surprising little detail, and may be a change inspired by indignation about that particular case.

The change in that one instance should not muddy the clarity of our view of the analyses in *Epps* and in *Malory*; they remain unacceptable for the reasons given in this chapter.

RECTIFICATION/ALTERATION UNDER THE LAND REGISTRATION ACT 2002: SUMMARY

Schedule 4 of the 2002 Act is much simpler than section 82 of the 1925 Act, despite its wordiness and repetitions. In our cases D, E and F (the ones concerned with indefeasibility) it can do the following:

—It can provide for the register to be altered where the transfer/charge to the current registered proprietor, Y in our example, involved a mistake; but where that amounts to rectification (ie prejudices the proprietor in possession) it will not normally be done if the current proprietor is innocent.[108] This is called qualified indefeasibility, and replicates the result under the 1925 statute but without any need to rely on cases decided under that Act. The word 'mistake', if it is interpreted as the authors of LC 271 intend, tells us when amendment must take place. There is still the inconsistency with the negative warranty of sections 29/30 (and only a small drafting amendment would have been needed to put that right) but that is perhaps a quibble. The new provisions continue the virtue of the position under the 1925 Act in protecting homes.
—It can provide deferred indefeasibility for Z, by a straightforward and internally consistent reading of sections 29/30 and Schedule 4 together. The virtue of this would be to reinforce dynamic security, in line with the whole thrust of the negative warranty, and to provide an interpretation consistent with one of the most important principles of title registration, the curtain principle, which protects a purchaser from hidden defects in past transactions.

Some of the outcomes of this may feel unfamiliar. Take our case F1 where one of two joint proprietors has forged a mortgage to Y. The approach urged here involves saying that if Y sells to Z, Z should take an indefeasible title because there is no mistake in the transfer to him. But recall that Y can only transfer (exercising

---

[107] [1993] Ch 116.
[108] Where rectification does take place, Y can have an indemnity; Schedule 8 para 1(2)(a) replicates the provision composed in answer to *Re Odell*; see n 24 above.

his power of sale) if he can give vacant possession; and if the victim of the forgery, X2, is not living at the property the case for rectification is much weaker.[109]

The alternative is to analyse Z's position in accordance with unregistered land principles, using the old precedent. In the context of a new law intended to embody the idea of 'title by registration, not registration of title' it is not hard to see which route the Adjudicator and the courts should take. The use of a consistent construction of the statute, unmuddied by pre-2003 precedent and without the intrusion of superfluous reasoning based on trusts will lead to at least qualified indefeasibility, as it will yield a plain answer in cases D2 and F2.

If that does not happen there will be a strange irony. The words just quoted are from the Australian case *Breskvar v Wall*,[110] a case that affirmed the Australian principle of immediate indefeasibility within the Torrens system. It is therefore perhaps a little strange to find these words describing what was achieved by LC 271, without a discussion of their context and without any intention to replicate the decision in the case from which they derive. Now the English law cannot go as far as have the Torrens systems here; qualified indefeasibility works much better for us. But if the courts fail to interpret the plain words of the 2002 Act so as to provide even deferred indefeasibility, it is hard to see how the words from *Breskvar v Wall* could possibly have appeared in LC 254.

FURTHER PROVISIONS

This chapter focuses upon the meat of the provisions for alteration and rectification, and it is not proposed to spend a great deal of time on the other details of sections 4 and 8.

Schedule 4, Paragraph 8

This paragraph reads:

> The powers under this Schedule to alter the register, so far as relating to rectification, extend to changing for the future the priority of any interest affecting the registered estate or charge concerned.'

The explanatory notes to the Bill appended to LC 271 say that the paragraph 'makes it clear that rectification of the register can affect derivative interests but that any such changes are prospective only'. The corresponding discussion in LC

---

[109] But can X2 get an indemnity in this case, rather than having to rely upon the remedy against X1? This is not clear; Schedule 8 para 1 refers to the availability of indemnity where someone has suffered loss by reason of a mistake whose correction would involve rectification, and there was a mistake in the registration of the disposition to Y. So it is suggested that there would be an indemnity here; rectification would have been available had it not been for the transfer to Z.

[110] (1971) 126 CLR 376, quoted in LC 254, 10.43.

271[111] relies on *Freer v Unwins Ltd*[112] and affirms the principle that change must be prospective only i.e. it must not affect third parties currently interested in the land who are not involved in the rectification itself (thus in *Freer*, the tenant was not affected by the addition of the restrictive covenant to the landlord's title). This is supposed to be achieved by the wording 'for the future'; but this is very ambiguous. Staying with *Freer*, it could mean that the change will only affect future tenants; or it could mean that it will affect the current tenant in future.

Translating that to a rather more serious example: take the forged transaction from X to Y, who then makes a disposition in favour of Z. Y is the forger, and it is clear that he must be vulnerable to rectification in X's favour. It has been argued above that Z should benefit from deferred indefeasibility, on a straightforward reading of the statute. Schedule 4 paragraph 8 could in fact be read so as to contradict this, by overriding sections 29/30 (which, as has been remarked, are about priorities[113]) and changing the effect of Z's title. This would re-muddy the waters; it is to be hoped that the provision will not be interpreted in this way.

The Proprietor in Possession

Section 131 Of the 2002 Act tells us when a proprietor is in possession. He is so not only when physically in possession of the land, but also when the land is in the possession of his tenant, mortgagee, licensee or beneficiary (in the latter case, when he is a trustee). Prima facie this is simply a provision making the qualified indefeasibility provisions more generous than they otherwise would be. But note the special significance of the mortgagee; section 131 entails that he can never actually be a proprietor in possession. This reinforces the virtue of the English approach to indefeasibility, which is to protect the home rather than to recover land for one whose interest is financial.

Indemnity

This is relatively straightforward, having been reformed already by the Land Registration Act 1997; LC 271 states that there is no significant alteration of substance in the indemnity provisions of Schedule 8, even though they have had to be re-cast to reflect the changed terminology of rectification and alteration.

The most obvious point has already been made, that indemnity is payable to anyone suffering loss because of rectification, or, equally, where there would have been rectification if the mistake in question had been corrected.[114] Not quite equally; for the former provisions on different measures of indemnity have been

---

[111] LC 271, 10.8.
[112] [1976] Ch 288; see above, n 44.
[113] See ch 5, under 'Priorities of interests inter se'.
[114] Schedule 8, para 1 (1)(a) and (b).

reproduced. Where loss arises because of rectification, the claimant gets the value of the estate or interest immediately before the rectification; where there is no rectification, he gets the value at the time of the mistake.[115] This has caused some indignation, but is justified in LC 271 on the grounds that the Land Registry will pay interest from the date of the mistake, and that it would otherwise be difficult to give fair compensation because the land might have been improved since the date of the mistake. The answer to this is obvious: interest does not match rising property prices; and improvements could be discounted.[116] As we might expect, there are provisions for the payment of costs,[117] and for an indemnity to be reduced or not paid at all if the claimant was at fault.[118]

It is not expected that indemnity will be an area of great controversy under the new Act; the challenge will be for the courts to decide where, among the various competing approaches, they stand so far as indefeasibility is concerned.

---

[115] Schedule 8, para 6.
[116] Smith, *Property Law*, 271.
[117] Schedule 8, para 4.
[118] Schedule 8, para 5.

7

Adverse Possession

T HE LAW RELATING to adverse possession has been changed fundamentally by the Land Registration Act 2002, and accordingly its position in the structure of land law has shifted. Formerly it was among the fundamental principles, because possession was the basis of title. Now it is relegated to two peripheral roles, functioning both as a way of making abandoned land marketable and also as an element in procedures for resolving boundary disputes. To understand this shift in the role of adverse possession we need to look, briefly, at the law of adverse possession in unregistered land, and then to explore how that law is affected by title registration.

ADVERSE POSSESSION IN UNREGISTERED LAND

Title to land in English law is based on possession; he who can show the longest period of possession is the one with the best title to it, which we colloquially call ownership. The origins of this go back centuries and are intimately linked with the forms of action and other medieval mysteries, but the law now is summed up in two rules. First, that possession of land is itself a fee simple. Thus when I take possession of your land, I have an estate in it, readily defeasible by you but not by anyone else. 'Possession is good title against all but the true owner'.[1] Thus I can sue in trespass or nuisance;[2] and my estate is a fee simple because I can leave it by will to whomsoever I please or allow it to pass on by the rules of intestacy. My fee simple co-exists with yours (or with whatever estate you happen to have, for example a life interest or a lease) until you evict me, or until the second rule takes effect. This is the statutory rule that actions to recover possession of land are barred after 12 years and the dispossessed proprietor's title is extinguished; this is now section 15 of the Limitation Act 1980, the latest in a long series of Limitation Acts.[3]

---

[1] Mellor J in *Asher v Whitlock* (1865) 1 LR QB 1; the judge's words nicely illustrate the tension between the relativity of title and the fact that the holder of the best title must, for practical purposes, be recognised as *the owner*. See also *Leach v Jay* (1878) 9 Ch D 42, and *Perry v Clissold* [1907] AC 73.

[2] *Chambers v Donaldson* (1809) 11 East 65, *Nicholls v Ely Sugar Beet Factory* [1931] 2 Ch 84; *Foster v Warblington Urban Council* [1906] 1 KB 648.

[3] The earliest statutes of limitation prescribe a well-known date such as the death of Henry I or the last voyage of Henry II to Normandy, and state that writs may not be purchased in respect of a cause of action that arose before then. The Limitation Act 1540, 32 Hen 8 c2, introduced the modern idea of a limitation period fixed by reference to the cause of action itself.

If your estate was less than a fee simple, mine will then co-exist with any prior estates. Thus if I dispossess a lessee, my fee simple supplants the lease and the statute extinguishes it after 12 years. My fee simple co-exists with the landlord's (and it is of course possible to construct complex examples with sub-tenancies); only when the lease expires, however many years hence that might be, does the landlord's own right to possession take effect, so that he then has 12 years[4] to recover possession from the squatter before his own title is barred. It seems that, following *Fairweather v St Marylebone Property Co Ltd*[5], after the tenant's title is barred he can nevertheless surrender his lease to the landlord, so accelerating the landlord's own ability to evict the squatter.

Adverse possession thus embodies another aspect of the fragmentation of title that is so characteristic of the common law: the fact that English land law is multi-titular.[6] There may in theory be any number of concurrent fees simple in a single piece of land, none deriving title from another.

There is a huge volume of case-law detailing what amounts to adverse possession, which is not our concern here;[7] but it is worth noting two things. First, that adverse possession has two elements, the factual and the issue of intention, or, as we used to say, *factus possidendi* and *animus possidendi. Animus* is particularly complex. What does the squatter have to intend to do? It is now established that he must intend to posses, and need not intend to own.[8] He must intend to possess to the exclusion of the whole world, including the true owner so far as is practicable;[9] thus knowledge of that owner's entitlement does not prevent his being in adverse possession.[10] Second, there is a recurring theme in the decisions—that deprivation by adverse possession is not welcomed by the judges, who have at times appeared to strive to make things difficult for the squatter by setting the requirements, both for factual possession and for the squatter's intention to possess, rather higher than they need be.[11]

---

[4] See *Fairweather*, n 5 below, at 544 as to the landlord's period of 12 years to recover possession following the ending of the lease.

[5] [1963] AC 510.

[6] Tony Honoré, 'Ownership', in AG Guest, ed (Oxford, Clarendon Press, 1961), 107 at 136–141.

[7] *Megarry and Wade* 21–001 ff.

[8] *Buckinghamshire County Council v Moran* [1990] Ch 623 at 643, CA; *JA Pye (Oxford) Ltd v Graham* [2002] UKHL 30, [42].

[9] *Powell v MacFarlane* (1977) 38 P & CR 452 at 471–2, *per* Slade J, approved in *JA Pye* (above, n 8) at [43].

[10] *JA Pye* (above, n 8); even, in this case, the possessor's willingness to pay rent if demanded did not prevent his being in adverse possession while no demand was made: [46] ff.

[11] Among the notorious cases have been *Littledale v Liverpool College* [1900] 1 ChD 268, *Leigh v Jack* (1879) 5 Ex D 264 and *Wallis' Cayton Bay Holiday Camp Ltd v Shell-Mex and BP Ltd* [1975] QB 94. Martin Dockray notes this trend and its dangers in 'Adverse Possession and Intention—I' [1982] *Conveyancer* 256. The judgments given in the House of Lords in *JA Pye* (above, n 8) show how the worst results of this judicial disapproval of the squatter have been corrected by subsequent cases and by statute (in particular, *Powell v McFarlane* (above, n 9) and *Buckinghamshire County Council v Moran* (above, n 8); and Schedule 1, para 8(4) of the Limitation Act 1980) while nevertheless making that disapproval very evident ([2002] UKHL 30 at [2]).

ADVERSE POSSESSION IN REGISTERED LAND

Two things make it difficult to absorb the law of adverse possession into title reg-istration. One is the basic principle that there is a state guarantee of title,[12] which sits ill with the idea that your registered title can be lost because someone else has taken possession of the land. The other is a practical problem of documentation; if title to registered land can be acquired by adverse possession, what happens to the registered title of the dispossessed owner, recorded fair and square on the register? The combination of these factors means that, while there is no logical difficulty in accommodating adverse possession within a system of registration of title,[13] there is a certain discomfort about it as well as some practical hurdles to be overcome.

The 1862 and 1875 title registration statutes answered these difficulties by mak-ing it impossible to challenge an absolute title by adverse possession. The difficulty with this simple solution is that it removes a convenient way of dealing with boundary disputes[14] and of getting abandoned land into marketable use. The Land Transfer Act 1897 allowed the squatter to apply for rectification of the register, but at the court's discretion.[15]

Solutions to the problem in other jurisdictions have been various. Most of the Australian Torrens statutes,[16] and the New Zealand statute,[17] allow title to be lost by adverse possession, regarding it as an exception to the principle of indefeasibil-ity which is so essential to those systems. Martin Dixon has argued persuasively that it is not a *necessary* feature of registered title;[18] Bruce Ziff comments: 'Adverse possession can put to rest other claims that Torrens will not'.[19]

---

[12] Whether expressed in English- or Torrens-style indefeasibility; see ch 6, above.

[13] In his first instance decision in *JA Pye (Oxford) Ltd v Graham* [2000] Ch 676, Neuberger J claimed, at 710, that it was illogical to say that an owner who has 'sat on his rights' should lose his land: 'Illogical because the only reason that the owner can be said to have sat on his rights is because of the existence of the 12-year limitation period in the first place'. The circularity is imagined: the feeling that one should not wait too long before enforcing rights was the cause, not the effect, of the Limitation Acts. Even the revised system under the Land Registration Act 2002 recognises a point when an owner must take action: see below.

[14] As important in registered as in unregistered land since registration does not guarantee bound-aries: s 60, Land Registration Act 2002, and all its predecessors.

[15] Land Transfer Act 1897, s 12.

[16] In Victoria, Western Australia and Tasmania the concept of adverse possession applies fully to reg-istered land; it applies in modified form in Queensland, South Australia and New South Wales, but not in the Northern Territory nor the Australian Capital territory; see *Bradbrook, MacCallum and Moore* [16.83] ff and LA McCrimmon, 'Whose Land is it Anyway? Adverse Possession and Torrens Title' in Grinlinton, *Torrens Conference Papers*. The Torrens systems in Canada similarly vary; Ziff, *Property Law*, 125.The authors of LC 271 say, of the new adverse possession provisions, 'Our starting point was the law applicable in Queensland, but our eventual model is very different.' (LC 271, 2.74, fn 146).

[17] Land Transfer Act 1952, amended to make this provision by the Land Transfer Amendment Act 1963.

[18] M Dixon, 'Substantive changes to property law under the Land Registration Act 2002: some prob-lems and some answers', in A Hudson, *New Perspectives on Property Law: Obligations and Restitution* (London, Cavendish, 2003).

[19] Ziff, *Property Law*, 125, fn 32.

THE 1925 SOLUTION

The Land Registration Act 1925 concentrated its efforts upon the production of a scheme that would overcome the practical difficulties caused by the ousting of a publicly documented title by an unrecorded one. Section 75 is worth quoting in full:

(1) The Limitation Acts shall apply to registered land in the same manner and to the same extent as those Acts apply to land not registered except that where, if the land were not registered, the estate of the person registered would be extinguished, such estate shall not be extinguished but shall be deemed to be held by the proprietor for the time being in trust for the person who, by virtue of the said Acts, has acquired title against any proprietor, but without prejudice to the estates and interests of any other person interested in the land whose estate or interest has not been extinguished by those Acts.

(2) Any person claiming to have acquired a title under the Limitation Acts to a registered estate in the land may apply to be registered as proprietor thereof.

(3) The registrar shall, on being satisfied as to the applicant's title, enter the applicant as proprietor either with absolute, good leasehold, qualified or possessory title, as the case may require, but without prejudice to any estate or interest protected by any entry on the register which may not have been extinguished under the Limitation Acts, and such registration shall, subject as aforesaid, have the same effect as the registration of a first proprietor . . .

The effect of this is that once the limitation period has passed, the registered proprietor's title is not extinguished (because it remains on the register) but is now 'deemed to be held on trust' for the squatter.

A trust is the English lawyer's natural response to a situation where true ownership and paper title diverge. As the Law Commission observed,[20] it was wholly unnecessary, given the provision in section 70(1)(f) that 'rights acquired or in the course of acquisition under the Limitation Acts'[21] are overriding interests. On expiry of the limitation period, the registered proprietor's title is held subject to the right of the squatter either to be registered as proprietor under section 75(2) or to demand a transfer following *Saunders v Vautier*,[22] and the status of the squatter's title as an overriding interest means that it binds purchasers too. The imposition of the trust raises more questions than it answers: what is the difference between being held on trust and being deemed to be held on trust? How far does the dispossessed owner, as trustee, have fiduciary duties?[23] If he sells the land, and

---

[20]   LC 254, 10.40.

[21]   The phrasing here betrays, perhaps, a misunderstanding. The fee simple arising from adverse possession is acquired at once, and cannot be said to be in the course of acquisition; it may or may not be strong enough to displace the dispossessed proprietor, depending upon its age. The wording of s 70(1)(f) seems to imply something more like prescription, where until the relevant period is completed the user of another's land can only be said to be in the course of acquiring an easement or profit (see *Megarry and Wade* 18–121 ff).

[22]   (1841) 10 LJ Ch 354. Cf *Bridges v Mees* [1957] 2 All ER 577.

[23]   It was held in *Central London Commercial Estates Ltd v Kato Kagaku Ltd (Axa Equity and Law Life Assurance Society plc, Third Party)* [1998] 4 All ER 948 that where the squatter has dispossessed a tenant, the limitation has expired but the squatter has not sought to register his title, the tenant cannot

reinvests the proceeds, might he have to account to the squatter for his profits? If the legal title is held jointly, can the squatter's estate be overreached?[24] And is it acceptable for the squatter to acquire, on expiration of the limitation period, the beneficial interest in the dispossessed proprietor's estate, in addition to the legal fee simple he already holds by virtue of his adverse possession? [25]

Once the limitation period has expired, a squatter can safely apply for registration.[26] The other notorious problem in this area is the consequence in registered land of dispossession of a lessee. In section 75(2) (above), does 'thereof' mean of the land or of the registered estate? Given the reference to acquisition of title *to a registered estate*—contrast unregistered land where one acquires title to land—we might suspect that registration is to be with title to *that estate*. If that is so, the position is very different from that in unregistered land where it is clear that the squatter keeps his own estate by adverse possession and that to speak of a 'Parliamentary conveyance' of the other party's title is incorrect.[27] On the other hand, the section goes on to speak of registration having the effect of a first registration, and the Land Registry gives the successful squatter a new title number; both these factors tend to the opposite conclusion, ie that the squatter takes a new estate.

Where the squatter dispossesses a freeholder the point does not really matter; where he has ousted a lessee it is crucial—is the newly registered squatter a freeholder or a leaseholder? We still do not quite know. It seems that practice has varied between District Land Registries, and that while in some areas the squatter takes a leasehold title and effectively becomes an assignee of the lease,[28] in others he is given a qualified freehold title, qualified by the landlord's right to recover possession which will accrue at some point in the future.[29] The latter policy is far

jeopardise the squatter's position by surrendering his lease (the *St Marylebone* manoeuvre, see n 5 above), since that would be a breach of trust. See the note by E Cooke at [1999] *Conveyancer* 136.

[24] This has never been litigated; it is hard to see how overreaching would not happen in such circumstances, bizarre as it is.

[25] These points are discussed by E Cooke in 'Adverse possession—problems of title in registered land' (1994) 14 *Legal Studies* 1. Whether or not the squatter's estate by adverse possession is legal rather than equitable after 1925 is a matter for discussion (*ibid*, 4–5), but it seems reasonably clear that it is legal. It is possible that the trust idea in s 75 sprang from an assumption that it was equitable; *Ruoff and Roper* still says this (29–02).

[26] He can do so beforehand, of course, when he holds a fee simple, albeit a very defeasible one; but he would not normally do so since the registrar would send notice of the application to the dispossessed proprietor, thus alerting him to the squatter's presence. See AJ Pain, *Adverse Possession—a Conveyancer's Guide* (London, Fourmat Publishing, 1992).

[27] *Doe d Jukes v Sumner* (1845) 14 M&W 39; *Tichbourne v Weir* (1892) 67 LT 735.

[28] As happened in *Spectrum Investment Co v Holmes* [1981] 1 WLR 221; note that the court was not called upon to decide whether or not the registration was correct. The decision does make it clear that in these circumstances the lease is transferred from the registered proprietor and vested in the squatter (Browne-Wilkinson J, as he then was, [1981] 1 WLR 221 at 228). This meant that the *St Marylebone* manoeuvre (n 5 above) was not available to the dispossessed lessee.

[29] See AJ Pain, n 26 above, at p 85. Whether or not this policy can stand after *Kato Kagaku* (see n 23 above) is unclear; Sedley J stated, at p 954, that the squatter 'is furnished . . . with the right to acquire and register as his own the usurped leasehold title'. As is noted at LC 271, 14.67, n 229, this is only an inference from s 75 of the 1925 Act; it is in any event obiter.

more consistent with unregistered land and with principle;[30] it is disliked by some because it means that the squatter is in a strange position, liable on the restrictive covenants in the lease but not otherwise subject to the tenant's covenants, and liable to forfeiture for non-payment of rent but not actually benefiting from the lease.[31] Giving the squatter the leasehold title is a pragmatic solution but inconsistent with principle. Moreover, where the squatter is given a fee simple, it is Land Registry practice to close the landlord's title;[32] this is completely anathematic to principle, but stems from a different anathema—that of fragmentation of title to land registration.

The weakness of section 75 is thus exposed in the awkward case, where a lessee is dispossessed; solutions might be various, but it was clear, after *Spectrum*,[33] that any reform of land registration must choose one.

THE LAND REGISTRATION ACT 2002

Since 1925 considerable thought has been given to the purpose of the law of limitation of actions to recover land. In a very general way it is summarised in the twenty-first report of the Law Reform Committee[34] as follows:

(a) to protect defendants from stale claims;
(b) to encourage plaintiffs to institute proceedings without unreasonable delay and thus enable actions to be tried when the recollection of witnesses is still clear;
(c) to enable a person to feel more confident, after the lapse of a given period of time, that an incident which might have given rise to a claim against him is finally closed.

The Limitation Acts, and the purposes behind them, apply as much to claims in tort and contract as to actions to recover land; unique to the latter, however, is the additional motivation: the facilitation of the conveyancing process.[35] Obviously, the shorter the limitation period, the shorter abstracts of title need to be. Thus today's requirement of a good root of title 15 years old[36] makes the title just a little longer than the limitation period of 12 years. In LC 254, the Law Commission and the Land Registry looked again at the function of the law of adverse possession, and concluded that the law of limitation of actions was almost irrelevant in

---

[30] Note that if even if this were adopted as universal practice, s 75 would still have to refer to the possibility of the squatter receiving a good or absolute leasehold title, to meet the unusual case where a squatter who is himself a tenant encroaches on to neighbouring land; he does so for the benefit of his landlord and accordingly takes his new land as an accretion to his own lease: *King v Smith* [1950] 1 All ER 553; *Perrot v Cohen* [1951] 1 KB 705; *Jarman v Hale* [1898] 1 QB 994.
[31] LC 271, 14.69.
[32] This is described in LC 254, at 10.38, as the 'necessary correlative' of this. It is not necessary at all; but the fact that it is supposed to be so reinforces the fact that a title registration system does not sit happily with fragmentation of ownership (see ch 1 at n 6).
[33] N 28 above.
[34] Law Reform Committee, *Twenty-first report: Final report on limitation of actions* (London, HMSO, 1977), 1.7.
[35] M Dockray, 'Why do we need adverse possession?' [1985] *Conveyancer* 272.
[36] Law of Property Act 1969, s 23.

registered land, where title must depend upon registration not on possession.[37] The facilitation of conveyancing by the linkage of the length of title to the limitation period is of course needed only for unregistered titles; and where title is registered, it was argued, it is unnecessary to encourage an owner not to sleep on his rights, because the security of his title through registration should entitle him to do just that.

The writers of LC 254 go on to say that the law of adverse possession in registered land remains useful where 'land ownership and possession are completely out of kilter' because a registered proprietor has abandoned his land[38] or where there have been 'dealings with registered land "off the register", so that the register no longer reflects the 'true' ownership of the land'.[39] It is also needed in respect of matters as to which the register is not conclusive, in particular boundaries,[40] and to prevent hardship, where the squatter has in his favour an equity by estoppel or an innocent mistake.[41]

The writers of LC 254 made it clear that reform of the law of adverse possession in registered land would take place, and that it would be a thorough one. The recommendations were twofold; first, some procedural reforms which would by themselves have made the law much more satisfactory, and second some thoroughly practical substantive changes on the basis of the points made about the purpose of the law of adverse possession. Respondents were asked to consider both aspects, on the understanding that they were not co-requisite; procedural reform without substantive change could take place. In the event, both were to go ahead, although the procedural reforms took quite a different form in LC 271 and the 2002 Act from that proposed in LC 254.

The approach to adverse possession seen in the Land Registration Act 2002 works very much in favour of the registered proprietor and of the integrity of the register. On the one hand, it represents an about-turn; the principle that possession is the basis of title has simply gone. Adverse possession *by itself* can never deprive a registered proprietor of his land. On the other hand, adverse possession still has limited effect in combination with other factors. It can be used to enable a squatter to acquire title to land that the registered proprietor has abandoned or shown no interest in; and it remains a tool in the resolution of boundary disputes. Registered title has therefore been rendered virtually squatter-proof.

Why? As we have seen, squatter-proofing is by no means always a feature of successful systems of registered title,[42] and the concerns about protecting defendants

[37] That of course is a very modern perspective on title registration and would not have been accepted in 1925, as the existence of s 75 of the Land Registration Act 1925 shows. LC 254, 10.5 ff.

[38] LC 254, 10.7.

[39] *Ibid.* The statement is an admission that title cannot depend solely upon registration; the inverted commas around the word 'true' perhaps indicate the difficulty of reconciling this with a commitment to registration as the basis of title.

[40] LC 254, 10.15.

[41] LC 254, 10.8, 10.16. In neither of the latter two cases is adverse possession actually necessary to prevent hardship.

[42] Above, n 16.

from stale claims (whatever 'stale' means) and taking action while evidence is still fresh are relevant in any context.[43] Yet there is a certain intellectual satisfaction in reducing the range of off-register events that can affect the registered title, so taking the register closer to the myth of perfection. And it is in this aspect of the 2002 Act that the authors of LC 254 have most clearly expressed their commitment to a system which is 'not a system of registration of title, but of title by registration.'[44] The practical purpose, of course, is to encourage voluntary registration. Large estates—family properties and local authority portfolios will account for most of them—will be the least likely to be registered pursuant to one of the statutory triggers; but equally they are the most vulnerable to adverse possession, and it would be in their interests to register voluntarily in order to pick up this advantage.[45]

Now to the detail.

SUBSTANTIVE CHANGES IN THE 2002 ACT

Section 96 provides that there is no longer a limitation period in respect of actions to recover possession of land.

Schedule 6 nevertheless provides that where someone has been in adverse possession for 10 years, and is still in possession,[46] he may apply to be registered as proprietor of the dispossessed proprietor's estate. Note the terminology here; the Land Registration Act 2002 insists that adverse possession is *of a registered estate*,[47] and title may be acquired to that registered estate; contrast the law of unregistered title where one is in adverse possession of land (whether one has dispossessed a freeholder or a leaseholder). The immediate consequence of the squatter's application is that notice is sent to the registered proprietor,[48] and to other interested parties such as mortgagees and landlords, enabling them to object to it. And in all but three excepted cases, where objection is made the squatter's application cannot proceed. All that the adverse possession gave the squatter was the right to make an application. From the proprietor's point of view, that gets rid of the application but not of the squatter, who still has a fee simple at common law; but it remains

---

[43]   As is acknowledged at LC 271, 14.54.

[44]   *Breskvar v Wall* (1971) 126 CLR 376, 385. Ironically, therefore, this principle is expressed in the 2002 Act through a change in the law relating to adverse possession of registered land, which is not essential to a title registration system; the subject matter of *Breskvar v Wall*, the issue of indefeasibility, is not addressed in a manner consistent with the decision in that case. See ch 6, n 110 and passim.

[45]   LC 254 at 10.19 expresses the hope that squatter-proofing will be an inducement to local authorities to register. See ch 8, below.

[46]   He must be still in possession, or have been in possession for the requisite 10 years and subsequently evicted by the registered proprietor, not pursuant to a judgment for possession and no more than six months before the date of his application: Sch 6 para 1(2). Note that the learning of centuries concerning the meaning of adverse possession remains relevant.

[47]   As did s 75 of the 1925 Act; it is not clear how far the 1925 draftsman thought through the implications of the wording.

[48]   Sch 6 para 2. There appears to be no provision in the Land Registration Rules 2003 as to the time within which the registrar must give such notice.

defeasible provided the proprietor acts promptly. If the squatter is still on the land two years later he may apply again and this time will succeed;[49] the registered proprietor therefore has two years to take steps to recover possession from the squatter,[50] or negotiate a sale to him if that suits them both.[51]

However, the squatter's application will succeed despite objection if:

—it would be unconscionable because of an equity by estoppel for the registered proprietor to seek to dispossess the squatter, and the circumstances are such that he ought to be registered as proprietor; or

—he has some other entitlement eg he is an unpaid vendor; or is entitled to the land under a will;

—he occupied the land under a reasonable mistake about a boundary.

The result of these provisions, taken together, is to allow adverse possession to transfer title to the squatter where land has been abandoned, and also to do so for a limited range of what we might call deserving squatters. The deliberate 'land thief' now has no opportunity to acquire title.

Of the three exceptions, two are cases where the squatter has a right to be registered anyway. Adverse possession is irrelevant to him because he has an *entitlement;*[52] but the provision enables the squatter to make use of the adverse possession procedure and, in particular, be heard by the Adjudicator rather than going to court.[53] Taking in order the three exceptions:

The First Exception: Estoppel

First, estoppel. Schedule 6, paragraph 5(2) reads:

(a) it would be unconscionable because of an equity by estoppel for the registered proprietor to seek to dispossess the applicant, and

(b) the circumstances are such that the applicant ought to be registered as proprietor.

The wording of the Bill had to be amended here—the words 'because of an equity by estoppel' were not originally there, and were added in the House of Lords in

---

[49] Sch 6 para 6(1).

[50] Sch 6 para 6(2) adds that the squatter may not make a further application if judgment for possession has been given against him in the last two years, or indeed if he is a defendant in possession proceedings; so the registered proprietor must commence proceedings in time and enforce judgment within two years of obtaining it. Obviously if the action is withdrawn, struck out, or compromised leaving the squatter still in possession, he may make his application under para 6(1). The aim of the provisions is to provide a swift resolution to the situation: LC 271, 14.55. Having been warned of the squatter's presence and intentions, the landowner must not sleep on his rights.

[51] Or to grant him a licence to use the land, if we are to believe *BP Properties Ltd v Buckler* (1987) 55 P & CR 337. This decision may have been overruled by *JA Pye (Oxford) Ltd v Graham* [2002] UKHL 30, [2002] 3 WLR 221 which stressed (at [32]) that it is the intention of the squatter, not of the proprietor, that is decisive.

[52] With the necessary qualifications in respect of estoppel: see below.

[53] See n 60 below.

order to prevent the sub-paragraph operating in favour of a squatter with a different equitable factor in his favour, such as laches.

Estoppel arises in favour of someone who was given some assurance about his entitlement, by words or silence, and has acted to his detriment on that basis so that it would be unconscionable for the proprietor not to act on his assurance by granting him an appropriate interest in the land.[54] This may or may not, according to estoppel principles, result in his taking on the registered estate of the person who made the assurance. Ownership of land may not have been promised; even if it was, there is no automatic entitlement. The courts do exercise their discretion with the aim of fulfilling the claimant's expectation in the absence of countervailing factors;[55] but they may choose to do so by giving a monetary equivalent rather than granting a property right.[56] Accordingly, the two separate sub-paragraphs mean that the squatter must show both unconscionability[57] and that he ought to be registered as proprietor; thus he must show that he has an equity by estoppel and that registration would be the appropriate response.[58] In relation to land, of course, estoppel is a cause of action in itself; whether or not combining it with adverse possession is useful is not clear. Take a case where neighbours Ed and Ted have discussed the siting of Ted's new garage, and Ed has agreed that Ted may encroach over his, Ed's, land by a few square feet in order to place the garage safely and conveniently. Thirteen years later Ed and Ted have a massive row about a football and a cucumber frame; Ed's parting shot is 'and you can take your garage off my land or you'll hear from my solicitor'. Ted's defence to a possession action is the estoppel; and he will counterclaim for the fee simple in the disputed land to

---

[54] *Megarry and Wade* 13–007 to 13–018.

[55] See S Gardner, 'The Remedial Discretion in Proprietary Estoppel' (1999) 115 *Law Quarterly Review* 438; R Smith, 'How Proprietary is Proprietary Estoppel' in F Rose (ed), *Consensus Ad Idem* (London, Sweet & Maxwell, 1996); E Cooke, 'Estoppel and the Protection of Expectations' (1997) 17 *Legal Studies* 258 and *The Modern Law of Estoppel* (Oxford, OUP, 2000) p 150 ff. Much is often made of the dictum of Scarman LJ in *Crabb v Arun DC* [1976] Ch 179 that the court must award the 'minimum equity to do justice'; but note that in *Crabb* the whole of the expectation aroused by the estoppel was met, and it does not appear to have been said with the intention of being restrictive.

[56] *Baker v Baker* [1993] 2 FLR 247. LC 271 lists this, at 14.40, among a range of cases where a transfer of land was not ordered; the important point is that, in this case, it was not promised. It is misleading to list the range of responses to estoppel without specifying in each case whether or not the response matched the claimant's expectation; in very nearly all cases it does.

[57] Any inquiry as to the meaning of unconscionability opens a can of worms. It is not clear whether unconscionability simply sums up the requirements of assurance and detrimental reliance (as in *Jon Richardson Computers Ltd v Flanders* [1993] FSR 497), or is an additional (undefined and variable) ingredient (*Elitestone v Morris* (1995) 73 P & CR 259 at 278); at times it even seems to be presented as an alternative to assurance and detrimental reliance, although this may be simply a matter of economy of expression (*Taylor Fashions Ltd v Liverpool Victoria Trustee Co Ltd* [1982] 2 QB 133 at 151). If, in an estoppel claim, the assurance and detrimental reliance are made out, but the circumstances are such that the claimant ought not to take the land, then the claim fails on unconscionability: *Sledmore v Dalby* (1996) 72 P & CR 196.

[58] The Adjudicator has an express power, under s 110(4), to make an order other than the registration of the applicant as proprietor; so has the court, on an appeal from the Adjudicator, under s 111(3). If the application were simply a claim for registration on the basis of an equity by estoppel, these provisions would be unnecessary; only the cloaking of the estoppel claim in an adverse possession claim makes them desirable for the avoidance of doubt.

be transferred to him. If he succeeds, the court will make an order for alteration of the register accordingly.[59] The Land Registration Act 2002 envisages that Ted might, instead, apply direct to the registrar for registration.

Whether or not this would save litigation is not at all clear. Where there is an objection to an application, such as Ted's, it must be referred to the Adjudicator, so the claim must be tried as it would be in court.[60] Ted could be given the right to have his estoppel claim heard by the Adjudicator without having to couch it in terms of adverse possession. More fundamentally, it is not at all clear that the squatter's possession has at any stage been adverse until the withdrawal of the assurance—he has been there by permission;[61] and estoppel claims come to a head precisely when the assurance is withdrawn, not 10 years later.

Thus the use of adverse possession to give an extra string to the bow of someone who has an equity by estoppel is odd, to say the least, and cases arising under this head will be read with great interest.

The Second Exception: Some Other Entitlement

Paragraph 5(3) of Schedule 6 reads:

The second exception [to the principle that the squatter's application will be dismissed if the registered proprietor objects to it] is that the applicant is for some other reason entitled to be registered as the proprietor of the estate.

This provision is intended, we are told,[62] to cover cases where the squatter has an independent entitlement to the land, for example under the will or intestacy of a deceased proprietor or pursuant to a vendor's lien. Again these are independent entitlements that would in themselves support an application for rectification; they may or may not coincide with adverse possession.[63] Whether or not the sublimely vague 'some other reason' will produce colourful litigation remains to be seen; it probably will not do so, since the word 'entitled' means that there will always be a free-standing cause of action. The intention is that this, and subparagraph (a), will be used for procedural reasons (it may prove quicker and cheaper to apply to the Adjudicator than to the court); the danger is that the

---

[59] S 65 and Sch 4, para 2. See ch 6; this is an example of bringing the register up to date, and so does not constitute rectification.

[60] S 73; the Adjudicator's office and jurisdiction are set out in ss 107 to 111. There is a right of appeal to the High Court.

[61] That is certainly the case in the examples given in LC 27 14.42. The idea that an estoppel claimant might use adverse possession may stem from remarks by Kenny J in *Cullen v Cullen* [1962] IR 268 at 292 and of RH Maudsley in a note at (1965) 81 LQR 183 at 184; see M Welstead, 'Proprietary Estoppel and the Acquisition of Possessory Title', [1991] *Conveyancer* 280. The only realistic possibility of an estoppel claimant being in adverse possession is the case where the assurance is withdrawn and then nothing happens for (now) 10 years.

[62] LC 271, 14.43.

[63] It is not clear that the possession either of an unpaid vendor or of a beneficiary under a will is adverse. Cf *Bridges v Mees* [1957] 2 All ER 577, but in that case the unpaid vendor still had the legal title and it was the purchaser who was in possession.

unnecessary addition of adverse possession to otherwise perfectly good claims will prove to be their downfall if adverse possession in fact does not exist.

The Third Exception: The Reasonable Mistake About a Boundary

Finally, paragraph 5(4) of Schedule 5 states:

The third condition is that—
(a) the land to which the application relates is adjacent to land belonging to the applicant,
(b) the exact line of the boundary between the two has not been determined under rules under section 60,[64]
(c) for at least ten years of the period of adverse possession ending on the date of the application, the applicant (or any predecessor in title) reasonably believed that the land to which the application relates belonged to him, and
(d) the estate to which the application relates was registered more than one year prior to the date of the application.

This is quite different from the preceding two sub-paragraphs, and rather more interesting. Boundary issues are productive of litigation; in a system such as the English one with general boundaries, adverse possession is an excellent way of sorting out disputes. If my fence has run along a particular line for (now) 10 years, there is obvious wisdom in a provision that it can stay in place on the basis that there is no need to determine where the boundary actually lay because if it was in fact on your land I have in any event now acquired title to it by adverse possession. What the provision here does is to salvage the pre-2002 law in this sort of case, albeit with a changed period and procedure—and *only* where there was reasonable mistake about the boundary.[65] Thus the squatter will be successful only if he has one particular form of the current spectrum of permissible intentions;[66] the intention found, for example, in *JA Pye (Oxford) Ltd v Graham*[67] will not work. Thus mingled with the practical issue of the need in some cases for adverse possession to sort out boundaries is a moral judgement; only honest, deserving, mistaken squatters need apply. The neighbour who moves his fence on purpose will have to put it back again if the registered proprietor objects. There is an assumption that we do not need adverse possession to resolve boundary problems where the applicant for registration was not under a reasonable mistake ie that in such cases the boundary is clear and can be resumed.[68] There may be some unfortunate results here, as a result of this overt mixing of practical and moral considerations. [69]

---

[64] S 60 and the rules thereunder make provision for the fixing of boundaries.

[65] An attempt was made to eliminate this item in the House of Lords at Committee stage, on the basis that it detracts from the authority of the register—presumably because the necessity for some such procedure in the absence of fixed boundaries was not understood. HL Deb 19/7/01 cols 1621 ff.

[66] LC 271, 14.51; and see nn 8–10 above.

[67] [2002] UKHL 30, [2002] 3 WLR 221.

[68] Suppose, for example, the applicant for registration knew that the boundary was unknown, and moved his fence in the belief that it did not matter, and/or that he would get title by adverse possession anyway. 'Mistake' implies a belief as to facts, which would be absent here.

[69] The idea of reasonable mistake leaves available the use of adverse possession to put into effect

Paragraph 5(4)(d) above ensures that a landowner is not caught out by a squatter's becoming entitled to make an application immediately on first registration of the title. The 10 year period in the Act is of course, shorter than the limitation period outside the Act, and so there would otherwise be a risk that the registered proprietor (whether a purchaser, or following voluntary registration) would lose his land the moment it is registered.[70] Moreover, we are told that it is intended to bring paragraph 5(4) of Schedule 6 into force one year after the rest of the Schedule, so that proprietors whose title is already registered will not be caught out by the sudden elevation of the squatter's title; before the Act he needed 12 years, now he needs ten, and so could become entitled immediately upon the Schedule's coming into force.[71]

Adverse possession in respect of registered title functions as a defence to an action for possession no less, and no more, than it gives an entitlement; thus section 98 preserves defences that correspond with entitlements in Schedule 6. It also provides that where a limitation defence has been successful, the court must order the registrar to register the squatter as proprietor of the relevant estate.

FORMAL CHANGES IN THE 2002 ACT

Just as interesting as the substantive changes are the formal changes made to the squatter's title. These are born from the dissatisfaction, noted above,[72] with the effects of the trust in section 75 of the Land Registration Act 1925, and with the uncertainty and confusion obtaining when there is adverse possession of registered leasehold land.[73] The formal changes are not the same as those envisaged in LC 254.

The Section 75 Trust Abolished

First, the trust in section 75 is gone; the squatter is protected in the event of sale by his overriding interest.

---

boundary agreements which have been in operation for many years and subsequently break down, because the parties usually believe that their agreement did effect a change in the boundaries. But there is doubt as to whether or not possession can be adverse, since *ex hypothesi* it is by agreement. See the note by E Cooke on *Burns v Morton* [2000] 1 WLR 347, at [2001] *Conveyancer* 191. However, such an agreement would certainly give rise to an estoppel, so that Sch 6 para 5(2) could be used.

[70] LC 271, 14.45. There is no need for such a provision for the other two exceptions, because they represent independent entitlements. For further comment on issues arising from the interface between registered and unregistered land, see below.

[71] LC 271, 12.103. Note that in this one respect, in cases falling under Sch 6 para 5(4), the position of squatters is improved by the Act, because the limitation period is effectively made shorter (but the improvement is worthless because extinction of the prior title is not automatic).

[72] Above, n 20.

[73] Above, n 28 ff.

The Parliamentary Conveyance Legitimised

Second, on registration the squatter takes the title of the dispossessed proprietor, not a new freehold title. This is a change from the proposals in LC 254, which accepted the technical position that a squatter takes an independent freehold title which may exist concurrently with, and be qualified by, any unbarred title such as that of a landlord.[74] The reason for the change of heart was the difficulty faced by squatters who had dispossessed lessees, and found that although they had a freehold title they were partially liable on the lease,[75] and of course that their freehold title was going to be terminable at some future date.

Thus when the squatter is registered as proprietor of the land he has taken—whether because no objection was made to his application, or because of a factor in paragraph 5 of Schedule 6, or after court proceedings—he steps into the shoes of the previous registered proprietor.[76] His fee simple by adverse possession is extinguished, and he takes the land as he finds it, subject to all estates and rights that bound the previous proprietor.[77] He takes it free of any registered charge, because the chargee had his own opportunity to object to the squatter's registration,[78] *unless* he succeeded because of a paragraph 5 factor.[79] Where the squatter is subject to a registered charge, or to a charge that is not a registered charge such as a charging order, there are provisions to allow him to have the charge apportioned, if it relates to land of which he now owns part, and to pay off the relevant proportion.[80]

Third, before their registration not all squatters will have an overriding interest in the land; there is no equivalent of the old section 70(1)(f). Instead, the squatter will have one only if he can bring himself within paragraph 2 of Schedule 1 or 3 by being in actual occupation of the land.[81] The idea here is to deny protection to squatters who subsequently abandon the land;[82] whether or not it will be effective in precisely that way is not clear, as abandonment may not be synonymous with not being in actual occupation.

SPECIAL CASES IN THE 2002 ACT

The Act makes provision for some special cases, which we must look at because they do raise some issues of principle.

---

[74] LC 254, 10.73. This has the effect of making it completely clear that the estate of a dispossessed tenant is extinguished for all purposes so that he has nothing to surrender; see above 5.

[75] LC 271, 14.69; and see above, n 31.

[76] Sch 6 para 4.

[77] Sch 6 para 9(1), (2).

[78] Sch 6 para 9(3).

[79] Sch 6 para 9(4); LC 271 does not say why this is so, but notes that if the squatter had an independent entitlement under para 5(3) or (4) he may in fact have priority over a chargee.

[80] Sch 6 para 10.

[81] See ch 5, above.

[82] See ch 5, text at n 106.

Dispossession of an Owner Under a Disability

First, there is protection for people dispossessed while under a disability, in paragraph 8 of Schedule 6. Where a squatter succeeds in an application for registration despite these provisions—as is very likely where the disability prevents an objection to the squatter's application—the intention is that the original proprietor's position will be able to be restored by an alteration of the register at a later date, or that compensation will be paid if rectification is impossible because the squatter has sold on and the new purchaser is a proprietor in possession.[83]

Adverse Possession Impossible Against Interests in Succession

Second, it is no longer possible to use adverse possession as a way of gaining title *at all* where registered land is held in trust for successive interests.[84] This is presented in LC 271[85] as a consequence of the principle that title is taken to a registered estate, so that it would not make sense to continue the present law that allows a squatter to acquire title to land against a beneficiary. The principle in unregistered land is that in these circumstances the squatter takes his own fee simple, which becomes vulnerable whenever a right of action accrues to someone (for example when the life tenant dies and a remainder falls in); the situation is thus similar to that arising in unregistered land where a tenant is dispossessed. The new approach of the 2002 Act changes the situation vis-à-vis tenants, by providing that the squatter steps into their shoes on the register. This cannot be done for a beneficiary who has no registered title, and where the squatter has dispossessed a life tenant under a trust of land it would be contrary to the principle of the new Act to give the squatter a registered fee simple while the trustees' title remained unbarred. Where the squatter dispossesses a life tenant under the Settled Land Act 1925,[86] he could of course take the latter's registered title; but the design of the new Act eschews the idea of registering him with a title qualified by the unbarred future interests that would make the title vulnerable in the future, and it would certainly produce inconsistencies to allow this in some settlements and not in others. The 2002 Act throws up its hands at the problem and simply provides that no one can be in adverse possession of land held on trust unless all the beneficiaries have interests in possession (as will be the case for ordinary co-ownership). This is perhaps

---

[83] LC 271, 14.30. fn 111. If the squatter himself is still in possession he might or might not suffer rectification, depending upon whether or not he was found to have caused or contributed to the mistake through fraud or lack of proper care: Sch 4, para 3(2)(a). The same considerations apply where a registered proprietor is dispossessed while he is an enemy or held in enemy territory: Sch 6 para 8(1).

[84] Sch 6 para 12.

[85] 14.92–14.94.

[86] An increasingly rare creature following the provision in the Trusts of Land and Appointment of Trustees Act 1996, but found, if at all, mostly on large estates which can be quite vulnerable to adverse possession.

an inevitable consequence of the new scheme, but it does mean that boundary disputes cannot be sorted out by adverse possession for these excepted trusts.[87]

There will, of course, be nothing to prevent the law of estoppel, and the law relating to other entitlements such as that of an unpaid vendor, from operating as they always have done in relation to trust property; but in relation to such property claimants will not be able to make procedural use of Schedule 6 by pretending to be adverse possessors.

The Foreshore

Third, the limitation period for Crown foreshore remains at 60 years. The Crown is one of the main victims of adverse possession, because of the ease of appropriating a chunk of beach, and so has enjoyed a longer limitation period, which is continued in the new provisions. The Crown should be one of the principal beneficiaries of the 2002 Act, since it is now enabled to register its land.[88]

Successive Squatters

Fourth, the law relating to successive squatters is altered slightly. For this we have to construct an example:

P is the freehold owner of land.
S1 takes possession of the land in 2010.
S2 takes possession of the land in 2014.

Where P's title is unregistered, it is barred in 2022, and whether S2 purchased S1's interest or dispossessed S1 the position is the same, S2 simply amalgamates the two periods.[89] But, outside the registration system (for there is nothing to oblige S2 to register), S2 remains vulnerable to proceedings by S1 until 2026. Now if P's title is registered it will not, of course, be barred automatically, but he may face an application by S2 in 2020; the change made by the Act is that this only works if S2 is a successor in title to S1, and not where S2 dispossessed S1.[90] However, if S1 regains the land later, say in 2019, by *whatever* means, he can then count S2's time together with his own.[91]

---

[87] Note also that trustees and beneficiaries (unless they are absolutely entitled) cannot be in adverse possession against each other, as a result of these provisions and of the rule in s 21(1)(b) of the Limitation Act 1980 that there is no limitation period for the recovery of land by beneficiaries from trustees.

[88] See ch 8, below.

[89] *Megarry and Wade*, 21–021 to 21–023; *Mount Carmel Investments Ltd v Peter Thurlow Ltd* [1988] 1 WLR 1078.

[90] Sch 6 para 11(2)(a).

[91] Sch 6 para 11(2)(b). There is nothing to prevent his doing so, it seems, even if S2 had been in possession for 12 years, extinguishing S1's title, presumably because there is now no special magic about 12 years so far as P is concerned.

At first sight it is difficult to see the point of such a complex rule.[92] It has been suggested that the aim is to prevent the registration of a squatter who could still be evicted by an earlier squatter; it might be felt undesirable to register the title of S2 in 2020 (assuming P failed to object, etc) when he might be evicted by S1 at any point up to 2024.[93]

This may be true, but if so not all possible instances have been eliminated. Recall that the *old* rules apply to unregistered estates. Taking our original example and supposing P's title to be registered, if S2 dispossesses S1, he can apply to be registered in P's place in 2024 under the new law. If he does not apply, or is not registered, S1 (as well as P) can evict him at any point until 2026. But if S2 is registered in P's stead in 2024 (unlikely as that is under the new law) what happens to S1's unbarred, unregistered fee simple? The combination of old and new rules will always yield a situation when a squatter in S2's situation is still liable for eviction by the previous squatter at the moment before registration, simply because the 10 year period is shorter than the 12 year limitation period. But once registered, S2 has P's registered estate. And that estate is not vulnerable to S1, because S1 is not in adverse possession and has not been for more than six months, so that he does not pass the threshold of the first two paragraphs of clause 1 of Schedule 6. What gives the right to apply for registration is not the squatter's estate by adverse possession but the fact that he is in adverse possession (or has very recently been evicted, paragraph 1(2)). Thus the moment S2 takes on P's registered estate, any unbarred estate of any previous squatter(s) becomes worthless and powerless.

The justification for not allowing S2 to tack on to S1's period if S2 dispossesses him may be simply to give the original proprietor a better chance of retaining his estate, by making longer the period before he loses it.

TRANSITIONS AND THE INTERFACE WITH UNREGISTERED LAND

The fact that the Land Registration Act 2002 amends another area of substantive law, but only for the purposes of its operation where title is registered, means that at two points quite complex transitional issues arise: first, for registered land when the new Act comes into force; second, when land first comes on to the register, voluntarily or otherwise, after the new Act is brought into force. In both cases a third party's position is affected (to put it neutrally) by the registration of another's title. There is a third case where transition is a problem, namely the one instance where a squatter's position is improved by the Act, under paragraph 5(4) of Schedule 6, and, as we have seen, there is special provision to ensure that the registered proprietor has a little extra time to take action against a potentially successful squatter.[94]

The changes effected by the 2002 Act, and the downgrading of adverse possession, may lead us to change our views of the squatter's status in unregistered land.

---

[92] Neither LC 271, nor the explanatory notes to the Land Registration Bill, explain the point.
[93] Smith, *Property Law*, 71.
[94] Text at n 71 above.

Before long, it is hoped, very nearly all title will be registered. It will then be true to say that adverse possession always gives, not a tender young fee simple that can ripen into an indefeasible title, but a plant that will almost inevitably wither when it meets the registration system, as it must. We may therefore in due course cease to regard adverse possession as giving a fee simple, and cease to regard it as a property right at all. The squatter's right to sue in nuisance and trespass[95] may therefore be compromised. This is conjecture, perhaps on a 50 to 100-year timescale.

Meanwhile, and with human rights considerations in mind, the Act makes strenuous efforts to avoid depriving any adverse possessor of accrued rights, either at the point when the Act comes into force or at a later point when first registration occurs.

Transitional Provisions for Title Already Registered

Transitional provisions belong in Schedule 12. The obvious question is: what happens to the squatter in registered land who has accrued his 12 years at the point when the Act comes into force but has not yet applied for registration? Schedule 12 paragraph 18 preserves his entitlement under section 75 of the 1925 Act; paragraph 11 gives that entitlement the status of an overriding interest for three years from the coming into force of Schedule 3, and thereafter he will have an overriding interest if he is in actual occupation of the land. There is thus a qualified preservation of old accrued rights; if the squatter has not registered his title after three years and the registered proprietor then sells, the squatter's title will only bind the purchaser if he remains in actual occupation. He would nevertheless be entitled to make an application under Schedule 6, but subject to the new rules and therefore with doubtful success.

There is thus a small chance of a deprivation of a possession, potentially contrary to Article 1 of the First Protocol to the European Convention for the Protection of Human Rights and Fundamental Freedoms. If the point is ever litigated, The Law Commission's reasons for making this change will be subjected to close scrutiny in any decision as to whether or not the deprivation is justified by the Article as a measure 'necessary to control the use of property in accordance with the general interest'.

Transitions on First Registration

Where title is registered for the first time, after the Act is brought into force, the newly registered proprietor is bound by the rights of any squatter (whatever they are, ie whether or not the limitation period has elapsed) as an overriding interest

---

[95] See n 2 above.

under Schedule 1 if the squatter is in actual occupation, and/or by notice of his right under section 11(4)(c).[96] The two may well be co-extensive. If at this point the squatter has not accrued his 12 years, he is automatically demoted. His possession is never now going to give him an automatic entitlement to the land; it will probably never give him any entitlement at all unless the registered proprietor fails to reply to notice received under the provisions of Schedule 6, or unless the squatter can bring himself within paragraph 5(4) of Schedule 6.

Could this be a deprivation of a possession, with human rights implications? Nothing has been taken away, the squatter still has his common law fee simple, but it has lost potential.

If the registered proprietor has somehow managed to achieve first registration at a point when a squatter has accrued his 12 years and so in fact, at the point immediately before first registration, held the fee simple in the land or part of it (this is easier to imagine in terms of a small part of a large estate), then *provided* that the registered proprietor is bound by his right (as an overriding interest or by notice)[97] then the squatter may apply to be registered as proprietor by an alteration of the register because of a mistake.[98] If he is not in actual occupation and the registered proprietor has no notice of his right, he is deprived of a fee simple in the land. The most likely scenario is that an adverse possessor in these circumstances may never realise what has happened. He may continue in adverse possession until some other event prompts him to seek registration under Schedule 6 and to discover that, whilst he had an indefeasible right just before registration, he has lost it. This is a serious deprivation. The fact that challenges on the basis of human rights are unlikely makes them none the less interesting.

The main instances of transitional provisions are illustrated in the table on page 152.

The Interface with Unregistered Land

Aside from transitional issues, for as long as some land remains unregistered there will be problems arising from the interface between the two different laws of adverse possession. The simplest case is where a squatter takes land, part of which is unregistered and part registered. The Law Commission contemplated this with equanimity.[99] More complex issues arise in leasehold land, where at any point there will be a freehold and at least one leasehold title, one of which may be unregistered.

---

[96] In addition, if first registration takes place within the first three years of Sch.1 coming into force, he will have an overriding interest no matter what the state of occupation or of notice until those three years elapse: Sch 12 para 7.

[97] Again, Sch 12 para 7 has effect for three years after Sch 1 comes into force.

[98] LC 271, 3.47; and see chs 5 and 6.

[99] LC 254, 10.18.

Period of possession, at the date at the head of each column	Possession against registered title; Land Registration Act 2002 comes into force in 2003	Possession against unregistered land, which is registered in 2005	Possession against unregistered land, which is registered in 2008
9 years	Lost potential.[100]	Lost potential.[2]	Lost potential.[2]
10 years six months	As above;[101] but if Schedule 6 paragraph 5(4) applies the right to be registered arises in a year's time when that subparagraph is in force[101]—a small acceleration of the entitlement.	As above;[3] but if Schedule 6 paragraph 5(4) applies the right to be registered arises in a year's time (paragraph 5(4)(d))[103]—a small acceleration of the entitlement.	As above[3] but if Schedule 6 paragraph 5(4) applies the right to be registered arises in a year's time (paragraph 5(4)(d))—a small acceleration of the entitlement.
13 years	The land is held on trust for the squatter[102] and he is entitled to registration as proprietor. This will be lost against subsequent purchasers if his title is still unregistered in three years' time unless he is in actual occupation of the land.[105]	The registered proprietor takes the land subject to the squatter's right to have the register altered until Schedule 1 has been in force for three years,[106] and thereafter only if the squatter is in actual occupation of the land[107] or the registered proprietor has notice of his rights.[108] As against a purchaser, he has an overriding interest if he is in actual occupation.[109]	The registered proprietor takes the land subject to the squatter's right to have the register altered, provided the squatter is in actual occupation of the land[7] or the registered proprietor has notice of his rights.[8] As against a purchaser, he has an overriding interest if he is in actual occupation.[9]

[100] The squatter's fee simple will never, now, mature into an indefeasible title unless he applies for registration and either the registered proprietor makes no objection, or he can bring himself within Schedule 6 para 5(4).
[101] See n 71 above.
[102] See n 70 above.
[103] See n 70 above.

[104] Schedule 12, para 18(1); s 75 of the Land Registration Act 1925.
[105] Schedule 12 para 11; Schedule 3 para 2.
[106] Schedule 12 para 7.
[107] Schedule 1 para 2.
[108] S 11(4)(c).
[109] Sch 3 para 2.

Provided the squatter dispossesses a tenant with a registered lease, of whatever length and whether or not it is a sub-tenancy, the Act's scheme applies without difficulty; the squatter simply takes the registered lease, which will run its course and then leave the squatter vulnerable, if he does not give up possession, to whatever superior interests exist at that point, registered or unregistered.

Where both lease and freehold are unregistered, the squatter will take a title under the old rules. It must be registered as a freehold title if the squatter makes an application because there is no registered lease; section 96 and Schedule 6 are irrelevant. But it will be vulnerable to the landlord's interest when the lease ends; if the registrar is aware of this, it is hard to see that anything other than a qualified freehold title will reflect the position adequately.[110] Note that the same issue will arise when a squatter dispossesses the beneficiary under a trust of unregistered land, where a later interest remains unbarred. Again the squatter will be entitled to register his fee simple, under section 3 of the Act, and it will become vulnerable afresh when later causes of action accrue.[111] In either case, it is very likely that the squatter will nevertheless be given an absolute rather than a qualified title (because he may not know, or may not tell, about the freeholder). In that event, once the landlord's, or the next entitled beneficiary's, cause of action accrues he will have to apply for the register to be altered/rectified. Will he succeed on the basis that the omission of the qualification was a mistake at the time of first registration,[112] or will an absolute title be taken to mean what it says it means? This takes us back to a debate already examined in chapter 6, which at some stage will have to be addressed by the courts.[113]

However, once the 2002 Act has been in operation for a relatively short time, there should be no unregistered leases longer than seven years, so that in theory adverse possession would be irrelevant to them. But short term tenants do hold over, and a periodic tenancy then arises. Suppose a squatter takes possession of a small area at the edge of something like a large farm, held on a periodic tenancy. On unregistered principles, there is no difficulty; his independent fee simple is irrelevant to the tenant, and will bar the landlord 12 years after the termination of the tenancy, which can take place at any point by notice or agreement.

---

[110] See above, n 29.

[111] Text at n 84 above.

[112] Sch 4. If this argument succeeds (and it should not, if indefeasibility is taken seriously), the alteration is likely to amount to rectification, as it is unlikely that it will not prejudice a proprietor in possession; if the squatter himself is in possession it may be that rectification will be ordered nonetheless on the basis of para 3(2)(a) of Sch 4, ie he may have caused or substantially contributed to the mistake by fraud or lack of proper care.

[113] See ch 6.

CONCLUSION

The law of adverse possession in registered land has been streamlined under the 2002 Act. The registered title is now much more secure. And the small intellectual satisfaction generated by the interplay of concurrent freeholds is sacrificed to the practical neatness of slotting the squatter into the dispossessed proprietor's title. A small change, but it moves our land law at a stroke to one where possession is no longer the basis of title.

8

After 2002: The Road Ahead

So THERE WE have the scheme of the 2002 Act: a new range of registrable inter-ests, a new approach to the powers of the registered proprietor, a more com-prehensive system of interest recording for unregistered interests, a slimmer set of overriding interests. The law on alteration of the register is re-drafted (although, as we have seen, the extent of the change is unclear) and the law relating to adverse possession is radically re-cast so as to strengthen the principle that registration is the basis of title.

All this comes into force in October 2003. But there is more to look forward to. This chapter considers the further changes that are likely to come about after the initial, and partial, implementation of the 2002 Act, of which the most prominent is the introduction of electronic conveyancing, or e-conveyancing. Indeed, it is possible to see the whole Act as a mechanism to enable the introduction of e-conveyancing although, as we shall see, the relationship between substantive and procedural change is much more subtle than that. None of the projected further changes can be regarded as a certainty, and they can be seen to depend upon quite fragile factors, including economic and political ones. This chapter discusses the elimination of unregistered conveyancing, the introduction of e-conveyancing, and the possible disappearance of the feudal system. These are all internal issues. The chapter that follows looks further afield, at land registration in Europe and the possibilities for further change that might bring the European systems, including our own, closer together.

THE DISAPPEARANCE OF UNREGISTERED CONVEYANCING

At the time of writing there are 18.8 million registered titles in England and Wales, and some 5 million unregistered titles.[1] But time is running out for unregistered title; LC 271 introduces new measures towards its elimination, and expresses a determination to complete that process. As things stand, this is to be achieved through the established 'trigger' mechanism, whereby certain events give rise to a requirement to register. The triggers have been contained in section 123 of the Land Registration Act 1925, as extended by the Land Registration Act 1997; they are now contained in section 4 of the 2002 Act. The section sets out the events that trigger a requirement to register a 'qualifying estate', ie a freehold estate in land, or

---

[1] March 2003; the writer is grateful to HM Land Registry for supplying these figures.

leasehold estate in land with more than seven years to run at the time of the event.[2] The length of the registrable lease has already been discussed[3] and represents a significant extension of the requirement to register; the land registry anticipates something like a 40 per cent rise in first registrations as a result from October 2003. The details of the triggering events were discussed in chapter 3, as was the sanction for non-registration: after two months, the legal estate jumps back whence it came.[4] We noted that nearly, but not quite, everything one does with a legal estate in land triggers registration.[5]

Not all qualifying estates will ever be caught by these provisions. Some land is never sold: local authority land, large rural estates, land belonging to universities and colleges. These are the properties most vulnerable to adverse possession, because of their extent, and, in some cases, the nature of their owners and uncertainties surrounding the title. Thus it is hoped that the new provisions relating to adverse possession, rendering registered land very nearly squatter-proof, will induce such landowners to register their titles. As we shall see, it appears that Crown land will be registered voluntarily.[6] Moreover, LC 271 recommends[7] that five years after implementation of the Act, if registration is not complete further measures be introduced to complete it.[8] Local authorities, for example, are easy targets for compulsion; there is anecdotal evidence that local authorities are, in any event, increasingly opting for voluntary registration. They are perhaps the ones who will reap the most benefit from registration, as their unregistered titles can be complex.[9] Registration offers them easier conveyancing and a significant saving in space for deeds storage.

One of the themes running through the Law Commission's explanation of the need to complete registration is the wish to dispense with the need for the skills of unregistered conveyancing. In LC 254 it is referred to as an 'increasingly unfamil-

---

[2] S 4(2).

[3] Ch 3, text at n 31.

[4] Invariably, an application to the registrar for an extension of the period will be granted, because the registrar *wants* titles to be registered. If such an application is made, and granted, after the expiry of the two months, the legal estate obediently jumps back to where it should be.

[5] Not quite: the transfer of the legal estate to new trustees of a trust of land is not caught. Land settled pursuant to the Settled Land Act 1925 will be caught within a generation of the Land Registration Act 1997 because a vesting assent triggers registration from 1997 onwards.

[6] See below, in the final section of this chapter.

[7] At para 2.13.

[8] Simpson, *Land Registration*, at 204, states that 'There is, in fact, no real prospect of systematic registration in England', because of the complexity of title in some areas. He cites TB Ruoff in 'The role of survey in land registration', 104 *Chartered Surveyor* (July 1971) 14: '. . . if we went in for systematic registration it would take hundreds, if not thousands, of years to register a small part of Lancashire'. Things are clearly looking up.

[9] Even after the right-to-buy legislation has enabled many public sector tenants to buy their homes, local authorities tend to own a vast range of properties with multiple separate titles. Any one property may have been owned by the same local authority in many different statutory forms since the nineteenth century. Thus the conveyancer may have to work out how to trace title from the last conveyance of the property to, say, the Poor Law Guardians in the nineteenth century, to the present authority, via transformations in numerous long-repealed statutes. Plans cause problems as it may be very difficult to relate them to what is now on the ground.

iar' process;[10] in LC 271 we are told 'Unregistered conveyancing must be given its quietus as soon as possible'.[11] It is hard to disagree with the fact that it is undesirable to have two systems of conveyancing in operation[12]—as has been the case since 1862. Taking the provisions of the Act as they stand, however, and even assuming that *all* freeholds will be registered, we can see that even then unregistered conveyancing will be needed for:

—Dealings with leases of seven years or less;
—Dealings with rentcharges, franchises and profits à prendre in gross where the proprietors have not chosen to register;
—Grants of, and dealings with, PPP leases;
—Dealings with manors.

Much of this will be whittled away. It seems safe to assume that the threshold for leases will come down to three years; that rentcharges will practically disappear; that PPP leases may do so; and that franchises and profits in gross will become compulsorily registrable. Manors and very short leases would remain. During the transitional period when unregistered title becomes increasingly rare, unregistered conveyancing skills will become expensive. They are not really so unfamiliar at present; but there will come a time when we cease to teach them. Yet it can be seen that it is almost impossible to eradicate unregistered conveyancing altogether in a statute devoted to registration. It has already been suggested that at some stage there will be a need for a reformed Law of Property Act. One of its objectives must be to ensure that the residual few unregistered titles can be dealt with without the need for disproportionately expensive skills.

ELECTRONIC CONVEYANCING

Electronic transactions are not, of course, an English invention. The pioneer of electronic transacting has been Ontario; it is being developed in many other jurisdictions[13] including, close at hand, Scotland. Thus although e-conveyancing was discussed rather tentatively in LC 254, by the time LC 271 was produced it had become a major objective. So much so that it is impossible to say which objective was the most important in the minds of those who produced LC 271: the elimination of unregistered title, the change in the nature of registered title, or the introduction of e-conveyancing. Perhaps everything tends towards the latter: unregistered title is to be eliminated, because no-one wants to be using two systems of conveyancing once registered title can be dealt with electronically;

---

[10] LC 254, 3.7, 3.8
[11] LC 271, 2.6.
[12] 'Absurd' says the Law Commission: LC 271, 2.6.
[13] The conference whose papers are to be published in Grinlinton, *Torrens Conference Papers* was convened to celebrate the completion of the electronic register in New Zealand, where e-conveyancing is being piloted.

registered title is made more secure, and in particular squatter-proof, to encourage voluntary registration and advance the elimination of title; thus both aim to bring about a comprehensive system of electronic conveyancing.

It cannot be as simple as that. Substantive change in the 2002 Act stands alone as an objective in itself; the Act is a classic instance of law reform that repeals an unsatisfactory statute and substitutes a better one, making the law more consistent and more workable. The hard truth is that had the substantive changes in the 2002 Act been proposed alone, and without e-conveyancing, it would not have been enacted. It would have been simply a vast piece of lawyers' law. It has been notoriously hard for Parliament to make time for Law Commission projects, and many have remained unimplemented. What e-conveyancing did was to make the legislation politically attractive. Parliamentary emotions have run high on the vexed question of the stress and delay of domestic conveyancing; legislation that claims to make this better may win votes, and so has a head start in the race on to the statute book. Recall that the Land Registration Bill was introduced in the House of Lords on 21 June 2001 even before LC 271 had actually been published; that government representatives made almost no concessions at all in the course of debate on the Bill; and that among the claims made for it was that it would reduce the time taken in leasehold conveyancing by about two-and-a-half hours per transaction.[14] Substantive change was necessary to get e-conveyancing to work; but e-conveyancing was the magic carpet that transported the Bill through Parliament.[15]

This book is about law rather than procedure, and it is not proposed to spend a great deal of time looking at the technical aspects of e-conveyancing.[16] Practitioners will have much better resources available to them. But e-conveyancing is an integral part of the 2002 Act and we need to consider the link between procedural and substantive change. After a general introduction to the proposed new procedures, this chapter addresses the further substantive changes that will be brought about by e-conveyancing once it is implemented, in particular the effect it will have upon unregistered interests and upon contracts. For e-conveyancing is not a neutral, procedural matter.

The Completion of the Electronic Register

Recall that although the whole of the 2002 Act is to be brought into force in October 2003, the provisions relating to e-conveyancing will not be activated

---

[14]   See ch 3 at n 17.

[15]   Whether e-conveyancing itself will actually make the conveyancing process any quicker is a moot point; delay is not really associated with the execution of documents. What could make domestic conveyancing much more efficient is the accompanying scheme for chain management. If all parties to a transaction are dealing on line, it is possible for a chain manager to ascertain what stage everyone has reached and to identify who is holding things up; see LC 271, 1.12, 2.52, and 13.63 ff.

[16]   See D Capps, 'Conveyancing in the Twenty-first Century: An Outline of Electronic Conveyancing and Electronic Signatures' [2002] *Conveyancer* 443.

because the necessary rules will not have been made.[17] The provisions in the Act are enabling provisions, leaving much to rules, but also include provision in section 93 for e-conveyancing to be made compulsory. As things stand, we are not quite ready for that.

The first step must be the completion of the electronic register. This has obviously been in hand for some time. At the time of writing, the land registry expects to have all the individual registers in electronic form by October 2003, all plans available on screen by March 2004, and all filed documents in electronic form by mid-2004.[18] Another step is access. At present, some firms of solicitors have direct access to the land registry intranet, through the Land Registry Direct service, and can both inspect the register and obtain official searches, paying for each activity. It is expected that later in 2003 access to the register will be available universally on the internet, with regular customers paying by key number and individuals by credit card for each activity. It is even possible to register the discharge of a mortgage electronically.[19]

Electronic Transactions

For transactions to be effected on line, a number of further steps are needed:

—Legislation is needed to enable documents which have hitherto been required to be made in writing or by deed to be made and signed electronically.[20] This has been managed, so far as statutory requirements are concerned, by the Electronic Communications Act 2002, section 8, and rules thereunder; section 91 of the 2002 Act goes further, in that it also disapplies formal requirements made by the common law. And section 93 enables rules to be made making electronic transaction compulsory for certain dispositions; rules, which have not yet been made, will specify which dispositions these are.

—Sophisticated software is needed to link solicitors with the land registry and enable the transactions. This is at an advanced stage of development and has been demonstrated to solicitors over the past two years by the land registry's e-conveyancing taskforce.

—Issues over the security of electronic signatures will have to be resolved. Secure electronic dealings have been achieved by the Stock Market for some years now under the CREST system, and do not seem to have given rise to problems. Nevertheless, the proposals for electronic dealing under the 2002 Act have

---

[17] Thus s 93, in particular, does not work until rules specify the dispositions to which it applies; this is not covered by the Land Registration Rules 2003 and is not intended to happen for some time.

[18] March 2003; again, the writer is grateful to HM Land Registry for this information.

[19] Land Registration Rules 1925, r 151A; but not, yet, to effect the whole tripartite transaction (transfer of funds plus registration of discharge) electronically.

[20] Law of Property Act 1925, s 52(1) and 53(1)(a); Law of Property (Miscellaneous Provisions) Act 1989, s 2.

aroused some disquiet. Documents are to be signed electronically by practitioners on behalf of their clients. It is clear that the internal security of the public/private key system[21] is probably unbreakable; but how will access to the system be governed? LC 271 indicates that a swipe card will be used;[22] thus the security of the system depends ultimately upon the honesty of the individual, as well as the care taken by him not to let, say, his secretary use his card or password.[23]

—Network access agreements will need to be put in place to regulate the access of practitioners to the system. These are discussed at length in LC 271, and would appear to be a potent form of control and regulation of the conveyancing profession.[24]

—Provision is made in the 2002 Act for the do-it-yourself conveyancer, who will have access to the system at an office of the land registry, where staff will give him technical but not legal assistance.[25]

It is envisaged that e-conveyancing will be piloted first, and then available on a voluntary basis; later, it will become compulsory, by rules made under section 93. Different kinds of transactions will be brought under section 93 in stages, but its eventual scope, as we shall see, is intended to be very wide. The section states, simply, that transactions specified by rules will only have effect when carried out by documents in electronic form and communicated electronically to the registrar.

What, then, will be the substantive legal changes brought about when electronic conveyancing becomes universal?

The Disappearance of the Registration Gap

From the outset of title registration, there was great potential for interesting things to happen between transfer and registration, in what is now called the 'registration gap', although it took decades for the catastrophic effect of the gap to be both realised and resolved in the courts.[26] What remains is the fact that when a registrable disposition is 'completed' by delivery of a deed, the legal estate nevertheless does not pass until the disposition is completed by registration. Thus section 27 of the 2002 Act; but the section will become obsolete as soon as section 93 is activated, making electronic transactions compulsory. At that point the delivery of executed documents and the registration of transaction will take place at the one moment when the practitioner completes the transaction—presumably by a mouse-click or keystroke.

---

[21] LC 271, 13.14.
[22] The New Zealand system is committed to passwords.
[23] Most solicitors delegate completions to their secretaries.
[24] LC 271, 13.36 to 13.58.
[25] LC 271, 13.72–3.
[26] *Lloyd's Bank Plc v Rossett* [1989] Ch 350; *Abbey National BS v Cann*]1991] 1 AC 56; and see *Megarry and Wade* 6–049.

At present there is some difference between different jurisdictions as to whether the completion of dispositions by practitioners actually effects the registration, or whether it merely effects an electronic submission of documents to the registry, where registration then takes place, albeit perhaps only a few seconds later. The latter is the practice in Ontario; in New Zealand, and in England and Wales, the former will be the case.[27] In practical terms there can be little or no difference. The function of the transaction software will be to check electronic documents as they are created—for consistency of names and addresses, for example—and, in the English system, to create a 'dummy register' showing the entries that will appear on the register once the transaction is completed. There is nothing left for the registry to check—of the things that a registry *can* check, leaving aside things that it cannot check such as fraud—once the dealing is ready to complete. The writer understands that in Ontario the transaction is regarded as completed, and settlement funds released, once the documentation is electronically transmitted to the registry. So although registration by solicitors—not to mention DIY conveyancers—seems alarming, in practice the system will check everything checkable before completion. We shall probably cease to think of completion and registration of a disposition as two separate events; registration will truly be completion.

Recorded Interests and E-conveyancing

A more direct effect on the various interests that can burden registered land is as follows. We do not know the range of transactions for which electronic conveyancing will be mandatory. Certainly it is not confined to registrable dispositions. Registrable dispositions are, of course, the creation of and dealings with registrable estates, and they take effect at law only when registered.[28] But section 93 expressly includes the possibility that dealings with interests which are merely recorded on the register will be among those specified in the rules.[29] Thus we may find that it is not possible to create or discharge, say, a restrictive covenant other than electronically. Thus while land registration cannot actually guarantee the validity of interests other than the registrable estates listed in section 2, it is nevertheless going to take control of their creation. The lack of guarantee remains significant, because while an interest may be created by the correct means there may be doubt as to its validity on other grounds; but the scope for doubt is reduced. The bringing of unregistrable interests within the electronic disposition requirements at least narrows the gap considerably between registration and recording.

---

[27] LC 271 insists that completion and registration will be simultaneous: 13.2.

[28] S 27.

[29] It specifies dispositions of both 'a registered estate or charge' and 'an interest which is the subject of a notice in the register'.

Electronic Contracts

Another very significant feature of section 93 is that it catches not only transactions but also contracts to make the transactions. This is startling. It is by no means a necessary element of an electronic conveyancing system; but it is the means by which conveyancing can become more efficient through the system of chain management which, as we have seen, was one of the ingredients that got the Bill through Parliament.[30] Whether or not this will ultimately take place is unclear. It does represent a huge erosion of freedom of contract and it may not be accepted happily. Our experience of the Law of Property (Miscellaneous Provisions) Act 1989 may be instructive. The 1989 Act provided that land contracts must be made in writing and are otherwise wholly void, rather than merely being unenforceable unless evidenced in writing as hitherto.[31] This has generated a number of tricky cases; it is clear that not all the effects of the new law had been thought out beforehand (in particular, the effect on options was potentially catastrophic but the problem was avoided by some nimble judicial reasoning[32]), but it does not seem that there have been major problems.

Consequences of Non-compliance with Section 93.

Section 93 states that a disposition specified by rules as being within the scheme of compulsory electronic conveyancing 'only has effect' if carried out electronically. This is intended to mean that transactions that do not meet the requirements of section 93 will have no effect at all, *at law or in equity*.[33] Now it is not clear that the drafting of the section actually forces this interpretation, ie the intention has not been translated into judge-proof drafting. But the fact that it does not say 'only has effect at law' (contrast section 27(1)) certainly implies the intended interpretation. If the section is interpreted as intended, we may find that entities such as equitable mortgages and equitable easements may simply cease to exist altogether, rather than being merely unlikely but possible as they are now.[34] Whether or not that interpretation will be endorsed by the courts remains to be seen; if it is, we shall be rid of the phenomenon of transactions that have missed the boat so far as legal validity is concerned nevertheless being rescued by equity. Proprietary interests, or at least most of them, will either exist or not exist, and certain interests will become

---

[30] See above.

[31] Thus repealing s 40 of the Law of Property Act 1925, which reproduced the still older provision of the Statute of Frauds 1677.

[32] *Spiro v Glencrown Properties Ltd* [1991] 64 P & CR 527.

[33] LC 271, 13.84.

[34] Much depends on the wording of the eventual statutory instrument. Will it say that a *charge* of registered land can only be created electronically; or a *legal charge*? If the latter, there is scope for the deliberate creation of an equitable mortgage, in writing, so as to avoid the registration trigger.

unable to exist in a second-rate form. This would bring to fruition a suggestion made some years ago by David Jackson.[35]

And that, if it happens, will have the curious effect of bringing the English system into a position that seems to have been advocated by Sir Robert Torrens in his plans for the original Torrens system in South Australia.[36] His speeches and writings were not wholly consistent, but he does seem to have intended a position where anything not on the register simply would not be able to exist as a proprietary right. His intention, assuming that was it, was not clearly expressed in the statute and the Torrens systems have all resisted what has become known as 'sterility'.[37] The European systems, by contrast, have no such issue, as they have no equitable proprietary interests at all; if the English e-conveyancing system has the effect suggested here, it would bring compatibility with Europe one step nearer.

The success of this approach depends upon the response of the courts. Law and Equity have fused, but both traditions remain very much alive; the courts' will to intervene when the law works injustice will hardly vanish overnight. What the courts have found very difficult, of course, is the interaction of their equity jurisdiction with statute. It is one thing to counter a common law injustice with an equitable maxim and its out-workings; it is quite another to override the expressed will of the legislature in a statute. Yet equity has ancient roots as the response to circumstances that the legislator had not thought of, so that modification of a statute by the courts is not inherently impossible,[38] although the courts have become increasingly reluctant to do it.[39] And it is not merely the courts' ability to create equitable interests that is in issue. Where individuals have failed to create either a legal or an equitable interest in land, and indeed when they have made something quite close to a contract but have not fulfilled the formal requirements for validity, the next recourse is the law of estoppel, which will give effect to representations where detrimental reliance has been placed upon them. It has been argued[40] that the introduction of electronic contracting may trigger an 'estoppel boom', as informal arrangements are outlawed. No such boom has followed the greatly increased regulation of land contracts in the Law of Property (Miscellaneous Provision) Act 1989,[41] and indeed the courts have expressed doubts as to the legitimacy of using estoppel to rescue purported contracts falling foul of that Act.[42] Will the courts use their equitable jurisdiction, including the law

---

[35] 'Registration of Land Interests—The English Version' (1972) 88 *Law Quarterly Review* 93, at 121.

[36] P O'Connor, 'Information, Automation and the Conclusive Register', in Grinlinton, *Torrens Conference Papers*, text at fn 69 ff.

[37] S Cooper, 'Equity and Unregistered Land Rights in Commonwealth Registration Systems' 2003 Oxford University Commonwealth Law Journal (forthcoming).

[38] *Kok Hoong v Leong Cheong Kweng Mines Ltd* [1964] AC 993, PC.

[39] *Godden v Merthyr Tydfil Housing Association* 15 Jan 1997, CA (unreported); *Actionstrength Ltd v International Glass Engineering IN.GL.EN. SpA* [2003] UKHL 17, [2003] All ER (D) 69.

[40] M Dixon: 'Proprietary Estoppel and Formalities in Land Law and the Land Registration Act 2002: A Theory of Unconscionability' in Cooke, *Modern Studies II*, 165.

[41] See above.

[42] *Godden v Merthyr Tydfil*, n 39 above. A more flexible approach is seen in *Yaxley v Gotts* [2000] Ch 162.

of estoppel, to combat the electronic contracting and conveyancing provisions? There is a very difficult line to be drawn here. The courts have the power to sabotage the new system, and it is to be hoped that they will find ways to balance the wish to remedy injustice in the individual case with the need to uphold the policy of the statute, reserving estoppel as a means of reversing injustice in cases involving unusual hardship or fraudulent behaviour, and interpreting fraud quite strictly.[43]

The Reduction of Overriding Interests

The network access agreement will include a provision that a solicitor who is aware of the existence of an overriding interest must inform the registrar, who will then enter a notice of that interest on the register.[44] We have seen that the 2002 Act reduces the categories of overriding interest;[45] there is also a wish to reduce the actual number of them, and the network access agreement is thus going to use solicitors as a tool to capture overriding interests and pin them down on to the register. In most cases this will be a matter of recording the interest, and thus protecting its priority but not its validity; presumably in the case of legal easements, if the registrar is satisfied as to the validity of an interest that has hitherto existed off-register, it may be registered rather than merely recorded.[46] Electronic conveyancing can thus be seen to have a streamlining effect, by means of a contractual by-product.

Electronic Fraud

A final comment on the legal effects of e-conveyancing concerns fraud. The potential for fraud should not be exaggerated. Electronic transaction in the Stock Exchange has not given rise to problems; and paper transactions are not at all fraud- or forgery-proof. Nevertheless there is a rational concern. For what electronic transaction does is to give every practitioner the ability to forge a transfer or mortgage of land *without the need for manual skill in forgery*. I cannot forge a signature on a paper transfer; I can swipe my card and press the button.

Obviously a solicitor who does this will be in breach of every possible rule of professional practice and of his network access agreement, as well as committing

---

[43] As they have done in cases where the formalities required by the Wills Act 1837 have not been complied with: *Wayling v Jones* (1993) 69 P & CR 170.
[44] This is the purpose of s 71. The interest can only be recorded if, of course, it is one that can be the subject of a notice; s 33 provides that certain interests cannot be, in particular beneficial interests under trusts of land.
[45] See ch 5.
[46] A simple example may be where registration was fairly recent and a solicitor becomes aware that a pre-registration easement benefiting the property was not picked up on first registration.

a criminal offence. But the ability remains, and doubtless there will be some crime as a result.[47] Very interesting is the provision, in section 91(6), that

If a document to which this section applies [ie an electronic document] is authenticated by a person as agent, it is to be regarded for the purposes of any enactment as authenticated by him under the written authority of his principal.

This would appear to mean—and there is of course no authority on the point—that if there is fraud in the shape of a solicitor dealing with a client's property without authority, the client's remedy for fraud will *not* be within the provisions for alteration/rectification of the register nor for indemnity under schedule 8. The document will be regarded, for the purposes of the 2002 Act, as having been executed by the solicitor under the client's written authority. The client will lose his land, and must look to the solicitor's insurance rather than to a land registry indemnity; and this must be a cause for concern because the land registry indemnity is probably far more reliable.[48]

THE DISAPPEARANCE OF THE FEUDAL SYSTEM

As mentioned above, the 2002 Act contains provisions that will enable Crown land to be registered.

This takes us back to the beginnings of our current legal system, when in 1066 all land in England and Wales became vested in the Crown—or so successive monarchs decided—and individuals were enabled to hold land in feudal tenure from the Crown and from each other.[49] The complexities of the system have been eliminated, in a long process completed in 1925; but still the estate in fee simple, held from the English Crown, is the nearest that the common law approaches to absolute ownership. The Crown itself—or the Queen herself—owns land in a number of different ways, as do the Duchies of Cornwall and Lancaster;[50] for the purposes of a discussion of registration, the main point is that much Crown land is owned 'in demesne', ie absolutely, not for an estate. This includes the foreshore, and land which has escheated to the Crown (ie reverted to it on the bankruptcy of the fee simple owner, or upon corporate insolvency or dissolution). And until the coming into force of the 2002 Act it has not been possible for Crown land held in demesne to be registered, because only an estate in land, freehold or leasehold, can

---

[47] Perhaps no more, or even less, than at present; for conversely, the ability of the skilled forger who is not a solicitor to create a document with someone else's purported signature will disappear. The great New Zealand case of *Frazer v Walker* [1967] 1 AC 569 (which resolved the contest, for New Zealand and, effectively, for Australia, as to whether their Torrens systems would operate deferred or immediate indefeasibility) could not happen under an electronic system; see ch 6, text at n 9.

[48] The writer hopes, both that she is wrong about this, and that it will never happen anyway.

[49] The same has happened since in the process of colonisation; presumably the Saxons in the eleventh and twelfth centuries felt as aggrieved as have the native populations under imposed feudalism in the former colonies.

[50] For the details, see LC 271, 11.3.

be registered; moreover, when land escheated to the Crown it had to be removed from the register.

In the preparation for the 2002 Act it was felt desirable that Crown land should be registered, and that land that escheats should stay registered—from the point of view of the policy of the legislation, so as to complete the registration of land in England and Wales, and from the point of view of the Crown, which would like the land to benefit from the squatter-proofing provisions of the 2002 Act (the foreshore is particularly vulnerable). Accordingly the 2002 Act provides, in section 79, for Her Majesty to grant herself a fee simple, for the purpose only of registering her land. It is anticipated that this will be done over a period of years, and that in the meantime the Crown will have specially extended powers[51] to protect its land by lodging a caution against first registration: section 81. The business of eliminating the requirement of the removal of escheated land from the register is left, by section 82, to rules; the intention is that escheated land should stay on the register until granted to someone willing to take responsibility for it, at which point the old register will be closed, and a new one, with a new title number, opened.[52] Section 130 of the 2002 Act even enables the registration of land covered by water, including submarine land out to the territorial limits of the United Kingdom.

Would it not have been simpler to amend, not the form in which Her Majesty holds land, but the forms of landholding that can be registered? The idea of her holding land feudally from herself is a little bizarre. The answer may be that if all land comes on to the register, and all registered land is held for an estate in fee simple or for a leasehold estate, it is then extremely simple to abolish the feudal system, once arrangements are in place for escheat and bankruptcy, etc, which do not depend upon feudal concepts.[53] All that is needed is a provision that the fee simple is transformed into ownership, just as the corresponding Scots provision has already done.[54] And this may be the intention.[55]

---

[51] See ch 3, n 62.

[52] LC 271, 11.28. This section of this chapter represents a vast over-simplification of the matters discussed in ch XI of LC 271.

[53] LC 271 envisages further reform, at 11.27.

[54] See ch 9.

[55] JE Hogg, *Australian Torrens System* (London, William Clowes & Sons, 1905), 21–22 remarked that title registration under the Torrens system pretty nearly created a non-feudal system of landholding: 'Were feudal tenure technically, as it has been practically, replaced by allodial ownership, the Torrens system of conveyance by registration would require but little alteration to transform it into a consistent system logically resting on intelligible principles' (cited in Simpson, *Land Registration*, 77).

9

After 2002: The Road to Europe?

IN CHAPTER 1 it was said that there are three families of title registration: the English, the Torrens, and the much older German family. So far, the comparative focus of this book has been the Torrens systems. They are so close to the English one that comparison is immensely useful as a source of understanding of what the 2002 Act does, and does not, do. They have in common the concepts of the estate and the trust, and fragmentation of ownership. By contrast, title registration in Europe (including Scotland) operates upon the Roman form of ownership, dominium. It does not have to wrestle with the coexistence of legal and equitable ownership, it is not expressed in English nor in terms that are readily translatable into English, and can appear inaccessibly foreign to an English lawyer.

It was perhaps a failure to be aware of these legal and psychological barriers that enabled Lord Harrison, in the House of Lords during the debate on the Land Registration Bill in 2001, to ask a very good question:

... the Bill applies to England and Wales, but it would be interesting to know to what degree it is compatible with the practice in Scotland and Northern Ireland. I also refer to the European Union.... We are talking about a modern world in which there is free movement of citizens and workers. We want to encourage the creation of a single market and make sure it works. I believe that each requires an efficient and transparent system of land registration throughout Europe.

In Europe, the common law sticks out like a sore thumb. The European Union has as its goal the free movement of goods and persons, and to that end has been seen to extend its own powers so as to encompass matters as apparently distant from its remit as family law.[1] Whatever our emotional response to the erosion of our legal system, it is in practice unlikely that our land law will remain immune from European influence for very long.

Work on the system to which Lord Harrison looked forward is already well under way. A considerable amount of comparative, survey-type work has been done;[2] and the EULIS project has been set up to develop a land information system throughout Europe, encompassing cadastres as well as title and deeds registers.[3] It

---

[1] See for example CMV Clarkson, 'Brussels III—Matrimonial Property European Style' [2002] *Family Law* 683; and Nigel Lowe's lecture in the 'Current Legal Problems' series, 27 February 2003: 'The Growing Influence of the European Union on International Family Law—A View From the Boundary'.

[2] See nn 30, 32 below.

[3] http://www.eulis.org.

is not possible in a book on this scale to reproduce the vast amount of information already accumulated by those surveys, nor to do comparative legal research on the scale being undertaken by EULIS. But some small-scale information may be useful. This chapter examines just a few of the European systems, concentrating on the issues of principle which have been the focus of this book.

It will come as no surprise that instant compatibility is not found. Even the grouping of the systems is not obvious. Northern Ireland and Ireland go together, as for historical reasons both have a common law system and both have a partial system of title registration with origins in the same statute. Then comes Scotland, with a continental, civil law system but a title registration statute on the English model. Then comes continental Europe, where title registration is based on the German model. After some general comments there follows a discussion of four of these systems. This chapter has been written in collaboration with European scholars, to whom the writer is immensely grateful; in particular, the sections on registration in Poland, Finland and The Netherlands have been written by Matti Niemi, Magdalena Habdas, and Lars van Vliet respectively. In each case we have tried to concentrate on the following points of comparison:

—The nature of registration: is it dispositive?
—What can be registered?
—How are third party rights treated?
—What is the position on indefeasibility?
—Can registered land be acquired by adverse possession?

Any attempt to make registration systems compatible must address at least these issues; but it is not always easy to find the answer in a legal system with different terminology and pre-occupations from those of the English and Torrens systems.

IRELAND AND NORTHERN IRELAND[4]

Deeds registration was established for the whole of Ireland by the Registration of Deeds (Ireland) Act 1707. This was of course contemporaneous with the establishment of the Middlesex and Yorkshire deeds registries;[5] like those systems, it was protective not dispositive. It evolved into a race-notice system; it is not possible to obtain priority over an earlier unregistered deed by registering if one has notice of the earlier deed.[6] Deeds registration continues in operation throughout Ireland and Northern Ireland, save where title registration has been established.

The first attempt at title registration was the Record of Title (Ireland) Act 1865; this was inspired not only by the enactment of the 1862 statute in England, but also

---

[4] See P Coughlan, *Property Law* 2nd edn (Dublin, Gill and Macmillan, 1998); S Witchell, *Residential Property in Northern Ireland* (Belfast SLS Legal Publications (NI), 2000); H Wallace, *Land Registry Practice in Northern Ireland* (Belfast, SLS Legal Publications (NI) 1987).

[5] See ch 2 n 20.

[6] *Agra Bank Ltd v Barry* (1859) 9 Ir Ch R 512 and (1874) LR 7 HL 135.

by the presence of Sir Robert Torrens himself, now home from Australia and eager to promote good registration legislation.[7] Torrens himself drafted a Bill which was introduced in Parliament in 1864, but it was withdrawn in favour of one prepared by the Government. The 1865 Act is very similar in style and content to the English 1862 statute;[8] like that statute, and unlike the one drafted by Torrens, it failed to introduce compulsion, it did not set up an insurance fund, and it left the landowner free to deal by deed.[9] It proved to be a failure, and in 1891 was replaced by the Local Registration of Title (Ireland) Act.

Turning to the separate development of Ireland and Northern Ireland in the twentieth century, the current Irish title registration statute is the Registration of Title Act 1964. It provides for the dispositive registration of freehold titles and of leaseholds of over 21 years; in the absence of the 1925 legislation section 27 enables registration of full ownership of freehold land or of limited ownership in the case of settled land, and similarly for leaseholds. Individual titles have the familiar tripartite registers. Third party rights are not among the registrable estates, but appear as burdens upon registered titles. Section 31 guarantees the validity of the registered title and its appurtenant rights and burdens. There is no distinction between the registration and recording of burdens. Section 72(1) lists overriding interests, among them the rights of any person in actual occupation of the land, save where enquiry has been made of him and he has failed to disclose his rights. Title to land can be acquired by adverse possession just as if the land was unregistered, and the squatter registered in place of the registered proprietor; the position is thus as it was under the English 1925 Act, though without the unnecessary interposition of a trust.

Section 31 adds the following proviso to its guarantee of title:

. . . nothing in this Act shall interfere with the jurisdiction of any court of competent jurisdiction based on the ground of actual fraud or mistake, and the court may upon such ground make an order directing the register to be rectified in such manner and on such terms as it thinks fit.

Section 32 enables the registrar to rectify any error in a registration where the error has originated in the Land Registry, and section 120 provides for compensation in the event of rectification of an error. Irish writers are untroubled by the issue of indefeasibility and it is not clear either from the statute or from comment upon it what would be the position of an innocent purchaser tracing title through a forged disposition. Either the matter has never arisen or it has been dealt with by the registrar and remain unreported. The likelihood is that an English approach would be taken, based upon the proviso to section 31.[10]

---

[7] For a full account of the introduction of title registration in Ireland, see A Dowling, 'Of Ships and Sealing Wax: the Introduction of Land Registration in Ireland', (1993) 44 *Northern Ireland Law Quarterly* 360.

[8] Moreover, both use the term 'caveat' rather than 'notice', as do the Torrens statutes.

[9] See A Dowling, n 7 above.

[10] There is no mention of the problem in B Fitzgerald, *Land Registry Practice* 2nd edn (Dublin, The Round Hall Press, 1995); nor in *Land Registry Centenary, 1892–1992* (Dublin, The Land Registry,

The modern Northern Irish statute is the Land Registration Act (NI) 1970, as amended by the Registration (Land and Deeds) Order (NI) 1992. Like the Irish statute it is based on the English model, and provides for the registration of freeholds and of leaseholds with 21 years or more to run; again, there is no 1925 legislation. There is an 'actual occupation' overriding interest[11] and adverse possession operates as in the Irish, and English 1925, statutes.[12] Section 83(1) states:

Subject to the provisions of this Act with respect to compensation and to registered dispositions for valuable consideration, any dealing with registered land which, if unregistered, would be fraudulent and void shall, notwithstanding registration, be fraudulent and void in like manner.[13]

Section 69 enables the rectification of the register where there has been an incorrect registration, and this has been interpreted to include void and voidable dispositions, and the approach to indefeasibility replicates the English one.[14] Section 69(3) restricts the availability of rectification against the registered owner in possession of the land—an issue that the Irish statute has failed to address.

Title registration is by no means universal in either Ireland or Northern Ireland. Some types of transaction, eg acquisitions by a statutory authority, trigger first registration; and there are a few designated areas of compulsory registration. Outside these parameters, deeds registration continues.

SCOTLAND[14a]

To the English lawyer, Scots land law presents a wonderful mix of concepts. Scotland is a civil law country, where ownership is represented as dominium and where, therefore, we should not expect anything of the fragmentation characteristic of the common law. There is no law/equity distinction. Yet feudalism has survived intact, with subinfeudation still possible and the feudal chain from Crown to mesne lord to vassal alive and well, right up to the Abolition of Feudal Tenures etc (Scotland) Act 2000. Thus it could be said in 1996:

Only in one country in the world does feudalism survive in any real sense, albeit attenuated to an extreme degree. That country is Scotland.[15]

This necessitated some conceptual juggling; dominium was split into *dominium directum* (the ownership of the feudal superior) and *dominium utile* (that of the vassal who is, of course, for practical purposes the owner); the Crown as ultimate

---

1992), which however gives an excellent all–round picture of the Registry's activities including 'Men's Soccer in the Land Registry', at 112.

[11] Sch 5 para 15.

[12] S 53.

[13] Contrast the similar, but significantly different, wording of the English 1875 statute; see ch 6, at n 22.

[14] This is clear from Chapter VIII of H Wallace, see n 4 above; the English cases are relied upon.

[14a] I am most grateful to Stewart Brymer, of Thorntons WS, for reading this section in draft and for his helpful comments; the errors that remain are my own.

[15] KGC Reid, *The Law of Property in Scotland* (Edinburgh, Butterworths, 1996), para 45.

feudal lord has *dominium eminens*.[16] The Abolition of Feudal Tenure (Scotland) Act 2000—not in force until 28th November 2004 ("the appointed day")—provides:

"2 Consequences of abolition

(1) An estate of *dominium utile* of land shall, on the appointed day, cease to exist as a feudal estate but shall forthwith become the ownership of the land and, in so far as is consistent with the provisions of this Act, the land shall be subject to the same subordinate real rights and other encumbrances as was the estate of *dominium utile*.

(2) Every other feudal estate in land shall, on that day, cease to exist.

(3) It shall, on that day, cease to be possible to create a feudal estate in land."

Feudal landholding was combined, by the Registration Act 1671, with a dispositive form of deeds registration. Thus a disposition did not create a real right unless registered,[17] although the system gave no guarantee of validity; priority of instruments was determined solely by the time of registration.[18]

Title registration did not begin in Scotland until 1979 with the enactment of the Land Registration (Scotland) Act. The statute established the Land Register of Scotland under the control of the Keeper of the Registers of Scotland (section 1). Section 2 provides for unregistered ownership rights (including the long lease, defined by section 28(1) as a lease of over 20 years) to be registered on the occurrence of triggering events, very much along the lines of the English statute but with a smaller range of events: thus sale, and the grant or assignment of a long lease, but not the grant of a mortgage nor transmission on death. As happened in England, the areas of compulsory registration in Scotland have been increased gradually, beginning with just the County of Renfrew; the process was completed in 2003.

Once land has been brought onto the register, dispositions can no longer be registered in the Sasines Register. But land whose title is currently unregistered has, of course, been the subject of registration in the latter for centuries; so it would be possible, now that compulsory registration has been extended throughout Scotland, to complete the register by administrative action, simply transferring titles from one register to the other.[19]

The individual registers are known as title sheets, and are prepared for ownership rights and not for subsidiary rights; the latter are noted on the title sheets. Once ownership has been registered, subsidiary rights become registrable (section 2(3)). The statute makes no distinction between the registration and recording of third party rights; but by section 12(3) losses arising from an inability to enforce a real burden or condition entered in the title sheet are excluded from the indemnity provisions unless the Keeper has expressly assumed responsibility for the enforceability of the burden; ie the validity of burdens and conditions is not guaranteed unless this is done expressly.

[16] Reid, see n 15 above, para 52.
[17] *Young v Laith* (1847) 9 D 932.
[18] Reid, see n 15 above, para 91.
[19] As has happened in Ontario, where titles have been transferred administratively from the deeds register to the titles register. The possibility is noted in R Rennie (*et al*), *Scottish Conveyancing Legislation* (Edinburgh, W Green, 1998; looseleaf update May 2002), at C.044.1.

Overriding interests are listed in section 28(3), (a) to (i); there is no equivalent of the English and Irish provisions for the rights of those in actual occupation to be overriding.[20]

The provisions for indefeasibility follow the English rather than the Torrens model both in drafting style and in substance. Thus section 3(1) states that registration shall have the effect of 'vesting in the person entitled to the registered interest a real right in the interest' *subject only* to adverse rights entered on the title sheet and to overriding interests.[21] Section 9(1) enables the Keeper to rectify 'any inaccuracy' in the register. 'Inaccuracy' is given a very wide meaning[22] so as to include forgery. Section 9(3) protects from rectification the proprietor in possession, except where rectification gives effect to an overriding interest, or where the inaccuracy has been caused by his fraud or carelessness. Section 12 provides for indemnity, along lines very similar to the English provisions. The approach taken to indefeasibility replicates the English one, ie anything that could render a document void or voidable in unregistered land does so in registered land, subject to the protection of the proprietor in possession, and supplemented by the provisions for indemnity.

Thus *Scottish Conveyancing Statutes*[23] cites the case of *Taylor v Taylor* (then unreported). Mrs T owned land; a transfer to a Mrs H was forged, and Mrs H then mortgaged it to the North of England Building Society. Obviously Mrs H must be unprotected; the Building Society was not a proprietor in possession, and so the register was rectified and Mrs T regained her land. This replicates the English position and is the reverse of *Frazer v Walker*;[24] had the eventual registered proprietor been a proprietor in possession the result in *Frazer v Walker* would have been replicated, as it would in England, but on the basis of principles quite different from those deduced from a Torrens statute. Further development of this is seen in the two cases of *Short's Trustee v Keeper of the Registers of Scotland*[25] and *Short's Trustee v Chung*[26] whose cumulative effect was that a trustee in bankruptcy was able to retrieve properties transferred at an undervalue by a bankrupt, during the period of two years before his sequestration.[27]

Acquisition of title to land by possession alone is not normally possible, whether or not the land is registered. It is possible only on the basis of the registration of an invalid or inaccurate deed in the Register of Sasines or in the Land Register.[28]

---

[20] *Kaur v Singh* [1997] SCLR 1075.

[21] Emphasis added; compare the English provision, see ch 6 nn 63, 64.

[22] *Brookfield Developments Ltd v The Keeper of the Registers of Scotland* (1999) SLT (Land Tr) 105. See Rennie, n 19 above, C.044.9 ff and Reid, n 15 above, para 607.

[23] See n 19 above, at C.044.10.

[24] [1967] 1 AC 569.

[25] (1996) SC (HL) 14.

[26] (1998) SC 105 (OH) and (1999) SLT 7 (IH).

[27] During which his dispositions were liable to be rescinded (the Scottish term is 'reduced'). Rennie, see n 19 above, says that the decision has 'serious implications for the registration process'. See also KGC Reid, 'Void and voidable Deeds and the Land Register' (1996) 1 *Scottish Law and Practice Quarterly* 265. The problem is addressed in the English legislation by s 26 of the Land Registration Act 2002 (and by s 85 for the period after the bankruptcy order).

[28] RRM Paisley, *Land Law* (Edinburgh, W Green/Sweet & Maxwell, 2000).

The Land Register of Scotland has been developing plans for Automated Registration of Title to Land (this is the title of the project), and electronic dealing has been piloted by solicitors working in conjunction with the Land Register; the intention at present is that only dealings with the whole of the land in a title should be effected electronically.[29]

CONTINENTAL EUROPE

Most, but not all, European countries have a title registration system. Reference was made in chapter 1 to an *Inventory* compiled for the United Nations Economic Commission for Europe, which gives very basic information about the registration systems in operation.[30] A related document,[31] *Study on Key Aspects of Land Registration and Cadastral Legislation,*[32] gives rather more detailed information about 43 jurisdictions in Europe and Canada. It is clear that title registration is prevalent, and that most systems involve dispositive registration with varying levels of 'guaranteed title'.

Two practical features of European property law and conveyancing are particularly unfamiliar to the English lawyer and have a profound effect on the nature of title registration. One is the existence of the cadastre. A cadastre is a land record compiled principally for taxation purposes. It consists of both map and documentation; it records surveyed parcels of land, and shows their ownership, use, value and, where appropriate, productivity. The cadastre, and not the land register, is thus the descendant of the Roman census.[33] A cadastre is maintained throughout Europe, whether or not true title registration is also maintained—for example, in France, where, as we have seen, the system is one of deeds registration rather than title registration. Where both are in existence, the legal system needs a way of keeping each up to date with the other. The close relationship between register and cadastre is seen in the *Inventory* and *Study* referred to above.

The other unfamiliar feature is the notary. Unlike the English notary, he is an important feature of continental conveyancing; every document transferring or creating rights in land must be read to the parties by a notary, explained by him,

---

[29] See the website of the Registers of Scotland: http://www.ros.gov.uk/solicitor/artl.html.

[30] *Inventory of Land Administration Systems in Europe and North America* 3rd edn, 2001, a survey produced for the United Nations Economic Commission for Europe (UN/ECE), financed and published by HM Land Registry in London on behalf of the UNECE Working Party on Land Administration, to be found at http://www.unece.org/env/hs/wpla/docs/wpla_inv3.pdf.

[31] But not, as its web address seems to imply, an earlier edition of the same.

[32] Again produced by HM Land Registry for the UNECE; to be found, in two volumes, at http://www.unece.org/env/hs/wpla/docs/wpla_inv2_p1.pdf and /wpla_inv2_p2.pdf.

[33] See ch 2, n 1. Recall that suggestions of attempting something similar in England met with opposition; the nearest we have to a cadastre is the Ordnance Survey, which by contrast is just a map, not a documentary record of parcels.

and signed in his presence.[34] He must be given proof of the identity of the parties, who normally have to execute documents before him in person; he acts for both parties, and is subject to strict professional regulation. This has implications for issues surrounding indefeasibility; it does not make forgery, or impersonation, impossible, but does make it rather less likely and provides a better safeguard than does the English system. This is an increased concern here in the light of the abolition of land certificates,[35] which did at least provide one more check on the identity of the client walking into the solicitor's office asking for conveyancing services. The English system is not specially rigorous in ensuring that the John Smith who walks in really is John Smith (and consider the difficulties posed by the client who can prove that he is John Smith but is not, in fact, the *right* John Smith. . .).

GERMANY[36]

The antiquity of the German system of title registration has already been remarked upon, as has its influence upon the developers of title registration in England and Australasia.[37] The modern form of registration in Germany was created out of the various ancient forms in the late nineteenth century when a unified Germany, after 1871, worked out its constitution and administration. Thus substantive land law is contained in the German civil code, the *Bürgerliches Gesetzbuch,* while the administrative regulation of the register, the *Grundbuch,* is to be found in the *Grundbuchordnung,* first compiled in 1897; title registration remains a matter for federal law, although it is administered by the local courts. All titles were registered, free of charge, by administrative action in the early twentieth century.[38]

The cadastre was developed during the nineteenth century, and enabled the completion of title register; the cadastre, however, is a matter for the law of the 16 individual states within Germany rather than for federal control. Nevertheless the *Grundbuch* and the *Kataster* are kept up to date with each other; transfers effected through the *Grundbuch* are communicated to the cadastre, while transfers of part of a parcel of land must be co-ordinated through both institutions.[39] Following

---

[34] As must, for example, marriage contracts.

[35] See ch 3, at n 27.

[36] This section has been written using NG Foster and S Sule, *German Legal System and Laws* 3rd ed, (Oxford, OUP, 2002) pp 440 ff, and the material and web pages cited below. I am most grateful to Jan-Bertram Hillig, Assessor, Universität zu Köln, for reading the section in draft and making comments and providing additional information and explanation.

[37] See ch 1, n 42.

[38] Simpson, *Land Registration,* 419.

[39] Simpson, *Land Registration,* 420–21; W Hawerk, 'Grundbuch and Cadastral Systems in Germany, Austria and Switzerland', at http://www.fig7.org.uk/events/Delft_seminar_95/paper3.html and W Hawerk, in 'ALKIS—Germany's way into a cadastre for the 21st century' at http://www.fig.net/figtree/pub/proceedings/korea/abstracts/pdf/session16/hawerk–abs.pdf

'Only Grundbuch and cadastre in combination are able to give a complete overview about legal and de facto land tenure. Both registers must be constantly updated and kept in correspondence with each other.'

the reunification of Germany in 1990, title registration and the cadastre were re-established in the former East German states.[40]

The Grundbuch and the cadastre are both now held in electronic form. Originally the map component of the cadastre and the descriptive component used incompatible software; currently software is being developed which will integrate the two aspects of the cadastre as well as being compatible with the *Grundbuch* software so that the two systems can, as we must be tempted to say, talk to each other.[41]

Turning to specific issues of title registration:

The Nature of Registration

The *Grundbuch* is made up, like the English Land Register, of individual registers of plots of land, each with a title number. The individual register is in three parts; the first part shows current and past owners; the second shows third party rights such as servitudes (easements); the third shows security rights. Registration under the *Grundbuchordnung* is dispositive; real rights arising from transactions between individuals have no effect unless they are registered.[42] The dispositive nature of registration is far more powerful than it can be in the English and Torrens systems, for there is no possibility of a property right existing in equitable form if it remains unregistered.[43] It simply cannot exist without *both* notarised agreement and registration. Certain charges and real rights arising under public law may nevertheless arise without registration, and a purchaser must make enquiries of Local Authorities—as he must in England. Equally, of course, the system must take account of off-register events such as the death of the registered proprietor, in which case the heirs become the owners without registration.[44]

Because the notarised agreement does not itself confer property rights, there is a 'registration gap',[45] as no proprietary rights are created until registration. Accordingly, at the point of application for registration a notice (*Auflassungsvormerkung*) is entered in the register, preventing adverse dispositions pending the registration in question.[46] This is the equivalent of the search with priority in the English and Torrens systems.

---

[40] W Hawerk, see n 39 above ('ALKIS'), states that this was an important element in the establishment of a market economy in the former socialist part of the country.

[41] W Hawerk, see n 39, ('Grundbuch . . .' and 'ALKIS') above.

[42] BGB para 873 requires both agreement and registration for validity.

[43] 'What is not in the "files" (Land Register) is legally not in the world'; German response to the UNECE *Study*, n 32 above, qu 11.

[44] G-S Hök, 'Law of Land Registration and Mortgages in Germany' (http:///www.eurojurislawjournal.net/Hypothekenrecht/Bericht–Deutschland.html) p 5.

[45] Again, of course, its nature is different from that in a common law system, because the notarised agreement (equivalent to the deed of transfer) has no proprietary effect without registration.

[46] G-S Hök, see n 44 above, p 2 and n 4.

What Can be Registered

Quite simply, ownership and all real rights over land. Thus the German system has reached the point to which the English one may perhaps be tending;[47] that either a right is registered and valid, or it is non-existent. Rights include servitudes, restrictive covenants, long leases,[48] condominium rights,[49] usufructs and security rights.

Treatment of Third-party Rights

All proprietary rights must be registered in order to be valid. There is no parallel at all to the English/Torrens concept of recording rather than registering third party rights. Priority is in order of registration.[50]

Security rights are of three kinds, recognised by the German civil code (the *Bürgerliches Gesetzbuch*, or BGB). The *Hypothek* is a straightforward mortgage and secures a debt.[51] The land charge (*Grundschuld*) is a charge over land which usually secures a debt but need not do so, and for that reason is rather more flexible than the *Hypothek*.[52] The annuity payment (*Rentenschuld*) secures payments of money at definite intervals.[53]

The *Hypothek* and the *Grundschuld* exist in two forms; the *Briefhypothek* and the *Buchhypothek*, the *Briefgrundschuld* and the *Buchgrundschuld*. All must appear on the *Grundbuch* in order to be valid; but the *Brief-* form, ie the form accompanied by a letter, is the normal form, and is easier to transfer. The entry on the register for the *Briefhypothek* does not state the identity of the creditor; and the security right can be transferred to a third party by handing over the *Brief*, the mortgage document, without making any entry in the *Grundbuch*.

An *Hypothek* cannot exist without a debt. But it may be transformed, as follows. Suppose that A owns a house; he has borrowed 20,000 Euro from B and 20,000 from C. Both claims are secured by an *Hypothek*, and B's has priority over C's. When A repays his debt to B, the *Hypothek* that secured it is transferred to A himself[54] and becomes an *Eigentümergrundschuld* (it cannot remain a *Hypothek* as there is no debt).[55] A now has a security right on his own house which takes

---

[47] See ch 8, text at n 35.

[48] These take the form of a 'heritable right to a building' (*Erbbaurechte*); the lease is of the building, not the land. They are normally of 75 or 99 years (German response to the UNECE *Study*, n 32 above, qu 16).

[49] Regulated separately by the *Wohnungseigentumsgesetz*. Flat owners co–own the land, while owning their apartment absolutely. See the German response to the UNECE *Study*, n 32 above, qu 14.

[50] G–S Hök, see n 44 above, p 10.

[51] BGB para 1113–1190.

[52] BGB para 1191 ff.

[53] BGB para 1199 ff.

[54] BGB para 1163, subs 1.

[55] BGB para 1177, subs 1.

priority to C's; when A wants to borrow again, he can offer the creditor, in English terms, a first mortgage.

Indefeasibility

The German registration system is uncompromising on the issue of indefeasibility; one of its fundamental principles is that the register is to be taken as correct in both the positive and negative senses for the purchaser in good faith.

The position is thus close to Torrens-style deferred indefeasibility, in its ethos and its practical application. For registration does not cure a defective transfer—eg one that is void or voidable; and the victim of fraud may apply to set a disposition aside. Once he discovers the wrongdoing, he may enter an objection (*Widerspruch*[56]) in the Register, which prevents a subsequent good faith acquisition, while the matter is sorted out. But in the absence of such proceedings, a purchaser may rely on the register. If, despite the safeguards of the notarial system, a forged transfer is registered, the purchaser who buys or takes any other disposition of the land in good faith is protected; provided he did not know of the mistake, fraud, etc he keeps the land.[57] The 'true' owner's title is extinguished[58] and he must seek a remedy in unjust enrichment against the person who was wrongfully registered.[59] The purchaser is not in good faith if he had actual knowledge of the incorrect entry, or when an objection is registered.

Where there has been an error in the register, caused by registry officials, an indemnity is payable to anyone who loses out as a result.[60]

Adverse Possession

It is not possible to acquire land by possession adverse to the registered owner. But a person wrongfully registered as owner will acquire title after 30 years' occupation in the absence of objection.[61] Boundary disputes are not dealt with by adverse possession; the cadastral system involves the assumption that surveyed boundaries can always be objectively determined.[62]

---

[56] BGB para 892.
[57] An example is given in G–S Hök, see n 44 above, p 3.
[58] BGB para 936.
[59] BGB para 816.
[60] German response to the UNECE *Study*, n 32 above, qu 22.
[61] BGB para 900.
[62] Compare those Torrens jurisdictions where adverse possession of a registered estate is not permitted; and note that throughout Australasia boundaries are surveyed.

POLAND

This section has been written by Dr Magdalena Habdas, of the University of Silesia.

The Nature of Registration

In Polish law, the main provisions concerning land registration are contained in the Land Register and Mortgages Act 1982 (LRM),[63] while more detailed matters have been dealt with in an Ordinance concerning the Implementation of the Land Register and Mortgages Act (OLRM).[64] According to article 1 of the LRM, the purpose of the land register is to evidence the legal state of the land in question. Consequently, a separate land register is to be kept for each parcel of land. This basic rule has not, however, been completely implemented and some land remains unregistered.

Entries in the register are, as a rule, not dispositive, ie it is not the entry itself which causes the change in title, but the legal activity undertaken by the parties. Ownership passes from one party to another by virtue of a concluded contract (the form of a notarial deed is obligatory), regardless of whether a suitable entry in the register is subsequently made or not.[65]

Such a situation is highly undesirable, since the goal of the register is to reflect the factual legal status of real property, not merely the identity of the current proprietor. Therefore the proprietor of land is obliged to file, without delay, a motion for a suitable entry of any changes in the legal status of the real property; if the title is not yet registered his application is treated as an application for first registration. Failure to do so may result in the proprietor's liability for losses third parties incur as a result of a violation of that obligation.[66]

In addition, if a notarised deed contains any changes of rights entered in the land register, the notary public is obliged to prepare a motion for suitable changes to be made in the land register.[67] Consequently, the danger of land register entries being obsolete is greatly diminished, though not completely removed.

Special legal provisions may, however, render an entry of a given right in the land register dispositive, i.e. necessary to effect legal changes in the legal status of a parcel of land. Currently, the following require a dispositive entry in the register:

1. The creation and transfer of the perpetual usufruct right.
   The perpetual usufruct resembles an English building lease. It allows the entitled person to use the land and to erect specified buildings. It is established for

[63] Dz.U.82, Nr 19, poz 147, with later amendments.
[64] Dz.U.92, Nr 29, poz 128, with later amendments.
[65] E Gniewek, *Prawo rzeczowe (Land Law)*, (Warsaw, CH Beck, 2000), 104–105.
[66] Art 35 s (1) and (2) LMR.
[67] Art 92 s (4) Notary Public Law Act 1991, Dz.U.91, Nr 22, poz 91 with later amendments.

a term certain, normally 99 years, but not less than 40 years. The entitled person pays an initial lump sum and then yearly rent. In Poland this right may only be created on land owned by the State Treasury or the local authority. It is a third party right, not ownership.[68]

2. The creation of a condominium right.
3. The creation of a right to demand a condominium right.
4. The transfer of a limited real right over land (e.g. usufruct, easements, mortgage) if the right is already entered in the land register.
5. The creation of a mortgage, and the rescission of a mortgage without the simultaneous rescission of the debt secured by the mortgage.[69]

The register kept for each separate parcel of land is tied to that land and not to its proprietor. It consists of four chapters, divided into parts and sections. The first chapter is divided into two parts. Chapter one, part one identifies the land (the most important information includes: data from the cadastre with survey numbers, the postal address, the area of the land, and the numbers of any previous registers kept for it).[70] Chapter one, part two enumerates rights tied to the right of ownership.[71]

Chapter two consists of three sections. They identify the proprietors of the land, and persons who have the right of perpetual usufruct. The legal bases for acquiring these rights are named (eg contract in the form of a notarial deed, a court order regulating inheritance matters, etc.).[72]

Chapter three is devoted to limited real rights over land (ownership or perpetual usufruct) other than mortgages, as well as to personal (obligation) rights.[73] Chapter four is dedicated to mortgages. It contains information about the amount secured by the mortgage and the legal relationship this amount is based on.[74]

Summarising the above: the Polish system of land registration allows interested parties to see in one document the details of the legal status of a given piece of land. The most important pieces of information include: the identity of the proprietor (owner), the rights burdening the right of ownership, and some (but not all) of the third-party rights (whether real or personal) burdening the land. There is no need to trace back a chain of title through previous transactions. Nevertheless, entries in the register are not, as a rule, dispositive, but are legally obligatory and their neglect may lead to civil liability.

---

[68] S Rudnicki, *Prawo obrotu nieruchomo_ciami (The law of conveyancing)*, (Warsaw, CH Beck, 1996), 43—69.

[69] See S Rudnicki, *Komentarz do ustawy o ksi_gach wieczystych i hipotece oraz do przepisów o post_powaniu w sprawach wieczystoksi_gowych (Commentary to the Land Register and Mortgage Act and to the provisions on the land register procedure)*, (Warsaw, Wydawnictwo Prawnicze, 2002), 17.

[70] §20 and §21 OLRM.

[71] §23 OLRM.

[72] §24 OLRM.

[73] §26 OLRM.

[74] §27 OLRM.

What Can be Registered?

Individual registers are kept for each parcel of land, although it is more precise to state that they are kept for separate ownership rights.[75] Consequently, the main right registered is the right of ownership. All other registered rights must in some way pertain to the right of ownership of the land.

The right of perpetual usufruct is a distinct real right. It is something less than ownership, and more than the so-called limited real rights. Its importance is reflected by the fact that it is entered in the second chapter of the register, along with the right of ownership. It is important to remember that the entry of perpetual usufruct in the register leads to the creation of this right. Entries in chapters three and four will relate to either the ownership right or to the right of perpetual usufruct. The entries will clearly denote which right is burdened.

The basic rule is that the land register reflects real rights (i.e. rights effective *erga omnes*, against all the world) pertaining to a given piece of land. The catalogue of these rights is a closed one and consists of the following rights: Ownership, perpetual usufruct, and limited real rights, namely: usufruct, easements (servitudes), right to residential premises in a co-operative, right to business premises in a co-operative, right to a single-family house in a co-operative, mortgage.[76]

For the three co-operative rights mentioned above, separate registers may be kept, as an exception to the rule that a book is kept only for the ownership right.[77] In such a case chapter two identifies the co-operative right in question, and chapters three and four reflect burdens over this right. In practice, a very important burden on the co-operative right is a mortgage, and indeed, a register is usually created when the holder of the co-operative right wishes to secure a mortgage on this right. This is because a mortgage is created not at the time of concluding a contract, but at the time of entry into the land register. It is not, however, compulsory to keep a register (book) on the co-operative limited real right.[78]

The remaining limited real rights (usufruct, easements, mortgage) are entered into chapter three or four of the register kept for the ownership (or ownership and perpetual usufruct) of a specific piece of land. They are treated as burdens on ownership or perpetual usufruct.

It is important to note that the creation (validity) of the right of usufruct and servitudes (easements) does not require the entry of these rights in the register. However, limited real rights entered in the register have priority over those not entered. In case of two or more limited real rights entered in the register, priority attaches to the right in respect of which the motion to make an entry was filed earlier. Also, as already mentioned, once a limited real right has been entered in the

---

[75] J Ignatowicz, *Prawo rzeczowe (Land Law)*, (Warsaw, PWN, 1994), 301–02.
[76] E Gniewek, see n 65 above, 20.
[77] Art 1§3 LRM.
[78] S Rudnicki, see n 68 above, 99.

register, any changes of that right must also be entered, in order to be legally effective (the entry is dispositive in nature).[79]

Despite the fact that land registers are maintained to reflect real rights, article 16 LRM allows for some personal rights and claims to be entered.[80] Examples include: a leasehold (in Polish law this is only an obligation right, not an interest in land), the right of pre-emption, the claim to transfer the ownership of property, etc. Once a personal right or a claim has been entered in the register it becomes effective against rights acquired subsequently.[81] Consequently, the lessee whose right is entered in the register, has a right effective not only against the original lessor, but also against the acquirer of the land.

Treatment of Third-party Rights

This question has been, to a large extent, addressed above. According to Article 3 LRM, it is rebuttably presumed that rights entered in the register (whether real, personal, or claims) are valid and that ones which have been deleted are no longer valid. The presumption does not, however, indicate that no other rights burden the right of ownership. This is a consequence of the principle that only some entries are dispositive in nature.

Indefeasibility

The question of indefeasibility is dealt with in article 5 LRM. The basic rule is, that when there is a discrepancy between the legal status shown in the register (the book) and the actual legal status, a person who acquired a right trusting the entry in the register is protected. There are, however, a number of conditions which have to be met:

1) the acquisition must be made through an act in law which is a *successio singularis* (sale, donation, exchange); acquisitions through administrative decisions, inheritance, long use, or execution proceedings are not protected.[82]
2) the acquisition must concern one of the rights entered in the register,[83]
3) the acquisition cannot be a gratuitous one (payment must be made),[84]
4) the acquirer (not the vendor!) must be in good faith (bad faith denotes a state in which the acquirer knew that there was a discrepancy between the register and the actual legal status, or who could have easily found out about this discrepancy).[85]

---

[79] Art 248 Polish Civil Code 1964 (PCC), Dz.U.64, Nr 16, poz 93, with later amendments.
[80] S Rudnicki, see n 68 above, 84.
[81] Art 17 LRM.
[82] Art 5 LRM.
[83] Art 5 LRM.
[84] Art 6 s (1) LRM.
[85] Art 6 s (2).

Article 5 can only work in *favour* of the acquirer in good faith. Therefore, if the register shows encumbrances which are no longer valid (eg usufruct, when the time it was created for has elapsed), they will still not become effective.[86] Conversely, if the register does not show encumbrances which are valid, and do exist, the acquirer will acquire ownership free from these encumbrances. Therefore, persons who choose not to enter their limited real rights, personal rights or claims on the register risk losing them if an acquisition under Article 5 LRM takes place. The above rule does not apply to four rights enumerated in Article 7 LRM (encumbrances which exist *ex lege*, the right of annuity, easement of necessary way,[87] easements created by administrative decisions). They remain valid, even if an acquisition under Article 5 LRM takes place, and these rights were not reflected in the register.

The most common type of discrepancy which may occur between the legal status shown in the register, and the actual legal status of the land is a situation in which X has transferred ownership to Y1, but before a notice of this is made in the register,[88] X transfers ownership to Y2, who is in good faith—the double conveyance situation. According to Articles 5, 6, and 7 LRM, if all the above conditions are met, Y2 acquires ownership, and Y1 loses his right. Y1 may only seek civil damages from X according to tortious or contractual liability; criminal liability may also arise. Y2's ownership need not be registered—his protection derives from reliance upon the register rather than upon his own registration.[89]

Where X transfers to Y and the transfer has been forged by someone else, X has no title. The transfer would probably be held to be void, and if any entry had been made in the register, that entry would be changed; X would have to apply to the court to establish that no contract existed. But if, before X took action, Y transferred to Z, who bought in good faith, Z's title would be secure.

The proper implementation of Article 5 LRM largely depends on the effectiveness of the courts that maintain the registers. The time which elapses between filing an application for an entry and the entry being made must be as short as possible. Unfortunately, in Poland this system is still not as effective as it should be, and there are some courts which do not even have the land register within a computerised system.

Adverse possession

According to Article 172 PCC it is possible to acquire ownership of land by long use if the following conditions are met:

---

[86] E Gniewek, see n 65, 292.

[87] It is created when land has no suitable access to a public road.

[88] A notice precedes the entry; if a notice is in the register, Art 5 LRM does not apply.

[89] Compare the Finnish system; contrast the position in Denmark and Norway where protection depends upon subsequent registration—see n 92 below. Contrast the German and Dutch systems, where the issue does not arise as Y2 cannot acquire without registration.

1. The person in question is an autonomous possessor (ie he possesses the land physically—*corpus*, and behaves as if he were the owner—*animus*)
2. He must be an autonomous possessor for 20 years if he is in good faith, and 30 years if he is in bad faith. The existence of good or bad faith is identified at the time possession was first obtained; if a person obtained possession in good faith, and later discovers that he is not the owner, that does not mean that he was in bad faith.

Once the required time period has elapsed, the person in question becomes the owner *ex lege*. However this fact should be confirmed by the court—only then will the new owner have proof of acquiring ownership and will be able to file a motion for an entry to be made in the land register.

It is possible to acquire the right of perpetual usufruct by long use, if the right has already been created, but a person other than the one originally entitled is in possession and behaves as if he were the perpetual usufruct holder. The requirements concerning time and good/bad faith are the same as described above with respect to ownership.[90] It is also possible to acquire easements by long use, but only if they involve the use of permanent and visible equipment, eg a paved road (but not an unmade road), a water well, etc.

FINLAND

This section has been written by Prof. Matti Ilmari Niemi, of the Lappeenranta University of Technology.

The Nature of Registration

The nature of registration of title is determined by the Finnish Real Estate Code (540/1995). The Finnish and Swedish systems are closely related; their laws have originated from the German system adopted in the German Civil Code. The German system was not, however, adopted as such in the Nordic Countries; for instance, the dispositive nature of registration was never adopted in Finland. Moreover, most of the leading principles of German Property Law are not recognised as such.

Finland adopted the continental legal system and therefore concepts such as common law or equity are unknown.

Traditionally and in accordance with the German model, the Nordic registration systems have been dualistic. The cadastre is called the Real Estate Register, and the register of title is the Title and Mortgage Register. Technically, the Title and Mortgage Register is based on the Real Estate Register. Both registers are public, centralised (national) and maintained by public officials.

[90] Art 237 PCC.

The ownership of land is transferred by way of a written document which must be attested by a notary. When in the hands of the transferee, the same document is a deed. Registration presupposes the existence of a formally valid deed. After having acquired land or a share thereof, the new owner is required to apply for the registration of his title, on pain of a fine and/or increased taxation.

The transferee's title is registered on the strength of the registered title of his predecessor and the valid deed of transfer; registration is sufficient proof of ownership. But registration only influences third-party relations and not those between the parties to the contract (although it may amend formal defects as between the parties: see below). Thus a registered title is not a necessary or an exclusive proof; the transferee can prove his ownership to individuals, including public officials, by producing the deed of transfer.

The transferee can rely upon the registered information in both the positive and negative senses. A registered title is sufficient proof of the validity of the ownership of the transferor and of the third-party rights that burden the land, subject, however, to the rules of constructive notice (the presupposition of good faith). Protection is provided on condition that the transferee did not know, nor should have known, that the transferor was not the rightful titleholder or that there were unregistered third-party rights. Similar rules apply to the grantees of special rights and liens (mortgages). The content of the Title and Mortgage Register is assumed to be public knowledge.

The contemporary Finnish Title and Mortgage Register exists in electronic form. It would be easy to adopt a system of electronic conveyances, but there are as yet no official plans for such an undertaking in Finland.

What Can be Registered?

The construction of the transfer of ownership is the point of departure in title registration. The acquisition of a title to a piece of land must be registered (again, on pain of financial penalties). Registration officials investigate both the formal and substantial validity of the transfer.

Nowadays, the information on land owners provided by the Title and Mortgage Register is comprehensive and updated sufficiently on the basis of information provided by the notary; registration has been compulsory for a very long time. All significant limited property rights over real property can be registered. Mortgages are used as security rights. The remaining rights are called special rights and are burdens on titles. An exhaustive list of these rights is given in the Code of Real Estate, although the *numerus clausus* principle, that is, the limited and distinct number of property rights, is not acknowledged at the general level. A lease or other kind of usufruct, the right to an annuity from land, the right to remove timber, and the right to extract land or mineral resources or other comparable rights of extraction may be registered; moreover, it is obligatory to register the most important usufructs. This obligation is applied when a lease or another usufruct is freely transferable and the lessee may build or owns buildings on the land. Such a right can be the object of a mortgage as well as of a lien. The possible terms for different kinds of leases are given in the Lease Act (258/1966).

Registration is necessary in order for real property to be used as security. The most important securities for loans are liens based on mortgages. An owner can apply for a mortgage over his land. When the mortgage is granted, the applicant will be issued with a mortgage instrument (a document that is a special kind of security deed). A lien is raised by submitting the mortgage instrument to a creditor as the security for a debt.[91]

In addition to liens established by the above-described agreements, statutory liens are acknowledged by the Finnish law. Under public law, land can be a security for a debt or fee by virtue of a special act. In this case, a statutory lien is entered into the register by public officials.

Treatment of Third-party Rights

According to section 1 of chapter 14 of the Code of Real Estate, all important limited property rights over land, other than liens, are registrable as special rights. As far as their priority and protection are concerned, they are, in principle, equivalent in strength to ownership. In situations of conflict, chronological priority is the principal rule. Exceptions can be made on the ground of constructive notice.

There are, however, other special rights as well, some of which may, but do not have to, be registered. As a rule, these special rights do not bind the transferee of land unless he has actual notice of them.

Registered easements and rights of ways are strong burdens on titles. They are not registrable in the Title and Mortgage Register but are entered into the Real Estate Register. As arrangements between pieces of land, they are seen as being parts of the extents of the estates and means of organising the use of these estates rather than the property rights that belong to certain persons.

Indefeasibility

Registration does not in any way restrict the voidability of conveyances between the contracting parties. Nordic countries have similar rules on the invalidity and adjustment of contracts (the Nordic Contract Acts, in Finland 228/1929); the consequences of a voidable disposition of land depend upon whether the reason for voidability was 'strong' or 'weak'. Where the reason was a weak one, for example X transfers to Y as a result of a fraudulent inducement by a third party, if Y is in good faith then the disposition is valid. A disposition which is invalid for a strong reason cannot be validated by the good faith of the transferee. Grave duress and forgery are examples of these strong reasons.

[91] Compare the German *Eigentümergrundschuld*, n 55 above.

What is the position where Y takes the land through a voidable disposition and transfers the land to Z? In that event, registration can amend the defect and give Z protection against the rightful titleholder. According to section 4 of chapter 13 of the Code of Real Estate an acquisition shall be permanent, even if Y was not the rightful titleholder due to a defect in his acquisition or in X's acquisition, if Y's title registered at the time of acquisition and Z at that time was not aware, nor should have been aware, that Y was not the rightful titleholder. This 'legitimation effect' takes place immediately upon the transfer to Z.[92] The same rule applies to a share and parcel of an estate and even to a registrable leasehold. Similar rules apply to the acquisitions of special rights and liens. However, where the transfer to Y was voidable for a 'strong' reason, Z is not protected; for example, if the transfer was forged or grave duress has been used. The same holds true if the transferor has been erroneously registered as the titleholder or if the entry in the register is not based on the decision of the registering authority.

There are also secondary and complementary rules for the state's liability for compensation. The Finnish state compensates damage caused by the indefeasibility of defective acquisitions and guarantees the trustworthiness of the Title and Mortgage Register. Where a person (X in our example) loses his title by virtue of the above-mentioned section 4, he has the right to compensation from state funds; conversely, a transferee or the holder of a lien or special right who loses their right to the land by virtue of a strong reason for voidability, has the same right to compensation.

As far as double conveyances are concerned, corresponding rules apply. The principal rule is chronological priority: the earlier acquisition prevails. According to section 3 of chapter 13 of the Code of Real Estate, the later conveyance, nevertheless, takes precedence if the purchaser's title is registered first, provided that he was not aware, nor should have been aware, of the previous conveyance. Similar rules apply to a share or a parcel of a piece of land and to acquisitions of special rights or liens when conflicting with a conveyance of real property. However, no state compensation is provided to the loser in this kind of a conflict.

Adverse Possession

One significant feature of the rules described above is that the protection of a transferee takes place immediately and no possession is required. These rules are, however, new in Finland. Before the new Code of Real Estate came into force (1.1.1997) in Finland, such protection was provided only on the ground of a fixed period of enjoyment (possession). Moreover, there were rules of immemorial enjoyment and prescription.

There is still one rule protecting enjoyment in the contemporary code (section 10 of chapter 13). A person whose title to a piece of land has been registered and

---

[92] As it does in Sweden, whereas in Denmark and Norway it does not take effect until registration of Z's title.

who remains in possession for 10 years may keep the land if, at the time of acquisition, he did not know, nor should have known, that the land had been taken from the rightful titleholder. It is noteworthy that this rule provides protection, even when there was a strong reason for voidability in a prior transfer, and it can amend defects between contracting parties. There are no corresponding rules for special rights or liens.

THE NETHERLANDS

The Netherlands is included here by way of contrast, as it has a deeds register which, in conjunction with the cadastre, very much resembles a title register. The following account has been written by Dr Lars van Vliet of the University of Maastricht.

The Nature of Registration

Dutch law has two closely connected registers for the administration of land which complement each other: the cadastre (*kadaster*) and the deeds register (*openbare registers*). The cadastre is an instrument of public law originally set up for reasons of taxation. It is based on the registration of separate plots of land which all have a unique number; a plot of land is called '*perceel*' (cf. 'parcel'). The entry of every parcel shows its owner and any limited real rights burdening the land, such as a hypothec. All rights other than full ownership appear in the cadastre as burdens on the right of ownership of a certain parcel. The cadastre also contains information about public law regulations (eg planning law).

The cadastre, however, is meant only to give easy access to the deeds register. The deeds register should be regarded as the genuine register. A transfer of ownership of land is valid only if the deed of transfer is registered in the deeds register, and ownership passes at the moment of registration in the deeds register. Some time after this registration the civil servants at the Registry will update the cadastre, which will not only mention the name of the new owner, but also the number of the deed transferring ownership to the current owner.

If the civil servants fail to update the register properly, this has no effect upon the passing of ownership. A third party relying solely on the cadastre will not be protected. He should always check the deeds register itself (see Article 3:23 BW[93]). The Registry, if its officials are at fault, will have to compensate any losses the third party incurred (Article 117 *Kadasterwet*). The provisions protecting third parties, which will be explained below, all refer to omissions or mistakes in the deeds register, not to omissions or mistakes in the cadastre.

---

[93] The Civil Code of 1992.

Before the transfer of land takes place the buyer of land, or of a real right, should check the deeds register. This register is in effect a huge pile of deeds each having its own individual number; the cadastre provides the number of the deed, without which it cannot be traced. The cadastre is searchable on name of the owner, parcel or address. In practice the notary acting for the transferor and acquirer will check the cadastre and deeds register. In principle he has to examine all deeds younger than 20 years (the longest limitation period in land law). In practice he will commonly check only the last deed giving the current owner his right of ownership, thus relying on correct examination of the register by the previous notary who in his turn relies on the work of his predecessor.[94]

In the following the deeds register will often be referred to as the register.

What Can be Registered?

To maximise reliability of the register every legal act by which a real right in land is created, transferred or released must be entered in the register in order to have legal effect. This rule applies equally to full ownership and limited real rights, such as the hypothec (which has the same function as a mortgage, but does not involve a transfer to the creditor).

The fact that registration of these legal acts is dispositive means that the legal effect of the notarial deed embodying the transfer, creation or release is postponed until the date of registration of the deed. It should be stressed that if the deed or the underlying contract on the basis of which the deed has been drafted is void or has been avoided, registration does not heal this defect. It does not turn a flawed transaction into a valid transaction. Moreover, real rights may exist off the register, and may affect third parties; on the other hand, real rights may appear on the register which do not exist or no longer exist.

In principle the register cannot be relied on. At the same time, important provisions exist which protect the innocent third party against flaws in the register. As a result, in many situations the third party will be protected. There is no State guarantee of title.[95] Nevertheless, the Dutch registration system gives fairly accurate information about the legal status of land.

Article 3:17 subsection 1 BW lists a number of rights and relevant facts that may be entered in the deeds register.[96] The creation, transfer and release of real rights do not work without registration, even between the parties; and all other facts mentioned in Article 3:17 subsection 1 BW can be registered voluntarily. Non-

---

[94] This has always been unacceptable in English conveyancing practice, which is why the nineteenth century reformers regarded the repetitive examination of title as one of the reasons for moving to title registration; see ch 2, n 39.

[95] However, the State or the Registry may under certain conditions be liable for compensation, for example if the register is incorrect or incomplete due to a mistake made by a civil servant working at the registry office (see Art 3:30 BW and Art 117 *Kadasterwet*).

[96] This list is not exhaustive as special legislation may make certain facts and rights capable of being registered.

registration, however, often entails the risk that the fact in question does not work against an innocent third party. Registration of these facts, although not compulsory, is prudent. An example of a fact which it is prudent to register is the assignment of a debt secured by a charge over land. The assignee of the debt automatically becomes the new holder of the charge. The assignor, however, is still registered as the holder of the charge. Another example is avoidance of a sale and transfer of land. Upon avoidance, ownership of the land automatically reverts to the transferor, but the transferee is still registered as the owner. He could therefore give a good title to an innocent third party until the register is rectified. To prevent third party protection the transferor should enter in the register that the transaction has been avoided. Similarly, if the transfer took place under a condition subsequent, fulfilment of the condition reverts ownership to the transferor. To prevent third party protection the transferor should have the fulfilment of the condition registered.

Treatment of Third-party Rights

This has been addressed above. Leases call for special mention, as their treatment is rather different from that in English law.

There are different forms of lease, some of which are seen as real rights[97] and some of which are seen as contracts.[98] The distinction derives from Roman law, under which the contractual forms did not bind third parties. This is no longer true in modern continental systems. The contract of lease binds the new owner, who automatically becomes the new landlord. He is subrogated to the contract. Accordingly the practical difference between contracts of lease and real rights of lease is less relevant than it used to be. Still, for different reasons, contracts of lease cannot be registered, whereas real rights of lease can and must be registered. Article 3:17 subsection 2 BW states that lease contracts and facts which create or release personal rights cannot be registered. No distinction is made between long and short leases. Enabling contractual leases to be registered would create a danger for tenants. True, the creation of the contract would be valid without registration, but an unregistered lease would not bind an innocent acquirer of the leased land. Most tenants would not think of having their contract registered. At present the contract binds even without registration. The acquirer's interests are subordinated to the tenant's interests.

Indefeasibility

The register does not guarantee that all rights and facts which appear in the register are valid or true. In principle the register cannot be trusted. Since 1992,

---

[97] *Erfpacht* (*emphytheusis*), *opstal* (comparable to building lease where building does not become a fixture).
[98] *Huur* and *pacht* (the latter is the agricultural lease).

however, third party protection has increased considerably. To a large extent innocent third parties are protected against incorrectness and incompleteness of the
register. The provisions giving this protection are very technical. Examples are as
follows:

Double Sale

X agrees to sell land to Y1. Afterwards, and before the transfer to Y1 takes place, X
sells the same land to Y2. The contract X-Y1 is not binding upon Y2, even if Y2
knows about it. Only in extreme cases, where Y2 misuses his personal relationship
with X to incite him to sell the same land to Y2, can Y1 obtain ownership of the
land in an indirect way: the fact that Y2 knowingly incites X to a breach of contract
in these circumstances is seen as a tort, and the judge can order Y2 to pay damages
in kind by ordering him to transfer ownership of the land to Y1.[99]

Defects in a Previous Transaction

Let us take the following example: X sells and transfers his land to Y. Subsequently,
Y sells and transfers the same land to Z. X entered into the contract X-Y under the
influence of a mistake, rendering the contract voidable[100] (rather than void from
the outset).[101] The mistake gives X the power to avoid the contract. After avoidance, which has retrospective effect, it is deemed that the contract has never been
valid. As a valid underlying contract is a requirement for a valid transfer of ownership, the transfer, ie the notarial deed, becomes void with retroactive effect as
well,[102] despite the registration in the deeds register. It is deemed that X has always
remained the owner of the land. As a result, Y has never been the owner of the land
and has therefore never been able to give a good title to Z under the *nemo dat* rule.
The transfer Y-Z is void because Y is not owner of the land.

The same problem occurs in the two following instances: the contract X-Y is
void from the outset, or, second, there is a defect in the *transfer* between X and Y
(formal requirements have not been fulfilled).

Z may nevertheless be protected under Article 3:88 BW and acquire ownership
if two conditions are met: he must have acquired the property in good faith, and
the voidness of the earlier transfer X-Y must not be the result of X having been
unauthorised to dispose of the land. Dutch law does not want to protect Z where

---

[99] HR 17 November 1967, NJ 1968/42 (Pos/Van den Bosch).

[100] Unlike in English law mistake renders the contract voidable rather than void.

[101] The same reasoning applies to contracts entered into under the influence of other defects of will,
such as fraud, duress and undue influence. The sanction in all these instances is voidability rather than
voidness.

[102] Dutch law has a so-called causal transfer system in which every transfer of property should be
based on a valid legal ground, commonly a valid contract preceding the transfer. If the contract is void,
the transfer is void as well. If the contract is voidable, avoidance of it will also avoid the transfer of property. See in general: LPW van Vliet, *Transfer of movables in German, French, English and Dutch law*,
(Nijmegen, Ars Aequi Libri, 2000), 24–25.

X, starting the sequence of transactions, was not the owner of the land or was unauthorised to dispose for another reason (e.g. X being insolvent). If X is not the owner, the transfer to Y is void from the outset. Z will not be protected, even though he is in good faith.

The protection of Article 3:88 BW will commonly apply where the defect in the transfer X-Y was caused by the voidness or the avoiding of the contract between X and Y (as in the above instance) or by a formal defect in the notarial deed embodying the transfer X-Y. In that event Z will become[103] or remain[104] owner of the land. In the above example Z will become owner of the land if he did not know, nor should have known of the mistake made by X. X will not be compensated by the Registry, but he may sue for damages in a personal action against Y.

Incompleteness of the Register

Article 3:24 BW offers a broad protection against incompleteness of the deeds register. If at the moment a transaction regarding land is registered a certain fact or right which can be registered has not yet been registered, this fact or right cannot be set up against the acquirer under the transaction, unless he knew of it. For example: X transfers ownership of his land to Y under a condition subsequent. By mistake the condition itself is not entered in the register. Afterwards Y transfers the same land to Z, who does not know the condition subsequent between X and Y. X is unable to set up the condition against Z.

Incorrectness of the Register

Article 3:25 BW protects against certain mistakes in notarial deeds. Let us look at the following example. X intends to sell and transfer someone else's land to Y using either a false passport or equivalent identification paper, or a false deed of mandate. A Dutch notary has the duty to check the identity of the persons signing any deed (a disposition or any other notarial deed). He has a similar duty to verify a written mandate giving X a power of agency.[105] The notary must verify X's and Y's passport or equivalent identification paper, and, if a mandate (an agency document) is used, the notary has to check the owner's signature on the written mandate.[106] In case of doubt, the notary should check the Verification Information System of the CRI (a criminal investigation department). If he does not thoroughly verify the identity of the relevant persons, the notary is liable for damages

---

[103] Where the earlier transaction is void.

[104] Where the earlier transaction is voidable.

[105] Art 39 Wet op het notarisambt. See P Blokland, *Teksten en toelichting op de Wet op het notarisambt*, 2nd edn, (Lelystad, WPRN, 2001), 88–90.

[106] In practice, if the mandator lives far away the notary will ask him to have a notarial deed of mandate made by a local notary. The local notary of course has the same duty to verify the mandator's identity.

(in tort).[107] This applies to all notarial deeds and thus to every disposition of land. If Y is in good faith, paid the purchase price and it turns out that X is a swindler, Y did not become and cannot become the owner of the land, as X is unable to give him a good title. Although Y is now the registered proprietor of the land, he has no legal title in reality. Y could sue X for breach of contract, but the more realistic option would be to sue the notary for damages. If, on the other hand, the passport is a stunning falsification, the notary is not to blame and is therefore not liable for damages. But the register gives Y no protection at all in this instance.

If Y (who is registered as being owner of the land) transfers or charges the land to Z or creates a charge in favour of Z, Article 3:25 will protect Z because as an outsider to the transaction X-Y he should be able to rely on the identity of X as ascertained officially by the notary. Note that the protection is not available to Y himself, as he is a party to the transaction X-Y rather than a third party.

Another article giving protection against incorrectness is Article 3:26 BW. If at the moment the acquisition of a right in land is registered an incorrect fact has been registered, the person who could reasonably have asked for rectification of the register cannot set up this mistake against a third party, unless the latter knew of the mistake or could have known the mistake when consulting the register.

Valuable Consideration and Possession

The protection given in the Articles 3:24, 25, 26 and 88 BW do not depend on the question whether the innocent third party acquired his right for valuable consideration nor on the question whether the third party or the owner is in actual possession of the land. Nor is actual possession relevant for rectification of the register.

Compensation

Under certain conditions Article 117 *Kadasterwet* offers compensation if civil servants of the cadastre and deeds registry make a mistake. Moreover, in rare instances, such as destruction of deeds by fire at the land registry, the State will give compensation (article 3:30 BW).

Adverse Possession

Although acquisition by adverse possession cannot be discovered from the register, it works against everyone, even against third parties in good faith. In English terminology this amounts to an overriding interest. Accordingly, the cadastral

---

[107] Hof's-Gravenhage 18 maart 1982, NJ 1983/273. See also P Blokland, n 105, 89 and WG Huijgen/AJH Pleysier, *De wetgeving op het notarisambt*, 2nd edn, (Deventer, Kluwer Law International 2001), p 155.

boundary is not decisive and may become outdated as a result of adverse possession. This amounts to an exception to the protection given by Article 3:24.[108]

CONCLUSIONS

When we look at the United Kingdom, Ireland, and the small snapshot of continental Europe as presented here, the following picture emerges.

First, dispositive registration is by no means pervasive and is not co-extensive
with title registration. The four continental systems described here show some
very interesting differences. Two—Germany and The Netherlands—practise dispositive registration—yet the system in The Netherlands is one of deeds registration, not title registration. In the Polish and Finnish title registration systems,
registration is not dispositive. England and Wales, Northern Ireland and Ireland
do practise dispositive registration, but with the important difference that what
does not work at law does work in equity.

Third party rights are registered in all the systems examined here. England and
Wales stands alone (but allied quite closely to the Torrens systems) in its use of
interest recording; and that must be a consequence of the law/equity split. The civil
law jurisdictions, with their more strictly applied *numerus clausus* and their innocence of the whole web of equitable interests that lurks potentially around any
English title, have far less need to hedge their bets about the validity of rights. The
English and both the Irish systems are unique in granting overriding status to the
rights of those in actual occupation; the other European systems, like the Torrens
systems, do not do this. This may be an issue we have to consider in the future; and
one of the questions that must be posed is: just how much real protection does
paragraph 2 of Schedule 3 give to those who need it, in the light of overreaching
and of post-*Boland* checks upon occupiers?[109]

When we come to indefeasibility, the picture is even more complex. Germany
and Poland have deferred indefeasibility; in our X-Y-Z sequence, Y is not protected, but Z is, provided that he is in good faith. Finland takes one step away from
this; transactions that are voidable for a 'weak' reason may be cured by a purchase
in good faith, so that Y is protected as well as Z; but where there is a 'strong' inval-
idating factor there is no protection either for Y or Z. In The Netherlands, similarly, there is no cure for a void disposition where the disponor was without
authority—in particular if there was a forgery or impersonation. But Z will be protected (deferred indefeasibility) where the transfer was vitiated by mistake or by a
formal defect.

None of the European systems examined here has anything resembling the
English concept of protection for the proprietor in possession. And in all instances
where a purchaser is protected, he must be in good faith; good faith seems rather

---

[108] Above, under '*Incompleteness of the register*'.
[109] See ch 5, after n 129.

closer to the concept of the 'purchaser without notice' than to the absence of 'fraud' in the Torrens sense, where something more than notice is required. Thus what is protected here is not simply purchase, as in the Torrens systems, nor purchase combined with possession, as in the English systems, but purchase and the absence of notice. The race-notice systems of the USA spring to mind.[110] The protection of possession may be a good concept for export; but compatibility with Europe is a further argument for combining this with the 'deferred indefeasibility' approach advocated here in chapter 6.

There is no consistent treatment of adverse possession. This is not something fundamental to any title registration system, and it would be possible to have a European register while maintaining different, but well-advertised, rules on adverse possession in different jurisdictions. What could not be maintained would be any difference in the dispositive effect of registration, nor in the effect of registering at least the most important third party rights (security rights and leases), nor in the protection of purchasers.

We are a long way apart, and perhaps standardisation is a pipe-dream. But a project for English law reform must be to examine the law/equity dichotomy, perhaps in the light of the streamlining effects of electronic conveyancing, and to endeavour to develop a system uncluttered by equitable proprietary rights, while nevertheless giving strong protection to those less able to benefit from conventional property rights. There is a lot to examine here; there are issues of feminism and of family protection, as well as economic factors—many European countries have a lower rate of owner-occupation and more rented family accommodation, so that deserted wives do not need an equity in a capital asset; and social security entitlement has a considerable effect on individual wealth and need. What is certain is that our contemplation of land ownership for the future must extend beyond our own borders.

---

[110] See ch 1, n 13.

Land Registration Act 2002

PART 1

PRELIMINARY

1. Register of title

(1) There is to continue to be a register of title kept by the registrar.

(2) Rules may make provision about how the register is to be kept and may, in particular, make provision about–
- (a) the information to be included in the register,
- (b) the form in which information included in the register is to be kept, and
- (c) the arrangement of that information.

2. Scope of title registration

This Act makes provision about the registration of title to–
- (a) unregistered legal estates which are interests of any of the following kinds–
  - (i) an estate in land,
  - (ii) a rentcharge,
  - (iii) a franchise,
  - (iv) a profit a prendre in gross, and
  - (v) any other interest or charge which subsists for the benefit of, or is a charge on, an interest the title to which is registered; and
- (b) interests capable of subsisting at law which are created by a disposition of an interest the title to which is registered.

PART 2

FIRST REGISTRATION OF TITLE

CHAPTER 1

FIRST REGISTRATION

Voluntary registration

3. When title may be registered

(1) This section applies to any unregistered legal estate which is an interest of any of the following kinds–
- (a) an estate in land,
- (b) a rentcharge,

(c) a franchise, and

(d) a profit a prendre in gross.

(2) Subject to the following provisions, a person may apply to the registrar to be registered as the proprietor of an unregistered legal estate to which this section applies if–

(a) the estate is vested in him, or

(b) he is entitled to require the estate to be vested in him.

(3) Subject to subsection (4), an application under subsection (2) in respect of a leasehold estate may only be made if the estate was granted for a term of which more than seven years are unexpired.

(4) In the case of an estate in land, subsection (3) does not apply if the right to possession under the lease is discontinuous.

(5) A person may not make an application under subsection (2)(a) in respect of a leasehold estate vested in him as a mortgagee where there is a subsisting right of redemption.

(6) A person may not make an application under subsection (2)(b) if his entitlement is as a person who has contracted to buy under a contract.

(7) If a person holds in the same right both–

(a) a lease in possession, and

(b) a lease to take effect in possession on, or within a month of, the end of the lease in possession, then, to the extent that they relate to the same land,

they are to be treated for the purposes of this section as creating one continuous term.

Compulsory registration

4. When title must be registered

(1) The requirement of registration applies on the occurrence of any of the following events–

(a) the transfer of a qualifying estate–

(i) for valuable or other consideration, by way of gift or in pursuance of an order of any court, or

(ii) by means of an assent (including a vesting assent);

(b) the transfer of an unregistered legal estate in land in circumstances where section 171A of the Housing Act 1985 (c. 68) applies (disposal by landlord which leads to a person no longer being a secure tenant);

(c) the grant out of a qualifying estate of an estate in land–

(i) for a term of years absolute of more than seven years from the date of the grant, and

(ii) for valuable or other consideration, by way of gift or in pursuance of an order of any court;

(d) the grant out of a qualifying estate of an estate in land for a term of years absolute to take effect in possession after the end of the period of three months beginning with the date of the grant;

(e) the grant of a lease in pursuance of Part 5 of the Housing Act 1985 (the right to buy) out of an unregistered legal estate in land;

(f) the grant of a lease out of an unregistered legal estate in land in such circumstances as are mentioned in paragraph (b);

(g) the creation of a protected first legal mortgage of a qualifying estate.

(2) For the purposes of subsection (1), a qualifying estate is an unregistered legal estate which is–

(a) a freehold estate in land, or

(b) a leasehold estate in land for a term which, at the time of the transfer, grant or creation, has more than seven years to run.

(3) In subsection (1)(a), the reference to transfer does not include transfer by operation of law.

(4) Subsection (1)(a) does not apply to–

(a) the assignment of a mortgage term, or

(b) the assignment or surrender of a lease to the owner of the immediate reversion where the term is to merge in that reversion.

(5) Subsection (1)(c) does not apply to the grant of an estate to a person as a mortgagee.

(6) For the purposes of subsection (1)(a) and (c), if the estate transferred or granted has a negative value, it is to be regarded as transferred or granted for valuable or other consideration.

(7) In subsection (1)(a) and (c), references to transfer or grant by way of gift include transfer or grant for the purpose of–

(a) constituting a trust under which the settlor does not retain the whole of the beneficial interest, or

(b) uniting the bare legal title and the beneficial interest in property held under a trust under which the settlor did not, on constitution, retain the whole of the beneficial interest.

(8) For the purposes of subsection (1)(g)–

(a) a legal mortgage is protected if it takes effect on its creation as a mortgage to be protected by the deposit of documents relating to the mortgaged estate, and

(b) a first legal mortgage is one which, on its creation, ranks in priority ahead of any other mortgages then affecting the mortgaged estate.

(9) In this section–

"land" does not include mines and minerals held apart from the surface;

"vesting assent" has the same meaning as in the Settled Land Act 1925 (c. 18).

5. Power to extend section 4

(1) The Lord Chancellor may by order–

(a) amend section 4 so as to add to the events on the occurrence of which the requirement of registration applies such relevant event as he may specify in the order, and

(b) make such consequential amendments of any provision of, or having effect under, any Act as he thinks appropriate.

(2) For the purposes of subsection (1)(a), a relevant event is an event relating to an unregistered legal estate which is an interest of any of the following kinds–

(a) an estate in land,

(b) a rentcharge,

(c) a franchise, and

(d) a profit a prendre in gross.

(3) The power conferred by subsection (1) may not be exercised so as to require the title to an estate granted to a person as a mortgagee to be registered.

(4) Before making an order under this section the Lord Chancellor must consult such persons as he considers appropriate.

6. Duty to apply for registration of title

(1) If the requirement of registration applies, the responsible estate owner, or his successor in title, must, before the end of the period for registration, apply to the registrar to be registered as the proprietor of the registrable estate.

(2) If the requirement of registration applies because of section 4(1)(g)–

    (a) the registrable estate is the estate charged by the mortgage, and

    (b) the responsible estate owner is the owner of that estate.

(3) If the requirement of registration applies otherwise than because of section 4(1)(g)–

    (a) the registrable estate is the estate which is transferred or granted, and

    (b) the responsible estate owner is the transferee or grantee of that estate.

(4) The period for registration is 2 months beginning with the date on which the relevant event occurs, or such longer period as the registrar may provide under subsection (5).

(5) If on the application of any interested person the registrar is satisfied that there is good reason for doing so, he may by order provide that the period for registration ends on such later date as he may specify in the order.

(6) Rules may make provision enabling the mortgagee under any mortgage falling within section 4(1)(g) to require the estate charged by the mortgage to be registered whether or not the mortgagor consents.

7. Effect of non-compliance with section 6

(1) If the requirement of registration is not complied with, the transfer, grant or creation becomes void as regards the transfer, grant or creation of a legal estate.

(2) On the application of subsection (1)–

    (a) in a case falling within section 4(1)(a) or (b), the title to the legal estate reverts to the transferor who holds it on a bare trust for the transferee, and

    (b) in a case falling within section 4(1)(c) to (g), the grant or creation has effect as a contract made for valuable consideration to grant or create the legal estate concerned.

(3) If an order under section 6(5) is made in a case where subsection (1) has already applied, that application of the subsection is to be treated as not having occurred.

(4) The possibility of reverter under subsection (1) is to be disregarded for the purposes of determining whether a fee simple is a fee simple absolute.

8. Liability for making good void transfers etc

If a legal estate is retransferred, regranted or recreated because of a failure to comply with the requirement of registration, the transferee, grantee or, as the case may be, the mortgagor–

    (a) is liable to the other party for all the proper costs of and incidental to the retransfer, regrant or recreation of the legal estate, and

(b) is liable to indemnify the other party in respect of any other liability reasonably incurred by him because of the failure to comply with the requirement of registration.

Classes of title

9. Titles to freehold estates

(1) In the case of an application for registration under this Chapter of a freehold estate, the classes of title with which the applicant may be registered as proprietor are–

    (a) absolute title,

    (b) qualified title, and

    (c) possessory title;

and the following provisions deal with when each of the classes of title is available.

(2) A person may be registered with absolute title if the registrar is of the opinion that the person's title to the estate is such as a willing buyer could properly be advised by a competent professional adviser to accept.

(3) In applying subsection (2), the registrar may disregard the fact that a person's title appears to him to be open to objection if he is of the opinion that the defect will not cause the holding under the title to be disturbed.

(4) A person may be registered with qualified title if the registrar is of the opinion that the person's title to the estate has been established only for a limited period or subject to certain reservations which cannot be disregarded under subsection (3).

(5) A person may be registered with possessory title if the registrar is of the opinion–

    (a) that the person is in actual possession of the land, or in receipt of the rents and profits of the land, by virtue of the estate, and

    (b) that there is no other class of title with which he may be registered.

10. Titles to leasehold estates

(1) In the case of an application for registration under this Chapter of a leasehold estate, the classes of title with which the applicant may be registered as proprietor are–

    (a) absolute title,

    (b) good leasehold title,

    (c) qualified title, and

    (d) possessory title;

and the following provisions deal with when each of the classes of title is available.

(2) A person may be registered with absolute title if–

    (a) the registrar is of the opinion that the person's title to the estate is such as a willing buyer could properly be advised by a competent professional adviser to accept, and

    (b) the registrar approves the lessor's title to grant the lease.

(3) A person may be registered with good leasehold title if the registrar is of the opinion that the person's title to the estate is such as a willing buyer could properly be advised by a competent professional adviser to accept.

(4) In applying subsection (2) or (3), the registrar may disregard the fact that a person's title appears to him to be open to objection if he is of the opinion that the defect will not cause the holding under the title to be disturbed.

(5) A person may be registered with qualified title if the registrar is of the opinion that the person's title to the estate, or the lessor's title to the reversion, has been established only for a limited period or subject to certain reservations which cannot be disregarded under subsection (4).

(6) A person may be registered with possessory title if the registrar is of the opinion–

(a) that the person is in actual possession of the land, or in receipt of the rents and profits of the land, by virtue of the estate, and

(b) that there is no other class of title with which he may be registered.

Effect of first registration

11. Freehold estates

(1) This section is concerned with the registration of a person under this Chapter as the proprietor of a freehold estate.

(2) Registration with absolute title has the effect described in subsections (3) to (5).

(3) The estate is vested in the proprietor together with all interests subsisting for the benefit of the estate.

(4) The estate is vested in the proprietor subject only to the following interests affecting the estate at the time of registration–

(a) interests which are the subject of an entry in the register in relation to the estate,

(b) unregistered interests which fall within any of the paragraphs of Schedule 1, and

(c) interests acquired under the Limitation Act 1980 (c. 58) of which the proprietor has notice.

(5) If the proprietor is not entitled to the estate for his own benefit, or not entitled solely for his own benefit, then, as between himself and the persons beneficially entitled to the estate, the estate is vested in him subject to such of their interests as he has notice of.

(6) Registration with qualified title has the same effect as registration with absolute title, except that it does not affect the enforcement of any estate, right or interest which appears from the register to be excepted from the effect of registration.

(7) Registration with possessory title has the same effect as registration with absolute title, except that it does not affect the enforcement of any estate, right or interest adverse to, or in derogation of, the proprietor's title subsisting at the time of registration or then capable of arising.

12. Leasehold estates

(1) This section is concerned with the registration of a person under this Chapter as the proprietor of a leasehold estate.

(2) Registration with absolute title has the effect described in subsections (3) to (5).

(3) The estate is vested in the proprietor together with all interests subsisting for the benefit of the estate.

(4) The estate is vested subject only to the following interests affecting the estate at the time of registration–

(a) implied and express covenants, obligations and liabilities incident to the estate,

(b) interests which are the subject of an entry in the register in relation to the estate,

(c) unregistered interests which fall within any of the paragraphs of Schedule 1, and

(d) interests acquired under the Limitation Act 1980 (c. 58) of which the proprietor has notice.

(5) If the proprietor is not entitled to the estate for his own benefit, or not entitled solely for his own benefit, then, as between himself and the persons beneficially entitled to the estate, the estate is vested in him subject to such of their interests as he has notice of.

(6) Registration with good leasehold title has the same effect as registration with absolute title, except that it does not affect the enforcement of any estate, right or interest affecting, or in derogation of, the title of the lessor to grant the lease.

(7) Registration with qualified title has the same effect as registration with absolute title except that it does not affect the enforcement of any estate, right or interest which appears from the register to be excepted from the effect of registration.

(8) Registration with possessory title has the same effect as registration with absolute title, except that it does not affect the enforcement of any estate, right or interest adverse to, or in derogation of, the proprietor's title subsisting at the time of registration or then capable of arising.

Dependent estates

13. Appurtenant rights and charges

Rules may–

(a) make provision for the registration of the proprietor of a registered estate as the proprietor of an unregistered legal estate which subsists for the benefit of the registered estate;

(b) make provision for the registration of a person as the proprietor of an unregistered legal estate which is a charge on a registered estate.

Supplementary

14. Rules about first registration

Rules may–

(a) make provision about the making of applications for registration under this Chapter;

(b) make provision about the functions of the registrar following the making of such an application, including provision about–

(i) the examination of title, and

(ii) the entries to be made in the register where such an application is approved;

(c) make provision about the effect of any entry made in the register in pursuance of such an application.

CHAPTER 2

CAUTIONS AGAINST FIRST REGISTRATION

15. Right to lodge

(1) Subject to subsection (3), a person may lodge a caution against the registration of title to an unregistered legal estate if he claims to be–

(a) the owner of a qualifying estate, or

(b) entitled to an interest affecting a qualifying estate.

(2) For the purposes of subsection (1), a qualifying estate is a legal estate which–

(a) relates to land to which the caution relates, and

(b) is an interest of any of the following kinds–

(i) an estate in land,

(ii) a rentcharge,

(iii) a franchise, and

(iv) a profit a prendre in gross.

(3) No caution may be lodged under subsection (1)–

(a) in the case of paragraph (a), by virtue of ownership of–

(i) a freehold estate in land, or

(ii) a leasehold estate in land granted for a term of which more than seven years are unexpired;

(b) in the case of paragraph (b), by virtue of entitlement to such a leasehold estate as is mentioned in paragraph (a)(ii) of this subsection.

(4) The right under subsection (1) is exercisable by application to the registrar.

16. Effect

(1) Where an application for registration under this Part relates to a legal estate which is the subject of a caution against first registration, the registrar must give the cautioner notice of the application and of his right to object to it.

(2) The registrar may not determine an application to which subsection (1) applies before the end of such period as rules may provide, unless the cautioner has exercised his right to object to the application or given the registrar notice that he does not intend to do so.

(3) Except as provided by this section, a caution against first registration has no effect and, in particular, has no effect on the validity or priority of any interest of the cautioner in the legal estate to which the caution relates.

(4) For the purposes of subsection (1), notice given by a person acting on behalf of an applicant for registration under this Part is to be treated as given by the registrar if–

(a) the person is of a description provided by rules, and

(b) notice is given in such circumstances as rules may provide.

17. Withdrawal

The cautioner may withdraw a caution against first registration by application to the registrar.

18. Cancellation

(1) A person may apply to the registrar for cancellation of a caution against first registration if he is–

(a) the owner of the legal estate to which the caution relates, or

(b) a person of such other description as rules may provide.

(2) Subject to rules, no application under subsection (1)(a) may be made by a person who–

(a) consented in such manner as rules may provide to the lodging of the caution, or

(b) derives title to the legal estate by operation of law from a person who did so.

(3) Where an application is made under subsection (1), the registrar must give the cautioner notice of the application and of the effect of subsection (4).

(4) If the cautioner does not exercise his right to object to the application before the end of such period as rules may provide, the registrar must cancel the caution.

19. Cautions register

(1) The registrar must keep a register of cautions against first registration.

(2) Rules may make provision about how the cautions register is to be kept and may, in particular, make provision about–

(a) the information to be included in the register,

(b) the form in which information included in the register is to be kept, and

(c) the arrangement of that information.

20. Alteration of register by court

(1) The court may make an order for alteration of the cautions register for the purpose of–

(a) correcting a mistake, or

(b) bringing the register up to date.

(2) An order under subsection (1) has effect when served on the registrar to impose a duty on him to give effect to it.

(3) Rules may make provision about–

(a) the circumstances in which there is a duty to exercise the power under subsection (1),

(b) the form of an order under that subsection, and

(c) service of such an order.

21. Alteration of register by registrar

(1) The registrar may alter the cautions register for the purpose of–
(a) correcting a mistake, or
(b) bringing the register up to date.
(2) Rules may make provision about–
(a) the circumstances in which there is a duty to exercise the power under subsection (1),
(b) how the cautions register is to be altered in exercise of that power,
(c) applications for the exercise of that power, and
(d) procedure in relation to the exercise of that power, whether on application or otherwise.
(3) Where an alteration is made under this section, the registrar may pay such amount as he thinks fit in respect of any costs reasonably incurred by a person in connection with the alteration.

22. Supplementary

In this Chapter, "the cautioner", in relation to a caution against first registration, means the person who lodged the caution, or such other person as rules may provide.

PART 3

DISPOSITIONS OF REGISTERED LAND

Powers of disposition

23 Owner's powers

(1) Owner's powers in relation to a registered estate consist of–
(a) power to make a disposition of any kind permitted by the general law in relation to an interest of that description, other than a mortgage by demise or sub-demise, and
(b) power to charge the estate at law with the payment of money.
(2) Owner's powers in relation to a registered charge consist of–
(a) power to make a disposition of any kind permitted by the general law in relation to an interest of that description, other than a legal sub-mortgage, and
(b) power to charge at law with the payment of money indebtedness secured by the registered charge.
(3) In subsection (2)(a), "legal sub-mortgage" means–
(a) a transfer by way of mortgage,
(b) a sub-mortgage by sub-demise, and
(c) a charge by way of legal mortgage.

24 Right to exercise owner's powers

A person is entitled to exercise owner's powers in relation to a registered estate or charge if he is–

(a) the registered proprietor, or

(b) entitled to be registered as the proprietor.

25 Mode of exercise

(1) A registrable disposition of a registered estate or charge only has effect if it complies with such requirements as to form and content as rules may provide.

(2) Rules may apply subsection (1) to any other kind of disposition which depends for its effect on registration.

26 Protection of disponees

(1) Subject to subsection (2), a person's right to exercise owner's powers in relation to a registered estate or charge is to be taken to be free from any limitation affecting the validity of a disposition.

(2) Subsection (1) does not apply to a limitation–

(a) reflected by an entry in the register, or

(b) imposed by, or under, this Act.

(3) This section has effect only for the purpose of preventing the title of a disponee being questioned (and so does not affect the lawfulness of a disposition).

Registrable dispositions

27 Dispositions required to be registered

(1) If a disposition of a registered estate or registered charge is required to be completed by registration, it does not operate at law until the relevant registration requirements are met.

(2) In the case of a registered estate, the following are the dispositions which are required to be completed by registration–

(a) a transfer,

(b) where the registered estate is an estate in land, the grant of a term of years absolute–

(i) for a term of more than seven years from the date of the grant,

(ii) to take effect in possession after the end of the period of three months beginning with the date of the grant,

(iii) under which the right to possession is discontinuous,

(iv) in pursuance of Part 5 of the Housing Act 1985 (c. 68) (the right to buy), or

(v) in circumstances where section 171A of that Act applies (disposal by landlord which leads to a person no longer being a secure tenant),

(c) where the registered estate is a franchise or manor, the grant of a lease,

(d) the express grant or reservation of an interest of a kind falling within section 1(2)(a) of the Law of Property Act 1925 (c. 20), other than one which is capable of being registered under the Commons Registration Act 1965 (c. 64),

(e) the express grant or reservation of an interest of a kind falling within section 1(2)(b) or (e) of the Law of Property Act 1925, and

(f) the grant of a legal charge.

(3) In the case of a registered charge, the following are the dispositions which are required to be completed by registration–

    (a) a transfer, and

    (b) the grant of a sub-charge.

(4) Schedule 2 to this Act (which deals with the relevant registration requirements) has effect.

(5) This section applies to dispositions by operation of law as it applies to other dispositions, but with the exception of the following–

    (a) a transfer on the death or bankruptcy of an individual proprietor,

    (b) a transfer on the dissolution of a corporate proprietor, and

    (c) the creation of a legal charge which is a local land charge.

(6) Rules may make provision about applications to the registrar for the purpose of meeting registration requirements under this section.

(7) In subsection (2)(d), the reference to express grant does not include grant as a result of the operation of section 62 of the Law of Property Act 1925 (c. 20).

Effect of dispositions on priority

28 Basic rule

(1) Except as provided by sections 29 and 30, the priority of an interest affecting a registered estate or charge is not affected by a disposition of the estate or charge.

(2) It makes no difference for the purposes of this section whether the interest or disposition is registered.

29 Effect of registered dispositions: estates

(1) If a registrable disposition of a registered estate is made for valuable consideration, completion of the disposition by registration has the effect of postponing to the interest under the disposition any interest affecting the estate immediately before the disposition whose priority is not protected at the time of registration.

(2) For the purposes of subsection (1), the priority of an interest is protected–

    (a) in any case, if the interest–

        (i) is a registered charge or the subject of a notice in the register,

        (ii) falls within any of the paragraphs of Schedule 3, or

        (iii) appears from the register to be excepted from the effect of registration, and

    (b) in the case of a disposition of a leasehold estate, if the burden of the interest is incident to the estate.

(3) Subsection (2)(a)(ii) does not apply to an interest which has been the subject of a notice in the register at any time since the coming into force of this section.

(4) Where the grant of a leasehold estate in land out of a registered estate does not involve a registrable disposition, this section has effect as if–

    (a) the grant involved such a disposition, and

    (b) the disposition were registered at the time of the grant.

30 Effect of registered dispositions: charges

(1) If a registrable disposition of a registered charge is made for valuable consideration, completion of the disposition by registration has the effect of postponing to the interest under the disposition any interest affecting the charge immediately before the disposition whose priority is not protected at the time of registration.

(2) For the purposes of subsection (1), the priority of an interest is protected–

    (a) in any case, if the interest–

        (i) is a registered charge or the subject of a notice in the register,

        (ii) falls within any of the paragraphs of Schedule 3, or

        (iii) appears from the register to be excepted from the effect of registration, and

    (b) in the case of a disposition of a charge which relates to a leasehold estate, if the burden of the interest is incident to the estate.

(3) Subsection (2)(a)(ii) does not apply to an interest which has been the subject of a notice in the register at any time since the coming into force of this section.

31 Inland Revenue charges

The effect of a disposition of a registered estate or charge on a charge under section 237 of the Inheritance Tax Act 1984 (c. 51) (charge for unpaid tax) is to be determined, not in accordance with sections 28 to 30 above, but in accordance with sections 237(6) and 238 of that Act (under which a purchaser in good faith for money or money's worth takes free from the charge in the absence of registration).

Part 4

Notices and restrictions

Notices

32 Nature and effect

(1) A notice is an entry in the register in respect of the burden of an interest affecting a registered estate or charge.

(2) The entry of a notice is to be made in relation to the registered estate or charge affected by the interest concerned.

(3) The fact that an interest is the subject of a notice does not necessarily mean that the interest is valid, but does mean that the priority of the interest, if valid, is protected for the purposes of sections 29 and 30.

33 Excluded interests

No notice may be entered in the register in respect of any of the following–

    (a) an interest under–

        (i) a trust of land, or

        (ii) a settlement under the Settled Land Act 1925 (c. 18),

(b) a leasehold estate in land which–

(i) is granted for a term of years of three years or less from the date of the grant, and

(ii) is not required to be registered,

(c) a restrictive covenant made between a lessor and lessee, so far as relating to the demised premises,

(d) an interest which is capable of being registered under the Commons Registration Act 1965 (c. 64), and

(e) an interest in any coal or coal mine, the rights attached to any such interest and the rights of any person under section 38, 49 or 51 of the Coal Industry Act 1994 (c. 21).

34 Entry on application

(1) A person who claims to be entitled to the benefit of an interest affecting a registered estate or charge may, if the interest is not excluded by section 33, apply to the registrar for the entry in the register of a notice in respect of the interest.

(2) Subject to rules, an application under this section may be for–

(a) an agreed notice, or

(b) a unilateral notice.

(3) The registrar may only approve an application for an agreed notice if–

(a) the applicant is the relevant registered proprietor, or a person entitled to be registered as such proprietor,

(b) the relevant registered proprietor, or a person entitled to be registered as such proprietor, consents to the entry of the notice, or

(c) the registrar is satisfied as to the validity of the applicant's claim.

(4) In subsection (3), references to the relevant registered proprietor are to the proprietor of the registered estate or charge affected by the interest to which the application relates.

35 Unilateral notices

(1) If the registrar enters a notice in the register in pursuance of an application under section 34(2)(b) ("a unilateral notice"), he must give notice of the entry to–

(a) the proprietor of the registered estate or charge to which it relates, and

(b) such other persons as rules may provide.

(2) A unilateral notice must–

(a) indicate that it is such a notice, and

(b) identify who is the beneficiary of the notice.

(3) The person shown in the register as the beneficiary of a unilateral notice, or such other person as rules may provide, may apply to the registrar for the removal of the notice from the register.

36 Cancellation of unilateral notices

(1) A person may apply to the registrar for the cancellation of a unilateral notice if he is–

(a) the registered proprietor of the estate or charge to which the notice relates, or

(b) a person entitled to be registered as the proprietor of that estate or charge.

(2) Where an application is made under subsection (1), the registrar must give the beneficiary of the notice notice of the application and of the effect of subsection (3).

(3) If the beneficiary of the notice does not exercise his right to object to the application before the end of such period as rules may provide, the registrar must cancel the notice.

(4) In this section–

"beneficiary", in relation to a unilateral notice, means the person shown in the register as the beneficiary of the notice, or such other person as rules may provide;

"unilateral notice" means a notice entered in the register in pursuance of an application under section 34(2)(b).

37 Unregistered interests

(1) If it appears to the registrar that a registered estate is subject to an unregistered interest which–

(a) falls within any of the paragraphs of Schedule 1, and

(b) is not excluded by section 33,

he may enter a notice in the register in respect of the interest.

(2) The registrar must give notice of an entry under this section to such persons as rules may provide.

38 Registrable dispositions

Where a person is entered in the register as the proprietor of an interest under a disposition falling within section 27(2)(b) to (e), the registrar must also enter a notice in the register in respect of that interest.

39 Supplementary

Rules may make provision about the form and content of notices in the register.
Restrictions

40 Nature

(1) A restriction is an entry in the register regulating the circumstances in which a disposition of a registered estate or charge may be the subject of an entry in the register.

(2) A restriction may, in particular–

(a) prohibit the making of an entry in respect of any disposition, or a disposition of a kind specified in the restriction;

(b) prohibit the making of an entry–

(i) indefinitely,

(ii) for a period specified in the restriction, or

(iii) until the occurrence of an event so specified.

(3) Without prejudice to the generality of subsection (2)(b)(iii), the events which may be specified include–

(a) the giving of notice,

(b) the obtaining of consent, and

(c) the making of an order by the court or registrar.

(4) The entry of a restriction is to be made in relation to the registered estate or charge to which it relates.

41 Effect

(1) Where a restriction is entered in the register, no entry in respect of a disposition to which the restriction applies may be made in the register otherwise than in accordance with the terms of the restriction, subject to any order under subsection (2).

(2) The registrar may by order–

(a) disapply a restriction in relation to a disposition specified in the order or dispositions of a kind so specified, or

(b) provide that a restriction has effect, in relation to a disposition specified in the order or dispositions of a kind so specified, with modifications so specified.

(3) The power under subsection (2) is exercisable only on the application of a person who appears to the registrar to have a sufficient interest in the restriction.

42 Power of registrar to enter

(1) The registrar may enter a restriction in the register if it appears to him that it is necessary or desirable to do so for the purpose of–

(a) preventing invalidity or unlawfulness in relation to dispositions of a registered estate or charge,

(b) securing that interests which are capable of being overreached on a disposition of a registered estate or charge are overreached, or

(c) protecting a right or claim in relation to a registered estate or charge.

(2) No restriction may be entered under subsection (1)(c) for the purpose of protecting the priority of an interest which is, or could be, the subject of a notice.

(3) The registrar must give notice of any entry made under this section to the proprietor of the registered estate or charge concerned, except where the entry is made in pursuance of an application under section 43.

(4) For the purposes of subsection (1)(c), a person entitled to the benefit of a charging order relating to an interest under a trust shall be treated as having a right or claim in relation to the trust property.

43 Applications

(1) A person may apply to the registrar for the entry of a restriction under section 42(1) if–

(a) he is the relevant registered proprietor, or a person entitled to be registered as such proprietor,

(b) the relevant registered proprietor, or a person entitled to be registered as such proprietor, consents to the application, or

(c) he otherwise has a sufficient interest in the making of the entry.

(2) Rules may–

(a) require the making of an application under subsection (1) in such circumstances, and by such person, as the rules may provide;

(b) make provision about the form of consent for the purposes of subsection (1)(b);

(c) provide for classes of person to be regarded as included in subsection (1)(c);

(d) specify standard forms of restriction.

(3) If an application under subsection (1) is made for the entry of a restriction which is not in a form specified under subsection (2)(d), the registrar may only approve the application if it appears to him–

(a) that the terms of the proposed restriction are reasonable, and

(b) that applying the proposed restriction would–

(i) be straightforward, and

(ii) not place an unreasonable burden on him.

(4) In subsection (1), references to the relevant registered proprietor are to the proprietor of the registered estate or charge to which the application relates.

44 Obligatory restrictions

(1) If the registrar enters two or more persons in the register as the proprietor of a registered estate in land, he must also enter in the register such restrictions as rules may provide for the purpose of securing that interests which are capable of being overreached on a disposition of the estate are overreached.

(2) Where under any enactment the registrar is required to enter a restriction without application, the form of the restriction shall be such as rules may provide.

45 Notifiable applications

(1) Where an application under section 43(1) is notifiable, the registrar must give notice of the application, and of the right to object to it, to–

(a) the proprietor of the registered estate or charge to which it relates, and

(b) such other persons as rules may provide.

(2) The registrar may not determine an application to which subsection (1) applies before the end of such period as rules may provide, unless the person, or each of the persons, notified under that subsection has exercised his right to object to the application or given the registrar notice that he does not intend to do so.

(3) For the purposes of this section, an application under section 43(1) is notifiable unless it is–

(a) made by or with the consent of the proprietor of the registered estate or charge to which the application relates, or a person entitled to be registered as such proprietor,

(b) made in pursuance of rules under section 43(2)(a), or

(c) an application for the entry of a restriction reflecting a limitation under an order of the court or registrar, or an undertaking given in place of such an order.

46 Power of court to order entry

(1) If it appears to the court that it is necessary or desirable to do so for the purpose of protecting a right or claim in relation to a registered estate or charge, it may make an order requiring the registrar to enter a restriction in the register.

(2) No order under this section may be made for the purpose of protecting the priority of an interest which is, or could be, the subject of a notice.

(3) The court may include in an order under this section a direction that an entry made in pursuance of the order is to have overriding priority.

(4) If an order under this section includes a direction under subsection (3), the registrar must make such entry in the register as rules may provide.

(5) The court may make the exercise of its power under subsection (3) subject to such terms and conditions as it thinks fit.

47 Withdrawal

A person may apply to the registrar for the withdrawal of a restriction if–
      (a) the restriction was entered in such circumstances as rules may provide, and
      (b) he is of such a description as rules may provide.

PART 5

CHARGES

Relative priority

48 Registered charges

(1) Registered charges on the same registered estate, or on the same registered charge, are to be taken to rank as between themselves in the order shown in the register.

(2) Rules may make provision about–
      (a) how the priority of registered charges as between themselves is to be shown in the register, and
      (b) applications for registration of the priority of registered charges as between themselves.

49 Tacking and further advances

(1) The proprietor of a registered charge may make a further advance on the security of the charge ranking in priority to a subsequent charge if he has not received from the subsequent chargee notice of the creation of the subsequent charge.

(2) Notice given for the purposes of subsection (1) shall be treated as received at the time when, in accordance with rules, it ought to have been received.

(3) The proprietor of a registered charge may also make a further advance on the security of the charge ranking in priority to a subsequent charge if–
      (a) the advance is made in pursuance of an obligation, and
      (b) at the time of the creation of the subsequent charge the obligation was entered in the register in accordance with rules.

(4) The proprietor of a registered charge may also make a further advance on the security of the charge ranking in priority to a subsequent charge if–
      (a) the parties to the prior charge have agreed a maximum amount for which the charge is security, and
      (b) at the time of the creation of the subsequent charge the agreement was entered in the register in accordance with rules.

(5) Rules may–

(a) disapply subsection (4) in relation to charges of a description specified in the rules, or

(b) provide for the application of that subsection to be subject, in the case of charges of a description so specified, to compliance with such conditions as may be so specified.

(6) Except as provided by this section, tacking in relation to a charge over registered land is only possible with the agreement of the subsequent chargee.

50 Overriding statutory charges: duty of notification

If the registrar enters a person in the register as the proprietor of a charge which–

(a) is created by or under an enactment, and

(b) has effect to postpone a charge which at the time of registration of the statutory charge is–

(i) entered in the register, or

(ii) the basis for an entry in the register,

he must in accordance with rules give notice of the creation of the statutory charge to such person as rules may provide.

Powers as chargee

51 Effect of completion by registration

On completion of the relevant registration requirements, a charge created by means of a registrable disposition of a registered estate has effect, if it would not otherwise do so, as a charge by deed by way of legal mortgage.

52 Protection of disponees

(1) Subject to any entry in the register to the contrary, the proprietor of a registered charge is to be taken to have, in relation to the property subject to the charge, the powers of disposition conferred by law on the owner of a legal mortgage.

(2) Subsection (1) has effect only for the purpose of preventing the title of a disponee being questioned (and so does not affect the lawfulness of a disposition).

53 Powers as sub-chargee

The registered proprietor of a sub-charge has, in relation to the property subject to the principal charge or any intermediate charge, the same powers as the sub-chargor.

Realisation of security

54 Proceeds of sale: chargee's duty

For the purposes of section 105 of the Law of Property Act 1925 (c. 20) (mortgagee's duties in relation to application of proceeds of sale), in its application to the proceeds of sale of registered land, a person shall be taken to have notice of anything in the register immediately before the disposition on sale.

55 Local land charges

A charge over registered land which is a local land charge may only be realised if the title to the charge is registered.

Miscellaneous

56 Receipt in case of joint proprietors

Where a charge is registered in the name of two or more proprietors, a valid receipt for the money secured by the charge may be given by–
    (a) the registered proprietors,
    (b) the survivors or survivor of the registered proprietors, or
    (c) the personal representative of the last survivor of the registered proprietors.

57 Entry of right of consolidation

Rules may make provision about entry in the register of a right of consolidation in relation to a registered charge.

PART 6

REGISTRATION: GENERAL

Registration as proprietor

58 Conclusiveness

(1) If, on the entry of a person in the register as the proprietor of a legal estate, the legal estate would not otherwise be vested in him, it shall be deemed to be vested in him as a result of the registration.

(2) Subsection (1) does not apply where the entry is made in pursuance of a registrable disposition in relation to which some other registration requirement remains to be met.

59 Dependent estates

(1) The entry of a person in the register as the proprietor of a legal estate which subsists for the benefit of a registered estate must be made in relation to the registered estate.

(2) The entry of a person in the register as the proprietor of a charge on a registered estate must be made in relation to that estate.

(3) The entry of a person in the register as the proprietor of a sub-charge on a registered charge must be made in relation to that charge.

Boundaries

60 Boundaries

(1) The boundary of a registered estate as shown for the purposes of the register is a general boundary, unless shown as determined under this section.

(2) A general boundary does not determine the exact line of the boundary.

(3) Rules may make provision enabling or requiring the exact line of the boundary of a registered estate to be determined and may, in particular, make provision about–

   (a) the circumstances in which the exact line of a boundary may or must be determined,

   (b) how the exact line of a boundary may be determined,

   (c) procedure in relation to applications for determination, and

   (d) the recording of the fact of determination in the register or the index maintained under section 68.

(4) Rules under this section must provide for applications for determination to be made to the registrar.

61 Accretion and diluvion

(1) The fact that a registered estate in land is shown in the register as having a particular boundary does not affect the operation of accretion or diluvion.

(2) An agreement about the operation of accretion or diluvion in relation to a registered estate in land has effect only if registered in accordance with rules.
Quality of title

62 Power to upgrade title

(1) Where the title to a freehold estate is entered in the register as possessory or qualified, the registrar may enter it as absolute if he is satisfied as to the title to the estate.

(2) Where the title to a leasehold estate is entered in the register as good leasehold, the registrar may enter it as absolute if he is satisfied as to the superior title.

(3) Where the title to a leasehold estate is entered in the register as possessory or qualified the registrar may–

   (a) enter it as good leasehold if he is satisfied as to the title to the estate, and

(b) enter it as absolute if he is satisfied both as to the title to the estate and as to the superior title.

(4) Where the title to a freehold estate in land has been entered in the register as possessory for at least twelve years, the registrar may enter it as absolute if he is satisfied that the proprietor is in possession of the land.

(5) Where the title to a leasehold estate in land has been entered in the register as possessory for at least twelve years, the registrar may enter it as good leasehold if he is satisfied that the proprietor is in possession of the land.

(6) None of the powers under subsections (1) to (5) is exercisable if there is out-standing any claim adverse to the title of the registered proprietor which is made by virtue of an estate, right or interest whose enforceability is preserved by virtue of the existing entry about the class of title.

(7) The only persons who may apply to the registrar for the exercise of any of the powers under subsections (1) to (5) are–

(a) the proprietor of the estate to which the application relates,

(b) a person entitled to be registered as the proprietor of that estate,

(c) the proprietor of a registered charge affecting that estate, and

(d) a person interested in a registered estate which derives from that estate.

(8) In determining for the purposes of this section whether he is satisfied as to any title, the registrar is to apply the same standards as those which apply under section 9 or 10 to first registration of title.

(9) The Lord Chancellor may by order amend subsection (4) or (5) by substituting for the number of years for the time being specified in that subsection such number of years as the order may provide.

63 Effect of upgrading title

(1) On the title to a registered freehold or leasehold estate being entered under section 62 as absolute, the proprietor ceases to hold the estate subject to any estate, right or interest whose enforceability was preserved by virtue of the previous entry about the class of title.

(2) Subsection (1) also applies on the title to a registered leasehold estate being entered under section 62 as good leasehold, except that the entry does not affect or prejudice the enforcement of any estate, right or interest affecting, or in derogation of, the title of the lessor to grant the lease.

64 Use of register to record defects in title

(1) If it appears to the registrar that a right to determine a registered estate in land is exercisable, he may enter the fact in the register.

(2) Rules may make provision about entries under subsection (1) and may, in par-ticular, make provision about–

(a) the circumstances in which there is a duty to exercise the power conferred by that subsection,

(b) how entries under that subsection are to be made, and

(c) the removal of such entries.

Alteration of register

65 Alteration of register

Schedule 4 (which makes provision about alteration of the register) has effect.
Information etc.

66 Inspection of the registers etc

(1) Any person may inspect and make copies of, or of any part of–
  (a) the register of title,
  (b) any document kept by the registrar which is referred to in the register of title,
  (c) any other document kept by the registrar which relates to an application to him, or
  (d) the register of cautions against first registration.
(2) The right under subsection (1) is subject to rules which may, in particular–
  (a) provide for exceptions to the right, and
  (b) impose conditions on its exercise, including conditions requiring the payment of fees.

67 Official copies of the registers etc

(1) An official copy of, or of a part of–
  (a) the register of title,
  (b) any document which is referred to in the register of title and kept by the registrar,
  (c) any other document kept by the registrar which relates to an application to him, or
  (d) the register of cautions against first registration,
is admissible in evidence to the same extent as the original.
(2) A person who relies on an official copy in which there is a mistake is not liable for loss suffered by another by reason of the mistake.
(3) Rules may make provision for the issue of official copies and may, in particular, make provision about–
  (a) the form of official copies,
  (b) who may issue official copies,
  (c) applications for official copies, and
  (d) the conditions to be met by applicants for official copies, including conditions requiring the payment of fees.

68 Index

(1) The registrar must keep an index for the purpose of enabling the following matters to be ascertained in relation to any parcel of land–
  (a) whether any registered estate relates to the land,
  (b) how any registered estate which relates to the land is identified for the purposes of the register,

(c) whether the land is affected by any, and, if so what, caution against first registration, and

(d) such other matters as rules may provide.

(2) Rules may–

(a) make provision about how the index is to be kept and may, in particular, make provision about–

(i) the information to be included in the index,

(ii) the form in which information included in the index is to be kept, and

(iii) the arrangement of that information;

(b) make provision about official searches of the index.

69 Historical information

(1) The registrar may on application provide information about the history of a registered title.

(2) Rules may make provision about applications for the exercise of the power conferred by subsection (1).

(3) The registrar may–

(a) arrange for the provision of information about the history of registered titles, and

(b) authorise anyone who has the function of providing information under paragraph (a) to have access on such terms as the registrar thinks fit to any relevant information kept by him.

70 Official searches

Rules may make provision for official searches of the register, including searches of pending applications for first registration, and may, in particular, make provision about–

(a) the form of applications for searches,

(b) the manner in which such applications may be made,

(c) the form of official search certificates, and

(d) the manner in which such certificates may be issued.

Applications

71 Duty to disclose unregistered interests

Where rules so provide–

(a) a person applying for registration under Chapter 1 of Part 2 must provide to the registrar such information as the rules may provide about any interest affecting the estate to which the application relates which–

(i) falls within any of the paragraphs of Schedule 1, and

(ii) is of a description specified by the rules;

(b) a person applying to register a registrable disposition of a registered estate must provide to the registrar such information as the rules may provide about any unregistered interest affecting the estate which–

    (i) falls within any of the paragraphs of Schedule 3, and

    (ii) is of description specified by the rules.

72 Priority protection

(1) For the purposes of this section, an application for an entry in the register is protected if–

    (a) it is one to which a priority period relates, and

    (b) it is made before the end of that period.

(2) Where an application for an entry in the register is protected, any entry made in the register during the priority period relating to the application is postponed to any entry made in pursuance of it.

(3) Subsection (2) does not apply if–

    (a) the earlier entry was made in pursuance of a protected application, and

    (b) the priority period relating to that application ranks ahead of the one relating to the application for the other entry.

(4) Subsection (2) does not apply if the earlier entry is one to which a direction under section 46(3) applies.

(5) The registrar may defer dealing with an application for an entry in the register if it appears to him that subsection (2) might apply to the entry were he to make it.

(6) Rules may–

    (a) make provision for priority periods in connection with–

        (i) official searches of the register, including searches of pending applications for first registration, or

        (ii) the noting in the register of a contract for the making of a registrable disposition of a registered estate or charge;

    (b) make provision for the keeping of records in relation to priority periods and the inspection of such records.

(7) Rules under subsection (6)(a) may, in particular, make provision about–

    (a) the commencement and length of a priority period,

    (b) the applications for registration to which such a period relates,

    (c) the order in which competing priority periods rank, and

    (d) the application of subsections (2) and (3) in cases where more than one priority period relates to the same application.

73 Objections

(1) Subject to subsections (2) and (3), anyone may object to an application to the registrar.

(2) In the case of an application under section 18, only the person who lodged the caution to which the application relates, or such other person as rules may provide, may object.

(3) In the case of an application under section 36, only the person shown in the register as the beneficiary of the notice to which the application relates, or such other person as rules may provide, may object.

(4) The right to object under this section is subject to rules.

(5) Where an objection is made under this section, the registrar–

    (a) must give notice of the objection to the applicant, and

(b) may not determine the application until the objection has been disposed of.

(6) Subsection (5) does not apply if the objection is one which the registrar is satisfied is groundless.

(7) If it is not possible to dispose by agreement of an objection to which subsection (5) applies, the registrar must refer the matter to the adjudicator.

(8) Rules may make provision about references under subsection (7).

74 Effective date of registration

An entry made in the register in pursuance of–
    (a) an application for registration of an unregistered legal estate, or
    (b) an application for registration in relation to a disposition required to be completed by registration,
has effect from the time of the making of the application.

Proceedings before the registrar

75 Production of documents

(1) The registrar may require a person to produce a document for the purposes of proceedings before him.

(2) The power under subsection (1) is subject to rules.

(3) A requirement under subsection (1) shall be enforceable as an order of the court.

(4) A person aggrieved by a requirement under subsection (1) may appeal to a county court, which may make any order which appears appropriate.

76 Costs

(1) The registrar may make orders about costs in relation to proceedings before him.

(2) The power under subsection (1) is subject to rules which may, in particular, make provision about–
    (a) who may be required to pay costs,
    (b) whose costs a person may be required to pay,
    (c) the kind of costs which a person may be required to pay, and
    (d) the assessment of costs.

(3) Without prejudice to the generality of subsection (2), rules under that subsection may include provision about–
    (a) costs of the registrar, and
    (b) liability for costs thrown away as the result of neglect or delay by a legal representative of a party to proceedings.

(4) An order under subsection (1) shall be enforceable as an order of the court.

(5) A person aggrieved by an order under subsection (1) may appeal to a county court, which may make any order which appears appropriate.

Miscellaneous

77 Duty to act reasonably

(1) A person must not exercise any of the following rights without reasonable cause–
   (a) the right to lodge a caution under section 15,
   (b) the right to apply for the entry of a notice or restriction, and
   (c) the right to object to an application to the registrar.
(2) The duty under this section is owed to any person who suffers damage in consequence of its breach.

78 Notice of trust not to affect registrar

The registrar shall not be affected with notice of a trust.

PART 7

SPECIAL CASES

The Crown

79 Voluntary registration of demesne land

(1) Her Majesty may grant an estate in fee simple absolute in possession out of demesne land to Herself.
(2) The grant of an estate under subsection (1) is to be regarded as not having been made unless an application under section 3 is made in respect of the estate before the end of the period for registration.
(3) The period for registration is two months beginning with the date of the grant, or such longer period as the registrar may provide under subsection (4).
(4) If on the application of Her Majesty the registrar is satisfied that there is a good reason for doing so, he may by order provide that the period for registration ends on such later date as he may specify in the order.
(5) If an order under subsection (4) is made in a case where subsection (2) has already applied, that application of the subsection is to be treated as not having occurred.

80 Compulsory registration of grants out of demesne land

(1) Section 4(1) shall apply as if the following were included among the events listed–
   (a) the grant by Her Majesty out of demesne land of an estate in fee simple absolute in possession, otherwise than under section 79;
   (b) the grant by Her Majesty out of demesne land of an estate in land–
      (i) for a term of years absolute of more than seven years from the date of the grant, and

(ii) for valuable or other consideration, by way of gift or in pursuance of an order of any court.

(2) In subsection (1)(b)(ii), the reference to grant by way of gift includes grant for the purpose of constituting a trust under which Her Majesty does not retain the whole of the beneficial interest.

(3) Subsection (1) does not apply to the grant of an estate in mines and minerals held apart from the surface.

(4) The Lord Chancellor may by order–

(a) amend this section so as to add to the events in subsection (1) such events relating to demesne land as he may specify in the order, and

(b) make such consequential amendments of any provision of, or having effect under, any Act as he thinks appropriate.

(5) In its application by virtue of subsection (1), section 7 has effect with the substitution for subsection (2) of –

"(2) On the application of subsection (1), the grant has effect as a contract made for valuable consideration to grant the legal estate concerned".

81 Demesne land: cautions against first registration

(1) Section 15 shall apply as if demesne land were held by Her Majesty for an unregistered estate in fee simple absolute in possession.

(2) The provisions of this Act relating to cautions against first registration shall, in relation to cautions lodged by virtue of subsection (1), have effect subject to such modifications as rules may provide.

82 Escheat etc

(1) Rules may make provision about–

(a) the determination of a registered freehold estate in land, and

(b) the registration of an unregistered freehold legal estate in land in respect of land to which a former registered freehold estate in land related.

(2) Rules under this section may, in particular–

(a) make provision for determination to be dependent on the meeting of such registration requirements as the rules may specify;

(b) make provision for entries relating to a freehold estate in land to continue in the register, notwithstanding determination, for such time as the rules may provide;

(c) make provision for the making in the register in relation to a former freehold estate in land of such entries as the rules may provide;

(d) make provision imposing requirements to be met in connection with an application for the registration of such an unregistered estate as is mentioned in subsection (1)(b).

83 Crown and Duchy land: representation

(1) With respect to a Crown or Duchy interest, the appropriate authority–

(a) may represent the owner of the interest for all purposes of this Act,

(b) is entitled to receive such notice as that person is entitled to receive under this Act, and

(c) may make such applications and do such other acts as that person is entitled to make or do under this Act.

(2) In this section–

"the appropriate authority" means–

(a) in relation to an interest belonging to Her Majesty in right of the Crown and forming part of the Crown Estate, the Crown Estate Commissioners;

(b) in relation to any other interest belonging to Her Majesty in right of the Crown, the government department having the management of the interest or, if there is no such department, such person as Her Majesty may appoint in writing under the Royal Sign Manual;

(c) in relation to an interest belonging to Her Majesty in right of the Duchy of Lancaster, the Chancellor of the Duchy;

(d) in relation to an interest belonging to the Duchy of Cornwall, such person as the Duke of Cornwall, or the possessor for the time being of the Duchy of Cornwall, appoints;

(e) in relation to an interest belonging to a government department, or held in trust for Her Majesty for the purposes of a government department, that department;

"Crown interest" means an interest belonging to Her Majesty in right of the Crown, or belonging to a government department, or held in trust for Her Majesty for the purposes of a government department;

"Duchy interest" means an interest belonging to Her Majesty in right of the Duchy of Lancaster, or belonging to the Duchy of Cornwall;

"interest" means any estate, interest or charge in or over land and any right or claim in relation to land.

84 Disapplication of requirements relating to Duchy land

Nothing in any enactment relating to the Duchy of Lancaster or the Duchy of Cornwall shall have effect to impose any requirement with respect to formalities or enrolment in relation to a disposition by a registered proprietor.

85 Bona vacantia

Rules may make provision about how the passing of a registered estate or charge as bona vacantia is to be dealt with for the purposes of this Act.

Pending actions etc.

86 Bankruptcy

(1) In this Act, references to an interest affecting an estate or charge do not include a petition in bankruptcy or bankruptcy order.

(2) As soon as practicable after registration of a petition in bankruptcy as a pending action under the Land Charges Act 1972 (c. 61), the registrar must enter in the register in relation to any registered estate or charge which appears to him to be affected a notice in respect of the pending action.

(3) Unless cancelled by the registrar in such manner as rules may provide, a notice entered under subsection (2) continues in force until–

(a) a restriction is entered in the register under subsection (4), or

(b) the trustee in bankruptcy is registered as proprietor.

(4) As soon as practicable after registration of a bankruptcy order under the Land Charges Act 1972, the registrar must, in relation to any registered estate or charge which appears to him to be affected by the order, enter in the register a restriction reflecting the effect of the Insolvency Act 1986 (c. 45).

(5) Where the proprietor of a registered estate or charge is adjudged bankrupt, the title of his trustee in bankruptcy is void as against a person to whom a registrable disposition of the estate or charge is made if–

(a) the disposition is made for valuable consideration,

(b) the person to whom the disposition is made acts in good faith, and

(c) at the time of the disposition–

(i) no notice or restriction is entered under this section in relation to the registered estate or charge, and

(ii) the person to whom the disposition is made has no notice of the bankruptcy petition or the adjudication.

(6) Subsection (5) only applies if the relevant registration requirements are met in relation to the disposition, but, when they are met, has effect as from the date of the disposition.

(7) Nothing in this section requires a person to whom a registrable disposition is made to make any search under the Land Charges Act 1972.

87 Pending land actions, writs, orders and deeds of arrangement

(1) Subject to the following provisions, references in this Act to an interest affecting an estate or charge include–

(a) a pending land action within the meaning of the Land Charges Act 1972,

(b) a writ or order of the kind mentioned in section 6(1)(a) of that Act (writ or order affecting land issued or made by any court for the purposes of enforcing a judgment or recognisance),

(c) an order appointing a receiver or sequestrator, and

(d) a deed of arrangement.

(2) No notice may be entered in the register in respect of–

(a) an order appointing a receiver or sequestrator, or

(b) a deed of arrangement.

(3) None of the matters mentioned in subsection (1) shall be capable of falling within paragraph 2 of Schedule 1 or 3.

(4) In its application to any of the matters mentioned in subsection (1), this Act shall have effect subject to such modifications as rules may provide.

(5) In this section, "deed of arrangement" has the same meaning as in the Deeds of Arrangement Act 1914 (c. 47).

Miscellaneous

88 Incorporeal hereditaments

In its application to–
    (a) rentcharges,
    (b) franchises,
    (c) profits a prendre in gross, or
    (d) manors,
this Act shall have effect subject to such modification as rules may provide.

89 Settlements

(1) Rules may make provision for the purposes of this Act in relation to the application to registered land of the enactments relating to settlements under the Settled Land Act 1925 (c. 18).

(2) Rules under this section may include provision modifying any of those enactments in its application to registered land.

(3) In this section, "registered land" means an interest the title to which is, or is required to be, registered.

90 PPP leases relating to transport in London

(1) No application for registration under section 3 may be made in respect of a leasehold estate in land under a PPP lease.

(2) The requirement of registration does not apply on the grant or transfer of a leasehold estate in land under a PPP lease.

(3) For the purposes of section 27, the following are not dispositions requiring to be completed by registration–
    (a) the grant of a term of years absolute under a PPP lease;
    (b) the express grant of an interest falling within section 1(2) of the Law of Property Act 1925 (c. 20), where the interest is created for the benefit of a leasehold estate in land under a PPP lease.

(4) No notice may be entered in the register in respect of an interest under a PPP lease.

(5) Schedules 1 and 3 have effect as if they included a paragraph referring to a PPP lease.

(6) In this section, "PPP lease" has the meaning given by section 218 of the Greater London Authority Act 1999 (c. 29) (which makes provision about leases created for public-private partnerships relating to transport in London).

PART 8

ELECTRONIC CONVEYANCING

91 Electronic dispositions: formalities

(1) This section applies to a document in electronic form where–

(a) the document purports to effect a disposition which falls within subsection (2), and

(b) the conditions in subsection (3) are met.

(2) A disposition falls within this subsection if it is–

(a) a disposition of a registered estate or charge,

(b) a disposition of an interest which is the subject of a notice in the register, or

(c) a disposition which triggers the requirement of registration,

which is of a kind specified by rules.

(3) The conditions referred to above are that–

(a) the document makes provision for the time and date when it takes effect,

(b) the document has the electronic signature of each person by whom it purports to be authenticated,

(c) each electronic signature is certified, and

(d) such other conditions as rules may provide are met.

(4) A document to which this section applies is to be regarded as–

(a) in writing, and

(b) signed by each individual, and sealed by each corporation, whose electronic signature it has.

(5) A document to which this section applies is to be regarded for the purposes of any enactment as a deed.

(6) If a document to which this section applies is authenticated by a person as agent, it is to be regarded for the purposes of any enactment as authenticated by him under the written authority of his principal.

(7) If notice of an assignment made by means of a document to which this section applies is given in electronic form in accordance with rules, it is to be regarded for the purposes of any enactment as given in writing.

(8) The right conferred by section 75 of the Law of Property Act 1925 (c. 20) (purchaser's right to have the execution of a conveyance attested) does not apply to a document to which this section applies.

(9) If subsection (4) of section 36A of the Companies Act 1985 (c. 6) (execution of documents) applies to a document because of subsection (4) above, subsection (6) of that section (presumption of due execution) shall have effect in relation to the document with the substitution of "authenticated" for "signed".

(10) In this section, references to an electronic signature and to the certification of such a signature are to be read in accordance with section 7(2) and (3) of the Electronic Communications Act 2000 (c. 7).

92 Land registry network

(1) The registrar may provide, or arrange for the provision of, an electronic communications network for use for such purposes as he thinks fit relating to registration or the carrying on of transactions which–

    (a) involve registration, and

    (b) are capable of being effected electronically.

(2) Schedule 5 (which makes provision in connection with a network provided under subsection (1) and transactions carried on by means of such a network) has effect.

93 Power to require simultaneous registration

(1) This section applies to a disposition of–

    (a) a registered estate or charge, or

    (b) an interest which is the subject of a notice in the register,

    where the disposition is of a description specified by rules.

(2) A disposition to which this section applies, or a contract to make such a disposition, only has effect if it is made by means of a document in electronic form and if, when the document purports to take effect–

    (a) it is electronically communicated to the registrar, and

    (b) the relevant registration requirements are met.

(3) For the purposes of subsection (2)(b), the relevant registration requirements are–

    (a) in the case of a registrable disposition, the requirements under Schedule 2, and

    (b) in the case of any other disposition, or a contract, such requirements as rules may provide.

(4) Section 27(1) does not apply to a disposition to which this section applies.

(5) Before making rules under this section the Lord Chancellor must consult such persons as he considers appropriate.

(6) In this section, "disposition", in relation to a registered charge, includes postponement.

94 Electronic settlement

The registrar may take such steps as he thinks fit for the purpose of securing the provision of a system of electronic settlement in relation to transactions involving registration.

95 Supplementary

Rules may–

    (a) make provision about the communication of documents in electronic form to the registrar;

    (b) make provision about the electronic storage of documents communicated to the registrar in electronic form.

96 Disapplication of periods of limitation

(1) No period of limitation under section 15 of the Limitation Act 1980 (c. 58) (time limits in relation to recovery of land) shall run against any person, other than a chargee, in relation to an estate in land or rentcharge the title to which is registered.

(2) No period of limitation under section 16 of that Act (time limits in relation to redemption of land) shall run against any person in relation to such an estate in land or rentcharge.

(3) Accordingly, section 17 of that Act (extinction of title on expiry of time limit) does not operate to extinguish the title of any person where, by virtue of this section, a period of limitation does not run against him.

97 Registration of adverse possessor

Schedule 6 (which makes provision about the registration of an adverse possessor of an estate in land or rentcharge) has effect.

98 Defences

(1) A person has a defence to an action for possession of land if–

(a) on the day immediately preceding that on which the action was brought he was entitled to make an application under paragraph 1 of Schedule 6 to be registered as the proprietor of an estate in the land, and

(b) had he made such an application on that day, the condition in paragraph 5(4) of that Schedule would have been satisfied.

(2) A judgment for possession of land ceases to be enforceable at the end of the period of two years beginning with the date of the judgment if the proceedings in which the judgment is given were commenced against a person who was at that time entitled to make an application under paragraph 1 of Schedule 6.

(3) A person has a defence to an action for possession of land if on the day immediately preceding that on which the action was brought he was entitled to make an application under paragraph 6 of Schedule 6 to be registered as the proprietor of an estate in the land.

(4) A judgment for possession of land ceases to be enforceable at the end of the period of two years beginning with the date of the judgment if, at the end of that period, the person against whom the judgment was given is entitled to make an application under paragraph 6 of Schedule 6 to be registered as the proprietor of an estate in the land.

(5) Where in any proceedings a court determines that–

(a) a person is entitled to a defence under this section, or

(b) a judgment for possession has ceased to be enforceable against a person by virtue of subsection (4),

the court must order the registrar to register him as the proprietor of the estate in relation to which he is entitled to make an application under Schedule 6.

(6) The defences under this section are additional to any other defences a person may have.

(7) Rules may make provision to prohibit the recovery of rent due under a rentcharge from a person who has been in adverse possession of the rentcharge.

PART 10

LAND REGISTRY

Administration

99 The land registry

(1) There is to continue to be an office called Her Majesty's Land Registry which is to deal with the business of registration under this Act.

(2) The land registry is to consist of–

    (a) the Chief Land Registrar, who is its head, and

    (b) the staff appointed by him;

and references in this Act to a member of the land registry are to be read accordingly.

(3) The Lord Chancellor shall appoint a person to be the Chief Land Registrar.

(4) Schedule 7 (which makes further provision about the land registry) has effect.

100 Conduct of business

(1) Any function of the registrar may be carried out by any member of the land registry who is authorised for the purpose by the registrar.

(2) The Lord Chancellor may by regulations make provision about the carrying out of functions during any vacancy in the office of registrar.

(3) The Lord Chancellor may by order designate a particular office of the land registry as the proper office for the receipt of applications or a specified description of application.

(4) The registrar may prepare and publish such forms and directions as he considers necessary or desirable for facilitating the conduct of the business of registration under this Act.

101 Annual report

(1) The registrar must make an annual report on the business of the land registry to the Lord Chancellor.

(2) The registrar must publish every report under this section and may do so in such manner as he thinks fit.

(3) The Lord Chancellor must lay copies of every report under this section before Parliament.

Fees and indemnities

102 Fee orders

The Lord Chancellor may with the advice and assistance of the body referred to in section 127(2) (the Rule Committee), and the consent of the Treasury, by order–

   (a) prescribe fees to be paid in respect of dealings with the land registry, except under section 69(3)(b) or 105;

   (b) make provision about the payment of prescribed fees.

103 Indemnities

Schedule 8 (which makes provision for the payment of indemnities by the registrar) has effect.

Miscellaneous

104 General information about land

The registrar may publish information about land in England and Wales if it appears to him to be information in which there is legitimate public interest.

105 Consultancy and advisory services

   (1) The registrar may provide, or arrange for the provision of, consultancy or advisory services about the registration of land in England and Wales or elsewhere.

   (2) The terms on which services are provided under this section by the registrar, in particular terms as to payment, shall be such as he thinks fit.

106 Incidental powers: companies

   (1) If the registrar considers it expedient to do so in connection with his functions under section 69(3)(a), 92(1), 94 or 105(1) or paragraph 10 of Schedule 5, he may–

   (a) form, or participate in the formation of, a company, or

   (b) purchase, or invest in, a company.

   (2) In this section–

   "company" means a company within the meaning of the Companies Act 1985 (c. 6);

   "invest" means invest in any way (whether by acquiring assets, securities or rights or otherwise).

   (3) This section is without prejudice to any powers of the registrar exercisable otherwise than by virtue of this section.

PART 11

ADJUDICATION

107 The adjudicator

(1) The Lord Chancellor shall appoint a person to be the Adjudicator to Her Majesty's Land Registry.

(2) To be qualified for appointment under subsection (1), a person must have a 10 year general qualification (within the meaning of section 71 of the Courts and Legal Services Act 1990 (c. 41)).

(3) Schedule 9 (which makes further provision about the adjudicator) has effect.

108 Jurisdiction

(1) The adjudicator has the following functions–

    (a) determining matters referred to him under section 73(7), and

    (b) determining appeals under paragraph 4 of Schedule 5.

(2) Also, the adjudicator may, on application, make any order which the High Court could make for the rectification or setting aside of a document which–

    (a) effects a qualifying disposition of a registered estate or charge,

    (b) is a contract to make such a disposition, or

    (c) effects a transfer of an interest which is the subject of a notice in the register.

(3) For the purposes of subsection (2)(a), a qualifying disposition is–

    (a) a registrable disposition, or

    (b) a disposition which creates an interest which may be the subject of a notice in the register.

(4) The general law about the effect of an order of the High Court for the rectification or setting aside of a document shall apply to an order under this section.

109 Procedure

(1) Hearings before the adjudicator shall be held in public, except where he is satisfied that exclusion of the public is just and reasonable.

(2) Subject to that, rules may regulate the practice and procedure to be followed with respect to proceedings before the adjudicator and matters incidental to or consequential on such proceedings.

(3) Rules under subsection (2) may, in particular, make provision about–

    (a) when hearings are to be held,

    (b) requiring persons to attend hearings to give evidence or to produce documents,

    (c) the form in which any decision of the adjudicator is to be given,

    (d) payment of costs of a party to proceedings by another party to the proceedings, and

    (e) liability for costs thrown away as the result of neglect or delay by a legal representative of a party to proceedings.

110 Functions in relation to disputes

(1) In proceedings on a reference under section 73(7), the adjudicator may, instead of deciding a matter himself, direct a party to the proceedings to commence proceedings within a specified time in the court for the purpose of obtaining the court's decision on the matter.

(2) Rules may make provision about the reference under subsection (1) of matters to the court and may, in particular, make provision about–

(a) adjournment of the proceedings before the adjudicator pending the outcome of the proceedings before the court, and

(b) the powers of the adjudicator in the event of failure to comply with a direction under subsection (1).

(3) Rules may make provision about the functions of the adjudicator in consequence of a decision on a reference under section 73(7) and may, in particular, make provision enabling the adjudicator to determine, or give directions about the determination of–

(a) the application to which the reference relates, or

(b) such other present or future application to the registrar as the rules may provide.

(4) If, in the case of a reference under section 73(7) relating to an application under paragraph 1 of Schedule 6, the adjudicator determines that it would be unconscionable because of an equity by estoppel for the registered proprietor to seek to dispossess the applicant, but that the circumstances are not such that the applicant ought to be registered as proprietor, the adjudicator–

(a) must determine how the equity due to the applicant is to be satisfied, and

(b) may for that purpose make any order that the High Court could make in the exercise of its equitable jurisdiction.

111 Appeals

(1) Subject to subsection (2), a person aggrieved by a decision of the adjudicator may appeal to the High Court.

(2) In the case of a decision on an appeal under paragraph 4 of Schedule 5, only appeal on a point of law is possible.

(3) If on an appeal under this section relating to an application under paragraph 1 of Schedule 6 the court determines that it would be unconscionable because of an equity by estoppel for the registered proprietor to seek to dispossess the applicant, but that the circumstances are not such that the applicant ought to be registered as proprietor, the court must determine how the equity due to the applicant is to be satisfied.

112 Enforcement of orders etc

A requirement of the adjudicator shall be enforceable as an order of the court.

113 Fees

The Lord Chancellor may by order–

(a) prescribe fees to be paid in respect of proceedings before the adjudicator;

(b) make provision about the payment of prescribed fees.

114 Supplementary

Power to make rules under this Part is exercisable by the Lord Chancellor.

PART 12

MISCELLANEOUS AND GENERAL

Miscellaneous

115 Rights of pre-emption

(1) A right of pre-emption in relation to registered land has effect from the time of creation as an interest capable of binding successors in title (subject to the rules about the effect of dispositions on priority).

(2) This section has effect in relation to rights of pre-emption created on or after the day on which this section comes into force.

116 Proprietary estoppel and mere equities

It is hereby declared for the avoidance of doubt that, in relation to registered land, each of the following–

(a) an equity by estoppel, and

(b) a mere equity,

has effect from the time the equity arises as an interest capable of binding successors in title (subject to the rules about the effect of dispositions on priority).

117 Reduction in unregistered interests with automatic protection

(1) Paragraphs 10 to 14 of Schedules 1 and 3 shall cease to have effect at the end of the period of ten years beginning with the day on which those Schedules come into force.

(2) If made before the end of the period mentioned in subsection (1), no fee may be charged for–

(a) an application to lodge a caution against first registration by virtue of an interest falling within any of paragraphs 10 to 14 of Schedule 1, or

(b) an application for the entry in the register of a notice in respect of an interest falling within any of paragraphs 10 to 14 of Schedule 3.

118 Power to reduce qualifying term

(1) The Lord Chancellor may by order substitute for the term specified in any of the following provisions–

(a) section 3(3),

(b) section 4(1)(c)(i) and (2)(b),

(c) section 15(3)(a)(ii),

(d) section 27(2)(b)(i),

(e) section 80(1)(b)(i),

(f) paragraph 1 of Schedule 1,

(g) paragraphs 4(1), 5(1) and 6(1) of Schedule 2, and

(h) paragraph 1 of Schedule 3,

such shorter term as he thinks fit.

(2) An order under this section may contain such transitional provision as the Lord Chancellor thinks fit.

(3) Before making an order under this section, the Lord Chancellor must consult such persons as he considers appropriate.

119 Power to deregister manors

On the application of the proprietor of a registered manor, the registrar may remove the title to the manor from the register.

120 Conclusiveness of filed copies etc

(1) This section applies where–

(a) a disposition relates to land to which a registered estate relates, and

(b) an entry in the register relating to the registered estate refers to a document kept by the registrar which is not an original.

(2) As between the parties to the disposition, the document kept by the registrar is to be taken–

(a) to be correct, and

(b) to contain all the material parts of the original document.

(3) No party to the disposition may require production of the original document.

(4) No party to the disposition is to be affected by any provision of the original document which is not contained in the document kept by the registrar.

121 Forwarding of applications to registrar of companies

The Lord Chancellor may by rules make provision about the transmission by the registrar to the registrar of companies (within the meaning of the Companies Act 1985 (c. 6)) of applications under–

(a) Part 12 of that Act (registration of charges), or

(b) Chapter 3 of Part 23 of that Act (corresponding provision for oversea companies).

122 Repeal of Land Registry Act 1862

(1) The Land Registry Act 1862 (c. 53) shall cease to have effect.

(2) The registrar shall have custody of records of title made under that Act.

(3) The registrar may discharge his duty under subsection (2) by keeping the relevant information in electronic form.

(4) The registrar may on application provide a copy of any information included in a record of title made under that Act.

(5) Rules may make provision about applications for the exercise of the power conferred by subsection (4).

Offences etc.

123 Suppression of information

(1) A person commits an offence if in the course of proceedings relating to registration under this Act he suppresses information with the intention of–
   (a) concealing a person's right or claim, or
   (b) substantiating a false claim.
(2) A person guilty of an offence under this section is liable–
   (a) on conviction on indictment, to imprisonment for a term not exceeding two years or to a fine;
   (b) on summary conviction, to imprisonment for a term not exceeding six months or to a fine not exceeding the statutory maximum, or to both.

124 Improper alteration of the registers

(1) A person commits an offence if he dishonestly induces another–
   (a) to change the register of title or cautions register, or
   (b) to authorise the making of such a change.
(2) A person commits an offence if he intentionally or recklessly makes an unauthorised change in the register of title or cautions register.
(3) A person guilty of an offence under this section is liable–
   (a) on conviction on indictment, to imprisonment for a term not exceeding 2 years or to a fine;
   (b) on summary conviction, to imprisonment for a term not exceeding six months or to a fine not exceeding the statutory maximum, or to both.
(4) In this section, references to changing the register of title include changing a document referred to in it.

125 Privilege against self-incrimination

(1) The privilege against self-incrimination, so far as relating to offences under this Act, shall not entitle a person to refuse to answer any question or produce any document or thing in any legal proceedings other than criminal proceedings.
(2) No evidence obtained under subsection (1) shall be admissible in any criminal proceedings under this Act against the person from whom it was obtained or that person's spouse.

Land registration rules

126 Miscellaneous and general powers

Schedule 10 (which contains miscellaneous and general land registration rule-making powers) has effect.

127 Exercise of powers

(1) Power to make land registration rules is exercisable by the Lord Chancellor with the advice and assistance of the Rule Committee.

(2) The Rule Committee is a body consisting of–

(a) a judge of the Chancery Division of the High Court nominated by the Lord Chancellor,

(b) the registrar,

(c) a person nominated by the General Council of the Bar,

(d) a person nominated by the Council of the Law Society,

(e) a person nominated by the Council of Mortgage Lenders,

(f) a person nominated by the Council of Licensed Conveyancers,

(g) a person nominated by the Royal Institution of Chartered Surveyors,

(h) a person with experience in, and knowledge of, consumer affairs, and

(i) any person nominated under subsection (3).

(3) The Lord Chancellor may nominate to be a member of the Rule Committee any person who appears to him to have qualifications or experience which would be of value to the committee in considering any matter with which it is concerned.

Supplementary

128 Rules, regulations and orders

(1) Any power of the Lord Chancellor to make rules, regulations or orders under this Act includes power to make different provision for different cases.

(2) Any power of the Lord Chancellor to make rules, regulations or orders under this Act is exercisable by statutory instrument.

(3) A statutory instrument containing–

(a) regulations under section 100(2), or

(b) an order under section 100(3), 102 or 113,

is to be laid before Parliament after being made.

(4) A statutory instrument containing–

(a) land registration rules,

(b) rules under Part 11 or section 121,

(c) regulations under paragraph 5 of Schedule 9, or

(d) an order under section 5(1), 62(9), 80(4), 118(1) or 130,

is subject to annulment in pursuance of a resolution of either House of Parliament.

(5) Rules under section 93 or paragraph 1, 2 or 3 of Schedule 5 shall not be made unless a draft of the rules has been laid before and approved by resolution of each House of Parliament.

129 Crown application

This Act binds the Crown.

130 Application to internal waters

This Act applies to land covered by internal waters of the United Kingdom which are–

(a) within England or Wales, or

(b) adjacent to England or Wales and specified for the purposes of this section by order made by the Lord Chancellor.

131 "Proprietor in possession"

(1) For the purposes of this Act, land is in the possession of the proprietor of a registered estate in land if it is physically in his possession, or in that of a person who is entitled to be registered as the proprietor of the registered estate.

(2) In the case of the following relationships, land which is (or is treated as being) in the possession of the second-mentioned person is to be treated for the purposes of subsection (1) as in the possession of the first-mentioned person–

(a) landlord and tenant;

(b) mortgagor and mortgagee;

(c) licensor and licensee;

(d) trustee and beneficiary.

(3) In subsection (1), the reference to entitlement does not include entitlement under Schedule 6.

132 General interpretation

(1) In this Act–

"adjudicator" means the Adjudicator to Her Majesty's Land Registry;

"caution against first registration" means a caution lodged under section 15;

"cautions register" means the register kept under section 19(1);

"charge" means any mortgage, charge or lien for securing money or money's worth;

"demesne land" means land belonging to Her Majesty in right of the Crown which is not held for an estate in fee simple absolute in possession;

"land" includes–

(a) buildings and other structures,

(b) land covered with water, and

(c) mines and minerals, whether or not held with the surface;

"land registration rules" means any rules under this Act, other than rules under section 93, Part 11, section 121 or paragraph 1, 2 or 3 of Schedule 5;

"legal estate" has the same meaning as in the Law of Property Act 1925 (c. 20);

"legal mortgage" has the same meaning as in the Law of Property Act 1925;

"mines and minerals" includes any strata or seam of minerals or substances in or under any land, and powers of working and getting any such minerals or substances;

"registrar" means the Chief Land Registrar;

"register" means the register of title, except in the context of cautions against first registration;

"registered" means entered in the register;

"registered charge" means a charge the title to which is entered in the register;

"registered estate" means a legal estate the title to which is entered in the register, other than a registered charge;

"registered land" means a registered estate or registered charge;

"registrable disposition" means a disposition which is required to be completed by registration under section 27;

"requirement of registration" means the requirement of registration under section 4;

"sub-charge" means a charge under section 23(2)(b);

"term of years absolute" has the same meaning as in the Law of Property Act 1925 (c. 20);

"valuable consideration" does not include marriage consideration or a nominal consideration in money.

(2) In subsection (1), in the definition of "demesne land", the reference to land belonging to Her Majesty does not include land in relation to which a freehold estate in land has determined, but in relation to which there has been no act of entry or management by the Crown.

(3) In this Act–

(a) references to the court are to the High Court or a county court,

(b) references to an interest affecting an estate or charge are to an adverse right affecting the title to the estate or charge, and

(c) references to the right to object to an application to the registrar are to the right under section 73.

Final provisions

133 Minor and consequential amendments

Schedule 11 (which makes minor and consequential amendments) has effect.

134 Transition

(1) The Lord Chancellor may by order make such transitional provisions and savings as he thinks fit in connection with the coming into force of any of the provisions of this Act.

(2) Schedule 12 (which makes transitional provisions and savings) has effect.

(3) Nothing in Schedule 12 affects the power to make transitional provisions and savings under subsection (1); and an order under that subsection may modify any provision made by that Schedule.

135 Repeals

The enactments specified in Schedule 13 (which include certain provisions which are already spent) are hereby repealed to the extent specified there.

136 Short title, commencement and extent

(1) This Act may be cited as the Land Registration Act 2002.

(2) This Act shall come into force on such day as the Lord Chancellor may by order appoint, and different days may be so appointed for different purposes.

(3) Subject to subsection (4), this Act extends to England and Wales only.

(4) Any amendment or repeal by this Act of an existing enactment, other than–

(a) section 37 of the Requisitioned Land and War Works Act 1945 (c. 43), and

(b) Schedule 2A to the Building Societies Act 1986 (c. 53),

has the same extent as the enactment amended or repealed.

SCHEDULES

SCHEDULE 1

UNREGISTERED INTERESTS WHICH OVERRIDE FIRST REGISTRATION

Leasehold estates in land

1 A leasehold estate in land granted for a term not exceeding seven years from the date of the grant, except for a lease the grant of which falls within section 4(1) (d), (e) or (f).

Interests of persons in actual occupation

2 An interest belonging to a person in actual occupation, so far as relating to land of which he is in actual occupation, except for an interest under a settlement under the Settled Land Act 1925 (c. 18).

Easements and profits a prendre

3 A legal easement or profit a prendre.
Customary and public rights
4 A customary right.
5 A public right.

Local land charges

6 A local land charge.

Mines and minerals

7 An interest in any coal or coal mine, the rights attached to any such interest and the rights of any person under section 38, 49 or 51 of the Coal Industry Act 1994 (c. 21).
8 In the case of land to which title was registered before 1898, rights to mines and minerals (and incidental rights) created before 1898.
9 In the case of land to which title was registered between 1898 and 1925 inclusive, rights to mines and minerals (and incidental rights) created before the date of registration of the title.

Miscellaneous

10 A franchise.

11 A manorial right.

12 A right to rent which was reserved to the Crown on the granting of any freehold estate (whether or not the right is still vested in the Crown).

13 A non-statutory right in respect of an embankment or sea or river wall.

14 A right to payment in lieu of tithe.

SCHEDULE 2

REGISTRABLE DISPOSITIONS: REGISTRATION REQUIREMENTS

PART 1

REGISTERED ESTATES

Introductory

1 This Part deals with the registration requirements relating to those dispositions of registered estates which are required to be completed by registration.

Transfer

2 (1) In the case of a transfer of whole or part, the transferee, or his successor in title, must be entered in the register as the proprietor.

(2) In the case of a transfer of part, such details of the transfer as rules may provide must be entered in the register in relation to the registered estate out of which the transfer is made.

Lease of estate in land

3 (1) This paragraph applies to a disposition consisting of the grant out of an estate in land of a term of years absolute.

(2) In the case of a disposition to which this paragraph applies–

(a) the grantee, or his successor in title, must be entered in the register as the proprietor of the lease, and

(b) a notice in respect of the lease must be entered in the register.

Lease of franchise or manor

4 (1) This paragraph applies to a disposition consisting of the grant out of a franchise or manor of a lease for a term of more than seven years from the date of the grant.

(2) In the case of a disposition to which this paragraph applies–

(a) the grantee, or his successor in title, must be entered in the register as the proprietor of the lease, and

(b) a notice in respect of the lease must be entered in the register.

5 (1) This paragraph applies to a disposition consisting of the grant out of a franchise or manor of a lease for a term not exceeding seven years from the date of the grant.

(2) In the case of a disposition to which this paragraph applies, a notice in respect of the lease must be entered in the register.

Creation of independently registrable legal interest

6 (1) This paragraph applies to a disposition consisting of the creation of a legal rentcharge or profit a prendre in gross, other than one created for, or for an interest equivalent to, a term of years absolute not exceeding seven years from the date of creation.

(2) In the case of a disposition to which this paragraph applies–

(a) the grantee, or his successor in title, must be entered in the register as the proprietor of the interest created, and

(b) a notice in respect of the interest created must be entered in the register.

(3) In sub-paragraph (1), the reference to a legal rentcharge or profit a prendre in gross is to one falling within section 1(2) of the Law of Property Act 1925 (c. 20).

Creation of other legal interest

7 (1) This paragraph applies to a disposition which–

(a) consists of the creation of an interest of a kind falling within section 1(2)(a), (b) or (e) of the Law of Property Act 1925, and

(b) is not a disposition to which paragraph 4, 5 or 6 applies.

(2) In the case of a disposition to which this paragraph applies–

(a) a notice in respect of the interest created must be entered in the register, and

(b) if the interest is created for the benefit of a registered estate, the proprietor of the registered estate must be entered in the register as its proprietor.

(3) Rules may provide for sub-paragraph (2) to have effect with modifications in relation to a right of entry over or in respect of a term of years absolute.

Creation of legal charge

8 In the case of the creation of a charge, the chargee, or his successor in title, must be entered in the register as the proprietor of the charge.

PART 2

REGISTERED CHARGES

Introductory

9 This Part deals with the registration requirements relating to those dispositions of registered charges which are required to be completed by registration.

Transfer

10 In the case of a transfer, the transferee, or his successor in title, must be entered in the register as the proprietor.

Creation of sub-charge

11 In the case of the creation of a sub-charge, the sub-chargee, or his successor in title, must be entered in the register as the proprietor of the sub-charge.

SCHEDULE 3

UNREGISTERED INTERESTS WHICH OVERRIDE REGISTERED DISPOSITIONS

Leasehold estates in land

1 A leasehold estate in land granted for a term not exceeding seven years from the date of the grant, except for–
    (a) a lease the grant of which falls within section 4(1)(d), (e) or (f);
    (b) a lease the grant of which constitutes a registrable disposition.

Interests of persons in actual occupation

2 An interest belonging at the time of the disposition to a person in actual occupation, so far as relating to land of which he is in actual occupation, except for–
    (a) an interest under a settlement under the Settled Land Act 1925 (c. 18);
    (b) an interest of a person of whom inquiry was made before the disposition and who failed to disclose the right when he could reasonably have been expected to do so;
    (c) an interest–
        (i) which belongs to a person whose occupation would not have been obvious on a reasonably careful inspection of the land at the time of the disposition, and

(ii) of which the person to whom the disposition is made does not have actual knowledge at that time;

(d) a leasehold estate in land granted to take effect in possession after the end of the period of three months beginning with the date of the grant and which has not taken effect in possession at the time of the disposition.

Easements and profits a prendre

3 (1) A legal easement or profit a prendre, except for an easement, or a profit a prendre which is not registered under the Commons Registration Act 1965 (c. 64), which at the time of the disposition–
(a) is not within the actual knowledge of the person to whom the disposition is made, and
(b) would not have been obvious on a reasonably careful inspection of the land over which the easement or profit is exercisable.

(2) The exception in sub-paragraph (1) does not apply if the person entitled to the easement or profit proves that it has been exercised in the period of one year ending with the day of the disposition.

Customary and public rights

4 A customary right.
5 A public right.

Local land charges

6 A local land charge.

Mines and minerals

7 An interest in any coal or coal mine, the rights attached to any such interest and the rights of any person under section 38, 49 or 51 of the Coal Industry Act 1994 (c. 21).
8 In the case of land to which title was registered before 1898, rights to mines and minerals (and incidental rights) created before 1898.
9 In the case of land to which title was registered between 1898 and 1925 inclusive, rights to mines and minerals (and incidental rights) created before the date of registration of the title.

Miscellaneous

10 A franchise.
11 A manorial right.

12 A right to rent which was reserved to the Crown on the granting of any freehold estate (whether or not the right is still vested in the Crown).

13 A non-statutory right in respect of an embankment or sea or river wall.

14 A right to payment in lieu of tithe.

SCHEDULE 4

ALTERATION OF THE REGISTER

Introductory

1   In this Schedule, references to rectification, in relation to alteration of the register, are to alteration which–
   (a) involves the correction of a mistake, and
   (b) prejudicially affects the title of a registered proprietor.

Alteration pursuant to a court order

2 (1) The court may make an order for alteration of the register for the purpose of–
   (a) correcting a mistake,
   (b) bringing the register up to date, or
   (c) giving effect to any estate, right or interest excepted from the effect of registration.
   (2) An order under this paragraph has effect when served on the registrar to impose a duty on him to give effect to it.

3 (1) This paragraph applies to the power under paragraph 2, so far as relating to rectification.
   (2) If alteration affects the title of the proprietor of a registered estate in land, no order may be made under paragraph 2 without the proprietor's consent in relation to land in his possession unless–
   (a) he has by fraud or lack of proper care caused or substantially contributed to the mistake, or
   (b) it would for any other reason be unjust for the alteration not to be made.
   (3) If in any proceedings the court has power to make an order under paragraph 2, it must do so, unless there are exceptional circumstances which justify its not doing so.
   (4) In sub-paragraph (2), the reference to the title of the proprietor of a registered estate in land includes his title to any registered estate which subsists for the benefit of the estate in land.

4 Rules may–
   (a) make provision about the circumstances in which there is a duty to exercise the power under paragraph 2, so far as not relating to rectification;
   (b) make provision about the form of an order under paragraph 2;
   (c) make provision about service of such an order.

Alteration otherwise than pursuant to a court order

5 The registrar may alter the register for the purpose of–
    (a) correcting a mistake,
    (b) bringing the register up to date,
    (c) giving effect to any estate, right or interest excepted from the effect of registration, or
    (d) removing a superfluous entry.
6 (1) This paragraph applies to the power under paragraph 5, so far as relating to rectification.
    (2) No alteration affecting the title of the proprietor of a registered estate in land may be made under paragraph 5 without the proprietor's consent in relation to land in his possession unless–
    (a) he has by fraud or lack of proper care caused or substantially contributed to the mistake, or
    (b) it would for any other reason be unjust for the alteration not to be made.
    (3) If on an application for alteration under paragraph 5 the registrar has power to make the alteration, the application must be approved, unless there are exceptional circumstances which justify not making the alteration.
    (4) In sub-paragraph (2), the reference to the title of the proprietor of a registered estate in land includes his title to any registered estate which subsists for the benefit of the estate in land.
7 Rules may–
    (a) make provision about the circumstances in which there is a duty to exercise the power under paragraph 5, so far as not relating to rectification;
    (b) make provision about how the register is to be altered in exercise of that power;
    (c) make provision about applications for alteration under that paragraph, including provision requiring the making of such applications;
    (d) make provision about procedure in relation to the exercise of that power, whether on application or otherwise.

Rectification and derivative interests

8 The powers under this Schedule to alter the register, so far as relating to rectification, extend to changing for the future the priority of any interest affecting the registered estate or charge concerned.

Costs in non-rectification cases

9 (1) If the register is altered under this Schedule in a case not involving rectification, the registrar may pay such amount as he thinks fit in respect of any costs or expenses reasonably incurred by a person in connection with the alteration which have been incurred with the consent of the registrar.

(2) The registrar may make a payment under sub-paragraph (1) notwithstanding the absence of consent if–

    (a) it appears to him–

        (i) that the costs or expenses had to be incurred urgently, and

        (ii) that it was not reasonably practicable to apply for his consent, or

    (b) he has subsequently approved the incurring of the costs or expenses.

SCHEDULE 5

LAND REGISTRY NETWORK

Access to network

1 (1) A person who is not a member of the land registry may only have access to a land registry network under authority conferred by means of an agreement with the registrar.

(2) An agreement for the purposes of sub-paragraph (1) ("network access agreement") may authorise access for–

    (a) the communication, posting or retrieval of information,

    (b) the making of changes to the register of title or cautions register,

    (c) the issue of official search certificates,

    (d) the issue of official copies, or

    (e) such other conveyancing purposes as the registrar thinks fit.

(3) Rules may regulate the use of network access agreements to confer authority to carry out functions of the registrar.

(4) The registrar must, on application, enter into a network access agreement with the applicant if the applicant meets such criteria as rules may provide.

Terms of access

2 (1) The terms on which access to a land registry network is authorised shall be such as the registrar thinks fit, subject to sub-paragraphs (3) and (4), and may, in particular, include charges for access.

(2) The power under sub-paragraph (1) may be used, not only for the purpose of regulating the use of the network, but also for–

    (a) securing that the person granted access uses the network to carry on such qualifying transactions as may be specified in, or under, the agreement,

    (b) such other purpose relating to the carrying on of qualifying transactions as rules may provide, or

    (c) enabling network transactions to be monitored.

(3) It shall be a condition of a network access agreement which enables the person granted access to use the network to carry on qualifying transactions that he must comply with any rules for the time being in force under paragraph 5.

(4) Rules may regulate the terms on which access to a land registry network is authorised.

Termination of access

3 (1) The person granted access by a network access agreement may terminate the agreement at any time by notice to the registrar.

(2) Rules may make provision about the termination of a network access agreement by the registrar and may, in particular, make provision about–
  (a) the grounds of termination,
  (b) the procedure to be followed in relation to termination, and
  (c) the suspension of termination pending appeal.

(3) Without prejudice to the generality of sub-paragraph (2)(a), rules under that provision may authorise the registrar to terminate a network access agreement if the person granted access–
  (a) fails to comply with the terms of the agreement,
  (b) ceases to be a person with whom the registrar would be required to enter into a network access agreement conferring the authority which the agreement confers, or
  (c) does not meet such conditions as the rules may provide.

Appeals

4 (1) A person who is aggrieved by a decision of the registrar with respect to entry into, or termination of, a network access agreement may appeal against the decision to the adjudicator.

(2) On determining an appeal under this paragraph, the adjudicator may give such directions as he considers appropriate to give effect to his determination.

(3) Rules may make provision about appeals under this paragraph.

Network transaction rules

5 (1) Rules may make provision about how to go about network transactions.

(2) Rules under sub-paragraph (1) may, in particular, make provision about dealings with the land registry, including provision about–
  (a) the procedure to be followed, and
  (b) the supply of information (including information about unregistered interests).

Overriding nature of network access obligations

6 To the extent that an obligation not owed under a network access agreement conflicts with an obligation owed under such an agreement by the person granted access, the obligation not owed under the agreement is discharged.

Do-it-yourself conveyancing

7 (1) If there is a land registry network, the registrar has a duty to provide such assistance as he thinks appropriate for the purpose of enabling persons engaged in qualifying transactions who wish to do their own conveyancing to do so by means of the network.

(2) The duty under sub-paragraph (1) does not extend to the provision of legal advice.

Presumption of authority

8 Where–

(a) a person who is authorised under a network access agreement to do so uses the network for the making of a disposition or contract, and

(b) the document which purports to effect the disposition or to be the contract–

(i) purports to be authenticated by him as agent, and

(ii) contains a statement to the effect that he is acting under the authority of his principal,

he shall be deemed, in favour of any other party, to be so acting.

Management of network transactions

9 (1) The registrar may use monitoring information for the purpose of managing network transactions and may, in particular, disclose such information to persons authorised to use the network, and authorise the further disclosure of information so disclosed, if he considers it is necessary or desirable to do so.

(2) The registrar may delegate his functions under sub-paragraph (1), subject to such conditions as he thinks fit.

(3) In sub-paragraph (1), "monitoring information" means information provided in pursuance of provision in a network access agreement included under paragraph 2(2)(c).

Supplementary

10 The registrar may provide, or arrange for the provision of, education and training in relation to the use of a land registry network.

11 (1) Power to make rules under paragraph 1, 2 or 3 is exercisable by the Lord Chancellor.

(2) Before making such rules, the Lord Chancellor must consult such persons as he considers appropriate.

(3) In making rules under paragraph 1 or 3(2)(a), the Lord Chancellor must have regard, in particular, to the need to secure–

(a) the confidentiality of private information kept on the network,

(b) competence in relation to the use of the network (in particular for the purpose of making changes), and

(c) the adequate insurance of potential liabilities in connection with use of the network.

12 In this Schedule–

"land registry network" means a network provided under section 92(1);

"network access agreement" has the meaning given by paragraph 1(2);

"network transaction" means a transaction carried on by means of a land registry network;

"qualifying transaction" means a transaction which–

(a) involves registration, and

(b) is capable of being effected electronically.

SCHEDULE 6

REGISTRATION OF ADVERSE POSSESSOR

Right to apply for registration

1 (1) A person may apply to the registrar to be registered as the proprietor of a registered estate in land if he has been in adverse possession of the estate for the period of ten years ending on the date of the application.

(2) A person may also apply to the registrar to be registered as the proprietor of a registered estate in land if–

(a) he has in the period of six months ending on the date of the application ceased to be in adverse possession of the estate because of eviction by the registered proprietor, or a person claiming under the registered proprietor,

(b) on the day before his eviction he was entitled to make an application under sub-paragraph (1), and

(c) the eviction was not pursuant to a judgment for possession.

(3) However, a person may not make an application under this paragraph if–

(a) he is a defendant in proceedings which involve asserting a right to possession of the land, or

(b) judgment for possession of the land has been given against him in the last two years.

(4) For the purposes of sub-paragraph (1), the estate need not have been registered throughout the period of adverse possession.

Notification of application

2 (1) The registrar must give notice of an application under paragraph 1 to–

(a) the proprietor of the estate to which the application relates,

(b) the proprietor of any registered charge on the estate,

(c) where the estate is leasehold, the proprietor of any superior registered estate,

(d) any person who is registered in accordance with rules as a person to be notified under this paragraph, and

(e) such other persons as rules may provide.

(2) Notice under this paragraph shall include notice of the effect of paragraph 4.

Treatment of application

3 (1) A person given notice under paragraph 2 may require that the application to which the notice relates be dealt with under paragraph 5.

(2) The right under this paragraph is exercisable by notice to the registrar given before the end of such period as rules may provide.

4 If an application under paragraph 1 is not required to be dealt with under paragraph 5, the applicant is entitled to be entered in the register as the new proprietor of the estate.

5 (1) If an application under paragraph 1 is required to be dealt with under this paragraph, the applicant is only entitled to be registered as the new proprietor of the estate if any of the following conditions is met.

(2) The first condition is that–

(a) it would be unconscionable because of an equity by estoppel for the registered proprietor to seek to dispossess the applicant, and

(b) the circumstances are such that the applicant ought to be registered as the proprietor.

(3) The second condition is that the applicant is for some other reason entitled to be registered as the proprietor of the estate.

(4) The third condition is that–

(a) the land to which the application relates is adjacent to land belonging to the applicant,

(b) the exact line of the boundary between the two has not been determined under rules under section 60,

(c) for at least ten years of the period of adverse possession ending on the date of the application, the applicant (or any predecessor in title) reasonably believed that the land to which the application relates belonged to him, and

(d) the estate to which the application relates was registered more than one year prior to the date of the application.

(5) In relation to an application under paragraph 1(2), this paragraph has effect as if the reference in sub-paragraph (4)(c) to the date of the application were to the day before the date of the applicant's eviction.

Right to make further application for registration

6 (1) Where a person's application under paragraph 1 is rejected, he may make a further application to be registered as the proprietor of the estate if he is in adverse possession of the estate from the date of the application until the last day of the period of two years beginning with the date of its rejection.

(2) However, a person may not make an application under this paragraph if–

(a) he is a defendant in proceedings which involve asserting a right to possession of the land,

(b) judgment for possession of the land has been given against him in the last two years, or

(c) he has been evicted from the land pursuant to a judgment for possession.

7 If a person makes an application under paragraph 6, he is entitled to be entered in the register as the new proprietor of the estate.

Restriction on applications

8 (1) No one may apply under this Schedule to be registered as the proprietor of an estate in land during, or before the end of twelve months after the end of, any period in which the existing registered proprietor is for the purposes of the Limitation (Enemies and War Prisoners) Act 1945 (8 & 9 Geo. 6 c. 16)–

(a) an enemy, or

(b) detained in enemy territory.

(2) No-one may apply under this Schedule to be registered as the proprietor of an estate in land during any period in which the existing registered proprietor is–

(a) unable because of mental disability to make decisions about issues of the kind to which such an application would give rise, or

(b) unable to communicate such decisions because of mental disability or physical impairment.

(3) For the purposes of sub-paragraph (2), "mental disability" means a disability or disorder of the mind or brain, whether permanent or temporary, which results in an impairment or disturbance of mental functioning.

(4) Where it appears to the registrar that sub-paragraph (1) or (2) applies in relation to an estate in land, he may include a note to that effect in the register.

Effect of registration

9 (1) Where a person is registered as the proprietor of an estate in land in pursuance of an application under this Schedule, the title by virtue of adverse possession which he had at the time of the application is extinguished.

(2) Subject to sub-paragraph (3), the registration of a person under this Schedule as the proprietor of an estate in land does not affect the priority of any interest affecting the estate.

(3) Subject to sub-paragraph (4), where a person is registered under this Schedule as the proprietor of an estate, the estate is vested in him free of any registered charge affecting the estate immediately before his registration.

(4) Sub-paragraph (3) does not apply where registration as proprietor is in pursuance of an application determined by reference to whether any of the conditions in paragraph 5 applies.

Apportionment and discharge of charges

10 (1) Where–

(a) a registered estate continues to be subject to a charge notwithstanding the registration of a person under this Schedule as the proprietor, and

(b) the charge affects property other than the estate,

the proprietor of the estate may require the chargee to apportion the amount secured by the charge at that time between the estate and the other property on the basis of their respective values.

(2) The person requiring the apportionment is entitled to a discharge of his estate from the charge on payment of–

(a) the amount apportioned to the estate, and

(b) the costs incurred by the chargee as a result of the apportionment.

(3) On a discharge under this paragraph, the liability of the chargor to the chargee is reduced by the amount apportioned to the estate.

(4) Rules may make provision about apportionment under this paragraph, in particular, provision about–

(a) procedure,

(b) valuation,

(c) calculation of costs payable under sub-paragraph (2)(b), and

(d) payment of the costs of the chargor.

Meaning of "adverse possession"

11 (1) A person is in adverse possession of an estate in land for the purposes of this Schedule if, but for section 96, a period of limitation under section 15 of the Limitation Act 1980 (c. 58) would run in his favour in relation to the estate.

(2) A person is also to be regarded for those purposes as having been in adverse possession of an estate in land–

(a) where he is the successor in title to an estate in the land, during any period of adverse possession by a predecessor in title to that estate, or

(b) during any period of adverse possession by another person which comes between, and is continuous with, periods of adverse possession of his own.

(3) In determining whether for the purposes of this paragraph a period of limitation would run under section 15 of the Limitation Act 1980, there are to be disregarded–

(a) the commencement of any legal proceedings, and

(b) paragraph 6 of Schedule 1 to that Act.

Trusts

12 A person is not to be regarded as being in adverse possession of an estate for the purposes of this Schedule at any time when the estate is subject to a trust, unless the interest of each of the beneficiaries in the estate is an interest in possession.

Crown foreshore

13 (1) Where–

(a) a person is in adverse possession of an estate in land,

(b) the estate belongs to Her Majesty in right of the Crown or the Duchy of Lancaster or to the Duchy of Cornwall, and

(c) the land consists of foreshore,

paragraph 1(1) is to have effect as if the reference to ten years were to sixty years.

(2) For the purposes of sub-paragraph (1), land is to be treated as foreshore if it has been foreshore at any time in the previous ten years.

(3) In this paragraph, "foreshore" means the shore and bed of the sea and of any tidal water, below the line of the medium high tide between the spring and neap tides.

Rentcharges

14 Rules must make provision to apply the preceding provisions of this Schedule to registered rentcharges, subject to such modifications and exceptions as the rules may provide.

Procedure

Rules may make provision about the procedure to be followed pursuant to an application under this Schedule.

SCHEDULE 7

THE LAND REGISTRY

Holding of office by Chief Land Registrar

1 (1) The registrar may at any time resign his office by written notice to the Lord Chancellor.

(2) The Lord Chancellor may remove the registrar from office if he is unable or unfit to discharge the functions of office.

(3) Subject to the above, a person appointed to be the registrar is to hold and vacate office in accordance with the terms of his appointment and, on ceasing to hold office, is eligible for reappointment.

Remuneration etc. of Chief Land Registrar

2 (1) The Lord Chancellor shall pay the registrar such remuneration, and such travelling and other allowances, as the Lord Chancellor may determine.

(2) The Lord Chancellor shall–

(a) pay such pension, allowances or gratuities as he may determine to or in respect of a person who is or has been the registrar, or

(b) make such payments as he may determine towards provision for the payment of a pension, allowances or gratuities to or in respect of such a person.

(3) If, when a person ceases to be the registrar, the Lord Chancellor determines that there are special circumstances which make it right that the person should receive compensation, the Lord Chancellor may pay to the person by way of compensation a sum of such amount as he may determine.

Staff

3 (1) The registrar may appoint such staff as he thinks fit.

(2) The terms and conditions of appointments under this paragraph shall be such as the registrar, with the approval of the Minister for the Civil Service, thinks fit.

Indemnity for members

4 No member of the land registry is to be liable in damages for anything done or omitted in the discharge or purported discharge of any function relating to land registration, unless it is shown that the act or omission was in bad faith.

Seal

5 The land registry is to continue to have a seal and any document purporting to be sealed with it is to be admissible in evidence without any further or other proof.

Documentary evidence

6 The Documentary Evidence Act 1868 (c. 37) has effect as if–

(a) the registrar were included in the first column of the Schedule to that Act,

(b) the registrar and any person authorised to act on his behalf were mentioned in the second column of that Schedule, and

(c) the regulations referred to in that Act included any form or direction issued by the registrar or by any such person.

Parliamentary disqualification

7 In Part 3 of Schedule 1 to the House of Commons Disqualification Act 1975 (c. 24) (other disqualifying offices), there is inserted at the appropriate place–

SCHEDULE 8

INDEMNITIES

Entitlement

1 (1) A person is entitled to be indemnified by the registrar if he suffers loss by reason of–

(a) rectification of the register,

(b) a mistake whose correction would involve rectification of the register,

(c) a mistake in an official search,

(d) a mistake in an official copy,

(e) a mistake in a document kept by the registrar which is not an original and is referred to in the register,

(f) the loss or destruction of a document lodged at the registry for inspection or safe custody,

(g) a mistake in the cautions register, or

(h) failure by the registrar to perform his duty under section 50.

(2) For the purposes of sub-paragraph (1)(a)–

(a) any person who suffers loss by reason of the change of title under section 62 is to be regarded as having suffered loss by reason of rectification of the register, and

(b) the proprietor of a registered estate or charge claiming in good faith under a forged disposition is, where the register is rectified, to be regarded as having suffered loss by reason of such rectification as if the disposition had not been forged.

(3) No indemnity under sub-paragraph (1)(b) is payable until a decision has been made about whether to alter the register for the purpose of correcting the mistake; and the loss suffered by reason of the mistake is to be determined in the light of that decision.

Mines and minerals

2 No indemnity is payable under this Schedule on account of–

(a) any mines or minerals, or

(b) the existence of any right to work or get mines or minerals,

unless it is noted in the register that the title to the registered estate concerned includes the mines or minerals.

Costs

3 (1) In respect of loss consisting of costs or expenses incurred by the claimant in relation to the matter, an indemnity under this Schedule is payable only on account of costs or expenses reasonably incurred by the claimant with the consent of the registrar.

(2) The requirement of consent does not apply where–

(a) the costs or expenses must be incurred by the claimant urgently, and

(b) it is not reasonably practicable to apply for the registrar's consent.

(3) If the registrar approves the incurring of costs or expenses after they have been incurred, they shall be treated for the purposes of this paragraph as having been incurred with his consent.

4 (1) If no indemnity is payable to a claimant under this Schedule, the registrar may pay such amount as he thinks fit in respect of any costs or expenses reasonably incurred by the claimant in connection with the claim which have been incurred with the consent of the registrar.

(2) The registrar may make a payment under sub-paragraph (1) notwithstanding the absence of consent if–

(a) it appears to him–

(i) that the costs or expenses had to be incurred urgently, and

(ii) that it was not reasonably practicable to apply for his consent, or

(b) he has subsequently approved the incurring of the costs or expenses.

Claimant's fraud or lack of care

5 (1) No indemnity is payable under this Schedule on account of any loss suffered by a claimant–
    (a) wholly or partly as a result of his own fraud, or
    (b) wholly as a result of his own lack of proper care.
    (2) Where any loss is suffered by a claimant partly as a result of his own lack of proper care, any indemnity payable to him is to be reduced to such extent as is fair having regard to his share in the responsibility for the loss.
    (3) For the purposes of this paragraph any fraud or lack of care on the part of a person from whom the claimant derives title (otherwise than under a disposition for valuable consideration which is registered or protected by an entry in the register) is to be treated as if it were fraud or lack of care on the part of the claimant.

Valuation of estates etc.

6 Where an indemnity is payable in respect of the loss of an estate, interest or charge, the value of the estate, interest or charge for the purposes of the indemnity is to be regarded as not exceeding–
    (a) in the case of an indemnity under paragraph 1(1)(a), its value immediately before rectification of the register (but as if there were to be no rectification), and
    (b) in the case of an indemnity under paragraph 1(1)(b), its value at the time when the mistake which caused the loss was made.

Determination of indemnity by court

7 (1) A person may apply to the court for the determination of any question as to–
    (a) whether he is entitled to an indemnity under this Schedule, or
    (b) the amount of such an indemnity.
    (2) Paragraph 3(1) does not apply to the costs of an application to the court under this paragraph or of any legal proceedings arising out of such an application.

Time limits

8 For the purposes of the Limitation Act 1980 (c. 58)–
    (a) a liability to pay an indemnity under this Schedule is a simple contract debt, and
    (b) the cause of action arises at the time when the claimant knows, or but for his own default might have known, of the existence of his claim.

Interest

9 Rules may make provision about the payment of interest on an indemnity under this Schedule, including–

(a) the circumstances in which interest is payable, and

(b) the periods for and rates at which it is payable.

Recovery of indemnity by registrar

10 (1) Where an indemnity under this Schedule is paid to a claimant in respect of any loss, the registrar is entitled (without prejudice to any other rights he may have)–

(a) to recover the amount paid from any person who caused or substantially contributed to the loss by his fraud, or

(b) for the purpose of recovering the amount paid, to enforce the rights of action referred to in sub-paragraph (2).

(2) Those rights of action are–

(a) any right of action (of whatever nature and however arising) which the claimant would have been entitled to enforce had the indemnity not been paid, and

(b) where the register has been rectified, any right of action (of whatever nature and however arising) which the person in whose favour the register has been rectified would have been entitled to enforce had it not been rectified.

(3) References in this paragraph to an indemnity include interest paid on an indemnity under rules under paragraph 9.

Interpretation

11(1) For the purposes of this Schedule, references to a mistake in something include anything mistakenly omitted from it as well as anything mistakenly included in it.

(2) In this Schedule, references to rectification of the register are to alteration of the register which–

(a) involves the correction of a mistake, and

(b) prejudicially affects the title of a registered proprietor.

SCHEDULE 9

THE ADJUDICATOR

Holding of office

1 (1) The adjudicator may at any time resign his office by written notice to the Lord Chancellor.

(2) The Lord Chancellor may remove the adjudicator from office on the ground of incapacity or misbehaviour.

(3) Section 26 of the Judicial Pensions and Retirement Act 1993 (c. 8) (compulsory retirement at 70, subject to the possibility of annual extension up to 75) applies to the adjudicator.

(4) Subject to the above, a person appointed to be the adjudicator is to hold and vacate office in accordance with the terms of his appointment and, on ceasing to hold office, is eligible for reappointment.

Remuneration

2 (1) The Lord Chancellor shall pay the adjudicator such remuneration, and such other allowances, as the Lord Chancellor may determine.

(2) The Lord Chancellor shall–

(a) pay such pension, allowances or gratuities as he may determine to or in respect of a person who is or has been the adjudicator, or

(b) make such payments as he may determine towards provision for the payment of a pension, allowances or gratuities to or in respect of such a person.

(3) Sub-paragraph (2) does not apply if the office of adjudicator is a qualifying judicial office within the meaning of the Judicial Pensions and Retirement Act 1993.

(4) If, when a person ceases to be the adjudicator, the Lord Chancellor determines that there are special circumstances which make it right that the person should receive compensation, the Lord Chancellor may pay to the person by way of compensation a sum of such amount as he may determine.

Staff

3 (1) The adjudicator may appoint such staff as he thinks fit.

(2) The terms and conditions of appointments under this paragraph shall be such as the adjudicator, with the approval of the Minister for the Civil Service, thinks fit.

Conduct of business

4 (1) Subject to sub-paragraph (2), any function of the adjudicator may be carried out by any member of his staff who is authorised by him for the purpose.

(2) In the case of functions which are not of an administrative character, sub-paragraph (1) only applies if the member of staff has a 10 year general qualification (within the meaning of section 71 of the Courts and Legal Services Act 1990 (c. 41)).

5 The Lord Chancellor may by regulations make provision about the carrying out of functions during any vacancy in the office of adjudicator.

Finances

6 The Lord Chancellor shall be liable to reimburse expenditure incurred by the adjudicator in the discharge of his functions.

7 The Lord Chancellor may require the registrar to make payments towards expenses of the Lord Chancellor under this Schedule.

Application of Tribunals and Inquiries Act 1992

8 In Schedule 1 to the Tribunal and Inquiries Act 1992 (c. 53) (tribunals under the supervision of the Council on Tribunals), after paragraph 27 there is inserted–
"Land Registration 27B. The Adjudicator to Her Majesty's Land Registry."
Parliamentary disqualification
9 In Part 1 of Schedule 1 to the House of Commons Disqualification Act 1975 (c. 24) (judicial offices), there is inserted at the end–
"Adjudicator to Her Majesty's Land Registry.";
and a corresponding amendment is made in Part 1 of Schedule 1 to the Northern Ireland Assembly Disqualification Act 1975 (c. 25).

SCHEDULE 10

MISCELLANEOUS AND GENERAL POWERS

PART 1

MISCELLANEOUS

Dealings with estates subject to compulsory first registration

1 (1) Rules may make provision–
    (a) applying this Act to a pre-registration dealing with a registrable legal estate as if the dealing had taken place after the date of first registration of the estate, and
    (b) about the date on which registration of the dealing is effective.
  (2) For the purposes of sub-paragraph (1)–
    (a) a legal estate is registrable if a person is subject to a duty under section 6 to make an application to be registered as the proprietor of it, and
    (b) a pre-registration dealing is one which takes place before the making of such an application.

Regulation of title matters between sellers and buyers

2 (1) Rules may make provision about the obligations with respect to–
    (a) proof of title, or
    (b) perfection of title,
of the seller under a contract for the transfer, or other disposition, for valuable consideration of a registered estate or charge.
  (2) Rules under this paragraph may be expressed to have effect notwithstanding any stipulation to the contrary.

Implied covenants

3 Rules may–

(a) make provision about the form of provisions extending or limiting any covenant implied by virtue of Part 1 of the Law of Property (Miscellaneous Provisions) Act 1994 (c. 36) (implied covenants for title) on a registrable disposition;

(b) make provision about the application of section 77 of the Law of Property Act 1925 (c. 20) (implied covenants in conveyance subject to rents) to transfers of registered estates;

(c) make provision about reference in the register to implied covenants, including provision for the state of the register to be conclusive in relation to whether covenants have been implied.

Land certificates

4 Rules may make provision about–

(a) when a certificate of registration of title to a legal estate may be issued,

(b) the form and content of such a certificate, and

(c) when such a certificate must be produced or surrendered to the registrar.

Part 2

GENERAL

Notice

5 (1) Rules may make provision about the form, content and service of notice under this Act.

(2) Rules under this paragraph about the service of notice may, in particular–

(a) make provision requiring the supply of an address for service and about the entry of addresses for service in the register;

(b) make provision about–

   (i) the time for service,

   (ii) the mode of service, and

   (iii) when service is to be regarded as having taken place.

Applications

6 Rules may–

(a) make provision about the form and content of applications under this Act;

(b) make provision requiring applications under this Act to be supported by such evidence as the rules may provide;

(c) make provision about when an application under this Act is to be taken as made;

(d) make provision about the order in which competing applications are to be taken to rank;

(e) make provision for an alteration made by the registrar for the purpose of correcting a mistake in an application or accompanying document to have effect in such circumstances as the rules may provide as if made by the applicant or other interested party or parties.

Statutory statements

7 Rules may make provision about the form of any statement required under an enactment to be included in an instrument effecting a registrable disposition or a disposition which triggers the requirement of registration.

Residual power

8 Rules may make any other provision which it is expedient to make for the purposes of carrying this Act into effect, whether similar or not to any provision which may be made under the other powers to make land registration rules.

SCHEDULE 11

MINOR AND CONSEQUENTIAL AMENDMENTS

Settled Land Act 1925 (c. 18)

1 Section 119(3) of the Settled Land Act 1925 ceases to have effect.

Law of Property Act 1925 (c. 20)

2 (1) The Law of Property Act 1925 is amended as follows.

(2) In section 44, after subsection (4) there is inserted–

"(4A) Subsections (2) and (4) of this section do not apply to a contract to grant a term of years if the grant will be an event within section 4(1) of the Land Registration Act 2002 (events which trigger compulsory first registration of title)."

(3) In that section, in subsection (5), for "the last three preceding subsections" there is substituted "subsections (2) to (4) of this section".

(4) In that section, at the end there is inserted–

"(12) Nothing in this section applies in relation to registered land or to a term of years to be derived out of registered land."

(5) In section 84(8), the words from ", but" to the end are omitted.

(6) In section 85(3), for the words from the beginning to the second "or" there is substituted "Subsection (2) does not apply to registered land, but, subject to that, this section applies whether or not the land is registered land and whether or not".

(7) In section 86(3), for the words from the beginning to the second "or" there is substituted "Subsection (2) does not apply to registered land, but, subject to that,this section applies whether or not the land is registered land and whether or not".

(8) In section 87, at the end there is inserted–

"(4) Subsection (1) of this section shall not be taken to be affected by section 23(1)(a) of the Land Registration Act 2002 (under which owner's powers in relation to a registered estate do not include power to mortgage by demise or sub-demise)."

(9) In section 94(4), for the words from "registered" to the end there is substituted "on registered land".

(10) In section 97, for "Land Registration Act 1925" there is substituted "Land Registration Act 2002".

(11) In section 115(10), for the words from "charge" to the end there is substituted "registered charge (within the meaning of the Land Registration Act 2002)".

(12) In section 125(2), for the words from "(not being" to "1925)" there is substituted "(not being registered land)".

(13) In section 205(1)(xxii)–

(a) for "Land Registration Act 1925" there is substituted "Land Registration Act 2002;", and

(b) the words from ", and" to the end are omitted.

Administration of Estates Act 1925 (c. 23)

3 In section 43(2) of the Administration of Estates Act 1925, for "Land Registration Act 1925" there is substituted "Land Registration Act 2002".

Requisitioned Land and War Works Act 1945 (c. 43)

4 (1) Section 37 of the Requisitioned Land and War Works Act 1945 is amended as follows.

(2) In subsection (2), for "Land Registration Act 1925" there is substituted "Land Registration Act 2002".

(3) Subsection (3) ceases to have effect.

Law of Property (Joint Tenants) Act 1964 (c. 63)

5 In section 3 of the Law of Property (Joint Tenants) Act 1964, for the words from "any land" to the end there is substituted "registered land".

Gas Act 1965 (c. 36)

6 (1) The Gas Act 1965 is amended as follows.

(2) In section 12(3), for "Land Registration Act 1925" there is substituted "Land Registration Act 2002".

(3) In sections 12(4) and 13(6), for the words from "be deemed" to the end there is substituted–

"(a) for the purposes of the Land Charges Act 1925, be deemed to be a charge affecting land falling within Class D(iii), and

(b) for the purposes of the Land Registration Act 2002, be deemed to be an equitable easement."

Commons Registration Act 1965 (c. 64)

7 (1) The Commons Registration Act 1965 is amended as follows.

(2) In sections 1(1), (2) and (3), 4(3) and 8(1), for "under the Land Registration Acts 1925 and 1936" there is substituted "in the register of title".

(3) In section 9, for "the Land Registration Acts 1925 and 1936" there is substituted "in the register of title".

(4) In section 12 (in both places), for "under the Land Registration Acts 1925 and 1936" there is substituted "in the register of title".

(5) In section 22, in subsection (1), there is inserted at the appropriate place–

"'register of title' means the register kept under section 1 of the Land Registration Act 2002;'.

(6) In that section, in subsection (2), for "under the Land Registration Acts 1925 and 1936" there is substituted "in the register of title".

Leasehold Reform Act 1967 (c. 88)

8 (1) The Leasehold Reform Act 1967 is amended as follows.

(2) In section 5(5)–

(a) for "an overriding interest within the meaning of the Land Registration Act 1925" there is substituted "regarded for the purposes of the Land Registration Act 2002 as an interest falling within any of the paragraphs of Schedule 1 or 3 to that Act", and

(b) for "or caution under the Land Registration Act 1925" there is substituted "under the Land Registration Act 2002".

(3) In Schedule 4, in paragraph 1(3)–

(a) for paragraph (a) there is substituted–

"(a) the covenant may be the subject of a notice in the register of title kept under the Land Registration Act 2002, if apart from this subsection it would not be capable of being the subject of such a notice; and", and

(b) in paragraph (b), for "notice of the covenant has been so registered, the covenant" there is substituted "a notice in respect of the covenant has been entered in that register, it".

Law of Property Act 1969 (c. 59)

9 In section 24(1) of the Law of Property Act 1969, for "Land Registration Act 1925" there is substituted "Land Registration Act 2002".

Land Charges Act 1972 (c. 61)

10 (1) The Land Charges Act 1972 is amended as follows.
   (2) In section 14(1), for the words from "Land Registration" to the end there is sub-stituted "Land Registration Act 2002".
   (3) In section 14(3)–
      (a) for the words from "section 123A" to "register)" there is substituted "section 7 of the Land Registration Act 2002 (effect of failure to comply with requirement of registration)", and
      (b) for "that section" there is substituted "section 6 of that Act".
   (4) In section 17(1), in the definition of "registered land", for "Land Registration Act 1925" there is substituted "Land Registration Act 2002".

Consumer Credit Act 1974 (c. 39)

11 In section 177(1) and (6) of the Consumer Credit Act 1974, for "Land Registration Act 1925" there is substituted "Land Registration Act 2002".

Solicitors Act 1974 (c. 47)

12(1) The Solicitors Act 1974 is amended as follows.
   (2) In sections 22(1) and 56(1)(f), for "Land Registration Act 1925" there is sub-stituted "Land Registration Act 2002".
   (3) Section 75(b) ceases to have effect.

Local Land Charges Act 1975 (c. 76)

13 In section 10(3)(b)(ii) of the Local Land Charges Act 1975, for "under the Land Registration Act 1925" there is substituted "in the register of title kept under the Land Registration Act 2002".

Rent Act 1977 (c. 42)

14 In section 136(b) of the Rent Act 1977, for the words from "charge" to the end there is substituted "registered charge (within the meaning of the Land Registration Act 2002)".

Charging Orders Act 1979 (c. 53)

15 In section 3(2) and (6) of the Charging Orders Act 1979, for "Land Registration Act 1925" there is substituted "Land Registration Act 2002".

Highways Act 1980 (c. 66)

16 Section 251(5) of the Highways Act 1980 ceases to have effect.

Inheritance Tax Act 1984 (c. 51)

17 In section 238(3) of the Inheritance Tax Act 1984, for paragraph (a) there is substituted–
    "(a) in relation to registered land–
       (i) if the disposition is required to be completed by registration, the time of registration, and
       (ii) otherwise, the time of completion,".

Housing Act 1985 (c. 68)

18(1) The Housing Act 1985 is amended as follows.
    (2) In section 37(5), for the words from "and" to the end there is substituted–
      "(5A) Where the Chief Land Registrar approves an application for registration of–
    (a) a disposition of registered land, or
    (b) the disponee's title under a disposition of unregistered land,
and the instrument effecting the disposition contains a covenant of the kind mentioned in subsection (1), he must enter in the register a restriction reflecting the limitation imposed by the covenant".
    (3) In section 154(5), for "Land Registration Acts 1925 to 1971" there is substituted "Land Registration Act 2002".
    (4) In section 157(7), for the words from "the appropriate" to the end there is substituted "a restriction in the register of title reflecting the limitation".
    (5) In section 165(6), for "section 83 of the Land Registration Act 1925" there is substituted "Schedule 8 to the Land Registration Act 2002".
    (6) In Schedule 9A, in paragraph 2(2), for the words from the beginning to "the disponor" there is substituted "Where on a qualifying disposal the disponor's title to the dwelling-house is not registered, the disponor".
    (7) In that Schedule, for paragraph 4 there is substituted–
    "4 (1) This paragraph applies where the Chief Land Registrar approves an application for registration of–
    (a) a disposition of registered land, or
    (b) the disponee's title under a disposition of unregistered land,
    and the instrument effecting the disposition contains the statement required by paragraph 1.
    (2) The Chief Land Registrar must enter in the register–
    (a) a notice in respect of the rights of qualifying persons under this Part in relation to dwelling-houses comprised in the disposal, and
    (b) a restriction reflecting the limitation under section 171D(2) on subsequent disposal."

(8) In that Schedule, for paragraph 5(2) there is substituted–
"(2) If the landlord's title is registered, the landlord shall apply for the entry in the register of–

(a) a notice in respect of the rights of the qualifying person or persons under the provisions of this Part, and

(b) a restriction reflecting the limitation under section 171D(2) on subsequent disposal."

(9) In that Schedule, paragraph 5(3) ceases to have effect.

(10) In that Schedule, in paragraph 6, for sub-paragraph (1) there is substituted–
"(1) The rights of a qualifying person under this Part in relation to the qualifying dwelling house shall not be regarded as falling within Schedule 3 to the Land Registration Act 2002 (and so are liable to be postponed under section 29 of that Act, unless protected by means of a notice in the register)."

(11) In that Schedule, in paragraph 9(2), for "Land Registration Acts 1925 to 1986" there is substituted "Land Registration Act 2002".

(12) In Schedule 17, in paragraph 2(2), for "Land Registration Acts 1925 to 1971" there is substituted "Land Registration Act 2002".

(13) In Schedule 20, in paragraph 17(2), for "Land Registration Acts 1925 to 1986" there is substituted "Land Registration Act 2002".

Building Societies Act 1986 (c. 53)

19(1) In Schedule 2A to the Building Societies Act 1986, paragraph 1 is amended as follows.

(2) In sub-paragraph (2), for "charge or incumbrance registered under the Land Registration Act 1925" there is substituted "registered charge (within the meaning of the Land Registration Act 2002)".

(3) Sub-paragraph (4) ceases to have effect.

(4) In sub-paragraph (5), the definition of "registered land" and the preceding "and" cease to have effect.Landlord and Tenant Act 1987 (c. 31)
20 In sections 24(8) and (9), 28(5), 30(6) and 34(9) of the Landlord and Tenant Act 1987, for "Land Registration Act 1925" there is substituted "Land Registration Act 2002".

Diplomatic and Consular Premises Act 1987 (c. 46)

21 (1) The Diplomatic and Consular Premises Act 1987 is amended as follows.

(2) In section 5, after the definition of the expression "diplomatic premises" there is inserted–
"'land" includes buildings and other structures, land covered with water and any estate, interest, easement, servitude or right in or over land,'.

(3) In Schedule 1, in paragraph 1–

(a) before the definition of the expression "the registrar" there is inserted–
"'registered land" has the same meaning as in the Land Registration Act 2002;', and

(b) the words from "and expressions" to the end are omitted.

Criminal Justice Act 1988 (c. 33)

22 (1) The Criminal Justice Act 1988 is amended as follows.

(2) In section 77(12)–

(a) for "Land Registration Act 1925" there is substituted "Land Registration Act 2002", and

(b) in paragraph (a), at the end there is inserted ", except that no notice may be entered in the register of title under the Land Registration Act 2002 in respect of such orders".

(3) In section 79(1) and (4), for "Land Registration Act 1925" there is substituted "Land Registration Act 2002".

Housing Act 1988 (c. 50)

23 (1) The Housing Act 1988 is amended as follows.

(2) In section 81, in subsection (9)(c), for "Land Registration Acts 1925 to 1986" there is substituted "Land Registration Act 2002".

(3) In that section, for subsection (10) there is substituted–

"(10) Where the Chief Land Registrar approves an application for registration of–

(a) a disposition of registered land, or

(b) the approved person's title under a disposition of unregistered land,

and the instrument effecting the disposition contains the statement required by subsection (1) above, he shall enter in the register a restriction reflecting the limitation under this section on subsequent disposal."

(4) In section 90(4), for "Land Registration Act 1925" there is substituted "Land Registration Act 2002".

(5) In section 133, in subsection (8)–

(a) for the words "conveyance, grant or assignment" there is substituted "transfer or grant",

(b) for the words "section 123 of the Land Registration Act 1925" there is substituted "section 4 of the Land Registration Act 2002", and

(c) in paragraph (c), for "Land Registration Acts 1925 to 1986" there is substituted "Land Registration Act 2002".

(6) In that section, for subsection (9) there is substituted–

"(9) Where the Chief Land Registrar approves an application for registration of–

(a) a disposition of registered land, or

(b) a person's title under a disposition of unregistered land,

and the instrument effecting the original disposal contains the statement required by subsection (3)(d) above, he shall enter in the register a restriction reflecting the limitation under this section on subsequent disposal."

Local Government and Housing Act 1989 (c. 42)

24(1) Section 173 of the Local Government and Housing Act 1989 is amended as follows.

(2) In subsection (8)–

(a) for the words "conveyance, grant or assignment" there is substituted "transfer or grant",

(b) for the words "section 123 of the Land Registration Act 1925" there is substituted "section 4 of the Land Registration Act 2002", and

(c) in paragraph (c), for "Land Registration Acts 1925 to 1986" there is substituted "Land Registration Act 2002".

(3) For subsection (9) there is substituted–

"(9) Where the Chief Land Registrar approves an application for registration of–

(a) a disposition of registered land, or

(b) a person's title under a disposition of unregistered land,

and the instrument effecting the initial transfer contains the statement required by subsection (3) above, he shall enter in the register a restriction reflecting the limitation under this section on subsequent disposal."

Water Resources Act 1991 (c. 57)

25 (1) Section 158 of the Water Resources Act 1991 is amended as follows.

(2) In subsection (5)–

(a) for paragraphs (a) and (b) there is substituted–

"(a) the agreement may be the subject of a notice in the register of title under the Land Registration Act 2002 as if it were an interest affecting the registered land;

(b) the provisions of sections 28 to 30 of that Act (effect of dispositions of registered land on priority of adverse interests) shall apply as if the agreement were such an interest;", and

(b) in paragraph (c), for "where notice of the agreement has been so registered," there is substituted "subject to the provisions of those sections,".

(3) In subsection (6), for "Land Registration Act 1925" there is substituted "Land Registration Act 2002".

Access to Neighbouring Land Act 1992 (c. 23)

26 (1) The Access to Neighbouring Land Act 1992 is amended as follows.

(2) In section 4(1), for "Land Registration Act 1925" there is substituted "Land Registration Act 2002".

(3) In section 5, in subsection (4)–

(a) in paragraph (b), for "notice or caution under the Land Registration Act 1925" there is substituted "notice under the Land Registration Act 2002", and

(b) for "entry, notice or caution" there is substituted "entry or notice".

(4) In that section, for subsection (5) there is substituted–

"(5) The rights conferred on a person by or under an access order shall not be capable of falling within paragraph 2 of Schedule 1 or 3 to the Land Registration Act 2002 (overriding status of interest of person in actual occupation)."

(5) In that section, in subsection (6), for "Land Registration Act 1925" there is substituted "Land Registration Act 2002".

Further and Higher Education Act 1992 (c. 13)

27 In Schedule 5 to the Further and Higher Education Act 1992, in paragraph 6(1)–
    (a) for "Land Registration Acts 1925 to 1986" there is substituted "Land Registration Act 2002", and
    (b) for "those Acts" there is substituted "that Act".

Judicial Pensions and Retirement Act 1993 (c. 8)

28 In Schedule 5 to the Judicial Pensions and Retirement Act 1993, there is inserted at the end–
    "Adjudicator to Her Majesty's Land Registry"

Charities Act 1993 (c. 10)

29 (1) The Charities Act 1993 is amended as follows.
    (2) In section 37, for subsections (7) and (8) there is substituted–
    "(7) Where the disposition to be effected by any such instrument as is mentioned in subsection (1)(b) or (5)(b) above will be–
    (a) a registrable disposition, or
    (b) a disposition which triggers the requirement of registration,
the statement which, by virtue of subsection (1) or (5) above, is to be contained in the instrument shall be in such form as may be prescribed by land registration rules.
    (8) Where the registrar approves an application for registration of–
    (a) a disposition of registered land, or
    (b) a person's title under a disposition of unregistered land,
and the instrument effecting the disposition contains a statement complying with subsections (5) and (7) above, he shall enter in the register a restriction reflecting the limitation under section 36 above on subsequent disposal."
    (3) In that section, in subsection (9)–
    (a) for "the restriction to be withdrawn" there is substituted "the removal of the entry", and
    (b) for "withdraw the restriction" there is substituted "remove the entry".
    (4) In that section, in subsection (11), for "Land Registration Act 1925" there is substituted "Land Registration Act 2002".
    (5) In section 39, in subsection (1), at the end there is inserted "by land registration rules".
    (6) In that section, for subsections (1A) and (1B) there is substituted–
    "(1A) Where any such mortgage will be one to which section 4(1)(g) of the Land Registration Act 2002 applies–
    (a) the statement required by subsection (1) above shall be in such form as may be prescribed by land registration rules; and
    (b) if the charity is not an exempt charity, the mortgage shall also contain a statement, in such form as may be prescribed by land registration rules, that the restrictions

on disposition imposed by section 36 above apply to the land (subject to subsection (9) of that section).

(1B) Where–

(a) the registrar approves an application for registration of a person's title to land in connection with such a mortgage as is mentioned in subsection (1A) above,

(b) the mortgage contains statements complying with subsections (1) and (1A) above, and

(c) the charity is not an exempt charity,

the registrar shall enter in the register a restriction reflecting the limitation under section 36 above on subsequent disposal.

(1C) Section 37(9) above shall apply in relation to any restriction entered under subsection (1B) as it applies in relation to any restriction entered under section 37(8)."

(7) In that section, in subsection (6), for the words from "and subsections" to the end there is substituted "and subsections (1) to (1B) above shall be construed as one with the Land Registration Act 2002".

Leasehold Reform, Housing and Urban Development Act 1993 (c. 28)

30 (1) The Leasehold Reform, Housing and Urban Development Act 1993 is amended as follows.

(2) In sections 34(10) and 57(11), for the words from "rules" to the end there is substituted "land registration rules under the Land Registration Act 2002".

(3) In section 97, in subsection (1)–

(a) for "an overriding interest within the meaning of the Land Registration Act 1925" there is substituted "capable of falling within paragraph 2 of Schedule 1 or 3 to the Land Registration Act 2002", and

(b) for "or caution under the Land Registration Act 1925" there is substituted "under the Land Registration Act 2002".

(4) In that section, in subsection (2), for "Land Registration Act 1925" there is substituted "Land Registration Act 2002".

Law of Property (Miscellaneous Provisions) Act 1994 (c. 36)

31 (1) The Law of Property (Miscellaneous Provisions) Act 1994 is amended as follows.

(2) In section 6 (cases in which there is no liability under covenants implied by virtue of Part 1 of that Act), at the end there is inserted–

"(4) Moreover, where the disposition is of an interest the title to which is registered under the Land Registration Act 2002, that person is not liable under any of those covenants for anything (not falling within subsection (1) or (2)) which at the time of the disposition was entered in relation to that interest in the register of title under that Act."

(3) In section 17(3)–

(a) in paragraph (c), for the words from "any" to the end there is substituted "the Adjudicator to Her Majesty's Land Registry", and

(b) for "section 144 of the Land Registration Act 1925" there is substituted "the Land Registration Act 2002".

Drug Trafficking Act 1994 (c. 37)

32 (1) The Drug Trafficking Act 1994 is amended as follows.

(2) In section 26(12)–

(a) for "Land Registration Act 1925" there is substituted "Land Registration Act 2002", and

(b) in paragraph (a), at the end there is inserted ", except that no notice may be entered in the register of title under the Land Registration Act 2002 in respect of such orders".

(3) In section 28(1) and (4), for "Land Registration Act 1925" there is substituted "Land Registration Act 2002".

Landlord and Tenant (Covenants) Act 1995 (c. 30)

33 (1) The Landlord and Tenant (Covenants) Act 1995 is amended as follows.

(2) In sections 3(6) and 15(5)(b), for "Land Registration Act 1925" there is substituted "Land Registration Act 2002".

(3) In section 20, in subsection (2), for the words from "rules" to the end there is substituted "land registration rules under the Land Registration Act 2002".

(4) In that section, in subsection (6)–

(a) for "an overriding interest within the meaning of the Land Registration Act 1925" there is substituted "capable of falling within paragraph 2 of Schedule 1 or 3 to the Land Registration Act 2002", and

(b) for "or caution under the Land Registration Act 1925" there is substituted "under the Land Registration Act 2002".

Family Law Act 1996 (c. 27)

34 (1) The Family Law Act 1996 is amended as follows.

(2) In section 31(10)–

(a) for "Land Registration Act 1925" there is substituted "Land Registration Act 2002", and

(b) for paragraph (b) there is substituted–

"(b) a spouse's matrimonial home rights are not to be capable of falling within paragraph 2 of Schedule 1 or 3 to that Act."

(3) In Schedule 4, in paragraph 4(6), for "section 144 of the Land Registration Act 1925" there is substituted "by land registration rules under the Land Registration Act 2002".

Housing Act 1996 (c. 52)

35 In section 13(5) of the Housing Act 1996, for the words from "if" to the end there is substituted "if the first disposal involves registration under the Land Registration Act 2002, the Chief Land Registrar shall enter in the register of title a restriction reflecting the limitation".

Education Act 1996 (c. 56)

36 In Schedule 7 to the Education Act 1996, in paragraph 11–
   (a) in sub-paragraph (a), for "Land Registration Acts 1925 to 1986" there is substituted "Land Registration Act 2002", and
   (b) in sub-paragraphs (b) and (c), for "those Acts" there is substituted "that Act".

School Standards and Framework Act 1998 (c. 31)

37 In Schedule 22 to the School Standards and Framework Act 1998, in paragraph 9(1)–
   (a) in paragraph (a), for "Land Registration Acts 1925 to 1986" there is substituted "Land Registration Act 2002", and
   (b) in paragraphs (b) and (c), for "those Acts" there is substituted "that Act".

Terrorism Act 2000 (c. 11)

38 In Schedule 4 to the Terrorism Act 2000, in paragraph 8(1)–
   (a) for "Land Registration Act 1925" there is substituted "Land Registration Act 2002", and
   (b) in paragraph (a), at the end there is inserted ", except that no notice may be entered in the register of title under the Land Registration Act 2002 in respect of such orders".

Finance Act 2000 (c. 17)

39 In section 128 of the Finance Act 2000–
   (a) in subsection (2), for the words from "rule" to the end there is substituted "land registration rules under the Land Registration Act 2002", and
   (b) in subsection (8)(a), for "Land Registration Act 1925" there is substituted "Land Registration Act 2002".

International Criminal Court Act 2001 (c. 17)

40 In Schedule 6 to the International Criminal Court Act 2001, in paragraph 7(1)–
    (a) for "Land Registration Act 1925" there is substituted "Land Registration Act 2002", and
    (b) in paragraph (a), at the end there is inserted ", except that no notice may be entered in the register of title under the Land Registration Act 2002 in respect of such orders".

SCHEDULE 12

TRANSITION

Existing entries in the register

1 Nothing in the repeals made by this Act affects the validity of any entry in the register.

2 (1) This Act applies to notices entered under the Land Registration Act 1925 (c. 21) as it applies to notices entered in pursuance of an application under section 34(2)(a).

    (2) This Act applies to restrictions and inhibitions entered under the Land Registration Act 1925 as it applies to restrictions entered under this Act.

    (3) Notwithstanding their repeal by this Act, sections 55 and 56 of the Land Registration Act 1925 shall continue to have effect so far as relating to cautions against dealings lodged under that Act.

    (4) Rules may make provision about cautions against dealings entered under the Land Registration Act 1925.

    (5) In this paragraph, references to the Land Registration Act 1925 include a reference to any enactment replaced (directly or indirectly) by that Act.

3 An entry in the register which, immediately before the repeal of section 144(1)(xi) of the Land Registration Act 1925, operated by virtue of rule 239 of the Land Registration Rules (S.I. 1925/1093) as a caution under section 54 of that Act shall continue to operate as such a caution.

Existing cautions against first registration

4 Notwithstanding the repeal of section 56(3) of the Land Registration Act 1925, that provision shall continue to have effect in relation to cautions against first registration lodged under that Act, or any enactment replaced (directly or indirectly) by that Act.

Pending applications

5 Notwithstanding the repeal of the Land Registration Act 1925, that Act shall continue to have effect in relation to an application for the entry in the register of a notice,

restriction, inhibition or caution against dealings which is pending immediately before the repeal of the provision under which the application is made.

6 Notwithstanding the repeal of section 53 of the Land Registration Act 1925, sub-sections (1) and (2) of that section shall continue to have effect in relation to an application to lodge a caution against first registration which is pending immediately before the repeal of those provisions.

Former overriding interests

7 For the period of three years beginning with the day on which Schedule 1 comes into force, it has effect with the insertion after paragraph 14 of–

"15. A right acquired under the Limitation Act 1980 before the coming into force of this Schedule."

8 Schedule 3 has effect with the insertion after paragraph 2 of–

"2A (1) An interest which, immediately before the coming into force of this Schedule, was an overriding interest under section 70(1)(g) of the Land Registration Act 1925 by virtue of a person's receipt of rents and profits, except for an interest of a person of whom inquiry was made before the disposition and who failed to disclose the right when he could reasonably have been expected to do so.

(2) Sub-paragraph (1) does not apply to an interest if at any time since the coming into force of this Schedule it has been an interest which, had the Land Registration Act 1925 (c. 21) continued in force, would not have been an overriding interest under section 70(1)(g) of that Act by virtue of a person's receipt of rents and profits."

9 (1) This paragraph applies to an easement or profit a prendre which was an overriding interest in relation to a registered estate immediately before the coming into force of Schedule 3, but which would not fall within paragraph 3 of that Schedule if created after the coming into force of that Schedule.

(2) In relation to an interest to which this paragraph applies, Schedule 3 has effect as if the interest were not excluded from paragraph 3.

10 For the period of three years beginning with the day on which Schedule 3 comes into force, paragraph 3 of the Schedule has effect with the omission of the exception.

11 For the period of three years beginning with the day on which Schedule 3 comes into force, it has effect with the insertion after paragraph 14 of–

"15. A right under paragraph 18(1) of Schedule 12."

12 Paragraph 1 of each of Schedules 1 and 3 shall be taken to include an interest which immediately before the coming into force of the Schedule was an overriding interest under section 70(1)(k) of the Land Registration Act 1925.

13 Paragraph 6 of each of Schedules 1 and 3 shall be taken to include an interest which immediately before the coming into force of the Schedule was an overriding interest under section 70(1)(i) of the Land Registration Act 1925 and whose status as such was preserved by section 19(3) of the Local Land Charges Act 1975 (c. 76) (transitional provision in relation to change in definition of "local land charge").

Cautions against first registration

14 (1) For the period of two years beginning with the day on which section 15 comes into force, it has effect with the following omissions–
    (a) in subsection (1), the words "Subject to subsection (3),", and
    (b) subsection (3).
    (2) Any caution lodged by virtue of sub-paragraph (1) which is in force immediately before the end of the period mentioned in that sub-paragraph shall cease to have effect at the end of that period, except in relation to applications for registration made before the end of that period.
    (3) This paragraph does not apply to section 15 as applied by section 81.
15 (1) As applied by section 81, section 15 has effect for the period of ten years beginning with the day on which it comes into force, or such longer period as rules may provide, with the omission of subsection (3)(a)(i).
    (2) Any caution lodged by virtue of sub-paragraph (1) which is in force immediately before the end of the period mentioned in that sub-paragraph shall cease to have effect at the end of that period, except in relation to applications for registration made before the end of that period.
16 This Act shall apply as if the definition of "caution against first registration" in section 132 included cautions lodged under section 53 of the Land Registration Act 1925 (c. 21).

Applications under section 34 or 43 by cautioners

17 Where a caution under section 54 of the Land Registration Act 1925 is lodged in respect of a person's estate, right, interest or claim, he may only make an application under section 34 or 43 above in respect of that estate, right, interest or claim if he also applies to the registrar for the withdrawal of the caution.

Adverse possession

18 (1) Where a registered estate in land is held in trust for a person by virtue of section 75(1) of the Land Registration Act 1925 immediately before the coming into force of section 97, he is entitled to be registered as the proprietor of the estate.
    (2) A person has a defence to any action for the possession of land (in addition to any other defence he may have) if he is entitled under this paragraph to be registered as the proprietor of an estate in the land.
    (3) Where in an action for possession of land a court determines that a person is entitled to a defence under this paragraph, the court must order the registrar to register him as the proprietor of the estate in relation to which he is entitled under this paragraph to be registered.
    (4) Entitlement under this paragraph shall be disregarded for the purposes of section 131(1).

(5) Rules may make transitional provision for cases where a rentcharge is held in trust under section 75(1) of the Land Registration Act 1925 immediately before the coming into force of section 97.

Indemnities

19 (1) Schedule 8 applies in relation to claims made before the commencement of that Schedule which have not been settled by agreement or finally determined by that time (as well as to claims for indemnity made after the commencement of that Schedule).

(2) But paragraph 3(1) of that Schedule does not apply in relation to costs and expenses incurred in respect of proceedings, negotiations or other matters begun before 27 April 1997.

Implied indemnity covenants on transfers of pre-1996 leases

20 (1) On a disposition of a registered leasehold estate by way of transfer, the following covenants are implied in the instrument effecting the disposition, unless the contrary intention is expressed–

(a) in the case of a transfer of the whole of the land comprised in the registered lease, the covenant in sub-paragraph (2), and

(b) in the case of a transfer of part of the land comprised in the lease–

(i) the covenant in sub-paragraph (3), and

(ii) where the transferor continues to hold land under the lease, the covenant in sub-paragraph (4).

(2) The transferee covenants with the transferor that during the residue of the term granted by the registered lease the transferee and the persons deriving title under him will–

(a) pay the rent reserved by the lease,

(b) comply with the covenants and conditions contained in the lease, and

(c) keep the transferor and the persons deriving title under him indemnified against all actions, expenses and claims on account of any failure to comply with paragraphs (a) and (b).

(3) The transferee covenants with the transferor that during the residue of the term granted by the registered lease the transferee and the persons deriving title under him will–

(a) where the rent reserved by the lease is apportioned, pay the rent apportioned to the part transferred,

(b) comply with the covenants and conditions contained in the lease so far as affecting the part transferred, and

(c) keep the transferor and the persons deriving title under him indemnified against all actions, expenses and claims on account of any failure to comply with paragraphs (a) and (b).

(4) The transferor covenants with the transferee that during the residue of the term granted by the registered lease the transferor and the persons deriving title under him will–

(a) where the rent reserved by the lease is apportioned, pay the rent apportioned to the part retained,

(b) comply with the covenants and conditions contained in the lease so far as affecting the part retained, and

(c) keep the transferee and the persons deriving title under him indemnified against all actions, expenses and claims on account of any failure to comply with paragraphs (a) and (b).

(5) This paragraph does not apply to a lease which is a new tenancy for the purposes of section 1 of the Landlord and Tenant (Covenants) Act 1995 (c. 30).

SCHEDULE 13

REPEALS

Short title and chapter	*Extent of repeal*
Land Registry Act 1862 (c. 53).	The whole Act.
Settled Land Act 1925 (c. 18).	Section 119(3).
Law of Property Act 1925 (c. 20).	In section 84(8), the words from ", but" to the end. In section 205(1)(xxii), the words from ", and" to the end.
Land Registration Act 1925 (c. 21).	The whole Act.
Law of Property (Amendment) Act 1926 (c. 11).	Section 5.
Land Registration Act 1936 (c. 26).	The whole Act.
Requisitioned Land and War Works Act 1945 (c. 43).	Section 37(3).
Mental Health Act 1959 (c. 72).	In Schedule 7, the entry relating to the Land Registration Act 1925.
Charities Act 1960 (c. 58).	In Schedule 6, the entry relating to the Land Registration Act 1925.
Civil Evidence Act 1968 (c. 64).	In the Schedule, the entry relating to the Land Registration Act 1925.
Post Office Act 1969 (c. 48).	In Schedule 4, paragraph 27.
Law of Property Act 1969 (c. 59).	Section 28(7).
Land Registration and Land Charges Act 1971 (c. 54).	The whole Act.
Superannuation Act 1972 (c. 11).	In Schedule 6, paragraph 16.
Local Government Act 1972 (c. 70).	In Schedule 29, paragraph 26.
Solicitors Act 1974 (c. 47).	Section 75(b).
Finance Act 1975 (c. 7).	In Schedule 12, paragraph 5.
Local Land Charges Act 1975 (c. 76).	Section 19(3). In Schedule 1, the entry relating to the Land Registration Act 1925.
Endowments and Glebe Measure 1976 (No. 4).	In Schedule 5, paragraph 1.

Administration of Justice Act 1977 (c. 38).	Sections 24 and 26.
Charging Orders Act 1979 (c. 53).	Section 3(3). Section 7(4).
Limitation Act 1980 (c. 58).	In section 17, paragraph (b) and the preceding "and".
Highways Act 1980 (c. 66).	Section 251(5).
Matrimonial Homes and Property Act 1981 (c. 24).	Section 4.
Administration of Justice Act 1982 (c. 53).	Sections 66 and 67 and Schedule 5.
Mental Health Act 1983 (c. 20).	In Schedule 4, paragraph 6.
Capital Transfer Tax Act 1984 (c. 51).	In Schedule 8, paragraph 1.
Administration of Justice Act 1985 (c. 61).	In section 34, in subsection (1), paragraph (b) and the preceding "and" and, in subsection (2), paragraph (b). In Schedule 2, paragraph 37(b).
Insolvency Act 1985 (c. 65).	In Schedule 8, paragraph 5.
Housing Act 1985 (c. 68).	Section 36(3). Section 154(1), (6) and (7). Section 156(3). Section 168(5). In Schedule 9A, paragraphs 2(1), 3 and 5(3).
Land Registration Act 1986 (c. 26).	Sections 1 to 4.
Insolvency Act 1986 (c. 45).	In Schedule 14, the entry relating to the Land Registration Act 1925.
Building Societies Act 1986 (c. 53).	In Schedule 2A, in paragraph 1, sub-paragraph (4) and, in sub-paragraph (5), the definition of "registered land" and the preceding "and". In Schedule 18, paragraph 2. In Schedule 21, paragraph 9(b).
Patronage (Benefices) Measure 1986 (No. 3).	Section 6.
Landlord and Tenant Act 1987 (c. 31).	Section 28(6). In Schedule 4, paragraphs 1 and 2.
Diplomatic and Consular Premises Act 1987 (c. 46).	In Schedule 1, in paragraph 1, the words from "and expressions" to the end.Land Registration Act 1988 (c. 3).The whole Act.
Criminal Justice Act 1988 (c. 33).	Section 77(13). In Schedule 15, paragraphs 6 and 7.
Housing Act 1988 (c. 50).	In Schedule 11, paragraph 2(3).
Finance Act 1989 (c. 26).	Sections 178(2)(e) and 179(1)(a)(iv).
Courts and Legal Services Act 1990 (c. 41).	In Schedule 10, paragraph 3. In Schedule 17, paragraph 2.
Access to Neighbouring Land Act 1992 (c. 23).	Section 5(2) and (3).
Leasehold Reform, Housing and Urban Development Act 1993 (c. 28). Section 97(3).	In Schedule 21, paragraph 1.
Coal Industry Act 1994 (c. 21).	In Schedule 9, paragraph 1.
Law of Property (Miscellaneous Provisions) Act 1994 (c. 36).	In Schedule 1, paragraph 2.

Drug Trafficking Act 1994 (c. 37).	Section 26(13). In Schedule 1, paragraph 1.
Family Law Act 1996 (c. 27).	Section 31(11). In Schedule 8, paragraph 45.
Trusts of Land and Appointment of Trustees Act 1996 (c. 47).	In Schedule 3, paragraph 5.
Housing Act 1996 (c. 52).	Section 11(4).
Housing Grants, Construction and Regeneration Act 1996 (c. 53).	Section 138(3).
Land Registration Act 1997 (c. 2).	Sections 1 to 3 and 5(4) and (5). In Schedule 1, paragraphs 1 to 6.
Greater London Authority Act 1999 (c. 29).	Section 219.
Terrorism Act 2000 (c. 11).	In Schedule 4, paragraph 8(2) and (3).
Trustee Act 2000 (c. 29).	In Schedule 2, paragraph 26.
International Criminal Court Act 2001 (c. 17).	In Schedule 6, paragraph 7(2).

Index